Music in Rural New England
Family and Community Life, 1870–1940

Revisiting New England: The New Regionalism
SERIES EDITORS

LISA MACFARLANE
University of New Hampshire

STEPHEN NISSENBAUM
University of Massachusetts at Amherst

DONA BROWN
University of Vermont

DAVID H. WATTERS
University of New Hampshire

This series presents fresh discussions of the distinctiveness of New England culture. The editors seek manuscripts examining the history of New England regionalism; the way its culture came to represent American national culture as a whole; the interaction between that "official" New England culture and the people who lived in the region; and local, subregional, or even biographical subjects as microcosms that explicitly open up and consider larger issues. The series welcomes new theoretical and historical perspectives and is designed to cross disciplinary boundaries and appeal to a wide audience.

Richard Archer,
Fissures in the Rock: New England in the Seventeenth Century

Nancy L. Gallagher,
Breeding Better Vermonters: The Eugenics Project in Vermont

Sidney V. James,
The Colonial Metamorphoses in Rhode Island: A Study of Institutions in Change

Diana Muir,
Reflections in Bullough's Pond: Economy and Ecosystem in New England

James C. O'Connell,
Becoming Cape Cod: Creating a Seaside Resort

Christopher J. Lenney,
Sightseeking: Clues to the Landscape History of New England

Priscilla Paton,
*Abandoned New England: Landscape in the Works of
Homer, Frost, Hopper, Wyeth, and Bishop*

Adam Sweeting,
Beneath the Second Sun: A Cultural History of Indian Summer

Mark J. Sammons and Valerie Cunningham,
Black Portsmouth: Three Centuries of African-American Heritage

Pauleena MacDougall,
The Penobscot Dance of Resistance: Tradition in the History of a People

Donna M. Cassidy,
*"On the Subject of Nativeness":
From Regionalism to Race in Marsden Hartley's Late Art*

Jennifer C. Post,
Music in Rural New England Family and Community Life, 1870–1940

Music in Rural New England Family and Community Life, 1870–1940

Jennifer C. Post

University of New Hampshire Press

DURHAM, NEW HAMPSHIRE

Published by University Press of New England

HANOVER AND LONDON

University of New Hampshire Press

Published by University Press of New England,

One Court Street, Lebanon, NH 03766

www.upne.com

© 2004 by Jennifer C. Post

Printed in the United States of America

5 4 3 2 1

Library of Congress Cataloging-in-Publication Data

Post, Jennifer C.

Music in rural New England family and community life, 1870–1940 / Jennifer C. Post.— 1st ed.

p.   cm. — (Revisiting New England)

Includes bibliographical references (p.   ) and index.

ISBN 1-58465-415-5 (cloth : alk. paper)

1. Music—New England—19th century—History and criticism.

2. Music—New England—20th century—History and criticism.

3. Community music—New England—History and criticism.

4. Music—Social aspects—New England.

5. Music—Religious aspects. I. Title. II. Series.

ML200.P67 2004

780'.974'09034—dc22   2004008430

To my family:
my parents, Avery and Margaret Post,
and my children, Alasdair and Margaret

Contents

Preface

When I moved to Middlebury, Vermont, in 1979 I was in the process of completing a doctoral dissertation on South Asian music. This study was the product of nearly a decade of research on music of Western India. As I settled into the region and submitted my research for the degree, my ethnomusicological training and work with library materials as a graduate research assistant enabled me to begin to organize the materials in the Helen Hartness Flanders Ballad Collection at Middlebury College. This collection, comprised of field recordings and supporting documentation, manuscripts, and a reference library of books and journals, had been neglected for a number of years, and the recordings and papers were in need of both preservation and organization. Initially I sought supporting information to aid my own understanding of the region's traditions. I quickly noted the dearth of historical and social information on musical practices in Maine, New Hampshire, and Vermont, especially from the period represented by the field recordings: the mid- to late-nineteenth century through the mid-twentieth century. Several regional collections of songs and song texts gathered between 1900 and 1965 provided valuable data on repertoires, but there was little contextual information to support them. Who were the performers whose songs were so carefully recorded and transcribed by the collectors of this period? How vital to the cultural landscape was the ballad repertoire that comprised the bulk of the collections? How significant were the dance tunes recorded from a selected group of performers? When and where were their songs and tunes performed? What was the character of the social life of the rural communities and how was music used to support relationships among the residents? As I became more familiar with the broad musical practices in the region, I began to wonder how representative of the repertoires the preserved collections were. What was missing? How did collections in the different periods affect our understanding of the historical record?

I quickly learned that the archive I was working with was one of four major northern New England music collections from this early period. The Helen Hartness Flanders Ballad Collection was established in 1930, when Flanders (1890–1972), a local poet active in Springfield, Vermont, social circles, was invited by a member of the Vermont Commission on Country Life to seek evidence of "old songs" in Vermont. She immediately enlisted the help of George Brown, a summer visitor who conducted a local orchestra, and over the years involved many others as well, including her daughter, Elizabeth Flanders Ballard, to help with collecting and transcribing her growing collection of songs. Of particular note were the contributions of conservatory-trained Marguerite Olney, who was hired in 1940 to curate the collection as it moved from Flanders's home in Springfield to the campus of Middlebury College. Olney remained with the collection for twenty years and conducted some of its most valuable fieldwork in northern New England during that time. I also discovered from correspondence and song notes connected to the Flanders material that a scholar based in Cambridge, Massachusetts, Phillips Barry (1880–1937), provided the primary intellectual and organizational framework for the collection. He had been gathering songs in northern New England and the Maritimes for several decades before Flanders began to work with him in 1930, and she sought both his scholarly advice and his moral support. Flanders and her team of collectors, friends, and scholars published seven books and one LP recording between 1930 and 1965. The major titles included *Vermont Folk Songs and Ballads,* first published in 1930 by Flanders and Brown, which focused on the character of Vermont's musical landscape and provided music and lyrics to a wide variety of ballads and songs; *The New Green Mountain Songster,* published in 1939 by Flanders, Ballard, Brown, and Barry, which used the character of an eighteenth-century manuscript of songs held by Dartmouth College (called *The Green Mountain Songster*) to frame its collection of songs from Vermonters; *Ballads Migrant in New England,* a collection of songs derived from the British Isles that were collected in all of the New England states, which was published in 1953 by Flanders and Olney; and *Ancient Ballads Traditionally Sung in New England,* a four-volume collection of all of the Child ballads gathered during a thirty-year period in all of the New England states, which was published between 1960 and 1965 by Flanders with critical commentary by folklorist Tristram P. Coffin and notes on the music by ethnomusicologist Bruno Nettl.[1]

As I looked beyond the Middlebury-based collection to seek supporting documentation for the Flanders material, I turned to the work of Phillips Barry, housed at the Houghton Library at Harvard. I found there a carefully documented collection of songs, recorded and transcribed, with limited notes on the performers but carefully developed ideas about the history of the songs and song types. Phillips Barry and Fanny Hardy Eckstorm (1865–1946) of Maine, whose papers are now collected at the University of Maine, Orono, were at the center of a small community of scholars exploring song and song transmission during the first four decades of the twentieth century. Their collecting followed the groundbreaking work of Francis James Child (1825–1896), who in his five-volume work *The English and Scottish Popular Ballads* (1882–1898) classified selected songs by story type based on his literary and historical research.[2] The Child ballads became the primary expressive form sought by collectors in rural America. The Barry and Eckstorm correspondence, notes, and publications show the dominance of the Child canon in their fieldwork. Their literature also contributed to an ongoing dialogue among collectors and compilers that was concerned with constructing ideas to explain the development and maintenance of Anglo-American song traditions in both oral and literary traditions. Possibly most importantly, they became part of a growing group of American scholars who were focusing on songs in a regional context. They gathered songs that also became part of a new canon, defined in print by G. Malcolm Laws who classified British broadside ballads in the United States and American-made ballads that were generally modeled on the British songs.[3] Eckstorm's song collecting acknowledges these categories but was also particularly closely tied to an interest in the Maine occupational sphere dominated in the late nineteenth and early twentieth centuries by lumbering; she also included songs of the sea. Her 1927 publication (with Mary Winslow Smyth) entitled *Minstrelsy of Maine: Folk Songs and Ballads of the Woods and the Coast* provided lyrics to over one hundred ballads and songs classed by type and historical period.[4] In 1929, Phillips Barry published with Eckstorm and Smyth a single volume of songs entitled *British Ballads from Maine: The Development of Popular Songs with Texts and Airs,* which represented a fraction of the collection of Child ballads Barry had amassed during the period.[5] Eckstorm and Barry published a diverse body of information on music in the region in their short-lived journal *Bulletin of the Folk-song Society of the Northeast.* From 1930 to 1937, the year of Barry's death, they provided focused explorations of categorized songs (dominated by ballads classified by Child), with a particular concern for musical characteristics and historical context. In 1939, *The Maine Woods Songster,* edited by Barry, was published posthumously. The volume collected fifty songs of the lumbermen and river-drivers of Maine.[6]

During the 1930s, Eloise Hubbard Linscott (1897–1978) also collected songs and tunes in northern New England. Her 1939 product of this fieldwork was the book *Folk Songs of Old New England,* in which she provided a broad view of musical traditions in the region.[7] In addition to chapters on ballads and songs, she included sections on play-party songs with game directions, and dance music with dance calls. Linscott offered more detailed notes on performers and other contextual information on performance practice than many of the other collectors had. She continued her fieldwork during the 1940s but did not have an opportunity to publish this material. Her recordings and notes are now housed at the Library of Congress.

Other early regional collections that contributed to my understanding of the practices in the region were compiled by individuals who had engaged in brief collecting trips in Vermont, Maine, and New Hampshire. In 1918, Elizabeth Burchenal published *American Country-Dances: Twenty-eight Contra-dances Largely from the New England States,* to some extent based on personal experience with local fiddlers and callers.[8] Edith B. Sturgis published *Songs from the Hills of Vermont* in 1919, a small edited selection of thirteen songs by James and Mary Atwood and Jenny Knapp of northern Vermont.[9] Roland Palmer Gray gathered songs from publications, broadsides, singers, and other collectors largely between 1900 and 1917 and published *Songs and Ballads of the Maine Lumberjacks with Other Songs from Maine* in 1924, a collection of song lyrics connected to lumbering in Maine.[10] In 1935, Robert Pike published an article in the *Journal of American Folklore* on folksongs he collected in Pittsburg, New Hampshire, with the lyrics to some of the local songs of this northern community.[11]

The practice of "collecting" the old Anglo-American songs and tunes as a preservation strategy slowed after the middle of the twentieth century. In the first place, access to the largely orally transmitted music became more difficult, because so many of the performers who had retained the practices had died. Also, the process of fieldwork in folklore and ethnomusicology had matured considerably by the 1970s and 1980s; scholars more readily recognized the significance of the singer and her life story as well as the overall importance of broadly defined contextual data in understanding performance practice, which introduced a new style of recording and interpreting music and dance performance for many scholars. One of the most important regional scholars to provide recordings and contextual information on regional traditions in this period was Edward (Sandy) Ives, whose studies of song-makers, and reflexive reporting on fieldwork in Maine and the Maritimes, has helped readers understand more clearly the social significance of song in northern New England. While he published a collection entitled *Folksongs from Maine* in 1966 as volume 7 of the journal *Northeast Folklore,* his later works, especially *Larry Gorman: The Man Who Made the Songs* (1964) and *Joe Scott: The Woodsman-Songmaker* (1978), focus on singers, songwriters, and the social significance of their songs.[12]

This study on northern New England music in family and community life has been influenced and informed by all of the previously cited historical literature: the published studies and collections as well as the archival material that supports them. Research was conducted in the Flanders Ballad Collection at Middlebury College, the Phillips Barry Collection at Harvard University, the archives at the Maine Folklife Center at the University of Maine, Orono, the Wilbur Collection in the Special Collections Department at the University of Vermont, and the Rauner Special Collections Library at Dartmouth College, the Maine Historical Society Library in Portland, the New Hampshire Historical Society Library in Concord, and the Vermont Historical Society Library in Montpelier. I also had access to the field recordings of Eloise Linscott and Phillips Barry housed at the Library of Congress, as well as the field recordings shared by Flanders and Alan Lomax (recorded between 1939 and 1941), for this study. The work of the early collectors encouraged me to seek contextual information during the 1980s and early 1990s from relatives of the performers they interviewed; most of this fieldwork was focused in New Hampshire and Vermont. In addition, Sandy Ives's interpretations of his field research in Maine, and the theoretical and place-based scholarship of a number of historians, folklorists, ethnomusicologists, and geographers, has influenced my interpretation of the archival and fieldwork data. Among the many scholarly sources that informed this study, I was affected especially by the ideas presented in the writings of Michael Pickering, Georgina Boyes, and Ruth Finnegan, who explore traditional music in its historical and social context; Roger Renwick's studies on ballad and folk poetry; Martin Stokes's work on music, identity, and place; the work of Barbara Allen, Gerald Pocius, and Kent Ryden, who theorize and apply concepts related to sense of place in folklore and anthropology; Thomas Hubka's careful look at farm life in Maine; Karen Hansen's interpretations of gendered social behaviors in local communities; Stephen Marini's work on religious sects in New England; and Joseph Conforti's focus on regional identity.[13]

In this study I explore facets of the forms and styles of musical expression that have sometimes been ignored by scholars in their efforts to record, reconstruct, and theorize the musical history of a nation. My goal has been to define significant cultural components that make this specific region of the United States distinct, while considering the complex historical terrain that is expressed in its music. I identify northern New England as a regional unit through its characteristic geography, its history as a frontier region, and the shared values that existed among its residents, who worked to establish and maintain their lifestyles while dealing with many social, cultural, and economic changes. The stories shared among these rural residents about experiences with music and dance echo from central Vermont to northern New Hampshire to central and northern Maine. I hope this study will offer opportunities for discussion on the use and interpretation of the literature presented. The historical information has been informed by contemporary field data, potentially modeling a practice that could contribute to a better understanding of continuity and change in performance in this region and others.

While the geographic and historical parameters of this study can be viewed as broad, it is not intended to be a comprehensive view of music in all of the segments of society during the periods covered. There are many more stories that northern New England families and communities have to tell about music during the nineteenth and twentieth centuries. For example, I present only limited information on the public music traditions of this period, expressed in the performances of the town bands that played an important role in many communities after the Civil War and the dance bands and hillbilly bands that emerged as both vaudeville and the radio became increasingly popular in rural regions. Most importantly, I chose to focus this study on the dominant social group in the region before the middle of the twentieth century: the Anglo-Americans. There is thus a wealth of research yet to be done on French Canadian song; Russian, Swedish, Italian, and other European musics; and Native American practices. More recently, there is emerging information about the musics of Asian and African groups from many different countries now residing in northern New England.

Financial support for this research was provided by a National Endowment for the Humanities Fellowship for College Teachers and Independent Scholars, an American Association for State and Local History (AASLH) grant to support archival research in Maine, and several Middlebury College research grants to support fieldwork in Vermont and New Hampshire.

I would like to acknowledge and thank all of the primary contributors to this study: the performers, and their friends and family members, who offered songs, tunes, and recollections of performances in their youths. The memories of literally hundreds of individuals contributed to this study; in addition to my own interviews with many regional residents, I felt I came to know the people interviewed by other researchers concerned with songs and tunes in their social contexts that were recorded in the 1970s, 1980s, and 1990s. While I know less about the many singers I heard in the historical interviews recorded between 1920 and the 1960s, their songs and tunes have contributed immensely to this research. I would especially like to acknowledge three individuals I worked with closely over several years: Marjorie Pierce, Florence Scott, and Clyde Covill. I made contact with all three because each had a parent that had recorded songs for the Helen Hartness Flanders Ballad Collection in the 1930s and 1940s. Marjorie Pierce's memories—informed by her close connection to family and a passion for local history—were some of the first to help me effectively link field data of the early and later periods; I valued her friendship immensely. Florence Scott's encouragement and her own determination to maintain connections between song and personal memory helped me to focus on her local community of Pittsburg, New Hampshire, among a large number of willing residents. And the extraordinary Clyde Covill's memories of family and community, diverse selection of songs and fiddle tunes, and—especially—humor will stay with me always.

J.C.P.
Middlebury, Vermont
June 2003

CHAPTER 1

Introduction:
The Geographic and Social Landscape

The Vermont Farmer's Song

A health unto the farmer who lives among the hills,
Where every man's a sovereign and owns land he tills;
Where all the girls are beautiful, and all the boys are strong,
'Tis my delight from morn 'til night to sing the farmer's song.

'Tis here the true merinos of pure imported stock
Are often seen to roam the green in many a noble flock;
Their forms are strong and beautiful, their wool is fine and long,
'Tis my delight from morn 'til night to sing the farmer's song.

You've often heard the stories of ancient Rome and Greece,
And of Jason's expedition to find the golden fleece,
Alonzo's got the fleece away and brought the sheep along,
'Tis my delight from morn 'til night to sing the farmer's song.

A health to the shearers, and many happy years,
Who with a will and ready skill propel the busy shears,
With conscience clear and hearts sincere and voices loud and strong,
'Tis my delight from morn 'til night to sing the farmer's song.

A health to old Bingham and all good shepherd men,
May heaven keep himself and sheep 'til shearing comes again,
When it comes may I be there to see and help the sport along,
'Tis my delight from morn 'til night to sing the farmer's song.[1]

Concerts of historical New England music held in Vermont, New Hampshire, and Maine during the last few decades feature performers who offer songs and tunes that conjure memories of rural life in America. The images conveyed in the lyrics, and in the music itself, often contrast sharply with the characteristics of life in the region today. Some of the views of rural life are constructed using a sentimental voice to set an idyllic scene; they provide a picture of a past that some

Illus. 1.1.   Weston, Vermont, landscape, early twentieth century (postcard view).

scholars today identify as partially or wholly invented. Historians and social scientists consider these imaginary landscapes, their invented histories and regional connections, to be products of both authors' and artists' nostalgia for a past that may in fact have been quite different from the one represented.

The dynamic relationships that yield forms of artistic expression in any communal environment are fueled by the shared values of individuals, family members, communities, and the nation, and those works of art often call on memories of past experience during both creation and performance. Songs constructed in a specific time sphere, then offered to an audience, carry social meanings that become increasingly complex as they are heard and interpreted by subsequent generations. Songs like "The Vermont Farmer's Song" *do* present an idyllic scene of the Vermont landscape for many contemporary listeners, and they also offered a different idealized view of life for listeners fifty or one hundred years ago.[2] The ever-changing meanings of these songs reflect the complex historical and social forces that have always existed in rural communities throughout the United States.

Before the middle of the twentieth century, the soundscape experienced by singers and audience members listening to ballads and dance tunes derived from the British Isles, or to newly created songs and tunes, was defined by the limited social spheres in which they and their music traveled. Performances were not broadcast widely beyond the local community; performance venues consisted largely of home, neighborhood, village, and workplace, and there were fewer opportunities than there are today for people from other regions to bring in new music, or for participants to take music outside the community. When the popular media began to dominate the musical information that reached an area after the 1930s and 1940s, public performances encouraged exchanges among musicians that broadened their spheres of influence, radically altering the local and regional musical landscape.

Prior to this diversification, musical life in rural northern New England existed within clearly delineated spheres created by local residents in conjunction with their needs and finely interwoven with the regional geography, local economy, established social practices, and family traditions. This period can be characterized by dominant musical and social activities that not only maintained music and dance traditions but also contributed to the economic health and the overall well-being of the local community.

It is not easy to gain access to information on music performed in rural homes during the nineteenth and early twentieth centuries. Musical traditions in the region existed largely outside the mainstream. The occasions for singing and dancing were part of daily social interaction, yet they escaped the attention of newspapers that announced or reported on public events. Today we find evidence that events took place only in brief diary entries, short introductory narratives on historical field recordings, or references by elderly residents today who relish their memories yet still struggle to recall performances that were so well integrated into their everyday community life.

During the nineteenth and early twentieth centuries the principal rural residents of northern New England were descendants of Irish, English, and Scottish settlers. They were farming families who came directly from their homelands, or moved up from southern New England or down from Canada, or returned east from settlements in the West. As families settled on hillsides and in villages, they became part of neighborhoods. To assure their own success as permanent residents, they adopted the practices of these communities, taking on identities in the social sphere that helped them to be part of a unit, whether family or household, neighborhood or town. Kent Ryden describes this process of establishing a sense of place and its character in *Mapping the Landscape*. He reminds us that a sense of place can be seen in a "strong sense of rootedness in a location, of identification with (and self-identification in terms of) that location, of membership in a unified place-based community, and of a common world view as a result of a common geographical experience" (Ryden 1993: 59).

Rural farming families remained in close proximity to one another in areas that were often framed by geographic features and then subsequently supported by neighborhood or district schools and village stores. The sense of place that individuals, families, neighborhoods, and villages developed was expressed in many ways through their cultural output. Furthermore, how women and men interacted within this social sphere was also reflected in their cultural expression. Placed in historical context, this framing of cultural life in a community context provided forms of expression through music and dance that were then maintained for many generations.

The important connections between landscape, social relations, and cultural expression were made especially clear to me in 1984 as I sat with an eighty-five-year-old Warren, Vermont, man on the front porch of the home in which he grew up. From where Ramon Gove and I sat, as far as we could see, the land was deeply scarred with condominiums in different stages of construction. Yet he appeared to ignore this as he talked about social life in his community when he was young.

Illus. 1.2. Calais, Vermont, neighborhood in the early years of the twentieth century (postcard view).

While he talked, he looked out at the land around us. And as he described social events, he pointed to the surrounding hills, to farms that were no longer there, and recreated the network of families that once lived within his view.

> We had a dance here—a party there—clear around the whole square where some of the neighbors was—every Saturday night. They'd have one here, then they'd go over to Stacy Jones's. They'd go down the hill to the house on the road up between the trees. Then you go there up to my sister's up on Plaicy Mountain. Then they'd come back down here . . .[3]

The families in these homes framed the social life of that neighborhood when Gove was young. They were involved in a network that both worked and played together, helped one another in times of need, gathered for a "sing" or a "kitchen dance" on a Saturday night, or celebrated together with a dance after a barn raising or corn husking.

Active musical traditions accompanied daily activities, provided entertainment, reinforced social roles, and contributed to the establishment and maintenance of a cultural identity. Anglo-American ballads and lyric songs, popular songs and tunes, hymns, and dance pieces dominated the diverse repertoires of the residents and were performed at events that took place regularly within families, neighborhoods, and occupational groups. Shared musical ideas in the family or household, and among neighbors and other members of the community, enriched each tradition. These practices continued until the mid-1940s, when major cultural, social, and economic changes finally moved northern New England musical traditions away from localized practices and into the mainstream.

The Geographic Sphere

On the Green Hills of Old Vermont

Guy Blood, Grafton, Vermont, 1930

I was born in Cham -plain Val -ley on a lit -tle hill -side farm. There I spent man -y hap -py day of yore. There I learned to love a maid -en with a heart so pure and true. That she won me by her gen -tle lov -ing way. There I read Green Mount -ain Boys and I learned with child -ish joys How my grand -sire fought by Al -len's side and fell. Now those boy -hood days are gone and I'm go -ing back a -lone Up a -mong the hills of Ver -mont I love so well.

I was at a city station, waiting there to take the train
That would take me back to old Vermont once more.
Thinking of the dear old homestead that I soon would see again
And the loving friends I knew in days of yore.

An old man standing near with gray beard and silvery hair
Said he, "In old Vermont I used to dwell."
And his eyes filled up with tears as he said, "It's forty years
Since I left the old green mountain state I love so well."

On the green hills of Vermont where the cool pine forests are
The arbuturis blossoms sweetly in the dell.
I have been in many climes since my boyhood happy times
But none are like the hills of old Vermont I love so well.

I was born in Champlain Valley on a little hillside farm
There I spent many happy day of yore.
There I learned to love a maiden with heart so pure and true
That she won me by her gentle loving ways.

There I read *Green Mountain Boys* and I cried with childish joys
How my grandsire fought by Allen's side and fell.
But those boyhood days are gone and I'm going back alone
Up among the hills of old Vermont I love so well.[4]

The geographical landscape that northern New England settlers adopted and adapted to was many layered. In the first place, the spatial organization of individuals and families who settled in the rural landscape was closely tied to its physical geography. The identity of the regional residents of northern New England was also connected to an understanding of their place in the cultural and symbolic landscape that framed their everyday lives.

In studies of regionalism in folklore and geography, we find common factors identified by authors seeking to consolidate disparate approaches to regional studies. In *A Sense of Place* Barbara Allen has identified four elements fundamental to distinguishing a region: the geographic entity, or *place;* the *people* who live and work in that location; the *history* of the relationship between the people and the place; and the *distinctiveness* of place in relation to surrounding regions (Allen 1990: 2). It is the geographic entity and the complex relationship between the residents and this changing landscape that frames their cultural expression. And as we will see, each of these elements exists within a functional and perceptual mode in the lives of the residents of northern New England.

THE PLACE

We identify the northern region of New England (as a geographic place) by its mountains, farmland, and bodies of water. The high proportion of rural land in relation to its more settled areas sets it apart from the other New England states, even today. The cold winters and cool, wet summers of the northern climatic zones also play a constant role in everyday life in these northern communities. Responses to the land and its weather form an important part of the common regional identity. Comments, stories, and lore related to weather and its effect on economic, social, and cultural life are frequent.

The northern border of the region is framed by Canada, where language and cultural practices, and differences imposed by nationality, create a boundary. While this physical border existed during the period of this study, for many residents in the northernmost towns it was transparent. Individuals moved freely between Canada and the United States to attend social events and even school in some communities.

To the south is the region often identified as "New England" by many social historians: all of Massachusetts, Connecticut, and Rhode Island, and sometimes the southernmost communities of Vermont, New Hampshire, and Maine. It is interesting that the northern regions are so often excluded from New England regional studies; the population was always small and, in fact, presented differences in historical patterns and lifestyles that were easier to ignore than to account for.

The forests and farmland, lakes and rivers, provided an environment for an active lumber industry throughout the nineteenth century. The industry thrived among the farmers, who made up the bulk of its labor force during the winters, when they harvested wood in the northern forests to be carried down the Connecticut, Androscoggin, Kennebec, and Penobscot rivers in the spring thaw, a less active farming season. Thus occupations were connected to the land as well: the forests provided opportunities for lumberers, the fields for farmers, and the water for growing industries that drew products from the land such as wool, marble, and granite.

While the physical landscape greatly affected every aspect of northern New Englanders' lives, the symbolic landscape that emerged from their unified experience is equally important. The language widely used by residents today to refer to where they live in relation to others to the south indicates a consciousness of a separate geographical sphere. When local residents talk about their location, the phrase "north country" emerges often. In fact, the north country in each state today refers to the region just below the Canadian border. For many, though, these boundaries are not clear, and the phrase has been used variably to describe different parts of the three northern states. The word "north" is used often, or implied by the phrase "up here" or "up this way," further signifying consciousness of *location*.

The dominant form of musical expression that has emerged among the residents indirectly reflects the physical landscape. Songs with texts that make direct references to known places or people in a region, that discuss the hardships of farming in Vermont, or that express the natural beauty of New England are actually relatively rare. Though musical culture in northern New England does reflect the society and its landscape, it does not always mirror it directly—instead, when we look closely, we find that its image is reflected back in obscure, almost oblique, ways. In *Everyday Culture: Popular Song and the Vernacular Milieu* Pickering and Green express this well:

> In studying the homological relations between songs and groups, we should not assume that we can simply read off song content as an inscription of the social values, attitudes, norms, and beliefs of particular groups. Indeed, song content may in part or in whole be discordant with the moral community, but of value precisely because it offers a symbolic, self-legitimizing counterpart to that community. Songs, along with other kinds of artistic expression or product, often provide visits to "other worlds" which interrupt the taken-for-granted pattern of everyday reality. (Pickering and Green 1987: 3)

These "other worlds" in northern New England include different times and places as well as extraordinary and impossible situations and events. Songs recount events in the lives of lords and nobles, occasionally involve the appearance of ghosts, and resolve impossible problems with improbable solutions. The Robin Hood ballads found in the region provide examples of a story type that encapsulates this fantasy yet retains elements of everyday reality for its residents as well.[5]

> Bold Robin Hood marched all on the highway,
> All on the highway marched he,
> Until he met a lady gay
> A-weeping all on the highway.
>
> "Oh, do you mourn for gold," he says,
> "Or do you mourn for fee,
> Or do you weep for any high knight
> That deserted your company?"
>
> "No, I don't you mourn for gold," she said,
> "Nor I don't you mourn for fee,
> Nor I don't mourn for any high knight
> That deserted my company,
>
> "But I do mourn for my three sons,
> Today they're condemned to die;
> In Nottingham town so fast they are bound,
> In Nottingham prison both lie."
>
> "Go home, go home," said Bold Robin Hood,
> "And weep no more today,
> And I will stand hangman this live long day
> To hang the squires all three."[6]

THE PEOPLE

Within each geographic sphere—a neighborhood on a hillside, the farmland in the Northeast Kingdom of Vermont, even the northern geographic zone stretching from the Maritimes through the Midwest—residents engaged in similar activities and were affected by common issues and constraints: the landscape and its remoteness, weather and its aberrations, seasonal activities connected to farming. The diverse and ever-changing population in the given region, and its volatile weather, provided opportunities for constantly changing dialogues between the people and their landscape. In response, they "organized their lives" in relation to "the environmental conditions and natural resources of that place" (Allen 1990: 2) and created domains that were delineated by characteristics they had some control over: family and neighborhood.

In a study of farm life in Maine, Thomas Hubka describes the farm neighborhood as an "informal and loosely defined social organization" that played an important role in the daily lives of families in the mid-nineteenth century (Hubka

1988: 13). The interrelationships among individuals and families within such a neighborhood domain affected the economic, social, and cultural spheres of everyday life for the residents. Together they struggled with the land, were victims of unexpected tragedies, and took on everyday responsibilities in their rural lives.

Farm neighborhoods throughout northern New England were comprised of networks of families who lived and farmed in a specific geographic area. These distinct social units consisted of small groups of farms located in a valley or on a hillside, sometimes in or near a village center. While the history of each neighborhood varied as families settled and swelled, moved out and were replaced by others, the overall character of the network—and the geographic entity in which distance between farms affected the character of social relations—remained the same.

The way neighborhood and small town residents interacted was defined also in relation to their everyday responsibilities. This in turn affected how the fabric of social relations and cultural expression was defined. Freeman Corey, Sr., a fiddler who grew up on a farm in Benson, Vermont, recalled in the 1980s the local dances during the early decades of the twentieth century. His memories are informed by his own experience as well as those of the older residents that taught him many of his tunes: "Back then the town wasn't separated. Everybody was like a big family, you know. This is where the big change came from horses to automobiles. You're dealing with a group that more or less stayed in a certain community because they just didn't have time to go that far out anyplace."[7]

Individuals and families assisted one other in many ways, cooperating "chiefly to facilitate their farming operations and thereby improve their overall quality of life" (Hubka 1988: 14).[8] They interacted particularly in times of need: during and after a flood, fire, or illness; through the settling-in period in a new home; or even while attending to necessary farm chores that seemed easier when working as a group. Stories of the reliance of one family on another were common.

Rural residents created domains based on social and economic need, developing critical relationships within the household and the community. These networks of neighbors and friends maintained their connections in many cases by visiting. Frequent visiting in New England rural families is evidenced in early diaries but also more recently in discussions with residents who recall social life earlier in the century. Visiting took place in homes and at neighborhood stores, community socials, town meetings, and church suppers. In her study on eighteenth- and nineteenth-century social life in New England, Karen Hansen describes the activity this way:

> Visits involved an individual or group going to another household. While there, visitors talked, occasionally worked, and sometimes ate food or drank tea. The many types of visiting ranged from pure socializing to communal labor; visitors took afternoon tea, made informal Sunday visits, attended maple sugar parties and cider tastings, stayed for extended visits, offered assistance in giving birth, paid their respects to the family of the deceased, participated in quilting parties, and raised houses and barns . . . It was through visiting, in fact, that they created their communities. (Hansen 1994: 80)

Town histories from the region also provide examples of these critical relationships, as in this description of nineteenth-century life in Dover, Vermont:

> With the growth of the settlement and with the arrival of newcomers, frequent barn-raisings meant fun for the whole neighborhood, along with hard work for the men; for the women working together, such events gave them the pleasure of providing them with food and drink. Exchange of work among the settlers—haying, reaping and binding, or cornhusking, according to the season—quickened as well as lightened the labor, and was pleasant beside. (Kull 1961: 55–56)

In some cases this sharing of work took place on a regular schedule adopted from a pattern more common in England before the twentieth century, where calendar customs were "finely intermeshed with the local economy and society" (Bushaway 1982: 35). In New England these customs ranged from barn raisings to box socials but were, like their English counterparts, always connected to the land and reinforced their sense of place.[9] Songs provide evidence of people's identification between place and specific events but also serve as reports on events that existed in a familiar pattern throughout the region. As a result, songs could easily be exchanged, with names changed, to serve various social, cultural, and economic purposes. "Jones' Paring Bee" recalls the significance of the personal relationships, family connections, community camaraderie, and geographic context shared in many northern locations:

Jones' Paring Bee

Oh Susan Jane do you remember
Down to Jones' parin' bee,
When I took you and your brother
Along with Sally Greer and me

Yes, Josiah, I remember
'Twas in winter time, you know,
As we wandered along the highway
Then we'd go up through the snow.[10]

The lines between work and social life were blurred in ways that do not apply to late-twentieth-century traditions in the region. This resulted first from need, but it quickly became a custom. When I asked Freeman Corey, Sr., where the support came from for a family who needed help, he responded: "Oh, just everybody pitched in, if something came about that was impossible for another to handle (in the fall of the year, of course, come time to put in fall season's growth of crops, it was an endless arrangement). They just helped one another. They spent more time helping one another than just doing their own work. And it got sort of a habit, I guess, to do it this way."[11]

While a spirit of cooperation played a significant role in maintaining communities and encouraging cultural expression in rural northern New England, social experience and access to knowledge was also often gendered. During large portions of the day, social interactions in the household or domestic sphere was divided by gender. Yet, the exchanges among women and among men were constantly interspersed with interactions taking place between women and men (as well as among several generations, and between individuals from both inside and outside the family). This affected the gendered spaces of the household and community, and it created a sphere that seems to transcend the dichotomy between public and private social spaces. Music and dance activities played an important part in the process of social and cultural exchange. Women and men regularly put aside some gender distinctions in order to get on with activities critical to the community's survival: they were involved in hard work and a lot of play.

HISTORY

Of course all of the activities in a family and neighborhood took place over time. Participants considered the importance of time and history in maintaining relationships and establishing and continuing their roles in community life; in fact, this shared experience has always played a critical role in binding people together in a neighborhood (Allen 1990: 161). There are many regional indications of place in historical context exhibited by local residents. Their sense of history appears in the shared experiences that link the present to the past. The landscape, of course, brings this into focus through family connections to the land, memories of specific events in particular places, and stories and songs that reinforce a relationship to the land. Songs are remembered in part to keep alive memories of the old times or of people who are no longer around. In fact, as in other parts of the country, many people representing rural traditions of the past—real or imagined—have adopted the phrase "old-time" to describe valued ways of life in northern New England.

The historical societies established in many communities indicate an awareness of a historical viewpoint, and have encouraged local residents to remember, reflect upon, and value the past. This is accomplished through objects of material culture such as tools or photographs but especially through memories that are recounted in narratives and song.

Retelling stories in song introduces a sense of history and rootedness in community tradition. As songs were recalled, they were often connected both to the singer and to the historical role the song had in relation to the singer, family, or broader community in which it was remembered. Remembering songs—and the act of performing music in general—was for many a way to hold on to older traditions. Songs, stories, and dance tunes reinforced these connections. Typical introductions to a song might be "Remember when so-and-so used to sing this song?" or "I remember when my father taught this to me." Dance tunes and the process of learning to play a musical instrument, especially the fiddle, are often marked by performers in northern New England; they both represent historical events in which the musician appreciates the significance of the opportunity to learn within a family or close-knit community tradition.

In any community there are those whose interests and cultural expressions indicate that they are primarily looking forward, while others maintain a worldview that more often includes memories of what is behind them. The old songs preserved by nineteenth- and early-twentieth-century collectors were generally also old songs when they were gathered; they constituted the repertoires of those residents who likewise relied primarily on memories of the old times. Scholars often use these old songs to better understand the cultural expression of the period, ignoring the fact that both old and new songs were part of many residents' repertoires. The songs and tunes preserved as representative of local identity and the sole form of cultural expression of a given time period result from the nostalgia of residents as well as collectors.

Connected also to a sense of history is the awareness of *change*. During the period of this study, the lives of residents in the region were undergoing a great deal of change due to many economic and social factors. These changes affected relationships to the land as well as social interactions, and they were expressed through musical performance in many ways.

DISTINCTIVENESS

The distinctiveness of northern New England as a region is to some extent in the eye of the beholder. While many people may consider northern New England a subregion of New England, the northern region does present unique geographical characteristics in climate and terrain, in settlement patterns, and in cultural expression. There is a significant internal uniformity in the social lives and cultural expression of northern residents in the late nineteenth and early twentieth centuries. These distinctive qualities emerge throughout this study of region and regional expression in music during a specific time period—in fact, without them, it could not be accomplished.

Musical traditions are linked to other regions but also distinguished from them through musical and social behaviors. Lyrical and musical references, ways of singing or playing, purposes for events and for musical expression, and extramusical aspects of performance, including the type of foods that participants choose to serve at social events, are all markers of this distinct identity.

One way that residents assure themselves of a distinct tradition in music is to leave marks of identification on their songs and tunes. Most songs were derived from other locations but adapted to fit the local landscape through its place names and real or imagined events. Similarly, dance tunes were named—or sometimes renamed—to mark a location or to remember individuals. Listeners continued to identify with the memory of a place, and its distinction, through the tune's name as it was passed from generation to generation.

A Changing Landscape

While we can identify a geographic sphere and fixed characteristic concepts related to place, people, history, and distinctiveness—the rural community also exhibited characteristics that were fluid in structure and function. During the late nineteenth and early twentieth centuries, the way of life for many people also included changes brought about (gradually in many rural areas) by factors including industrialization, the growing urban population, and changing American values that impacted rural communities both directly and indirectly.

In the home, the family was extended by blood relatives, but also by the presence of hired help. Some households regularly changed with the seasons, as fathers and brothers went to the lumber camps in the winter months (sometimes staying from fall until spring) or farm and household workers arrived and then left again. The communal space and the shared ideas that resulted from these fluid social environments produced particular sets of cultural characteristics.

It is easy to think of New England in the nineteenth and early twentieth centuries as the starting point for westward journeys rather than as a location for new settlements. In fact, families arrived in the northern states from all directions during this period. Many were drawn to the area because of opportunities to work in the lumber, marble, and granite industries, or in the textile mills. The opportunity for farming was also an attraction for many settlers, especially as land became oversettled and overcultivated in the southern regions.

Industrial development that impacted the region most strongly took place particularly in the broadly defined activities of the lumber industry, and the mills for manufacturing cotton and wool. The industries were responsible for many changes to the land and the people that ultimately affected their economy and their social and cultural values.

During the first three decades of the twentieth century, national and regional concern about the rural environment spurred social movements that sought to survey, emulate, and modify rural life during a period of radical change in the social and industrial fabric of American life. Theodore Roosevelt's Country Life Commission of 1908 was established to evaluate and improve rural life in America—and to assure agricultural health for both rural and urban residents. This was followed in the 1920s by a Vermont Commission on Country Life that had a similar goal.[12] Throughout this period a back-to-the-land movement encouraged some urban dwellers to take up residence in rural America, including locations in northern New England, but it also reinforced a nostalgia for rural life through some of the views of cultural and social realms that were emerging from the literature produced by the commissions. By glorifying the past and reaching to historical cultures to frame an idealized identity, the participants in these movements (including some of the collectors who provided data for this study) affected the forms and styles of cultural expression of rural regions throughout the United States.

The effect of urban growth in southern New England during the nineteenth and twentieth centuries on residents of the north was felt both directly and indirectly. Overdevelopment in the southern New England states encouraged movement within this population to the north, thereby changing the character of that population. But the urban values that slowly moved into the entire region from elsewhere in the United States had a greater effect on cultural output and expression. It would be inaccurate to say that northern New England was spared the changes that affected the social and cultural lives of Americans during the late nineteenth and early twentieth centuries. Yet the character of the land, the people, the economy, and the social structure affected these influences in unique ways to create what can be described as a separate geographic region.

After the 1940s

Music flourished as an active and interactive tradition during the late nineteenth and early twentieth centuries in rural communities. While music and musical experience in communities were protected from some of the changes that occurred earlier in more highly populated towns and cities, those rural communities began to move into the musical mainstream during the early years of the twentieth century.[13] By the 1930s the process of transformation had begun to affect the nature and (in some cases) continuation of some of the local traditions. Contrasting directly with earlier practices, whose source was the socially, economically, and culturally interactive community, musical influences began to come from less interactive sources such as traveling stage performers, printed sources (sheet music and song books especially, but also more widely circulated newspapers and magazines), and the radio and recorded media, which were growing in popularity.

During the earlier period, most musicians who contributed to local music lived within the community and were supported by a local audience. Relative geographical isolation discouraged widespread travel, and it was common for families and neighbors to provide entertainment for each other on a daily, weekly, or seasonal basis. When standards for performance were no longer family or community generated but instead arose more from an aesthetic outside the community, they left the social sphere for a broadly defined public arena that lacked the human contact to maintain them.

By the 1930s and 1940s, musical standards for many people in this region were set by national radio programs and the hillbilly song industry. This affected community values that influenced the reduction and rejection of repertoires, the relative importance of song and instrumental traditions, even what men, women, and children did with their leisure time. For many people these newer traditions became a source for family tradition, supplanting older practices.

Certainly, music events in rural northern New England in the latter part of the twentieth century exhibit some of the characteristics of earlier traditions. Many dance tunes are closely connected to old tunes, and public singing continues in some locations. Yet the environment in which the songs of the earlier period were learned and shared is gone; there are few reports of household singing in what was once a common private sphere of music making. Yet while community continues to play a role, especially at dance events in the region, it is *not* often derived from a group of people that is intergenerational in composition, that has familial connections and lives in close proximity, that exhibits continuous need for mutual support. These changes influence the overall character of the musical output of each social group and the perception of meaning in each performance. Given the close relationship between repertoire, performance practice, and community, it is not surprising that the changes that took place (including the loss of traditions) would be so extreme.

Residents of rural northern Vermont, New Hampshire, and Maine lived in spatial domains defined by the physical geography, over which they had little control, and by the cultural geography established and contributed to by the communities themselves. Members of the community depended upon one another for support, camaraderie, and socialization, and social obligation became a critical factor in their everyday lives. The resulting reciprocity turned into a pattern of farm mutuality that was the primary element in family and community survival. Music was an essential element in the mutuality in these communities, providing the means and environment for socialization, communication, creativity, and the maintenance and reinforcement of tradition.

CHAPTER 2

The Musical Landscape: Singing Traditions

*T*he unique character of music in rural regions is reflected in community repertoires and performance practice. Historical collections often present an inaccurate picture of the northern New England musical landscape by indicating a narrowly defined tradition that consists primarily of Anglo-American ballads and old-time dance tunes.[1] Michael Pickering identifies this as an issue of representation and control in *Village Song and Culture,* his 1983 study on nineteenth- and twentieth-century rural English communities. He comments on contributions made by collectors like Janet Blunt (1859–1950), who collected in the northern Oxfordshire region of England between 1907 and 1919:[2]

> Rural working class life was far more culturally dynamic when it comes to music than collections such as that made by Janet Blunt, based upon pre-selected criteria, would tend to suggest, and it may well be that folk-song, as conventionally defined, and the idea of a 'folksinger' confining himself or herself only to the hallowed material of oral tradition, are in some ways products of a cultural conspiracy. (Pickering 1983: 51)

Recent interviews with northern New England performers and their families, information compiled from nineteenth- and twentieth-century diaries and manuscript collections, and historical recordings provide evidence that in fact musical traditions in the region were not fully represented by the collections compiled by American collectors between 1920 and 1965. Musical repertoires were broad; furthermore, they were fluid and flexible in performance practice, enriched by musical ideas shared within the family unit and among neighbors and other community members.

Like their lifestyles, the music that rural northern New England families and communities preserved and shared had connections to the traditional music of their homelands, which they had adapted over time to their own social and physical landscape. Song repertoires and social functions maintained flexible lines within culturally defined parameters. The diverse and constantly changing repertoires were drawn from songs passed orally in families for generations, from broadsides and songbooks, and from radio programs and commercial recordings. The repertoires in many families included the British and American ballads valued by early collectors as well as a rich tradition of popular songs, play-party songs, hymns, and dance tunes.

Contexts for Singing

Descriptions of musical performance during work and at events associated with leisure are retained in the memories of individuals who lived in rural households during the late nineteenth century and the early years of the twentieth century. In *Village Song and Culture*, Pickering isolates two types of musical events associated particularly with English traditional song: first, when people gathered specifically to sing, and second, when singing was "part of an accepted pattern, following or preceding or falling between other events of equal, perhaps greater importance" (Pickering 1983: 23, 59). In the narratives of northern New England residents, we find that singing and other musical performance played a range of social roles in their communities, ranging from the central activity in a family context or a gathering of neighbors to one of several forms of cultural and social expression at an event attended by family, friends, or the wider community. Music was often associated with specific events and event types, and there is a clear correlation between activity type (leisure vs. work) and the relationship of song to event, as well as a relationship between performance space and specific musical genres. While there is, of course, variation in the character of occasions during which music was performed in families and neighborhoods in each community, we find enough similarity throughout the region to establish patterns that are common to northern New England.

GATHERINGS SPECIFICALLY TO SING

Events that took place *exclusively* for performing music in the household or the neighborhood context were relatively rare. Instead, there were many events during which singing or music making was a significant activity, but other activities (socializing, storytelling, card playing, and dancing) played an equally important—and sometimes greater—role. There are frequent references, however, to family members who gathered in the kitchen or parlor in the evening during the week specifically to sing. In Middlebury, Vermont, Elizabeth Vaara talked to me about her father's music at home in Ripton, Vermont, during the first few decades of the twentieth century:

> Sometimes, you know, when we had company, and sometimes when we was all alone he used to sit there and sing those songs. And he taught us the "Woodmen's Song" there, and that's how we learned our ABC's, I guess. . . . Or in the dining room we had a big table, of course, for a big family and we used to sit around that and sing. And then sometimes we'd go in what they called the parlor—the livin' room. And my brother and my sister'd play the organ and we'd sing.[3]

In the wider community, neighbors and families would gather to socialize in a similar way. The "sing" was an informal occasion for sharing songs that took place in families, neighborhoods, and work-related groups. These events invariably occupied times of leisure, after work was done for the day or week, in neighborhood homes or a common room in the lumber camps (the dining room or bunkroom). The repertoire offered at these events included ballads, popular songs, play party songs, and hymns. In the neighborhood this was often referred to as "having a sing" or a "party." Sometimes the event revolved around a singer or singers especially known for their renditions of certain songs. I asked Clyde Covill, from northern New Hampshire, about gatherings at the home of one of his neighbors:

> Lots of people used to come back when they had them parties, that's the way they used to handle them parties, lots of times. They would have a singalong with it, you know. And they'd asked people to sing—that was "a sing"—someone that they knew that really could. And that was quite a lot of entertainment. And once in a while they'd spring a song the rest hadn't heard, then oh boy! That was wonderful. It's probably the song they learnt when they were younger, before that they knew them.[4]

Neighbors, family, and friends also gathered to sing, recite stories, or, less often, offer an instrumental tune. The expressed purpose of the event was social, but not specifically for singing. These events took place both in the home and in the occupational sphere. Referencing performance practices in northern New Hampshire in the early years of the twentieth century, Ardes Haynes remembered the varied repertoires: "A lot of the entertainment back then was people would get together in the evening, there might be two or three that would speak pieces, then some of 'em would sing. They'd entertain each other. That was the entertainment."[5]

In the lumbercamps, gatherings specifically for entertainment took place with regularity. Ives, in his study of "woodsman song-maker" Joe Scott in Maine, reports that men assembled on Saturday evenings after a long week of work in the woods. A "formal entertainment context" for performance did not exist in every camp, but when it did, the performances included singing as well as stepdancing, instrumental music (primarily fiddle and harmonica), storytelling, and recitations (Ives 1978: 375). Ives describes the environment reported by many men who spent winters in the woods:

> Sometimes Saturday-night entertainment would be highly organized and would involve the entire crowd. Angus Enman . . . had worked for years over in the Androscoggin watershed in Maine and New Hampshire, and when I asked him about singing in the camps, he replied, "Saturday night, you see, when you'd come into the camp after supper you had to tell a story or sing a song or dance. If you didn't, they'd ding you; they'd put the dried codfish to you . . . They had these old dried codfish, and if you wouldn't sing or dance or do something . . . they'd take the dried codfish and two or three would throw you down and whale you with it . . . Hit you! Hard! Yeah . . . If you couldn't sing, you could tell a good story [or] perhaps you could

dance. There'd be a fella have a fiddle there, see, and give a tune . . . Oh yes, somebody he'd go round: 'Now boy, come on. Do what you're going to do.' " (Ives 1978: 380)

Singing was also a central activity at organized events such as singing schools, hymn sings, and camp meetings and revival meetings. While early diaries indicate that people gathered regularly to sing at singing schools in northern New England during the eighteenth and early nineteenth centuries, by the mid-nineteenth century, camp and revival meetings were also becoming popular and by the early twentieth century hymn sings at homes and in churches, in addition to the established camp meetings were also found in some communities.

SINGING AS AN ADJUNCT TO OTHER ACTIVITIES

Singing also took place in conjunction with other activities, including events accompanied occasionally by song, and others where there is a clear relationship between song and activity. Music was not the central activity in either case. Kathryn Fogg of Pittsburg, New Hampshire, expressed this well when I asked her about her family's songs: "If my mother was singing and we felt like singing, well, we did. But we never had any time set aside for this."[6]

Singing While Working

Singing played an important role in the daily lives of both women and men, yet when I spoke with residents about singing at work I discovered that more women than men could recall this. Ardes Haynes of Pittsburg, New Hampshire, remembered: "A lot of people would sing at home where today you hardly ever hear anybody singing at work—but lots of people used to sing while they were doing their work. And it might be just a snatch or part of a song and it might be a full song."[7] Singing was used often during work bees and while residents were doing indoor and outdoor household chores. Thelma Neill of Warren, Vermont, remembered singing with her mother: "Yes, sometimes doing dishes we'd sing. Sometimes she and I would sing after the rest of them was gone—and we'd sing when we were doing our work."[8]

When women sang at work, they were singing both to themselves and to their children. The songs distracted them from the pressures of their work and kept the children occupied while completing their household chores. In a 1931 interview with Helen Hartness Flanders, Nellie Richardson of Springfield, Vermont, remembered her mother dancing around the kitchen singing her version of "The Auld Soldier."[9] Marjorie Pierce of North Shrewsbury remembers her mother singing songs while doing her kitchen chores: "She sang when she was doing dishes, washing, or working around the house. I think she sang for company, and to make the work lighter, and so on—you know, the time goes more rapidly. And I presume when we were young she was alone—it kind of kept her company."[10]

Gerard Richards from northern New Hampshire learned songs from his grandfather at work when he lived with his grandparents as a young child. He describes his grandfather, a blacksmith, singing the ballad "Old Kelly's Blood" ("The Irish Patriot"): "Grandpa, he'd be banging away on the anvil—with a song at the top of his voice. And like this 'Old Kelly's Blood,' I've heard him sing it time and time again."[11]

On the farms, children were involved in household chores in the women's domain as well as with their fathers in the barn or on the land.[12] The repertoire and singing style found inside the house and in the outbuildings of a farm was not always the same, because women and men tended to adopt different songs, and to express themselves differently in song. Children, then, heard and learned various songs and ways of singing in each context.

Despite the close association of singing with work, the traditional "work song" was found only in limited geographic and social spheres in northern New England. Referring to lumbercamp singing, Edward Ives comments:

> It was not something to time the blows of the axes or to keep men moving together while they were rolling or lifting logs on the drives or on the yards or landings. In this way the lumberman's life contrasts sharply with what we read about the sailor's life, where the shanties were work songs and were very distinct from the songs men sang for pleasure in the forecastle off watch. There were no work songs in the woods at all, in the strictest sense of the word. (Ives 1978: 374)

On the Maine coast, on the other hand, shanties were typically used to regulate specific activities such as raising and lowering sails and other operations on sailing vessels.[13] In some homes women who were engaged in spinning and wool processing occasionally used songs to regulate this work too.

SINGING ASSOCIATED WITH COMMUNAL ACTIVITIES

Communal functions often grew out of the cooperative activities in the farm sphere that contributed to the economic health and wellbeing of the community. These functions expanded during the nineteenth and early twentieth centuries to include events sponsored by local, regional, and national organizations, such as local fairs, church events, town meetings, and Grange-sponsored events. Some gatherings were gender specific and others were made up only of young couples, but many were broad, intergenerational affairs.

Music was associated with many types of communal activities, but it was not always their main purpose and more often consisted of instrumental music and dance rather than singing. Events ranged from informal work bees to loosely organized gatherings that provided opportunities for family, neighbors, and friends to maintain the social networks during both work and play.

From the social networks arose the pattern of entertainment that was often locally referred to as the "kitchen dance." This was a chance for neighbors, relatives, and friends to gather to dance, socialize, share food, and sometimes sing.[14] In 1934, Martin Leonard of Shaftsbury Hollow, Vermont, remembered that the songs "The Lamented Cowboy" and "Miss Clara Noble's Ball" were sung at kitchen dances. In 1931, Annie Adams of Springfield, Vermont, recalled learning "The Old Oak Tree" at a kitchen dance in Quebec: "When we girls would get tired of dancing, first one, then another of the company would sing old songs."[15]

While some activities were followed by dances, certain local seasonal customs within a community included singing as well. In many communities, singing played a role similar to card playing or conversation. People described a gathering following a work bee that would included a meal followed by a game of cards or the sharing of songs.

Where Songs Were Learned and How They Were Remembered

Family and community members learned songs that originated in both the oral and printed media throughout the period. Sources for their songs included other family members, itinerant workers, teachers, neighbors, and coworkers, but also the radio, phonograph records, sheet music, hymnbooks, broadsides, and songsters, all of which played an increasing role in people's lives. Songs were also remembered and transmitted orally within a family or community context, or individuals and families used copybooks to preserve them.

Unfortunately, until quite recently, song collectors were interested primarily—if not exclusively—in material learned orally from family or community members. They avoided songs that informants admitted were learned from books or the radio, or that had been retained using songsheets or copybooks. Songs that had been learned from media sources were seldom recorded for collections during the early years of the century. Instead, they remain frozen in their printed and commercially recorded form, and their development as they moved into oral tradition was not documented. We therefore must recognize first that early collectors and their historical collections provide us with a limited view of song transmission.

In addition, we must rely today on interview data from the early twentieth century and interviews with singers' relatives who are today in their seventies, eighties, and nineties. Sources of songs were not always recorded in the early years, and today singers are frequently unable to recall where they or their relatives learned them.

Among singers that do recall where they learned their songs, we find that they identify sources ranging from different family and other household members to public gatherings. For example, Lona Bourne Fish of East Jeffrey, New Hampshire, learned songs from an itinerant singer, her parents, her grandparents, her mother-in-law, and the church.[16] In Vermont, Myra Daniels records her mother, her father, a woodsman, a neighbor, a friend, and her grandfather, respectively, as sources for six different songs.[17] In Burlington, Maine, Mrs. Norris Moore in 1936 included as her sources for songs "an old lady, her brother, men in the woods, her grandfather, her mother, and other women in the community.[18]

The records seldom indicate that singers pursued individuals as sources for songs (although occasionally a singer will mention this, saying "I wanted to get all the words to that song!"). Singers often expressed a great appreciation for the opportunities they had to hear—and therefore learn—a song from a specific singer, but songs were more often presented as learned by chance in singers' everyday lives during their work or leisure time.

Despite the limited data, information on some of the sources for songs transmitted orally can enrich our view of music in the lives of individuals. A sampling of historical recordings from the region made between 1924 and 1960 indicates that family members were the most important sources of these songs (parents, grandparents, and siblings, especially brothers, are the primary sources).[19] This is true of both women and men, although many men who worked in the woods learned their songs from co-workers in the camps as well. Songs recorded by collectors were most often learned from immediate and extended family members in a home environment and least often in the public sphere that included schools, Grange hall, and the town hall. In the sample, 51 percent of the songs were learned from immediate family members; when extended family members are included, this increases to 70 percent. Churches, schools, and other public gathering places are seldom noted as sources of songs.[20] This does not mean that songs were not learned in these more public spaces, but we can infer that songs, and memories associated with them, were most valued when learned from individuals.

This sampling is affected by the collectors' personal values that developed during a period when popular songs learned from public forums or songs learned from books, records, or the radio were not as highly valued as oral sources for information on historical practice.

The Songs

When scholars established categories for songs that they were collecting in the nineteenth and early twentieth centuries, they provided a convenient method for identifying and discussing their technical elements. These scholars' enthusiasm for certain repertoires, though, also encouraged a generation of collectors to value some song types more than others. Since the singers and other community members appear not to have considered their categories before the collectors' arrival, historical collections that are maintained in the scholarly community do not fully represent vernacular music culture of the period. Instead they convey a concept that developed in literary circles in Great Britain and the United States and was then maintained by the collectors and administrators during the first half of the twentieth century. Although we like to think that families in rural communities sat around and exclusively sang old Child ballads like "Lord Bateman" or "Barbara Allen," in fact there was often little or no apparent distinction made between the Child and broadside or parlor and American ballads; the "folk" and "popular" musics so designated by scholars. Families enjoyed humor, suspense, and human tragedy in the songs they sang. Both the old songs of the seventeenth to eighteenth centuries as well as the more contemporary popular songs provided this for them.

It was not unusual in the late twentieth century to hear an elderly singer recall how a family member sang an old ballad—sometimes even one revered by collectors in the 1930s and 1940s. It was even more common, though, to hear them express fond memories of singing other American popular songs and old turn-of-the-century hymns in the same social contexts. In the early 1940s a Bethel, Vermont, woman corresponded with the collector Helen Hartness Flanders about her family songs when she was young. Of her mother's contribution she said, "My mother . . . used to amuse us children by reciting poems and singing good old Watts hymns and drinking songs with equal gusto, taking just about as much stock in one as the other."[21]

In fact, research reveals that performances often included popular songs learned from both printed and oral sources, and that the older ballads sought by collectors were not as familiar as many of them led the public to believe. In the early 1930s, Ida B. Morgan of Jeffersonville, Vermont, responded to Flanders's request for "old ballads":

> I have tackled my friends about old songs, but even the musical ones don't know any that have not been printed. There are plenty like "Are We Almost There," "I'm Sitting on the Stile Mary," "Nellie Gray," "Mary's Dream," "Gentle Annie," etc., but I have clipped most of those from the Family Herald and Weekly Star.
>
> I have never seen nor heard of "False Lamkin," "Lord Banner," "Robin Hood Ballads," "The Greenwood Side."
>
> "The Fox and the Grapes," grandmother used to sing to me and I never heard anyone else sing it and never saw it anywhere.
>
> That day of Judgment hymn, "Sinners You Will Tremble," mother used to sing me to sleep with. It was a strange lullaby, but I liked it.
>
> Mother told me of another song written by one of her uncles about "Uncle Hall's Barn." It was of purely local interest and probably known only in that neighborhood. [22]

Data compiled on musical traditions in the region indicate that Morgan's narrative presents a more typical repertoire of the period than repertoires identified by scholars at the time. While informants responded to collector's requests for the old songs, they remembered songs more by their subject matter and social function than by their category. Their repertoires were broad and fluid, as varied as events in their lives. Rural performers sang ballads that included vivid details about local murders and other tragic community events. Yet they also sang about fictional characters and events that seemed to have little relationship to everyday life.[23] Men who worked in the lumber camps sang what are sometimes described as "sentimental" songs about home and family, along with ballads that narrated the details of accidents that occurred all too frequently in the woods.[24] Yet the men also challenged one another with satirical songs about coworkers and friends, performed solo dances, and sang erotic, humorous, or tall-tale songs. Women working in the kitchen sang very long ballads learned in their families or clipped from newspapers to keep themselves distracted and to occupy their children; or they sang hymns learned at church or religious meetings. Yet they also gathered in the family or the neighborhood to sing popular songs learned from songbooks, the radio, or the Victrola. Children at play parties or on the playground, teenagers, and even adults at socials sang and danced to play party songs using nonsense, humor, and mime.[25] Yet they also sang songs that sometimes focused on the death of children through dramatic play/performance. Many of these families gathered together to dance to lively tunes on a Saturday night at neighborhood and town events, sometimes dancing all night after a long day of work, returning in the morning just in time to get the cows milked and begin the other morning chores.

Altogether these songs and tunes described the individual's and community's life experience: prescriptions for socially acceptable behavior; a constant and close relationship to the geographic and social landscape; the risk and reality of tragedies or accidents in everyday lives; local history maintained by recollecting people and events. These performances took the singers and listeners, dancers and instrumentalists temporarily away from their everyday lives even as they focused on those lives in song.

Ballads

Collectors combing the hills of Appalachia and New England during the early years of the twentieth century sought information on the "ancient ballads" derived from European traditions of the sixteenth and seventeenth centuries. Discovery of the songs in the homes of the rural residents reinforced connections to relatives and ancestors, many from the British Isles, fewer from France (via Canada). In fact, when asked to recall the singing traditions of their childhood, many older regional residents, who were interviewed during the twentieth century, referred to narrative songs that were once popular in their families. These ballads were enjoyed by children and adults in a variety of contexts and were part of the repertoire of tales passed along within families in both spoken and sung form.

Ballads included captivating stories, moral tales, and narratives about people and events. Singers sometimes personalized or localized the recounted events, making slight changes in the lyrics by adding or inserting identifying elements from within their community. Audience members also made a personal connection to the songs by finding names, experiences, and emotions that were familiar to them. When tragedies were recounted in song, singers and their audiences related to the event itself, sometimes recognizing that it *could* have taken place in their community, even when it did not.

The localized versions of the Anglo-American ballads that have been identified with rural life in Appalachia and New England share the unique characteristics exhibited by ballads of this period in both Europe and the New World. They generally tell a story with a single theme in strophic form, and some include a refrain. Typically they rely upon formulaic verse, specific meters, and thematic uniformity to move their stories from complication to climax to resolution (Renwick 1980: 113). Musically, some of the early ballads share common or similar contours and use the older European modes, while later ballads adopt the more widely used major and minor scales. Between the late nineteenth and mid-twentieth centuries, scholars organized ballads found in the United States among English language speakers by story type and placed them into categories that were indicative of their imagined and (sometimes) documented history. These categories have been broadly termed *Child* (today they sometimes referred to as the "classical" ballads), *broadside,* and *regional* (once referred to as "Native American").[26] It is important to emphasize, though, that singers seldom indicated an interest in or any knowledge about ballad or song classification and were instead simply concerned with the entertainment the songs provided.

Today the historical view of this song culture is the product of the relationship between the performers' and the collector-scholars' views, which are virtually impossible to separate. Most of the information that is available on the songs has been categorized, and singers and their relatives today have adopted through contact with the early collectors and through the literature that their music exists in different categories and is valued in relation to them. While performers do not acknowledge ballad classification, the consideration of these narrative songs and scholars' categorical divisions helped them to understand stylistic difference, historical practice, and social function, as well as to document local and regional change.

CHILD BALLADS

The ballads compiled in the nineteenth century by Francis James Child (who believed he was gathering and preserving the oldest narrative songs of the British Isles) are identified musically by their modality, and textually by the way their stories are told.[27] Generally they are more impersonal than many of the other songs in northern New England collections. The dramatic retelling of a tale may contain dialogue and nearly always includes exaggeration; the language is stylized and uses formulaic phrases and stanzas. These characteristics in practice produced long, lyrical stories that both singers and listeners were drawn to again and again.

When collectors in the rural southern and northeastern states began to look for evidence of traditional songs, they made it clear to their informants that they were primarily concerned with recovering the Child ballads from oral tradition.[28] This intense search for a particular ballad type, while ignoring other categories of songs, did allow scholars to learn a great deal about these narrative song traditions in a particular historical and geographic context. Between 1920 and 1965 regional collectors in northern New England, including Phillips Barry, Fannie Hardy Eckstorm, Eloise Linscott, and Helen Hartness Flanders, found the evidence they sought: many of the Child ballads were known in rural northeastern families. Of the 305 unique titles that Child identified and numbered, there is evidence—in the ballads themselves, fragments, and references to singing—that nearly half of them were found in some form in New England. A typical example of a well-known ballad of this type, popular in New England and other parts of the country, is "Lady Isabel and the Elf Knight" (Child 4). As with many of the other ballads, the title and internal details varied but were unified by a common story. In northern New England the song had various titles, especially "The Outlandish Knight" but also "Castle by the Sea," "Daughter of Old England," "The False-Hearted Knight," "He Followed Me Up He Followed Me Down," "Pretty Polly," "The Pretty Colin," and "Six Kings' Daughters." The ballad tells the story of a young woman (Polly or Nancy) who was spirited away by a false-hearted man (often identified as a knight). She thwarts his attempt to murder her with her creative responses to his careless actions (illustrated in the excerpt below as sung by Jonathan Moses of Orford, N.H.), ultimately causing the death that he had wished upon her.

"Take off, take off your gay clothing,
And leave it here with me,
For I think they are too rich and too costly
For to rot all in the salt sea."

"Oh, turn your back to the deep blue sea
And your face to the willow tree,
For I don't think it's fit for a ruffing like you
A naked lady to see."

He turned his back to the deep blue sea,
And his face to the willow tree,
And she grabbed him round the middle so small
And plunged him into the sea.

"Lie there, lie there, you false-hearted wretch,
Lie there instead of me.
If there's six kings' daughters you have drownded here,
Go keep them company."[29]

The popularity of this ballad, and others with similar themes ("Lady Isabel" was recorded by nearly twenty singers in all three states between 1908 and 1960), suggests shared community values in its structure, use of language, and the views it reinforces. Ballads of this kind were maintained during the nineteenth and early twentieth centuries across the region.

Also popular both locally and nationally is "Young Beichan" (Child 53), commonly known as "Lord Bateman," "Lord Bakeman," or "Lord Bacon," which recounts an adventure of a "noble lord" who traveled from India to Turkey, where he was jailed and finally freed by the jailer's daughter. His freedom came with a pact that neither he nor the daughter would marry for seven years. At the end of the allotted time, she arrives at the nobleman's estate in India to find that his marriage to another woman has taken place that very day. The man is thus torn between two women.

Then up spoke the young bride's mother,
Who never was heard to speak so free.
"Don't you forget my only daughter,
Although Sophia has crossed the sea."

"I own I've made a bride of your daughter
She's none the better or worse for me,
She came to me on a horse and saddle
She may return in a coach and three."

Then another marriage was prepared
With both their hearts so full of glee,
"I'll rove no more to foreign countries
Since Sophia has crossed the sea for me."[30]

These and other ballads such as "The Farmer's Curst Wife" (with the uniform title "The Old Scolding Wife," Child 278), "The Golden Vanity" ("The Sweet Trinity," Child 286), and "Bonny Barbara Allen" (Child 84) were well known in both rural and urban communities not only because they were passed orally in families but because they were some of the most popular ballads printed in songbooks and on broadsides. Performers of these songs provided their communities with endless variations on the basic theme, as exemplified in the lyrics on a broadside printed in New York at the end of the nineteenth century and a version of the same song sung by Hattie Smith in Springfield, Maine, in 1942.

Barbara Allen

In Scarlet Town where I did dwell,
There was a maiden dwelling;
Young Jimmy Grove did love her well;
Her name was Barbara Allen.

On the fifteenth day of May,
The green fields were a-blooming;
This young man on his death-bed lay
For the love of Barbara Allen.

So slowly she put on her gown,
So slowly she went to him;
And all she said when she got there
Was, "Young man, you are a-dying."

"For death is printed on your face
And sorrow on your bearing;
You never will be none the better for me,
Nor the love of Barbara Allen."

She had not got far out of town
Before the bells were tolling,

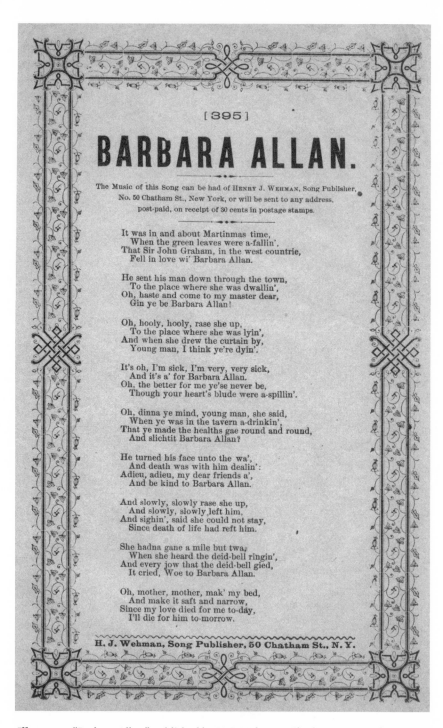

[395]

BARBARA ALLAN.

The Music of this Song can be had of Henry J. Wehman, Song Publisher, No. 50 Chatham St., New York, or will be sent to any address, post-paid, on receipt of 30 cents in postage stamps.

It was in and about Martinmas time,
When the green leaves were a-fallin',
That Sir John Graham, in the west countrie,
Fell in love wi' Barbara Allan.

He sent his man down through the town,
To the place where she was dwallin',
Oh, haste and come to my master dear,
Gin ye be Barbara Allan!

Oh, hooly, hooly, rase she up,
To the place where she was lyin',
And when she drew the curtain by,
Young man, I think ye're dyin'.

It's oh, I'm sick, I'm very, very sick,
And it's a' for Barbara Allan.
Oh, the better for me ye'se never be,
Though your heart's blude were a-spillin'.

Oh, dinna ye mind, young man, she said,
When ye was in the tavern a-drinkin',
That ye made the healths gae round and round,
And slichtit Barbara Allan?

He turned his face unto the wa',
And death was with him dealin':
Adieu, adieu, my dear friends a',
And be kind to Barbara Allan.

And slowly, slowly rase she up,
And slowly, slowly left him,
And sighin', said she could not stay,
Since death of life had reft him.

She hadna gane a mile but twa,
When she heard the deid-bell ringin',
And every jow that the deid-bell gied,
It cried, Woe to Barbara Allan.

Oh, mother, mother, mak' my bed,
And make it saft and narrow,
Since my love died for me to-day,
I'll die for him to-morrow.

H. J. Wehman, Song Publisher, 50 Chatham St., N. Y.

Illus. 2.1. "Barbara Allan," published by H. J. Wehman, Chatham, New York.

And with the tolling of the bells
Laughed cruel Barbara Allen.

She turned about to get her breath
And spied the funeral coming;
She laughed to see him pale in death.
O cruel Barbara Allen!

When he was buried in his grave,
Her heart did burst with sorrow.
"O mother, mother, make my bed,
For I shall die tomorrow!"

"Now maidens all a warning take
And shun the way I fell in,
Or else your heart like mine will break;
Farewell!" said Barbara Allen.[31]

The well-known ballads were also found in collections and newspaper columns during the early years of the twentieth century that printed nostalgic songs enjoyed by readers. The interest in these titles by collectors and revivalists of this period was also responsible for their maintenance in local New England communities.[32]

The region also retained ballads that were not often heard in other parts of the country (or even the British Isles during the twentieth century). "Willie O Winsbury" (known locally as "Johnny Barbour" or "Fair Mary" and popular in Vermont in the 1930s; Child 100) relates the story of a father's objection to his daughter's plan to marry a mere sailor. The issue is resolved when the sailor reveals that he is actually the Duke of Cumberland. Other rare ballads include the farcical "The Keach i' the Kreel" (Child 281), recovered only in fragmentary form in New Hampshire and Maine, and "Hind Horn" ("The Old Beggarman," Child 17), recorded in Maine in 1928 and 1942.[33] The most complete regional version of this song, cited in Barry's *British Ballads from Maine,* was recorded by Eckstorm in 1928 (Barry 1929: 73–75):

Hind Horn

"Whence came ye, or from what counteree?
Whence came ye, or where were you born?"
"In Ireland I was bred and born
Until I became a hele and his horn.

"I gave my love a gay gold watch
That she might rule her own counteree,
And she gave me a gay gold ring,
And the virtue of this was above all things.

"If this ring bees bright and true,
Be sure your love is true to you;
But if this ring bees pale and wan,
Your true love's in love with some other man."

He set sail and off went he,
Until that he came to a strange counteree.
He looked at the ring, it was pale and wan,
His true love was in love with some other one.

He set sail and back came he,
Until that he came to his own counteree,
And as he was riding along the plain,
Who should he meet but an old beggar man.

"What news, what news, you old beggar man?
What news, what news have you got for me?"
"No news, no news," said the old beggar man,
"But tomorrow is your true love's wedding day."

"You lend me your begging rig,
And I'll lend you your riding stage."
"Your riding stage ain't fit for me,
Nor my begging rig ain't fit for you."

"Whether it be right, or whether it be wrong,
The begging rig they must go on.
So come, tell to me as fast as you can
What's to be done with the begging rig."

"As you go up to yonder hill,
You may walk as fast as 'tis your will,
And when you come to yonder gate,
You may lean upon your staff with trembling step.

"You may beg from Pitt, you may beg from Paul,
You may beg from the highest to the lowest of them all;
But from them all you need take none
Until you come to the bride's own hand."

She came trembling down the stairs,
Rings on her fingers and gold in her hair,
A glass of wine all in her hand,
Which she gave to the old beggar man.

He took the glass and drank the wine,
And in the glass he slipped the ring.
"Oh, where got you this, by sea or by land,
Or did you get it off a drowned one's hand?"

"Neither got I it by sea or land,
Neither did I get it off a drowned one's hand;
I got it in my courting gay,
And gave it to my love on her wedding day."

Rings from her fingers she did pull off,
Gold from her hair did she let fall,
Saying, "I'll go with you forever more
And beg my bread from door to door."

Between the kitchen and the hall
The diner's coat he did let fall,
All a-shining in gold amongst them all,
And he was the fairest in the hall.

By the time northern New England collectors were systematically recording songs in Vermont, Maine, and New Hampshire in the 1930s and 1940s, singers had put aside many of the Child ballads in favor of songs disseminated through the popular music industry. While the musical and lyrical characteristics of the newer songs were sometimes different, the overriding focus on human relationships remained.

BROADSIDE BALLADS

Many of the ballads rejected by Child for inclusion in his collection were also derived from singing traditions in seventeenth- and eighteenth-century England, Ireland, and Scotland. While the songs that came to be known as "broadside ballads" are often characterized as "newer" than the Child ballads, this is not always true.[34] Printed on one side of a single sheet of paper, they were also found in "chapbooks," small booklets that held the words (but rarely the music) for several ballads. Hawkers sold the song sheets and chapbooks on the streets in the cities of Great Britain as early as the sixteenth century, and similarly in American cities (especially Philadelphia, Boston, and New York) during the eighteenth and nineteenth centuries. Many of the songs that today are considered broadside ballads were passed orally in families for many generations before being printed, or they were created by printers in the style of the most popular ballads that were already in oral tradition.

While Child and broadside ballads share a number of stylistic elements, some scholars differentiate the broadside ballads from Child ballads because they are more descriptive and show some lyrical patterns not often seen in the classical songs, including a "come-all-ye" opening and a greater inclination to complete the song with a moralizing stanza. These stanzas embody both the social nature of the song—the call to the listener to heed—and the mark of identity left sometimes by singers who add their own final "warning." In 1941, Charles Finnemore of Bridgewater, Maine, began his very lyrical version of the broadside ballad "The Female Smuggler" this way:

The Female Smuggler

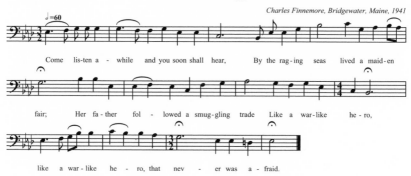

Come listen awhile and you soon shall hear,
By the raging seas lived a maiden fair;
Her father followed a smuggling trade
Like a war-like hero, like a war-like hero, that never was afraid.[35]

Tunes of the songs were generally not included on the song sheets, and the performance practice exhibited by Finnemore in this recording includes clearly stated lyrics and a loosely structured meter; his voice projects confidence and challenges his audience to *listen*. These elements typified many of these ballads sung to entertain a group—for example, lumbermen, neighbors, or children in the singer's family. The absence of tunes on the song sheets also encouraged singers to use well-known tunes to sing the ballads, sharing melodies among groups of songs that were metrically related. During the period that broadside ballads were popular, the repertoires of performers included diverse styles—not only ballads codified by Child and Laws but other popular songs as well. Thus the tunes that were used were drawn from the singers' varied experiences with many styles.

Laws's designations of British broadsides in the United States indicate at least 290 titles found before the 1950s. Inventories compiled by collectors in northern New England reveal that they in turn found nearly 200 of these ballads in the region. One, a variation of "The Bold Privateer" (Laws O32), was collected in fragmentary form in Colebrook, New Hampshire, in 1943.

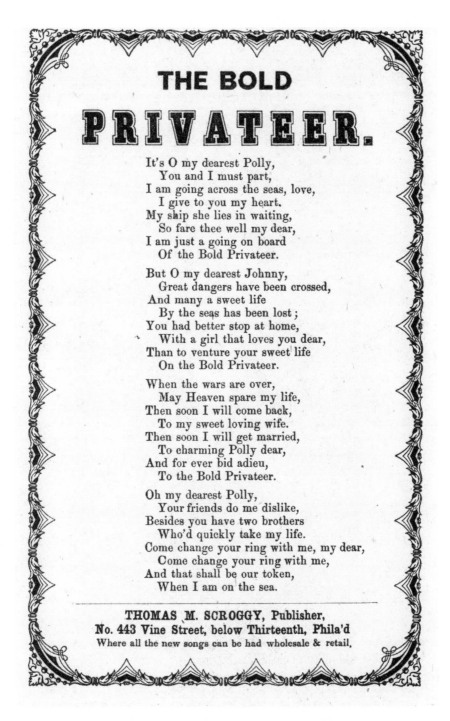

THE BOLD
PRIVATEER.

It's O my dearest Polly,
    You and I must part,
I am going across the seas, love,
    I give to you my heart.
My ship she lies in waiting,
    So fare thee well my dear,
I am just a going on board
    Of the Bold Privateer.

But O my dearest Johnny,
    Great dangers have been crossed,
And many a sweet life
    By the seas has been lost;
You had better stop at home,
    With a girl that loves you dear,
Than to venture your sweet life
    On the Bold Privateer.

When the wars are over,
    May Heaven spare my life,
Then soon I will come back,
    To my sweet loving wife.
Then soon I will get married,
    To charming Polly dear,
And for ever bid adieu,
    To the Bold Privateer.

Oh my dearest Polly,
    Your friends do me dislike,
Besides you have two brothers
    Who'd quickly take my life.
Come change your ring with me, my dear,
    Come change your ring with me,
And that shall be our token,
    When I am on the sea.

THOMAS M. SCROGGY, Publisher,
No. 443 Vine Street, below Thirteenth, Phila'd
Where all the new songs can be had wholesale & retail.

Illus. 2.2. "The Bold Privateer," Thomas M. Scroggy, Philadelphia.

The Bold Privateer

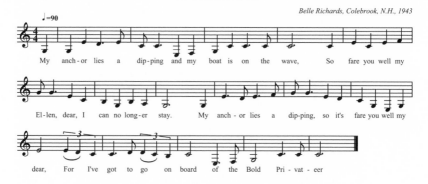

Belle Richards, Colebrook, N.H., 1943

My anchor lies a dipping and my boat is on the wave,
So fare you well my Ellen, dear, I can no longer stay.
My anchor lies a dipping, so it's fare you well my dear,
For I've got to go on board of the Bold Privateer.[36]

The British broadside ballads that were especially popular in northern New England before the middle of the century cover a broad array of topics dealing with relationships and issues that were often related in some way to the singers' lives. Some of these include "The Drowsy Sleeper" also known as "The Silver Dagger" (Laws M4) and "The Bold Soldier (Laws M27), both songs about parental opposition to a daughter's lover;[37] "The Boston Burglar" (Laws L16b),[38] a narrative of a repentant thief; and "Mary of the Wild Moor" (Laws P21), a story about a daughter who has a child out of wedlock and dies at her father's door attempting to return home. Also well known in the region is "The Dark Eyed Sailor" (Laws N35). Here is how James Shepard of Baltimore, Vermont, sang it in 1933.

The Dark Eyed Sailor

James Shepard, Baltimore, Vermont, 1933

It was of a comely lady fair
Was walking out to take the air;
She met a sailor upon the way
And I paid attention, and I paid attention
To hear what they did say.

Music in Rural New England Family and Community Life

He says, "Fair lady, why do you roam alone
For the night is come and day's far gone?"
She said, while tears from her eyes did fall,
"It's my dark eyed sailor, it's my dark eyed sailor
That cause me my downfall.

"It's three long years since he left this land.
A gold ring he took from off my hand.
He broke the token in half with me
The other is rolling, and the other is rolling
In the bottom of the sea."

Says Willie, "Drive him from your mind
As good a sailor as he you'll find.
Love turns aside and cold doth grow
Like a winter's morning, like a winter's morning
When the hills are clad with snow."

These words did poor Phoebe's heart inflame.
"Young man, on me you will play no game."
She drew a dagger and then did say,
"For my dark eyed sailor, for my dark eyed sailor
A maid I'll live and die."

Then Willie he did the ring unfold.
She seemed distracted with joy and woe.
"You are welcome, Willie. I have lands and gold,
For my dark-eyed sailor, for my dark-eyed sailor
So manly, true and bold."

In a cottage down by the riverside
In peace and harmony they do reside.
So girls, be true while your love's away.
Ofttimes a cloudy morning, ofttimes a cloudy morning
Brings forth a pleasant day.[39]

Shepard's concluding moralizing stanza contributes to the song's social function as a source of entertainment and education for both families and communities.

AMERICAN BALLADS

A third group of ballads sought by the collectors was comprised of songs resulting from the influence of both Child and broadside ballads on cultural expression and imagination in the region and in North America as a whole. Musically and textually, they are patterned after British ballads, yet they retain a separate identity, with local language and melodies used freely (borrowed from various melodic traditions).

Generally, American ballads present events that local singers related to directly: details of a murder, drowning, train accident, fire, or flood, or events that occurred (or could have taken place) at war or in the regional occupational realms of cowboys, lumbermen, and sailors.

The ballads were transmitted both orally and in print during the nineteenth and early twentieth centuries. While many composers introduced their songs orally, thereby rapidly moving them into oral tradition in occupational and other social communities, some were established (and even maintained) in print form. Some were composed by "professional" ballad writers and printed on broadsides like their English and Irish counterparts; more commonly, printed lyrics in the rural areas were transmitted through magazines and newspapers, where weekly columns offered readers new songs and poems.

Many American ballads, like the British ballads, opened with a "come-all-ye" stanza and sometimes included moralizing comments in their last verses. This characteristic encouraged singers to adapt their first and last verses to their own comments on the story's subject. Songs varied from singer to singer, or region to region. Also, like the broadside ballads, American ballads adopted popular tunes that fit the meter of the lyric. It is not uncommon to hear the same, or similar, tunes used for several ballads (especially those with related content).

G. Malcolm Laws classified American ballads according to story type in the mid-twentieth century.[40] Songs in nearly all his categories (which include war, cowboys and pioneers, sailors, tragedies and disasters) have been recovered in northern New England, with the largest representation on the subject of war, tragedies and disasters, murder, and especially lumbering. Among the lumbering ballads, there are many that recount stories about men who died on the river drives or in the northern woods of New England, New York, the Midwest, or Canada.[41] Many of the ballads invite the listener in a "come-all-ye" style. "Jam on Gerry's Rock" begins typically:

> Come all you true born shanty boys and list while I relate
> Concerning a young riverman and his untimely fate.[42]

Similarly, "The Drowning of John Roberts" (Laws C3) begins:

> Come fellow men and lend an ear, a melancholy tale to hear
> About one poor mortal, he who has sunk and gone to eternity.[43]

A variation on the call for attention introduces the singer (as subject). "Peter Amberley" or "Peter Emberley" (Laws C27) often begins:

> My name is Peter Emberley as you will understand.
> I was born on Prince Edward Island, down to the ocean strand;
> In eighteen hundred and eighty one, when the flowers were in brilliant hue,
> I left my native country my fortune to pursue.[44]

"The Bonshee River" ("Jimmie Judge" or "Jimmie Judd," Laws C4), recorded in the early 1940s by Richard Smith of Menardo, Maine, includes many of the elements cited by Edward Ives in *Joe Scott: The Woodsman-Songmaker*, including the come-all-ye opening, a description of the accident and the efforts to find the lumberjack, a description of his mangled body, responses of those closest to him (his mother, father, and girlfriend), and a final theological reference (Ives 1978: 159). This example also provides clear evidence of the sentimentalism that was so common in this group of songs.[45]

Bonshee River

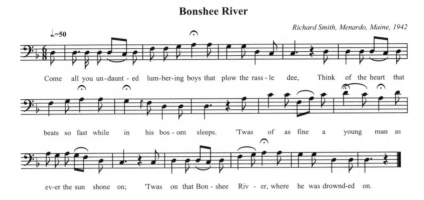

Richard Smith, Menardo, Maine, 1942

Come all you undaunted lumbering boys that plow the rassle dee,
Think of the heart that beats so fast while in his bosom sleeps.
'Twas of as fine a young man as ever the sun shone on;
'Twas on that Bonshee River, where he was drownded on.

'Twas on that Bonshee River, a little below and fro,
Where he went down to break a jam and with it he went through.
He tried his whole activity, his precious life to save;
'Twas on that Bonshee River he met his watery grave.

It was early the next morning the raftsmen all a-joined,
To search this river all over, the young man for to find,
To search this river on every side, where the water does swiftly glide;
A fisher boy, so I've been told, the floating corpse did spy.

It would melt the hearts of pity when he was brought on shore,
To see his love-lie features all mangled, cut, and torn;
To see as fine a young man cut down all in his bloom;
'Twas on that Bonshee River he met his dreadful doom.

There stood his aged mother, crying, "My darling son."
Likewise his aged father saying, "I am undone."
But the girl that loved him dearly her hair in anger torn
Crying, "My love is drownded, and I ne'er shall see him more."

Oh, Jimmy Judge was this young man's name, I mean to let you know.
I mean to sound his praises wherever I may go.
His hair hung down in ringlets brown; his teeth were as white as the snow;
He was admired by old and young wherever he did go.

I hope his soul in heaven may shine and happy yet may be;
I hope his soul in heaven may shine through all eternity,
For God is our Creator; His name I shall adore;
I hope his soul in heaven may shine for now and evermore.

Typically, the lumbering ballads are performed at a slow tempo using a deliberate pace. Listeners are given the opportunity to hear an engaging story by singers who extend the note values according to the lyrics sometimes giving the overall effect that time is suspended in a performance.

The nineteenth-century lumbercamp origins for these songs have been traced and retraced by scholars and historians since the first few decades of the twentieth century.[46] While specific locations (and sometimes composers) have been identified for some of the songs, researchers generally see many of the stories as a recounting of the collective experience of woodsmen in Canada (the Maritimes, Quebec, and Ontario especially), the Midwestern states of Michigan and Minnesota, northern New York, Vermont, New Hampshire, and Maine.

Other lumbering ballads and songs from the region provide a direct link to its geographic and social landscape. They recall the lives in the woods and the camps: "Little Brown Bulls" (Laws C16), for example, provides information on log skidding as well as the competitive spirit among men in the woods.[47] A version of "Blue Mountain Lake" (or "Belle of Long Lake"; Laws C20) gives a glimpse of forms of entertainment and captures the camaraderie among people both inside and outside the camp context:

Blue Mountain Lake

When the God of all wisdom did fashion our land,
The logmaker's beauty he did understand,
The choicest of them in his hand he did take,
And fashioned the region of Blue Mountain Lake,
Derry down, down, down, derry down.

Mountains in their grandeur round this Eden rise,
The pines wave their branches and point to the skies,

Disease is not cured by potion or pills,
The strength of our God is the strength of the hills,
Derry down, down, down, derry down.

At last the bright, happy New Year it did come,
The boys had some whiskey and planned to have fun,
Some played the fiddle and some danced and sang,
Till the walls of the shanty with their music rang,
Derry down, down, down, derry down.

Now Mitchel Camfield who kept the shanty,
Was the meanest damn crank that you ever did see;
He'd hang round the shanty all day and at night,
If a man said a word he was ready to fight,
Derry down, down, down, derry down.

At the stroke of eleven brave Mitchel did say,
We have had enough racket I'm sure for one day,
And besides I have quite a pain in my head,
So put up your fiddles and go straight to bed,
Derry down, down, down, derry down.

Up spoke Patsy McDonough the boss of the gang,
He could cut down the logs as he whistled and sang,
"To command me to silence any man I defy,"
In his voice there was courage and red in his eye,
Derry down, down, down, derry down.

Mitchel then attempted to put Patsy out,
But Pat with his fist did soon put him to rout;
His wife standing near if the truth I would tell,
She was tickled to death to see Mitchel get hell,
Derry down, down, down, derry down.

So they kept up the racket, the noise and the din,
Till the bright happy Now Year, they did usher in;
Canfield is a much different man it is said
And is troubled no more with a pain in his head.
Derry down, down, down, derry down.

A lumberman's life is the best life of all,
With the boys ever ready to serve at your call;
There seems to be health in each breath that I take,
I will die and be buried near Blue Mountain Lake,
Derry down, down, down, derry down.[48]

"Banks of Gaspereaux" (Laws C26) demonstrates simultaneously connections to a familiar place (Littleton, Maine) and to the broader ballad traditions of the period with its come-all-ye opening, idealized characters, formulaic phrases, and dialogic style.

Banks of Gaspereaux

Come all you jolly lumbermen, I mean to let you know,
Those Yankees they will ne'er return to drive the Gaspereaux.
You told them all the lies you could; you were their bitter foe.
Nor dares attend those wild galloots, down on the Gaspereaux.

You told them all the lies you could to fill our hearts with fear.
You said that they would not get to lumbering the first year.
Says the boss unto his men, "We'll let those galpins know."
In seven days those Yankee boys, they drove the Gaspereaux.

Now the miller had a daughter, she very handsome, too,
Was she much admired by all the Yankee crew;
Because she wore a purple dress with aperun also,
They called her "Robin Redbreast" on the banks of Gaspereaux.

"Now Robin, lovely Robin, if you and I can agree,
I'll show you a short cut to my counteree.
I'll dress you all in riches my bride you'll be also,
And we would leave these lonely scenes down on the Gaspereaux."

"Oh, no, no," this young girl cries, "With you I cannot go.
My sisters they would weep for me, my parents they would know.
But you go ask my father, and to the church we'll go.
I'll be your kind companion on the banks of the Gaspereaux."

Straightway to her father he went with no delay:
"I want to wed your daughter, an answer please, I pray."
"Oh yes, oh yes," the old man cried, "but from me she can't go.
She can be your kind companion on the banks of the Gaspereaux."

"Oh, no, no," this young man cried, "This place I cannot bear.
We'll go over to the State of Maine, and we'll be happy there."
"Oh yes, oh yes," the old man cried, "but from me she can't go.
She can be your kind companion on the banks of the Gaspereaux."

Now these two have parted, and sorely they complain.
One of them's in the Gaspereaux, the other, the state of Maine.
I roam this wide world over, and I'll travel to and fro,
But I'll ne'er forget that girl I left on the banks of the Gaspereaux.[49]

Other American ballads that were passed into communities on broadside sheets recounted tragic events: local accidents and murders, fires and floods. Some became part of the oral tradition and were sometimes recited or sung in local and regional communities. The sheets themselves, though, were also retained to become parts of individual, family, or community history. Examples of the songs and poems printed in New England presses address events that occurred in Auburn, Bangor, Bucksport, Deer Isle, E. Bridgewater, Palmyra, Waterville, and Windham, Maine; Dover, Grafton, Hookset, Manchester, Meredith, Nashua, and Nottingham, New Hampshire; and Calais, Cambridge, E. Poultney, and Hartford, Vermont.[50] The "Wild River Tragedy," found in broadside form, was sung in northern New Hampshire to a dirgelike melody. One fragmentary version of this ballad was performed in Berlin, New Hampshire, in 1940.

Wild River Tragedy

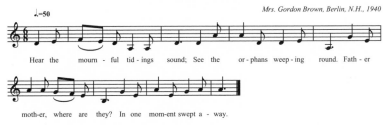

Locally created ballads were not always preserved in broadside form. The songs also provided narratives of everyday events, offered social commentary on behaviors exhibited to a local community, and included stories of local tragedies, often acting as warnings to local listeners. "The Calais Disaster" describes a drowning in Calais, Vermont, in 1873; "The Suncook Town Tragedy" or "Josie Langmaid" (Laws F21) recounts the details of the brutal murder of a schoolgirl in Pembroke, New Hampshire, in 1875. The "Murder of Sarah Vail" (Laws F9) describes a murder that took place in New Brunswick, Canada, in 1868, but it was sung also in Maine and Vermont.

Illus. 2.3. "Wild River Tragedy," published in Lancaster, N.H.

Murder of Sarah Vail

A. Tolin, Chester, Vermont, 1934

Come all you peo - ple lend an ear, A dread-ful stor - y you shall hear. This murder-ous
deed was done of late, In eight-een hund-red and six - ty eight.

Come all you people lend an ear
A dreadful story you shall hear
This murderous deed was done of late
In eighteen hundred and sixty eight.

There was a man called John Monroe
Who did Miss Vale a courting go,
This girl was handsome, young, and fair
Few with her that could compare.

Monroe was married it is true,
He had a wife and children, too,
But still Miss Vale he went to see
Not caring what the talk might be.

In course of time an offspring came,
Which brought to light their hidden shame,
But still together they did go
Until he proved their overthrow.

He led her to that lonely spot,
And there he fired the fatal shot,
A bullet buried in her brain,
She fell in death, there to remain.

Then killed the baby with a rush
And covered them with moss and brush,
And hurried off with rapid flight
Not thinking it would come to light.

The jury found it very plain
Miss Vale and baby had been slain,
The jury found it plain, also
That they were killed by John Monroe.[51]

Compare this with a version of "Josie Langmaid" collected from Alice Dodge
Titus in Hardwick, Vermont, in 1954, given below. Both songs share the characteristic conventions found in obituary (or funeral) ballads of the time, including a

common metrical pattern (iambic tetrameter) and rhyme scheme (AABB) and the come-all-ye opening stanza followed by the narrated details of the event.[52] Many of these ballads also conclude with a homiletic stanza (as in the final lines: "And we must all examples make / Until crimes shall cease in the Granite State").

'Twas on the morning very clear,
When Josie started for her school.
For many a time this way she passed
When little she thought this time her last.

'Twas at the foot of Pembroke Street
LePage lay ambushed with a stake
Long time ago his plans were laid
To take the life of this fair maid.

The mother watched with tender care
Hoping her daughter would appear
But as the evening shades drew near
Her darling child did not appear.

The anxious father and the son
All through the forest search begun
And found at last to his surprise
His murdered child before his eyes.

Her head was from her body tore
Her clothes were all a crimson gore
And on her body marks did show
Some skillful hand had dealt the blow.

The one that did this awful deed
Was one LePage a chopper by trade
And oft had he outrages made
And taken the lives of two fair maids.

And now LePage your work is done
And you like Evans must be hung
And we must all examples make
Till crimes shall cease in the Granite State.[53]

PARLOR SONGS

The storytelling style of the older songs was continued in later American popular songs performed in homes and public venues in northern New England. Scholars categorize these songs in the nineteenth century as parlor or sentimental songs; publishers attached "ballad" to many of their titles, although not all are narrative. Considered the product of the nineteenth-century music industry, these songs were composed using parameters set in urban contexts, but they quickly spread into the rural regions as well, where they remained popular for several generations.

Characterized first by sentimentalism, parlor songs shared meter, formula, melodic style, and regional singing styles with some of the other ballads of the period. The songs in this broad category were typically published in sheet music form with keyboard accompaniment; they were also transmitted to rural communities by traveling performers. As the popular music industry developed, related song traditions were spread in the region (and other parts of the country) through the media, including the radio and commercial recordings. Some of the songs quickly took on a life of their own in the oral tradition. Collectors and other researchers have not consistently documented the songs, despite their importance to many individuals in the region, because of a bias in favor of the older ballads. Scholars did not often consider these songs significant, sometimes due to their clear origin in the printed and/or vaudeville tradition. Collectors, then, shied away from them during the twentieth century, making it clear to their informants that they were less interested in them. This had an enormous impact on how singers (and later students and scholars) valued the songs during that period, and how long they were retained in the collective memory of residents.

Research in the region in the 1980s revealed a wide range of titles in this category, used in various social circumstances. One popular song in the home was "The Blackberry Girl." When I asked eighty-eight-year-old Clyde Covill of Pittsburg, New Hampshire, if he recalled a song "about a girl picking berries to buy a gown," he responded, "My grandfather—my mother's father—used to sing that. 'The Blueberry Girl,' he called it. Phoebe was her name." He sang:

> Now Phoebe if you'll take the time
> That is given you to play.
> And gather blueberries along the line
> And carry them to town

That was one of mother's songs. She used to sing that quite a while— "Where are your berries child?" She had an accident somewhere. I forget how that did work in. She spilt some berries and they went in the dirt and she couldn't get 'em out. They wouldn't be no good and she wouldn't have time to get back home. [Laughs.] Phoebe, her name was Phoebe.

I've heard the story about them, too. 'Twarnt because he was awfully poor, but he had quite a big family and it took all the money that he could possibly scrape to keep 'em going! There was a lot more to the song. We always called it "The Blueberry Girl."[54]

A reconstruction of Clyde's melody for "The Blueberry Girl" as he remembered pieces of it during our interview is on page 47.

Marjorie Pierce of North Shrewsbury, Vermont, remembered "The Blackberry Girl" as well. She recalled it as a recitation, reading twenty verses of what she described as part one of her mother's piece. Her lyrics were nearly identical to those found in an 1821 manuscript housed in the Flanders Collection, shown here:

THE BLACKBERRY GIRL.

"Why Phebe are you come so soon ?
  Where are your blackberries child ?
You cannot, sure, have sold them all,
  You had a basket pil'd."

No, mother, as I climb'd the stile,
  The nearest way to town,
My apron caught upon a stake,
  And so I tumbled down.

I scratch'd my arm, & tore my hair,
  But still did not complain:
And had my blackberries been safe,
  Should not have car'd a grain.

But when I saw them on the ground,
  All scatter'd by my side,
I pick'd my empty basket up,
  And down I sat & cried.

Just then a pretty little Miss,
  Chanc'd to be walking by;
She stopp'd & look'd so pitiful—
  And beg'd me not to cry.

"Poor little girl, you fell," said she,
  "And must be sadly hurt—
Oh no, I cried, but see my fruit,
  All mix'd with sand & dirt.

"Well, do not grieve for that, she said—
  "Go home & get some more ;"
Ah, no, for I have stripp'd the vines,
  These were the last they bore.

My father, Miss, is very poor—
  He works in yonder stall—
And has so many little ones,
  He cannot clothe us all.

I always long'd to go to church,
  But never could I go ;
For when I ask'd him for a gown,
  He always answerd "no".

There's not a father in the world
  That loves his children more,
I'd get you one with all my heart,
  But, Phebe, I am poor."

But when the blackberries were ripe,
  He said to me one day,
"Phebe, if you will take the time,
  That's given you to play ;

12. And gather blackberries enough,
  (And carry them to town,)
To buy your bonnet & your shoes,
  I'll try & get the gown?

13. Oh, Miss, I fairly jump'd for joy—
  My spirits felt so light ;
And so, when I had leave to play
  I pick'd with all my might.

14. I sold enough to get my shoes,
  About a week ago;
And these, if they had not been spilt,
  Would buy a bonnet too.

15. But now they're gone they all are gone,
  And I can get no more—
And Sundays I must stay at home
  Just as I did before.

16. And, mother, then I cried again,
  As hard as I could cry,—
And looking up I saw the tears
  Were glist'ning in her eye.

17. She caught her bonnet from her head,
  "Here, here, she cried, take this!"
Oh, no, indeed I fear your Ma'
  Would be offended, Miss.

18. "My Ma'! no, never, she delights
  "All sorrow to beguile—
"And 'tis the sweetest joy she feels
  To make the wretched smile.

19. "She taught me when I had enough,
  "To share it with the poor :
"And never let a needy child
  "Go empty from the door.

20. "So take it, for you need not fear
  "Offending her, you see—
"I have another, too, at home,
  "And one's enough for me."

21. So then I took it—here it is—
  For pray, what could I do ?
And mother, I shall love this Miss,
  As long as I love you.

Proverbs VIII. 32, 33, 34, 35 & 36. Now therefore hearken unto me, O ye children : for blessed are they that keep my ways. Hear instruction, & be wise, & refuse it not. Blessed is the man that heareth me, watching daily at my gates, waiting at the posts of my doors. For whoso findeth me findeth life, & shall obtain favour of the LORD. But he that sinneth against me wrongeth his own soul : all they that hate me love death.

Any little Girl who shall commit to memory what is on this paper, shall receive "Watts' Divine & Moral Songs" as a reward.

                        David Clixbe.

Illus. 2.4. "Blackberry Girl," manuscript, 1821.

The Blueberry Girl

Clyde Covill, W. Stewartstown, N.H., 1987

Other popular songs of this type, referred to by many in the region, include "The Drunkard's Child," words by Mary A. Kronsbein, music by J. L. Feeney (1882); "The Letter Edged in Black," words and music by Hattie Nevada (1897); "Two Little Girls in Blue," words and music by Charles Graham (1893); and "The Engineer's Child," by Neal Andrews Kind (1926).

Gussie L. Davis authored two sentimental songs in the 1890s that were particularly popular in many northern New England communities: "The Baggage Coach Ahead" and "The Fatal Wedding." Both used the death of a family member and its effect on relatives and community members as a primary theme. Hattie Eldred's version of "The Baggage Coach Ahead" from Hardwick, Vermont, was recorded in 1958.[55]

The Baggage Coach Ahead

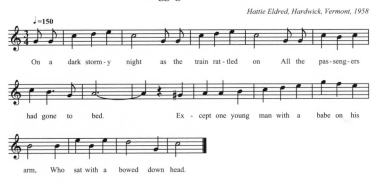

Hattie Eldred, Hardwick, Vermont, 1958

On a dark stormy night as the train rattled on,
All the passengers had gone to bed.
Except one young man with a babe on his arm,
Who sat with a bowed down head.

While the train rolled onward, a husband sat in tears,
Thinking of the happiness of just a few short years.
And baby's face brings pictures of a cherished hope that's dead,
For baby's cries can't waken her in the baggage coach ahead.

The innocent one commenced crying just then,
As though its poor heart would break.
One angry man said "Make that child stop its noise,
It's keeping us all awake."

"Put it out," said another, "don't keep it in here,
We paid for our berths and want rest."
But never a word said the man with the child,
As he fondled it close to his breast.

"Oh where is its mother, go take it to her,"
A lady then softly said.
"I wish that I could," the man sadly replied,
"But she's dead in that coach ahead."

Everyone long arose to assist with the child,
The mothers and wives on that train.
And soon was the little one then sleeping in peace,
With no thought of sorrow or pain.

Every eye filled with tears as his story he told
Of the wife who was faithful and true.
He told how he'd saved up his earnings for years,
Just to build up a home for two.

And when heaven had sent them this sweet little babe,
Their young happy lives were blest.
In [thought] he broke down as he mentioned her name
And in tears tried to tell them the rest.

Next morn at the station, he bade all goodbye.
"God bless you," he softly said.
And each had a story to tell in their homes
Of the baggage coach ahead.

Sentimental songs also entered the oral tradition through the radio, especially due to popular performers like Bradley Kincaid, as Elwin Corey of Benson, Vermont, recalled.

> I can remember years ago when radios first came. We had a battery radio and back when we used to get WLS—I don't know whether Nashville come in at that time or not. We used to listen to WLS and Bradley Kincaid—bet you ever heard of him or not—well, he always sung those old ballads. And we sat and got a book of his old ballads, I don't know if his old book is around or not, but we got that sort of thing. And of course we got to hear him play those and sing those. We got so we might sing 'em, you know, but we never set to the piano and sung like a lot of people. Like her mother always played the piano, and she could play music—and they sung around this piano. But in my particular case, well, it was different. I learned a lot of those old tunes, as I say, from my father, friends, and people that I knew.[56]

A popular radio personality from 1938 to 1947, Bradley Kincaid reinforced with his voice and publications what was increasingly being identified as a "mountain"

Illus. 2.5. *My Favorite Mountain Ballads and Old Time Songs* by Bradley Kincaid, distributed in various editions during the 1920s or 1930s.

repertoire from the south. Many of the Anglo-American songs he offered, though, had been popular in families in the northeast as well, and his performances played a role in strengthening them as well as introducing related songs and versions to many regional families. Kincaid's publications were generated to support his image as a folksinger and made his songs available to an even wider public. Songs were published in songbook and sheet music formats (some with piano accompaniment and guitar chords). For example, Kincaid offered "A Fatal Wedding" in a 1928 edition of *My Favorite Mountain Ballads*. A version of this ballad was sung from memory in the 1980s by Bill Hook in northern New Hampshire; he remembered singing it in the woods. In fact, he spoke the last few words of the song in a style typically found among northern New England woods singers. His lyrics and melody were remarkably similar to the published version of over fifty years before.

A FATAL WEDDING

The wedding bells were ringing
On one moonlight winter night;
The church was decorated,
All around was clear and bright.
A woman with her baby came
And saw the lights aglow;
She remembered how those same bells chimed
For her three years ago.

I'd like to be admitted, sir,
She told the sexton bold,
Just on account of baby
To protect him from the cold.
This wedding is not for the poor,
But for the rich and grand;
So, with the eager watching crowd,
Outside you'll have to stand.

She begged the sexton once again
To let her pass inside.
For baby's sake you may step in,
The gray haired man replied.
Has any one a reason why this couple should
not wed?
Speak now or hold your peace forever
Soon the preacher said.

I must object, the woman cried,
In voice so meek and mild.
The bride-groom is my husband, sir,
And this our little child.
What proof have you, the preacher said.
My infant, she replied.
She held it up, then knelt to pray,
The little one had died.

Chorus:

While the wedding bells were ringing,
While the bride and groom were there
Marching up the aisle together
While the organ pealed an air,
Telling tales of fond affection
Vowing never more to part,
Just another fatal wedding,
Just another broken heart.

The parents of the bride then took
The outcast by the hand,
A home have you thru life said they,
You've saved our child from harm.
The bride and parents, outcast wife,
Then quickly drove away.
The husband died by his own hand
Before the break of day.

No wedding feast was spread that night;
Two graves were made next day:
One for the little baby
And in one the father lay.
This story has been oft retold,
By fireside warm and bright,
Of the wasted life of the outcast wife,
That Fatal Wedding Night.

Illus. 2.6. "The Fatal Wedding" from Bradley Kincaid's 1928 collection published for WLS Radio in Chicago.

Lyric Songs

Lyric songs adopted from European traditions are identified not by their narrative content (although narration may be implied) but by their expression of an emotional reaction to an experience or idea. Metaphor and other symbolic devices are also more widely used in lyric songs than in ballads. Often delivered in the first person, lyric songs present interpersonal relationships and tend to speak in general terms (while ballads often relate specific situations). Like ballads, lyric songs use formulaic phrases and stanzas (sometimes called "floating stanzas").

The lyric songs in the region further demonstrate the adaptability of songs to the needs of singers and their audiences. The sharing between Child and broadside traditions, British and American narrative songs, and ballad literature and lyric song is clear in the songs of northern New England. Like some of the broadside ballads, lyric songs can also be characterized by their borrowed and adapted tunes and texts.

An example of this kind of borrowing is found in "A-Walking and A-Talking," which is derived from the narrative tradition. Like other lyric songs, it exhibits a flexible form using texts and tunes that grow and shrink with individual and regional tradition and practice. Like the version found in many locations in the United States, Canada, and Great Britain, this Vermont version includes lines and stanzas related to "The Cuckoo," "The Unconstant Lover," "Irish Molly-O," and other lyric songs.

A-Walking and A-Talking

A-walking and a-talking and a-walking went I
To meet my sweet William; he's coming by'n by;
To meet him in the meadow is all my delight,
To walk and talk with him from morning 'til night.

A meeting is a pleasure, but parting is grief,
And an unconstant lover is worse than a thief;
For a thief will but rob you and take all you have
While an unconstant lover will carry you to the grave

The grave it will mold you and turn you to dust.
There is scarce one in twenty that a fair maid can trust;
Oh they'll coax and they'll flatter you, and tell as many lies
As the fish in the ocean or stars in the skies.

The cuckoo is a pretty bird; she sings as she flies,
She brings us glad tidings and she tells us no lies,
She sucks the sweet flowers to make her voice clear
And when she sings "cuckoo" the summer draws near.

Come all you pretty fair maids, take warning by me,
Don't place your affections on the green willow tree
For the tree will but wither, and the roots they will die.
Oh, if I am forsaken, I know not for why.

If I am forsaken, it's only by one
And he's greatly mistaken if he thinks I'm undone;
I can place as little by him as he can by me,
So adieu to these young men who court two and three.[57]

While ballads describe specific events, lyric songs are more adaptable to the needs of the singer and audience. Songs that express a connection with a social group or society (departure from homeland or family, political or economic conditions) are less common than those that express a relationship between individuals, especially between women and men (love songs). The songs recalled by residents that express a connection with place often speak of loss, as in "Leaving Old Ireland." They sometimes use popular or traditional tunes, even borrowing lyrics. Information on this song type is limited, though; its absence in collections may relate more to its relative lack of value for collectors than for informants.

Leaving Old Ireland

There's a dear spot in Ireland that I long to see
'Tis my own native birthplace, once heaven to me;
My poor aged mother lives there all alone
With my brothers and sisters was a bright and happy home.

We hadn't much money, but my mother dear
Pressed a kiss on my cheek, bade me of good cheer;
I bade them good-bye on that rocky old shore,
And I left Ireland, left mother, because we were poor.[58]

Other popular lyric songs in the region include love songs such as "Paper of Pins." This and other dialogue songs also could be performed as duets, a practice possibly inspired by vaudeville performances that were popular in the region during the early years of the twentieth century.

Paper of Pins (Excerpt)

I'll give to you the paper of pins,
If that's the way that love begins;
If you will marry me, me, me,
If you will marry me.

Oh I won't accept your paper of pins,
If that's the way that love begins;
Nor I shan't marry you, you, you,
Nor I shan't marry you.

Illus. 2.7. Floyd and Bea Shatney perform "Paper of Pins" in West Stewartstown, New Hampshire, 1987.

I'll give to you a nice blue dress,
Trimmed all 'round with a nice silver thread;
If you will marry me, me, me,
If you will marry me.

Oh I won't accept your nice blue dress,
Trimmed all 'round with a nice silver thread;
Nor I shan't marry you, you, you,
Nor I shan't marry you.[59]

WORK SONGS

While there is a great deal of evidence that songs were performed at work in the region, there is limited indication that work songs, defined here by their direct lyrical and metric connection to regulating or coordinating work, were widely performed in northern New England. Along the coast of Maine, though, chanties were performed in connection with maritime activities. In 1941, David Kane and other retired seamen of Searsport, Maine recalled the following well-known song. Before singing, Kane said, "I used to hoist the mast in the yard up there."

Blow the Man Down

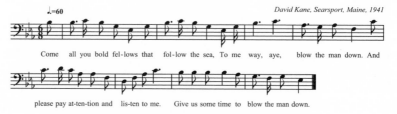

Come all you bold fellows that follow the sea,
To me way, aye, blow the man down.
And please pay attention and listen to me.
Give us some time to blow the man down.

On board the Black Baller where I served my time,
On board the Black Baller I wasted my time.

There were tinkers and tailors and sailors and all,
Who shipped for good seaman on board the Black Ball.

'Twas starboard and larboard yer jump to the call,
For Skipper Jack Williams commands the Black Ball.[60]

In the household, work songs were used while spinning, reeling, and waulking (or beating) wool. In 1930, Mr. A. B. Cheney of Dorset, Vermont sang a reeling song that substituted for counting he heard his aunts use while reeling yarn during the 1870s. He described the process: "Grandmother sat in front of swifts [reels] which set in a heavy block. Well, then, these swifts would whirl. She would start them after tying a thread from the spindle from spinning wheel onto swifts in skeins. After forty-eight threads she would tie these forty-eight threads together, in indigo blue. So many knots, stop and tie off to make skein. Linktem blue was a knot."

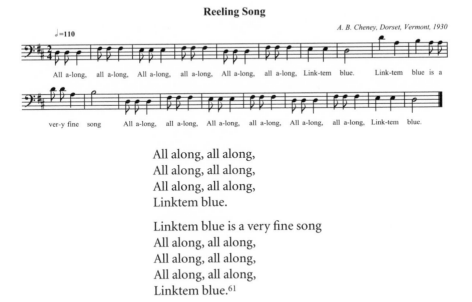

Reeling Song

A. B. Cheney, Dorset, Vermont, 1930

All along, all along,
All along, all along,
All along, all along,
Linktem blue.

Linktem blue is a very fine song
All along, all along,
All along, all along,
All along, all along,
Linktem blue.[61]

PLAY-PARTY SONGS

We should not underestimate the importance of what are often referred to as "play-party songs" in the lives of families and neighbors in many communities. Identified as products of the playground in the latter part of the twentieth century, historically these songs have been found to be popular as well among adults, who used them for entertainment, and teenagers, who used them for courting; only later were they associated exclusively with young children. The play-party as a social dance was popular in the nineteenth and twentieth centuries in communities throughout the Midwestern, southern, and northeastern United States. A repertoire of songs that can be connected to Anglo-American traditions includes "We Are Marching Down to Old Quebec," "London Bridge," "Go In and Out the Window," "The Needle's Eye," and "Green Carpet." Many of these songs played multiple social roles, including reinforcing gender roles in the community.

Green Carpet

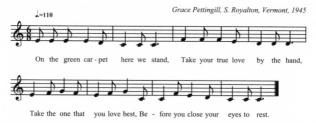

On the green carpet here we stand
Take your true love by the hand
Take the one that you love best
Before you close your eyes to rest.

Now you are married, you must obey.
You must be careful what you say.
So give her a kiss and send her away
And tell her to come some other day.

We marched 'round the circle: take your true love. And then you take them in: give her a kiss and send her away. Oh, and then face the opposite way, and when everyone had been chosen, the game was over.[62]

And "The Needle's Eye," remembered by Sadie Harvey of Monticello, Maine, in 1942, was also recalled in the 1980s as a song popular at socials.

The Needle's Eye

The needle's eye that does comply
That carries the thread so true
We have caught many a smiling lass
But now we have caught you.

She dresses so neat
And she kisses so sweet,
We do intend be-fore we end
To see this company.[63]

"King William was King George's Son" ("King William was King John's Son")
has been recorded in Vermont, New Hampshire, and other New England states.
The following version was recorded in Cornish, New Hampshire, by Minnie Dillon Crane who had learned it in Newfoundland in her youth.

King William was King George's son
And in the royal race he run.
On his breast a star he wore
It pointed to the governor's door.
Come choose to the east
Come choose to the west,
Come choose the very one
That you love best.
And she is not here
To take her part
Come choose another one
With all your heart

Down on the carpet you may kneel
Just as the grass grows in the field
Kiss your partner as your sweet
And you may rise upon your feet.

The first to go into the center of the ring chooses a partner. Then the first in
the ring comes out and the partner chooses a new partner, and the game
goes on.[64]

One song that may be have been more exclusively associated with childhood
games is "Water, Water Wild Flowers." The roots of this piece are in the English
song tradition, and it was popular as a game song in nineteenth- and early-
twentieth-century America. This fragment was remembered by a South Royalton,
Vermont, woman in 1945.

Water, Water Wild Flowers

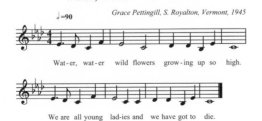

Water, wat-er wild flowers grow-ing up so high.

We are all young lad-ies and we have got to die.

The Musical Landscape: Singing Traditions

> Water, water wild flowers growing up so high
> We are all young ladies and we have got to die.
>
> Except Susie Blank, she is so fond of flowers
> Fie, fie, fie for shame, turn your back and tell his name.

We march 'round in a circle and then take the one player that you pick out, call her into the center, and she has to turn her back and tell his name, and then she is put out and the circle grows smaller as each one goes out until the end. [65]

Another fragmentary version of this song was collected in nearby Barnet, Vermont, in 1944.

> Water, water wild flowers growing up so high
> We are all young ladies and we have got to die
>
> Mother, mother I am sick, send for the doctor quick, quick, quick
> Doctor, doctor shall I die? Yes my darling, but don't you cry.[66]

Forty years later, in Barre, Vermont, Cordelia Cerasoli remembered this version from her childhood:

> Water, water wild flowers growing up so high
> We are all young ladies and we are sure to die
> Excepting Mrs. Lucy, an' a fie for shame an' a fie for shame
> Turn your back and tell a boy's name
>
> Walter Pidgeon's a nice young man
> He comes to the door with a hat in his hand
> Down comes she all dressed in silk
> A rose on her bosom as white as milk
> Water, water wildflowers growing up so high.

We would all hold hands and when we called her name she had to turn her back and tell a boy's name.[67]

Changes

By the middle of the twentieth century the new generation of "old songs" in northern New England communities referred not simply to Child and broadside ballads, or even to local or regional ballads and early lyrical songs, but to turn-of-the-century and World War I popular songs that were sung along with the older ballads and songs in many communities. At the same time, the popularity of early country songs, in the form of hillbilly music, and versions of the old ballads popularized by singers like Bradley Kincaid provided opportunities for listeners to connect simultaneously with the older traditions yet move easily into contemporary country music performances. The songs that had been part of individuals' and families' traditions for so long, while no longer sung, remained in the characteristic sentiment of country music performances.

The songs shared by northern New England residents, regardless of their origin or category, remain an important part of the social and cultural landscape. They express common sentiments understood by participants during each performance. While repertoires vary from community to community and family to family, northern New England has displayed a characteristic body of popular, traditional, and religious songs, as well as traditional and popular dance tunes, that were performed throughout the region in conjunction with social and occupational events.

CHAPTER 3

Religious Singing

I remember her standing at the end of the stove, a lot of times with her arm up on the warming oven, and she'd stand there with her head over on her hand and she'd sing and sing and sing. Hymns like "Rock of Ages" and "The Rock That Is Higher Than I." When we used to go over to visit Annie Scott, over in that neighborhood, they always made a point of singing that hymn together. I think they probably learned them when they went to the different meetings and there was a group of the ladies that were always there. I think that they learned them more right from the meeting 'cause they went a lot— not only just on Sundays, but during the week they had meetings—and people made a point of going. That was more or less their social get-togethers really. Men went to them too, but I remember her talking about these different women and how they'd group together and sing.[1]

Many U.S. libraries with historical Americana house large collections of nine-teenth- and early-twentieth-century hymnals and songbooks. Often the hymn books are tattered, some are even carefully rebound in leather or cloth—and these too are worn. When an owner's name and town is written on the inside of the front or back cover, or a number in the upper right hand corner indicates a connection to a church or community group, there are also often marks in pen or pencil next to selected titles in the tables of contents or next to the songs themselves, suggesting hymns with particular significance to the owner and/or the community. Can we correlate information found in these collections to the narrative data provided by local residents? Interviews show that hymns were often sung in clearly delineated social groups: women, family members or neighbors, and believers. In fact, hymnody played an important role in socialization during this period, and, as Stephen Marini has argued, hymnody was a significant factor in the development and maintenance of the evangelical movement in the region beginning in the eighteenth century (Marini 1996: 118). He states elsewhere, "More than any other medium, hymnody constructed a common symbolic language for Evangelicalism. Whether employed as a device in private meditation, as a vehicle for family devotions, or as a unifying frame for congregational worship, hymnody supplied an indispensable structure for the articulation of Evangelical faith" (Marini 1982: 158).

In rural northern New England, although protestant churches dotted the countryside, the series of religious revivals that occurred between 1780 and the 1840s were embraced by local residents and promoted a continuation of the evangelical movement in the following decades. Utilizing hymnody widely, the movement's practices encouraged a diversity of religious expression greater than that offered in many of the denominational settings. The collected information we have on regional religious practices and the attendant hymnody, from both oral and printed sources, reinforces Marini's claim and demonstrates once again that the fluid and flexible lifestyles of regional residents yielded diverse repertoires of religious musics drawn from a variety of religious denominations.

Hymn singing in homes, schools, and camp meetings, as a social activity and a forum for sharing musical information, contrasted in many ways with the practices in regional churches. The dominant denominational groups, Congregationalists, Methodists, and Baptists, established and maintained specific structures in worship and social organization that encouraged the adoption of specific hymns derived from a sanctioned repertoire; when sung, these hymns in turn became referential of the social and performance tradition established and maintained in the national church context. Alternative sites for the performance of hymns reflected locally constructed social patterns that provided opportunities for more diverse traditions to be maintained in the family and neighborhood. The memories of hymn singing presented by respondents in the early and later part of the twentieth century were dominated by a wide range of hymns and diverse social contexts for learning and sharing religious music. Taken together, they indicate a clear pattern that is aligned with other value systems identified with this rural sphere.

History

The early religious music traditions in New England can be traced from psalm singing in the colonies during the seventeenth and eighteenth centuries through the singing school traditions and shape note hymnody of the eighteenth and nineteenth centuries. While remnants of these practices continued in northern New England during the late nineteenth and early twentieth centuries, the increasingly sectarian environment, which encouraged hymn singing not only in churches but also in homes and other community contexts, helped to establish and maintain the practice of folk hymnody in the region.

SINGING SCHOOLS

Hymn singing in social gatherings was established in New England with the singing schools of the eighteenth and nineteenth centuries. These community gatherings were led by itinerant and resident singing masters, some of whom were authors of the characteristically oblong songbooks sold to participants. While musical performance at local churches took place in an environment that fused worship and singing based on the tenets of a specific denomination, the singing schools were typically nondenominational and their goals were not religious but musical, social, and economic (providing opportunities for songwriters and publishers to benefit financially from their productions). Furthermore, by the nineteenth century the hymnals used in the singing schools indicate that they were increasingly sites for sharing both secular and sacred music.[2] While the tradition was waning by the late nineteenth century, mid- to late-century diary entries and town histories from the rural regions reference singing schools frequently. They typically occurred during winter months and were sometimes held once or twice each week. Few diarists provide details on the events, and local historians seldom indicate whether the music taught was religious or secular. From the information we do have, though, we learn that events were held in schools or other public buildings, and sometimes in homes. While some classes were unaccompanied, there are also references to participants bringing instruments, or to instrumental accompaniment provided by one of the song leaders. Participants in the schools were often but not always youth in the community. As an example, Charles Cobb (1835–1903) of Woodstock, Vermont, provided information on his attendance at "singing school" in his mid-nineteenth-century diary.[3] He notes that the earliest singing school he went to was in 1845, and in 1850 he was reluctant to go during a period when his voice was changing. He went often with his mother during this period (though he also noted that his mother attended on her own as well). In 1854 he wrote about a friend who attended the singing school with him, providing rare details of the event that include references to issues pertaining to economic value, sociability, aesthetic concerns, lyrical content, and performance practice:

> He has bought a singing book & paid 58 cents and is impatient to get his money's worth. He starched up & went to singing school Jan. 1—I went also—they bawled some psalm tunes, out of tune, in such a manner that the words could barely be heard only by those who had them before their eyes, and to close off, the singing master (Oscar Perkins), Harvey Vaughn and Smith the schoolmaster sung some funny songs accompanying on Vaughn's melodeon. After such a monotonous and universal howling it was a treat to hear some singing. (Cobb 1849–50: 1084–85)

In the rural regions some singing schools were not established until mid-century, as in Somesville, Maine, where the first singing school began in 1845 with an agreement signed by members of the town and an effort to raise funds to hire a singing teacher (Somes-Sanderson 1982: 161–62). And in Colebrook, New Hampshire, singing schools may not have begun until 1870, after which schools led by a series of teachers took place over a twenty-year period (Gifford 1970: 257).

While in general the singing schools had an impact on musical literacy, the greatest effect was probably on repertoire. It was through the instruction and the music books that were introduced to these communities that local residents learned hymns connected to early psalmody, as well as newer folk-like tunes developed by some of the singing masters in an effort to encourage wider interest in religious singing. The *American Vocalist*, published in the 1840s, continued to be

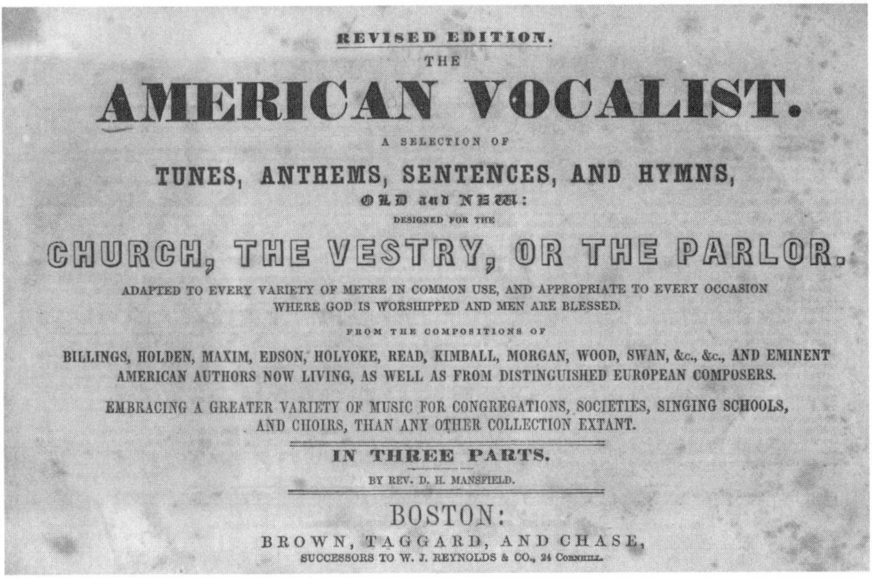

REVISED EDITION.

THE

AMERICAN VOCALIST.

A SELECTION OF

TUNES, ANTHEMS, SENTENCES, AND HYMNS,

OLD and NEW:

DESIGNED FOR THE

CHURCH, THE VESTRY, OR THE PARLOR.

ADAPTED TO EVERY VARIETY OF METRE IN COMMON USE, AND APPROPRIATE TO EVERY OCCASION WHERE GOD IS WORSHIPPED AND MEN ARE BLESSED.

FROM THE COMPOSITIONS OF

BILLINGS, HOLDEN, MAXIM, EDSON, HOLYOKE, READ, KIMBALL, MORGAN, WOOD, SWAN, &c., &c., AND EMINENT AMERICAN AUTHORS NOW LIVING, AS WELL AS FROM DISTINGUISHED EUROPEAN COMPOSERS.

EMBRACING A GREATER VARIETY OF MUSIC FOR CONGREGATIONS, SOCIETIES, SINGING SCHOOLS, AND CHOIRS, THAN ANY OTHER COLLECTION EXTANT.

IN THREE PARTS.

BY REV. D. H. MANSFIELD.

BOSTON:

BROWN, TAGGARD, AND CHASE,

SUCCESSORS TO W. J. REYNOLDS & CO., 24 CORNHILL.

Illus. 3.1. "American Vocalist," Rev. D. H. Mansfield, 1849.

popular in northern New England for several decades; its musical effect on families who continued to transmit songs orally probably reached to the end of the nineteenth century.[4] *The American Vocalist* provided singers with psalms, fuguing tunes, and various hymn types drawing from a wide range of styles and belief systems. Divided into three sections, the collection offers 522 tunes that range widely in nature, as is described on the title page: "Designed for the church, the vestry, or the parlor." In the first section is formal church music, beginning with Martin Luther's "Old Hundred" but also including hymns by New England composers William Billings, Daniel Read, Lowell Mason, Justin Morgan, and many others; this is followed by a section of vestry music, with hymns that include "O Land of Rest," "When Shall We Meet Again," "The Bower of Prayer," and "Star in the East," many of which are set to traditional airs ("When Marshalled on the Nightly Plain" is set to "Bonny Doon"); the last section has parlor hymns that include "Canaan," "The Garden Hymn," and "Will You Go."[5]

The Folk Revival in Northern New England

The migration of southern New Englanders to the outlying regions of New England after the American Revolution provided many opportunities for the growth and development of religious beliefs connected to revivalism, because the resulting social and economic instability allowed for radical sectarianism. At the same time, this environment encouraged even greater religious pluralism. The neighborhood gatherings in which church, school, and hymns were shared, and the impact of charismatic leadership connected to the growing sects (especially the Adventists) made it possible for the fluid and flexible traditions noted previously in secular forms to be adopted in the religious sphere as well.

The folk revival hymns that were characteristic of this period emerged from the Protestant evangelical activity of John Wesley. Using popular and folk (or folk-like) melodies to accompany traditional hymn texts, and ultimately fusing the concepts behind spirituals and hymns, these revival hymns were bound up in the Protestant evangelicalism of the nineteenth century, a movement that, while iden-tified especially with the South, affected many communities in northern New En-gland (the northern "frontier") as well. Many of the resulting hymns of this era comprise the primary expressive forms referenced by individuals interviewed for this project.[6]

Land of Canian

Lena Bourne Fish, E. Jaffrey, N.H., 1943

To - geth - er let us sweet - ly live, I am bound for the land of Ca - ni - an. To-geth - er let us sweet - ly die, I am bound for the land of Ca - ni - an. O Ca - ni - an, bright Ca - ni - an, I am bound for the land of Ca - ni - an. O Ca - ni - an, it is my hap - py home, I am bound for the land of Ca - ni - an.

Together let us sweetly live,
I am bound for the land of Canian.
Together let us sweetly die,
I am bound for the land of Canian.

Chorus:
O Canian, bright Canian,
I am bound for the land of Canian.
Canian, it is my happy home,
I am bound for the land of Canian.

If you get there before I do,
Look out for me I'm coming too.

I have some friends before me gone,
So I'm resolved to travel on.

Illus. 3.2. Lena Bourne Fish, East Jaffrey, New Hampshire, 1940s. Helen Hartness Flanders Ballad Collection.

Our songs of praise shall fill the skies,
While higher still our joys they rise.

Then come with me beloved friend,
The joys of heaven shall never end.[7]

The hymn known to Lena Bourne Fish of East Jaffrey, New Hampshire, as "Land of Canian" was more widely known as "Canaan" and is found in numerous revival sources. She sings it at a moderate tempo using an unembellished singing style. Like other revival hymns, the piece is characterized by its use of a folk-like tune, and a refrain plays a significant role musically and lyrically. These characteristics typify historical recordings of revival hymns of the northern New England region. Information on part singing the hymns, as they are so often represented in published form, has been more difficult to find. The rural performances of hymns

Illus. 3.3. "Canaan," from *Revival Melodies, or Songs of Zion,* 1843.

during the period of this study are primarily presented by the performers with their melodies only, and some have identified the songs as sung in unison (sometimes with accompaniment on piano, organ, or fiddle).

The revival tune book version of "Canaan" represents a harmonic setting in the refrain only. Its style is not unlike the early tune books used by singing masters who did not follow the stringent rules established by European choral tradition, instead offering a new texture to performers and listeners.

In another well-known folk hymn, "O Sing To Me of Heaven," recorded in 1945, Lena Bourne Fish uses a melody that is a variation on one found in a shape-note hymnal nearly one hundred years before.

O Sing to Me of Heaven

Lena Bourne Fish, E. Jaffrey, N.H., 1945

O sing to me of Heaven
When I am called to die,
Sing songs of Holy ecstasy
To wrap my soul on high.

Chorus:
There'll be no sorrow there,
There'll be no sorrow there.
In heaven above where all is love,
There'll be no sorrow there.

When cold and sluggish drops
Roll off my marble brow,
Break forth in songs of joyfulness,
Let Heaven begin below.

When the last moment comes,
To watch my dying face.
To catch the bright seraphic glee,
Which o'er my feature plays.[8]

Gene Staples of Dixfield, Maine, who was eighty-four in 1941 when this recording was made, recalled the hymn "When the Roll Is Called Up Yonder"; he said he learned it from a schoolteacher in his youth.[9] While the lyrics and tune of this widely known Methodist Sunday-school hymn were written by James Milton

Black in 1893,[10] its ultimate adoption by a number of denomination and sects contributed to its development. Staples's variation on the original lyrics, and—especially—his treatment of the melody demonstrate a flexibility in the tradition.

When the Roll Is Called Up Yonder

O come my children sing with me,
When the general roll is called I'll be there;
Our blessed savior soon we'll see
When the general roll is called I'll be there.

I'll be there, I'll be there
O when the general roll is called I'll be there.

You'll bury this body under the ground
When the general roll is called I'll be there;
For I'll come up when the trumpets sound
When the general roll is called I'll be there.

You pray for me, I'll pray for you
For that's the way the Christians do.

Revival hymns and spirituals were offered widely to children and adults, compiled in hymn books aimed at children (for use in schools and homes), in social singing books aimed at families and community groups, and in hymn and choral collections for congregations and church choirs.

The revival hymn books of the mid- and late nineteenth century provide an important connection between oral data and printed sources; these well-worn collections contain many of the songs referred to by regional residents. *Revival Melodies: Songs of Zion,* a small, paper-covered collection published in 1843 that contains a selection of hymns, is dedicated to Baptist evangelist Jacob Knapp. Similarly, *The Millennial Harp: or Second Advent Hymns,* by Joshua V. Himes, is a small collection of revival hymns, many of them drawn from European and

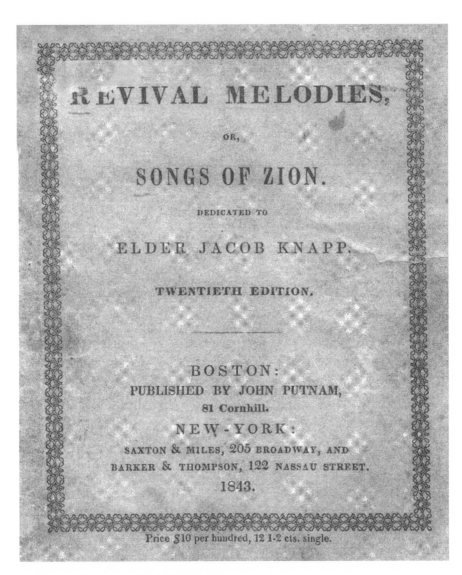

Illus. 3.4. *Revival Melodies, or Songs of Zion, 1843.*

American sources and sometimes altered for use in the Adventist church. Both of these collections contain a wide range of hymns, clearly drawn from different evangelical traditions.

Revival Melodies offers, for example, "Canaan," "When I Can Read My Title Clear," "All is Well," "The Young Convert," "Christ in the Garden," and some of the popular hymns better known by their first lines, including, "Invitation" ("We're traveling home of Heaven above—Will you go"), "The Happy Land" ("On Jordan's banks I stand"), "Judgment Hymn" ("O there will be mourning, mourning,

mourning"), "Lenox" ("Arise my soul arise"), and "Expostulation" ("O turn ye"). All have been recorded or referenced by northern New England residents as significant to them and their communities.

MILLERITES

Among the indigenous sects that emerged in rural northern New England, the Adventists have had the most lasting effect on the region. This millennialist revival movement was established in the mid-nineteenth century by William Miller (1782–1849), who predicted that the second coming of Christ would occur in 1843, and then 1844. Following this period, several separate Adventist sects connected to Miller's established belief system emerged, including the Advent Christian Church in 1860 and the Seventh-day Adventists in 1863. Their beliefs in prophetism and messianism, along with the "millennial expectation" they shared with other nineteenth-century sects, can be identified in the hymns that they adopted for their use (Marini 1982: 157).

Many of the songs and religious practices noted by individuals interviewed in the early and later years of the twentieth century can be connected to this movement, through direct reference to family membership or indirectly through hymns connected to the sect. One of the hymns most frequently referenced from this era is referred to as the "Millennial Hymn" or the "Judgment Hymn." Ora Knapp of Putney, Vermont, submitted a handwritten version of this song with its music to Helen Hartness Flanders in 1940, stating that he remembered his mother and father singing it to him when he was a child in the 1850s and 1860s.[11]

O there will be weep - ing, weep - ing, weep - ing, weep - ing

O there will be weep - ing, at the judg - ment day to see

Friends and neigh - bors there will part Friends and neigh - bors there will part

Friends and neigh - bors there will part There will part to meet no more.

Nearly ten years earlier, Ida Morgan of Jeffersonville, Vermont, had also submitted a version of this hymn, often identified with the Millerites, saying: "I got it from Mrs. Annie Munson, Morrisville, Vermont. She must be about seventy-five years old, and this was in a book that belonged to her mother."[12] The revival hymn book *Millennial Harp* provides a more complete version of this hymn; its lyrics are expressive of the values of the mid-nineteenth-century movement.

Parents and children there will part, Will part to meet no more.

2. O there will be mourning, mourning, mourning, mourning,
O there will be mourning at the judgment seat of Christ.
Wives and husbands there will part, Wives and husbands there will part,
Wives and husbands there will part, Will part to meet no more.

3. O there will be mourning, mourning, mourning, mourning,
O there will be mourning at the judgment seat of Christ.
Brothers and sisters there will part, Brothers and sisters there will part,
Brothers and sisters there will part, Will part to meet no more.

4. O there will be mourning, mourning, mourning, mourning,
O there will be mourning at the judgment seat of Christ.
Friends and neighbors there will part, Friends and neighbors there will
Friends and neighbors there will part, Will part to meet no more. [part,

5. O there will be mourning, mourning, mourning, mourning,
O there will be mourning at the judgment seat of Christ.
Pastors and people there will part, Pastors and people there will part,
Pastors and people there will part, Will part to meet no more.

6. O there will be mourning, mourning, mourning, mourning,
O there will be mourning at the judgment seat of Christ.
Devils and sinners there will meet, Devils and sinners there will meet,
Devils and sinners there will meet, Will meet to part no more.

7. O there will be glory, glory, glory, glory,
O there will be glory at the judgment seat of Christ.
Saints and angels there will meet, Saints and angels there will meet,
Saints and angels there will meet, Will meet to part no more.

1. O there will be mourning, mourning, mourning, mourning,

O there will be mourning at the judgment seat of Christ,

Parents and children there will part, Parents and children there will part,

Illus. 3.5. Judgment Hymn, *Revival Melodies, or Songs of Zion,* 1843.

Related to this is a hymn that Margaret Shipman of East Bethel, Vermont, re-membered when recalling the gatherings of the Millerites in her town:

Millerite Hymn

You will see the world a-burn-in' You will see the world a-burn-in' You will see the world a-

— burn-in' In the old church — yard. And the band of mu-sic And the band of

mu-sic And the band of mu-sic How they'll sound it through the air.

You will see the world a-burnin'
You will see the world a-burnin'
You will see the world a-burnin'
In the old churchyard.

And the band of music
And the band of music
And the band of music
How they'll sound it through the air.

You'll see Gabriel with his trumpet
. . . .
You will see the Lord a-comin'
. . . .
You will see the graves all openin'
. . . .
You will see the dead a-risin'

You will hear a mighty wailin'
You will hear a mighty wailin'
You will hear a mighty wailin'
And a gnashin' of the teeth.[13]

In the early 1930s, Ella Doten of North Calais, Vermont, talked about the Ad-ventist gatherings that she witnessed as a child during the 1870s, recalling the hymn "Salem's Bright King."

The Adventists used to gather at Maple Grove in Woodbury over fifty years ago. Several ministers and people from surrounding towns came and were baptized in the mill-pond. The old mill and brook and lake, surrounded by hills, made a lovely picture. They always sang this hymn.

Salem's Bright King

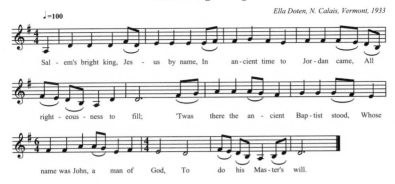

Ella Doten, N. Calais, Vermont, 1933

♩=100

Sal - em's bright king, Jes - us by name, In an - cient time to Jor - dan came, All right - eous - ness to fill; 'Twas there the an - cient Bap - tist stood, Whose name was John, a man of God, To do his Mas - ter's will.

> Salem's bright king, Jesus by name,
> In ancient time to Jordan came,
> All righteousness to fill;
> 'Twas there the ancient Baptist stood,
> Whose name was John, a man of God,
> To do his Master's will.
>
> Down in old Jordan's rolling stream,
> The Baptist led the holy lamb,
> And there did him baptize;
> Jehovah saw his darling Son,
> And was well pleased with what he'd done,
> And owned him from the skies.[14]

This hymn is also found in the revival compilation *The Millennial Harp*, although it is published without a melody.[15] Ella Doten's melody has all the characteristics of the folk-like tunes that borrowed their style not only from early secular songs but dance tunes as well.

CAMP MEETINGS

People learned many of their hymns at camp meetings held throughout the region. Camp meeting grounds dotted the northern New England landscape and provided significant sites for combining music learning, performance, and socialization in a nondenominational environment. Camp meetings are often identified with American frontier life in the south and west, and it thus not surprising that on the New England frontier these sites would have flourished as well.

An interview in the 1980s with one central Vermont couple went from hymns to a discussion about the camp meetings that took place on the nearby Camp Meeting Road in the early part of the twentieth century. Ray Grimes said that he had

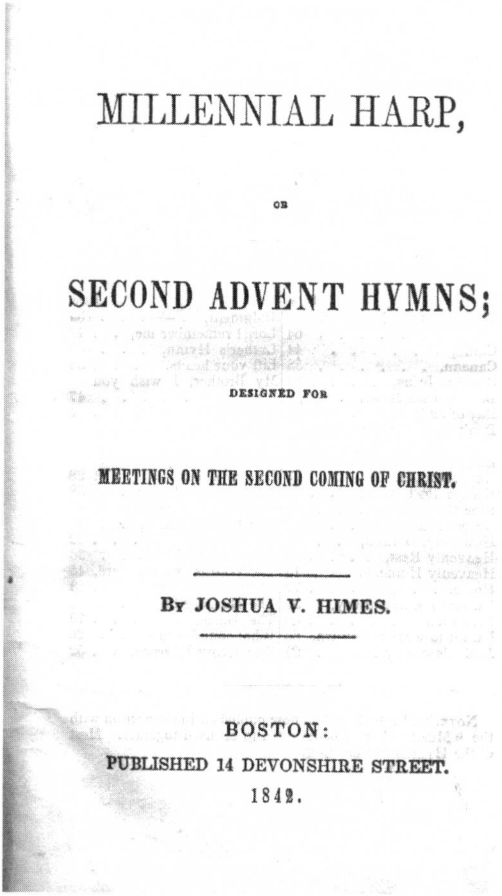

MILLENNIAL HARP,

OR

SECOND ADVENT HYMNS;

DESIGNED FOR

MEETINGS ON THE SECOND COMING OF CHRIST.

By JOSHUA V. HIMES.

BOSTON:
PUBLISHED 14 DEVONSHIRE STREET.
1842.

Illus. 3.6. *Millennial Harp: Designed for the Meetings on the Second Coming of Christ,* Joshua Himes.

attended the events a few times out of curiosity ("'cause everybody else did"). He described what he remembered: "They had a hall, a large hall where they held meetings. Ministers from different churches would all be there—take part in it. It was a—revival meeting . . . I don't remember the music part of it. We'd ride out there on our bicycles Sunday afternoon. There were quite a lot of little bungalows out there. There was sort of a little village."[16]

His wife, though, recalled her own experience at the camps, where she attended a week at a time and was taught music and "religion," learning songs such as "In the Garden," "Beyond the Sunset," "Whispering Hope," "Throw Out the Life Line," "Rock of Ages," and "Sweet Hour of Prayer": "The same old songs that we have [today]. They did more singing. They didn't use that many instruments, as I remember it."[17] The hymns cited by Mrs. Grimes represent a collection of hymns popular especially between the late nineteenth century and the 1940s. Most were anthologized in revival collections supporting a number of denominations including Baptists, Mennonites, and Adventists.

Family Singing

Many of the hymnals and songbooks published in the mid- to late nineteenth and early twentieth centuries were directed at revival and prayer meetings held in family and neighborhood contexts. Their titles and contents reveal the range of hymns and performance practices. The link between social singing and the singing of hymns collected in hymn books and song collections that were identified with sectarian worship is most readily found in the family and neighborhood. While most of the respondents for this project noted that their songs were learned in a variety of contexts, the opportunities provided by family, friends, and communities who readily shared songs of all kinds gave women and men, individually and together, a chance to identify hymns that broadly expressed their values. Their repertoires of hymns, in general, were connected to religious belief systems but not driven by them.

Hymns were taught in many families as a form of entertainment and as a way of maintaining sociability within the family context. For some people, hymns were remembered as one of the primary genres shared by their parents, set not in the context of religious teaching but in the experience of sharing songs. Thelma Neill of Warren, in central Vermont, recalled that her father, a farmer, "used to come in and hold us kids and sing . . . mostly all hymns. My mother too, she used to sing hymns. We used to all get together around the organ and she'd play. She'd play and we'd all sing."[18]

The published collections that once sat in parlors or were used in churches and at camp meetings were important sources for hymns shared in family and community contexts. The hymn books and hymn collections of the late nineteenth and early twentieth centuries served multiple purposes. Adopted in churches, singing schools, and singing societies, but especially when purchased for use in homes, the books were handed down in families like heirlooms or identified by respondents like Katherine Fogg as "lost" connections to their past:

> Yes, she had a lot of hymn books, and I have often wondered what became of them, because I don't know where they went. She had a lot of the old hymnals—thick hymnals—'course they were getting very much on the worn side, she may have just disposed of them, which she did with a lot of her things which she thought—well, you know, what will become of them, and she'd just get rid of them. It's too bad now that we don't have 'em.[19]

While the hymn books continued to be valued, the social unit selected specific hymns from these collections and was therefore the most important source for their regeneration. The hymns sung in this region were not so much connected to a denomination or sect as to the belief in the power of social singing.

CHAPTER 4

The Musical Landscape: Social Dance Music

When I first started attending local fiddler's club meetings in Vermont's Champlain Valley in the early 1980s, the highly structured practice of playing a carefully chosen repertoire of tunes in old-time fiddlers' contest format surprised me.[1] I felt at first that this formal practice ultimately contrasted with the character of the wide range of tunes musicians played and the varied performance practices they exhibited. The formalized tradition was evidence that participants were concerned about maintaining a remembered—and sometimes imagined— practice. Was the clear concern for authenticity at these meetings an indication that repertoires and performance practices had always been broadly conceived? The older fiddlers and dancers from the region that I subsequently interviewed may have answered this. In 1985, one longtime member of the Champlain Valley Fiddlers' Association, who had learned to play in his youth and was still playing occasionally at kitchen dances in central Vermont, said to me: "But back then you learned such a variety. When a man went out to play for a dance years ago—even old fiddlers—they played everything from hymns right up through to waltz, fox-trots, polkas, and two steps, and all this sort of thing."[2]

As I continued to attend meetings and became more familiar with the local repertoire, I was increasingly fascinated by the combination of tunes and playing style that merged French Canadian and what many refer to as "Yankee" practices. In one family I observed two brothers who played separate styles influenced by the dual ethnic heritage tied to the region; one the family-connected and family-identified Scots-Irish tradition, the other the Franco-American rhythm, repertoire, and playing style.

The characteristics of the dance music tradition of northern New England have been shaped by the location and the residents' willingness to accept influence from a broad spectrum of sources. The Anglo-Celtic tradition, French-speaking Canada, and popular styles heard through the media all affected emerging syncretic traditions in both music and dance. In these northern regions, cooperation among friends and neighbors came out in their shared social dance traditions throughout the period of this study.

Like the singing, the predominant dance music traditions in northern New England came from Europe, brought by settlers during the eighteenth, nineteenth, and twentieth centuries. Settlers in the region over the centuries held on to these traditions to contribute to their identities as they established residence in the towns and cities. Music and dances were performed at events that took place regularly in small and extended family groups as well as in neighborhoods and lumbercamps.

As they have with singing practices, scholars and the popular press may have misrepresented instrumental traditions as well, generalizing about New England dance music and romanticizing country life (and rural life in general). New England contradance and its accompanying music have come to represent the primary (and sometimes the only) old New England dances of the nineteenth and early twentieth centuries. While contradancing may have dominated during a period of time in the eighteenth and nineteenth centuries, interviews and manuscripts reveal that other dance forms and dance tunes were popular as well, especially in the late nineteenth and twentieth centuries. In fact, an increasingly diverse music and dance repertoire was adopted in the region to support the changing musical culture throughout the period of this study.

Scholars seeking information on social dancing in New England during the eighteenth and nineteenth centuries have used dance manuals and historical references to regional dance practices.[3] A careful look at the sources, though, reveals that their descriptions are generally limited to practices that took place in the cities and larger towns. We have less consistent data on dancing and instrumental music in the rural regions in this period and even up to the middle of the twentieth century. Interviews supplemented with historical recordings of dance tunes provide evidence of a clear contrast between urban and rural traditions, with significant differences in social function and performance practice.

Many popular instrumental tunes, and their associated dances, existed in the region throughout the nineteenth and twentieth centuries. In fact, the dance music repertoire in the region presents a more continuous tradition than we find in the song genres, which were quite radically altered by the end of the twentieth century. Yet we have even less consistent information on instrumental music and popular dances than we do on the singing, especially in the period before the 1940s or 1950s. This is because collectors in northern New England focused almost exclusively on finding ballads and songs; the dance music they recorded was neither frequently nor systematically compiled.[4]

The misrepresentation of rural traditions in popular literature, influenced by the romanticized ideals connected to country life and cultural revival, has also radically affected our understanding of the nature and diversity of these traditions. The information that we do have reveals that the dance and dance music traditions were (and still are) a vital part of the cultural lives of many northern New England rural residents. The dances and their accompanying music represent a continuation of European styles and repertoire. Like the songs, dance tunes in the nineteenth and early twentieth centuries exhibit a core Anglo-Celtic repertoire that is constantly being adapted to the region to accommodate the specific cultural, social, and spatial concerns of families and communities during different time periods. During the period of this study, though, dance music demonstrates an increasingly syncretic tradition that has combined regional and ethnic styles of playing, instrumentation, and repertoire.

Instrumental music and social dancing in northern New England were so closely intertwined during the nineteenth and early twentieth centuries that it is difficult to talk about one without the other. There is little evidence that instrumental traditions—separate from dancing—were as widely practiced as singing was in rural regions during the eighteenth and nineteenth centuries.[5] The instrumental music that was maintained most widely throughout the period had a specific social function: to accompany dancing. As in the songs, the connection between social life, geographic landscape, and cultural expression was clearly demonstrated in the performances. There was a dynamic relationship among tunes, dance steps and figures, rhythms, social bonds, and other interactions in space and time that was constantly being negotiated.

In the nineteenth and early twentieth centuries, dance and dance music in rural northern New England was performed in an environment that, like the singing traditions, can be described as musically, socially, and spatially flexible. Dances took place in a variety of locations depending on availability and space, but at first the most common place for a social time on a Saturday night was a neighborhood home. Often the whole house was used, with dancing in one room and socializing and singing in another; the youngest children would be put to bed in one of the remaining rooms, as Elwin Corey of Fair Haven, Vermont, recalls: "They'd clear out the livin' room, and part of the kitchen, and maybe another room, a dining room if they happened to have one, and they'd have a bedroom downstairs and one upstairs. And the kids would be asleep upstairs. It was just a matter of a family affair, you know—a community thing. And those old dances were carried on much different than they are today."[6]

A home with a central staircase permitted dances utilizing all of the downstairs spaces by allowing dancers to move in a circular pattern from room to room. Dancing took place in the kitchen, the living room, and sometimes the bedroom, or *from* the kitchen *to* the living room, as Thelma and Albert Neill of Warren, Vermont, recall: "We used to dance in the sittin' room . . . and we had just a curtain between the two rooms, and we'd move my father and mother's bed to one side, and we'd dance in the sittin' room—we'd go right down through—down the center."[7]

Neighborhood and community social events that featured dance and instrumental music ranged from local gatherings to formal dances. The overall social and musical characteristics of these events varied. While the informal dances collected together a very specific social group tied to neighborhoods and other local communities that had been invited to participate and share their music and companionship, the public dances drew participants from a variety of social circles and a wider geographic sphere.

Among the informal events were family gatherings and dances following work bees and other social events. Town histories, diary entries, and personal recollections provide evidence that cooperative activities such as corn huskings, barn raisings, or apple parings in farm neighborhoods were often followed by gatherings that included or featured instrumental music and dance. They also took place during the pauses between the many farm chores or at the end of a long day or week. Tamworth, New Hampshire, resident Charlie Bennett remembers them well:

I remember a husking bee we had one night. There must have been seventy-five people there and we husked eighty bushels of corn. They put a plank down both sides and the corn was in the middle and everybody husked and threw the butts away. Most people brought something for it. My sister got the dinner and there was a dance afterwards. We danced in the house, not in the barn. We could open all the doors and dance right around the chimney through the room around it. It was a ring play. Everybody took hold of hands and went right and left and then would turn and go the other way![8]

The Neills remembered a neighborhood husking event. Their narrative provides evidence of the relationship between highly organized communal labor and informal recreation.

Albert: Well, we had to look for red ears. Every time you got a red ear you tap a girl on the shoulder, she turn around and you give her a kiss, see. You keep that red ear, and pretty soon you'd get another one—it'd be the same one.

Thelma: One night we went over to—where the road was to Roxbury Mountain, round the corner there in East Warren, fellow called and wanted to know if Albert would bring a fiddle. And I said, "Yes, he'll bring his violin." So he took his fiddle and got over there and we'd go out in the barn and husk all the corn there was. There must have been seventy-five of us there. They had seats, you know, all the way down through. And we got the corn all husked. Went into the house. And he said "Well, come on into the house now. Maybe we can dance and have some lunch." So we went into the house and he said "Albert, I think they want to dance. You want to get your fiddle?" And Albert says, "Whose gonna play?" And he said "The fat you won't." [She laughs.] So he and I played. I played chords the best I could. If we weren't playin' they'd dance just the same.[9]

Events such as these were directly connected to cooperative labor but were also reflective of individual roles and social relationships established to maintain the health of the community. They represented the complex network of social, cultural, and economic relations that connected individuals to neighborhoods and other communities in the rural sphere. The regular gatherings of families, neighbors, and friends provided an opportunity for introduction and renewal of relationships that were extremely important to the maintenance of community.

KITCHEN DANCES

Lois Greeley of Springfield, Vermont, echoed the memories of others in the region when she described a practice found in many rural American communities in the nineteenth and early twentieth centuries:

They used to have—years ago—kitchen dances. Move everything out of the dining room, the bedroom, and have a dance. Most everybody in those olden days had an organ, and usually their daughter could play the organ; if she had left home, why, a neighbor could do it, and they'd get a fiddler and sometimes a young kid would pick up drums. That was the music for our kitchen dances . . . In the winter time, somebody would hitch up a team of horses, put a lot of hay on it, get their old blankets out, and gather everybody up and go up to their house for a kitchen junket. We had some nice ones. And sometimes, if we couldn't go [by sleigh], we'd walk a couple miles to get there. My uncle, he liked to dance some. He'd take my sister and I up. We had about a half a dozen during the winter months. During the summer, everybody was too busy in their gardens, in their cornfields, the potato fields, they were too busy.[10]

The kitchen dance, also referred to as "kitchen junket" in northern New England rural communities, was an important community social event when close neighbors gathered to socialize, sometimes to sing, and always to dance.[11] Like the dances following work bees, this event was a source of entertainment but also reinforced social bonds that formed through mutual help during times of need. Entire neighborhoods would arrange, sometimes on a regular basis, to gather at a home on a Saturday night. Usually a man in the neighborhood (or a close relative of one of the families) played the fiddle, and a local woman would accompany with chords on piano or organ. It was not uncommon for a dance to begin in the evening and continue until the early morning hours. Interviews with residents, anecdotal town histories, and social histories all provide information on this formalized practice. While there were local and regional distinctions in dances, dance styles, tunes, and other social patterns, there are also some broad generalizations that can be made about these events to identify them as regional expressions of identity. While the events were molded by each neighborhood, they maintained some consistent characteristics, including the locality and time, participation and description, and the characteristics of dance and music performed.[12]

Elwin Corey described in 1985 the dances in his community:

Back in those days you take from fall to spring, there was house dances all over the community. My family would have a house party this week and the next week it would be up the road at a neighbor's and on up through and back and forth all the way along. And there was somebody, usually in the neighborhood, that played violin. They called 'em kitchen hops. And I learned to dance there first when I was dancin' with my mother. My mother started me dancin'. 'Course we used to go to them back years ago.[13]

The neighborhood often framed the social and geographic parameters for the kitchen dances. The proximity of participants in relation to one another dictated the viability of attending events. When people were limited to those events they could attend by walking (or traveling by sleigh), their experience was connected to the specific landscape they all shared. The event was also shared among neighbors as it moved from one house to another on successive weekends (taking place especially in homes that were practical for dancing [i.e., large enough to accommodate line and square dancing] and that had barns to store the horses and sleighs of the visitors in winter time).

The place, date, and time of the local dances were generally set by mutual agreement within the neighborhood. Dances took place more often during the winter months than during the summer, and they were generally held on a Saturday night. The event began in the evening, with a break for a meal around midnight, and often continued into the early hours of the morning. Participants frequently describe returning home between 4:00 and 6:00 A.M., "just in time to do the morning chores." Clearly it would be more difficult for farming folk to be as socially active during planting, haying, and harvest seasons.

Participants at the local dances were limited to nearby neighbors, who used the time to socialize. Even the musicians were local—often from within the family or neighborhood group. Activities included dancing, singing, talking, card playing, and sharing food. While there was an informality about the neighborhood event, participants also played clearly delineated roles necessary to its success. The fiddler, whose presence was almost always essential, was respected for his musical skill; he was the musical soloist, sometimes acted as caller, and chose the music and often the dances. The accompanist was generally closely connected to the fiddler (his wife or daughter) and played a valuable role in providing the underpinning for the dance music. The organizers and food providers were often the women who planned the events, which wouldn't happen without them. The dancers and other attendees were multigenerational participants who represented the community. All were players in the social network; their roles in the kitchen dance were reflected in their everyday lives as well.

A wide variety of dances were represented at these local affairs, although participants were constrained somewhat by the physical space needed to execute line dances or form squares. The music was drawn from a specific repertoire chosen by the fiddler but clearly supported by the community. Local and regional differences were inevitable, as repertoires, instrumentation, and refreshments were each affected by local custom or preference and by the landscape itself. Since the musicians that accompanied kitchen dances were usually local, the instrumentation for dances varied with who was available. Generally a fiddle and keyboard (piano or organ) were essential, but other instruments were also popular in some communities: drums, a second fiddle, a lone brass instrument (trumpet), and later the accordion, mandolin, or banjo. Each neighborhood seemed to have preferences for the kinds of dances performed as well. Food, especially beverages served, differed from region to region. For example, serving hard apple cider was popular in the apple-growing areas of Vermont.

Albert Neill of Warren, Vermont, describes the spirit of cooperation that characterized one of the first dances he played for:

And I played for corn huskings on the hill—different parties—different houses where every Saturday night around we'd have a party. One night a fellow got lit up pretty well and he dropped his violin right in the middle of a set. Mrs. Sommerville was playing the chords. She says, "Fred," she says (she went and got him some coffee), "Have some coffee." "No, thank you, Mrs. Sommerville. I don't very often drink coffee." Boys took him out to get him another drink, and Irving Jones was calling a set, wanted to know if I could finish it up. I told him I'd make some noise at it. So I picked up Fred's fiddle and went at it.[14]

The camaraderie was evidence of the close social relationship among family and friends who shared responsibilities within the community. Ardes Haynes in Pittsburg, New Hampshire, also communicated the spirit of cooperation at the dances she attended:

One night I was to a party and they wanted to dance what they called "The Soldier's Joy." And nobody there could call changes. Well, I knew the changes, but I couldn't keep up—I didn't know the music enough to do it right. But I says I can call the changes but it may not be right. And so I called the changes and there was probably thirty or forty people there and they were dancin' to my callin' changes.[15]

House parties, *soirées,* or *veillées* were also popular in many Franco-American families. Parties took place on weekends, on a Sunday or holiday, or during a celebration such as a wedding. Brigitte Lane, in a study of Franco-American traditions in Lowell, Massachusetts, notes the significance of these gatherings in the social lives of French Canadian immigrants and their descendants. She describes events in Lowell on Saturday nights in spacious kitchens that are markedly similar to the descriptions of kitchen dance in the rural northern communities (Lane 1980: 158–59).

In Manchester, New Hampshire, Philip LeMay described family gatherings that were typical of many Franco-American residents who had arrived to farm or work in the mills in northern New England during the early years of the twentieth century: "We had family reunions, mostly on Sunday, to amuse ourselves. They were real *veillées canadiennes* and we certainly enjoyed ourselves. We sang without piano accompaniment, songs of Old Quebec, danced square and round dances and jigs, played games like *L'assiette tournante* (Spin the Platter) for forfeits, and played cards for the fun of it, mostly euchre, a game we learned here" (quoted in Doty 1985: 28).

Similarly, for the Beaudoin family of Burlington, Vermont, New Year's Day gatherings featured family, food, music, and celebration. Participants of all ages, both women and men, were caught up in dance events. Julie Beaudoin remembers: "There'd be dancing, or dancing the broom. The little kids even do it. They stand a broom between their legs and jump over it right in keeping time with the music. Some of the men were good step dancers, and some of them were good singers, and so they would join the party and we would make music."[16]

From the late nineteenth to the mid-twentieth centuries dances grew with the changing social focus from neighborhoods to town, regional, and national organizations. The new environments for the events, including town halls, Granges, and later, dance halls, had an effect on music, dances, and social purpose. At the neighborhood dances, local musicians generally were not paid for their services, except with a good meal and a drink. Yet in many communities as transportation became easier (and the supply of fiddlers smaller), a fiddler might be brought in from outside the circle. He was paid for his services with money gathered by passing a hat.[17] If the fiddler was well known, people from a wider sphere began to seek invitations to the gatherings. In time, these gatherings became too large (and wild) for a private home and were discontinued or moved to a large barn or the town hall, where admission was charged at the door. The historical movement from a small gathering of neighbors to a large public dance represents a movement from one social context to another with different characteristics. Charles E. Wakefield of Cherryfield, Maine, describes this:

> In Cherryfield and vicinity many related families by the name of Stout began having "kitchen breakdowns." These gatherings were held around at the individual houses. We would set up the drums and tune up and play for dancing. We had a number of these gatherings, and they were all characterized by much gaiety. The Strouts finally wound up hiring the old K. of P. hall because the families and guests multiplied so rapidly that the family homes would not accommodate them. (Wakefield 1978: 22)

This progression from a small gathering of neighbors to a large dance held in a public hall represents a movement along the continuum from a private to a public performance context. The social networks established in conjunction with the rural sphere and cultural expression then changed as well, altering the meaning, function, and often overall character of the events.

PUBLIC DANCES

> In the second half of the nineteenth century, traditional neighborhood gatherings were supplemented by activities beyond the immediate farm network. An increasing number of communal functions were sponsored by granges, churches, agricultural fairs, and numerous fraternal organizations. Many of these activities, however, continued to be conducted within the neighborhood district. (Hubka 1988:19)

Dances outside of the home sphere were held in common buildings in villages and towns throughout the region. The social dances that at first supplemented, then replaced, the kitchen junkets included events at local town halls, schools and churches, grange halls and fraternal lodges, and, increasingly, dance halls and pavilions. Those who attended both neighborhood and town dances report that the character of the public events was very different from the kitchen junkets. In the first place, they were larger. They were attended by more people and accompanied by bigger, and more diverse, musical ensembles. The larger space and musical diversity help the continuation of the dances within a community, even as other neighborhood traditions were waning. At the same time, these factors affected the events' overall function, social relationships, and forms of musical expression.

The public dances drew participants from a wider social circle and not all who attended knew each other well. This introduced new behaviors and changed social functions. At the neighborhood dances, participants had developed relationships that were based on communal responsibility. The behavior of attendees who had too much to drink, for example, was controlled within the community (by elders or the individual). At the public events, historical evidence shows that dances were increasingly marred by drunken behavior that sometimes had to be dealt with by village law enforcement. In fact, many dances were stopped because of the aberrant behavior of attendees who came from outside the once tight-knit social circle.

The mutuality of the neighborhood dances also changed because the halls were hired, not shared (as homes were), and the musicians were nearly always paid. The admission that was charged at the door for most of the events was necessary for their success, but it replaced the mutual responsibility for organizing, inviting, providing refreshments and musical accompaniment that was reinforced in the regular events in the neighborhood.

The ensembles that accompanied public dances were larger and more diverse than those in the homes; they were often referred to as "dance bands" or "orchestras" even though they often comprised only four or five players. During the nineteenth and early twentieth centuries the growing popularity of marching bands, hillbilly bands, dance bands, and orchestras encouraged residents to develop local bands to accompany the public dances even in the most rural northern New England communities. Dance bands and hillbilly bands used local talent on brass, strings, and percussion in addition to the fiddle. The influence of music heard on the radio, on recordings, and from traveling groups was clear in the larger ensembles. While some groups continued to play the older dance tunes, many included newer tunes, and by the 1930s some were playing the popular tunes exclusively, abandoning the fiddle for an ensemble that emulated the urban bands more closely. Roy Clark of Bristol, Vermont, describes his involvement during the 1940s: "I had a round and a square dance band that played at the Basin Harbor Club on Lake Champlain for a number of years . . . For the round dances we would use two trumpets, trombone, three saxes, bass, piano, and drums. And then for square dances we would use piano, drums, bass, or violin or fiddle. And then we would have a caller. And it was really quite interesting."[18]

In Chelsea, Vermont, Densmore's Band, also sometimes known as Densmore's Cotillion Orchestra, was popular during the second half of the nineteenth century. Instruments in this group included fiddle, clarinet, string bass, and trumpet.[19] In Milo, Maine, Charles Overlock began a dance ensemble that performed from the late nineteenth until the mid-twentieth century. The Charles Overlock Orchestra regularly performed with three or four musicians from among the following instruments: fiddle, piano, banjo, saxophone, trumpet, and drums. In Farmington, Maine, during the early decades of the twentieth century, Mosher's Orchestra included fiddle (played by George Mosher), accompanied by piano, trombone, trumpet, and drums.

Illus. 4.1. Lake Bomoseen dance pavilion, early twentieth century (postcard view).

Throughout the period, town halls and especially grange halls increasingly became settings for local dances. Most of these village-centered buildings had two stories, and the dancing took place on the second floor. Dances were organized as separate events and as events to follow town meetings or Grange meetings. Fraternal lodges also sponsored or housed dance events, as in this description of 1872 Lovell, Maine: "The Odd Fellows Lodge had what was described as a 'fine hall' at No. 4. It had a store on the first floor and a hall and anterooms above. A large stable with accommodations for the members' horses was part of the property" (Moore 1970: 191).

In Hancock, Maine, dances were held at a local hotel, the town hall, or local schoolhouses. "The most popular hall, however, was Albert Blackstone's Pavilion at Franklin Roads which was noted for its 'floating' dance floor and considered one of the best in the area." Harry Johnston and his Nighthawks, which included Johnston on fiddle, along with accordion, trumpet, sax, piano, harmonica, piano, and drums, played at "schools, churches, village greens, town hall, Townsend Hall, the Franklin Roads Pavilion, and during holiday celebrations and town meeting days" (Sesquicentennial Committee 1978: 200).

Local families, seeing the changes in social patterns and recognizing a need for dance space and an opportunity for income, sometimes renovated spaces or built single-story structures that became dance halls and pavilions. Open-air summer pavilions were also popular, especially in lake regions, where summer visitors assured proprietors (and musicians) of an income during those months. Both large and small lakes were sites for these popular halls. Elwin Corey recalled the pavilions on nearby lakes in Central Vermont: "Back when I was growing up there was a dance pavilion here on Lake Hortonia—you remember that? One on Lake Hortonia, Bomoseen, and there was a big pavilion on Lake Dunmore. And there was another pavilion on Lake Champlain."[20]

The character of the dances at the pavilions and dance halls varied with the population. "You see when they went into a pavilion—like that pavilion that was on Bomoseen there. They went more for the rounds; they did a lot of work on the rounds. But when they were running dances at Lake Hortonia, now they'd play a square dance set and then they'd play rounds . . . And it revolved in that way. It was split. But they did old traditional square dancing."[21]

Balls, which were held in many of the same venues were also popular, although they were more often limited to a distinct population. Graduation balls, masquerade balls, and anniversary balls were more formal affairs with music provided by members of the dance bands or dance orchestras; many people traveled some distance to take part in the event, as this history of East Montpelier, Vermont, relates:

> One of the most gala events of the year was the annual East Montpelier "Oyster Supper and Dance." This February event was held at Hammet's Hall in East Village and, during the 1880s, at the Pavilion in Montpelier. Music was provided by a seven-piece band; the price of admission was two dollars and fifty cents . . . A similar, formal "New Year's Ball" was also held at Hammet's Hall. In 1850 the ball commenced at four o'clock P.M., and music was provided by Robinson's Band from Stowe. The Montpelier and Wells River Railroad provided half fare to an East Montpelier Social Dance held at Montpelier's Pavilion Hotel in March 1883. Cotillion parties were equally popular. On December 23, 1890, Waterman's Orchestra of Montpelier played music until four o'clock A.M. at J. B. Wylie's in North Montpelier. The bill was fifty cents for the hall, seventy-five cents per couple for the supper, and fifteen cents for horsekeeping. (Hill 1983: 211)

While historical society libraries today hold evidence that many balls took place in northern communities, with posters, invitations, newspaper announcements, and dance cards that present details on date, time, place, and sometimes performers and their repertoires, few of the people interviewed for this study referred to balls or other formal events of this type. Information on these events comes to us primarily from the musicians who took part in dance bands that traveled to perform at various formal events. The oral data indicates that this type of event may have had less significance in the lives of most rural farming family members, possibly because it was so removed from their everyday lives. The local dances had a greater social purpose that was critical to the maintenance of well being in their communities.

History of the Dances and Their Music

The rural dances in nineteenth-century New England included group, couple, and individual dances adopted from European traditions and shared in both informal and formal, private and public contexts, from family and neighborhood social dances to town dances and sometimes organized balls or assemblies. Most common in this region were neighborhood dances accompanied by a small group of instrumentalists that nearly always included a solo fiddle backed by piano or organ; other instruments were added only when community members could offer them. The rural dances and their accompanying music exhibited a flexibility in format and style and shifted with the changing U.S. relationship with Europe and Canada, with perceptions of independence, with the involvement of dancing masters and their itinerancy, and innovation, and according to the social and cultural needs of each community.

The adopted dances and tunes in the region represent a direct relationship with Europe, especially the British Isles, but also France and French-speaking Canada. European dances popular in nineteenth- and twentieth-century rural regions often included mixed-sex group dances derived from England and developed in France, performed in line or square formations. Couple dances, including the waltz, polka, *schottische,* and *galop* to some extent emerged from these dances, representing influence from Germany (*schottische*) and Eastern Europe (polka) as well. The individual step dances, often competitively performed, were derived from Ireland, Scotland, and France. As the dances and their tunes were adopted, new forms were developed that were expressive of local, regional, and national identities.

EUROPEAN DANCE TRADITIONS

The earliest detailed documentation of the English country dance or social dance tradition is in John Playford's *English Dancing Master,* a volume first published in 1651 but modified numerous times between 1652 and 1728 to reflect changing dance patterns and styles.[22] The country dances noted by Playford were primarily the longways dances that dominated England in the seventeenth and eighteenth centuries, but square and round dances were represented as well.

In the longways dances, women and men faced each other in two lines. The head couple moved down the line as each figure was completed and a new head couple was established; this gave each dancer an opportunity to "lead." In relation to the performance, it allowed the figure (and tune) to be repeated as many times as there were couples in a line.

While longways dances remained popular in England through the eighteenth century, the adoption in France of the country dances (contradances, then *contradanse*) in the late seventeenth century encouraged the inclusion of more square-formation dances in the repertoire. This called for an even number of couples, typically four. In developing the square form of the *contradanse,* the French extended the length of the dance by adopting a series of movement figures (changes) that allowed dancers to repeat the square figure more than once. By the mid to late eighteenth century these *cotillons* dominated in France. The *cotillon* did not have set tunes associated with it and was often accompanied by a medley of popular tunes; by the nineteenth century, this medley freely integrated waltzes, polkas, and *galops.*

The quadrille in eighteenth-century France was known as the *contradanses françaises*[23] and was not always clearly distinguished from the cotillon. Like the cotillon, there were set figures that were strung together to create a complete dance. In the early nineteenth century, a set of six popular cotillon figures was introduced in London and became known as the French quadrille.

The waltz and other couple dances (sometimes referred to as "round" or "turning" dances) broke away from the context of the French *contradanse* in the late eighteenth century and were adopted as separate—and very popular—dances throughout the nineteenth century. The two step (a variation on the *galop*) was adopted in the late nineteenth century.

The individual dances popular in Europe included different forms of step dancing, which were often considered percussive dance genres because of the rhythmic sounds produced by the feet in time to the music. The dance existed in solo form and as an integral part of group dancing. The Irish jig, a fast solo dance that originated in Ireland, was also in use in Morris dancing in England as early as the seventeenth century. The Scottish group dances, including the set dance (related to the French quadrille) have used step dancing since the eighteenth century.

BALANCE FOUR IN A LINE.

Illus. 4.2. Illustration from Elias Howe's *American Dancing Master, 1882.*

The French gigue was popular in seventeenth- and eighteenth-century European courts and is found in the ballroom and theatre repertoire of the same period.

NEW ENGLAND DANCES

In the northern New England social landscape, group, couple, and individual dances were initially adopted from the European forms. The genres reached the region directly from Europe, Canada, and urban New England and were recorded in printed dance manuals that were used and even published in the northern regions to spread the popular dances and styles.[24] While we can find a direct (and possibly continuous) historical connection between dances popular throughout the twentieth century in rural New England and urban dances performed in the nineteenth century, it is clear that many of these traditions were informed largely by social practices and literature generated to support a dance revival.[25] The popular dance manuals of the nineteenth and early twentieth centuries reinforced the importance of specific dances and also illustrated a formality that circumscribed cultural and social practices in the urban-based traditions, as seen in Elias Howe's *American Dancing Master* of 1862.

The longways or country dances are referred to in the literature as "contra," "country," or "contry" dances, but locally they were known as "string" or "line"

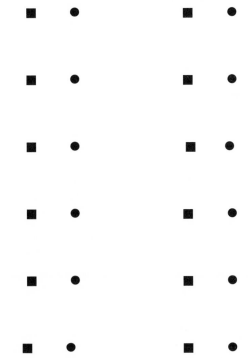

Illus. 4.3.   Typical line formation for contradances.

dances. Like the popular country dances in England, they were performed by two lines of dancers who faced each other to form a set. Participants were numbered alternately and identified as active or inactive as they progressed in the dance. Typically women were on one side and men on the other or, for some dances, women and men alternated along the line.[26]

Longways dances provided an opportunity for participants to interact in lines of dancers, repeating the figures as many times as there were couples. The dance music continued until all of the couples had an opportunity to be at the head of the line. Participants were also less confined to a limited group than in squares (they moved up and down the long line of dancers). Furthermore, women and men also moved independently of one another during the dances. This relatively informal structure may have appealed to more people in rural communities, as evidenced by the longer period of time during which this dance genre was popular. It, of course, mirrored the informality that pervaded their social and cultural lives.

Contrasting in social structure to the contras were the square-formation dances. Cotillions (from the French *cotillon*) and quadrilles, distant relatives of today's square dances, were couple square-formation dances that included a sequence of figures. Both dances, like their European sources, were executed by a set group of couples, generally four, although some quadrilles were danced with eight.[27] The traditional number of figures (or changes) was five with four intermissions, like the

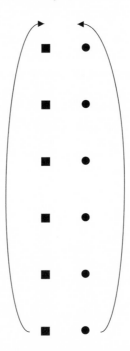

Illus. 4.4. Movement of the dancers from the bottom of the top of the set. Women and men moved independently.

Music in Rural New England Family and Community Life

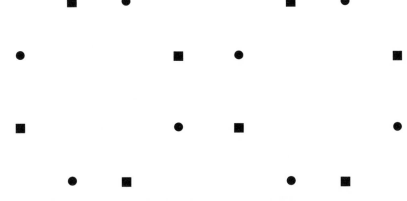

Illus. 4.5.   Typical formation for the quadrille: a small social group.

European model, and each figure was supported with a separate tune. The New England dances were often shortened to three figures (with two intermissions).

The community of dancers established for the length of the dance provided an opportunity for social exchange among a small group of couples. The squares recreated a social community in which couples remained in their designated places (in relation to one another) throughout most of the dance (moving away only briefly to greet or swing their neighbor but returning immediately to their partner). There were fewer opportunities for women to move separately from their partners and in general a more limited and unchanging set of social relations maintained for the dance than in the longways-style dances.

Calling, by separate prompter or by the fiddler, was adopted in North America during the early years of the nineteenth century, and by the second half of the century it was an accepted—even expected—practice in many communities. The formulaic language that represented the changes allowed more figures to be incorporated into the dances. Calling provided a greater opportunity for the creative development of cultural expression—the prompter could alter steps, make comments, chant or sing the changes, and even generate new dances.

The Northern New England prompts were functional, yet they exhibited individual creativity as well. In separate performances, Edson Cole of Freedom, New Hampshire, and Ed Larkin of Chelsea, Vermont, call "Chorus Jig," a popular longways dance in the 1930s and 1940s. Their contrasting performances represented in the following diagrams demonstrate the integration of calling into the overall performance and show how calling can affect the performance experience for the participants. The frameworks present calling events within the four- and eight-bar framework; the brief statement of direction for a period typically occurs at the very end or very beginning of a musical phrase. Edson Cole's calling sequence was reported by Eloise Linscott in *Folk Songs of Old New England,* a collection based on fieldwork in the 1930s, while Ed Larkin's was recorded by Helen Hartness Flanders and Alan Lomax in 1939.

Chorus Jig

Edson Cole, Freedom, N.H.

Chorus Jig

Ed Larkin, Chelsea, Vermont, 1939

"Chorus Jig"[28]		"Chorus Jig"[29]	
Edson Cole	*32 bars*	*Ed Larkin*	*32 bars*
First couple down the outside and back	8 bars	First couples outside	8 bars
Down the center and back	8 bars	Sashay	4 bars
		Second cast off	4 bars
Swing contra corners	8 bars	And swing country corners	8 bars
Balance six	4 bars	And forward and back six	4 bars
Turn in place	4 bars	And swing your partner half round	4 bars

Illus. 4.6. "Balance four," illustration from *Country Dance Book,* by Beth Tolman and Ralph Page, 1939. Publisher: A. S. Barnes, New York; reprinted by Stephen Green Press, Brattleboro.

Both contradances and square-formation dances traditionally prescribed specific steps that corresponded to the tune and were prescribed by social convention. Yet in rural New England, the variety demonstrated by prompters and dancers in both current and historical dance contexts provides evidence that there was ample opportunity for creative development and stylized and individualized dancing. This is captured in the illustrations for Beth Tolman and Ralph Page's *Country Dance Book,* published in 1937 (Tolman 1937: 90–91).

Other popular dances in rural communities include round and solo dance forms. The most popular dances, the waltzes, marches, *schottische, galop,* and polka, were sometimes performed at kitchen dances, but they were more often associated with dances at local halls. Step dancing in the region was connected to the specific traditions of the dominant residents: the Irish, Scottish, and French.[30] In general, step dancing existed both as a solo form and as an integral part of group dances. The *gigue* or "dancing the jig," originally a solo dance form often associated with men's performance, was performed by both women and men in New England. Step dance figures are used for competition, for entertainment, and often by Franco-American fiddlers who while seated step to accompany their fiddling. Passed along in families from parent or grandparent to child, the *gigue* was performed in the lumbercamps and at family gatherings, and it is performed today with great enthusiasm at social events, including local fiddlers' club meetings.

In some communities, adults at family or neighborhood gatherings performed sung circle dances. These dances are often associated with children's games, although in New England families, adults also performed the dances; sometimes they relied on the singing of participants rather than instrumental accompaniment.

In Franco-American communities the quadrille, *contredanse, rond, danses carrées,* and *gigue* were all popular dances. The quadrille is executed in parts, and dancers use square, circle, and longways formations. While a form of the quadrille evolved to become the American square dance, among French Canadians it is known as *la danse carrée.*

The core tradition preserved in the dance music in the region can be described as Anglo-Celtic, although French-Canadian styles also played an increasingly important role. The dance music in both the rural and urban communities during this period was in a constant state of change, expanding with the influx of new residents and the popularity of new styles and forms of dancing and entertainment. While British, Irish, and Scottish music dominated in the nineteenth century, a number of factors altered the social landscape and therefore the local repertoires and playing styles by the early twentieth century. A primary influence for many was the French-Canadian style that was brought with settlers from Quebec and heard throughout the airwaves in Maine, New Hampshire, and Vermont. The Quebecois instrumental style quickly became fused with the local repertoire and playing style in many communities. The tradition was also fluid because fiddlers constantly created new variations on the old tunes, ultimately generating a new, expanded repertoire as they had with the American material.[31]

INSTRUMENTATION

The fiddle was—and still is—the primary accompanying instrument for country dancing. And it is the fiddle, its tunes, and the dances they embody that dominate our perception and understanding of nineteenth- and twentieth-century rural dance music in the United States. The fiddle enjoyed widespread use throughout North America, though distinct stylistic traditions can be identified by region based on tunes, repertoires, playing style, and overall performance practice. The fiddle was typically played as the solo instrument in an ensemble, and most of the other instruments established a harmonic framework for the soloist, although some also doubled the melody. The dominant accompanying instruments in the ensembles changed in each historical period and location. Often the keyboard (piano or organ, in the nineteenth century) was the only instrument used in the kitchen dances, but increasingly the guitar, banjo, mandolin, trumpet, trombone, and drums were added. In the Franco-American ensemble the primary instruments that supported the fiddle were guitar, mouth organ, accordion, and spoons. In the Quebec-derived ensembles, the fiddler also typically provided rhythmic support with his own clogging. Paul Wells describes Louis Beaudoin's fiddling in Burlington, Vermont, during the second half of the twentieth century: "Louis' skill at providing this danceable rhythm has been shaped by many nights of playing for old-time kitchen dances, sitting on the kitchen table and fiddling all night with no accompaniment apart from his own clogging" (Wells 1976a).

The accordion popular in the Franco-American ensembles became an occasional participant—and in some communities a substitute for the fiddle—in the dance ensemble. In general, locally available instruments were used to provide music for the dances. Mike Pelletier of Old Town, Maine, remembers the "kitchen breakdowns" in his community: "We used to have whatever kind of music was available. Somebody might have a fiddle, or maybe it would be an accordion or a Jew's Harp. Sometimes we sang songs. If there wasn't room for square dancing, we'd dance clogs."[32]

Philippe Lemay of Manchester, New Hampshire, reinforces the casual approach to instrumentation and performance practice: "For our round and square dances as well as jigs, the music was furnished by a fiddler who always played the same tune as long as you wanted him to—he knew no other—and by a fellow who played the accordion, but they never played together because their tunes were different. We didn't care about that and we danced and had great fun."[33]

Instrumentation for the dance ensembles developed in relation to other popular ensembles that residents either observed or participated in. The most significant changes came from instrumentation introduced by cotillion, quadrille, and marching bands, which were established in the second half of the nineteenth century in many communities; traveling musicians (including minstrel shows) that reached the region in the early years of the twentieth century; dance bands of the 1920s, 1930s, and 1940s; and music heard on the radio in many families after the 1920s. Popular additions to the instrumental ensemble during the period reflected these influences as well as the music industry's response to developing American styles. The guitar, mandolin, and banjo were introduced through their popularity in minstrel shows, dance bands, and hillbilly bands; the trumpet, trombone, and drum set came from military and other marching bands, and then the increasingly popular dance bands; the accordion and spoons—as well as clogging while playing the fiddle, as a form of rhythmic accompaniment—came from French-Canadian performance practice.

REPERTOIRE

While a systematic study that parallels Child's or Laws' song classifications has not been completed for dance music, this absence encourages us to focus more directly on the regional traditions. Both scholars and local musicians informally identify a specific instrumental repertoire with New England. Their sources for this include nineteenth- and early-twentieth-century manuscripts, early-twentieth-century fieldwork data, music and dance traditions documented during Henry Ford's revival of country dancing in the 1920s and 1930s, and the activities of older musicians after World War II who became involved in renewing and reinforcing older traditions, including the repertoires.

We can identify a core repertoire for the region that emerged during the nineteenth and early twentieth centuries by examining the popularity of specific tunes. Some of the tunes were connected to New England as early as the eighteenth century, while others were adopted later from contact with traveling musicians and the media.[34] Older pieces that are sometimes referred to today as "old-time tunes" include "Chorus Jig," "Soldier's Joy," "Durang's Hornpipe," "Portland Fancy," "Devil's Dream," "Fisher's Hornpipe," and "Money Musk."

Considering the significance of repertoire and its variation over time, we can observe that a version of "Fisher's Hornpipe" from *Asa Willcox's Book of Figures,* a commonplace book dated 1793 from Connecticut, is very close to the S. Daily manuscript of dance tunes from Pittsburg, New Hampshire, dated circa 1850.[35]

Fisher's Hornpipe

Willcox ms., 1793

Fisher's Hornpipe

S. Daily ms., Pittsburg, N.H., c. 1850

Similar comparisons can be made with many tunes that can be identified with a core repertoire in the region. The tune "Devil's Dream" in the S. Daily manuscript from Pittsburgh, New Hampshire, is also nearly identical to one in a manuscript compiled in 1915 by John A. Taggart originally of Sharon, New Hampshire.[36] What is more important, though, is a consideration of this data in light of recorded performances of these tunes. It helps us to also recognize that the tunes preserved in written format can only provide a snapshot of the music of the period. Quechee, Vermont, resident Elmer Barton recorded a version of the same tune that illustrates a New England style using sparing embellishments. His performance clearly exhibits the variation that is behind the skeletal tunes found in local manuscripts.

Music in Rural New England Family and Community Life

The Devil's Dream

S. Daily ms., Pittsburg., N.H., c. 1850

The Devil's Dream

John Taggart ms., 1915

The Devil's Dream

Elmer Barton, Quechee, Vermont, 1945

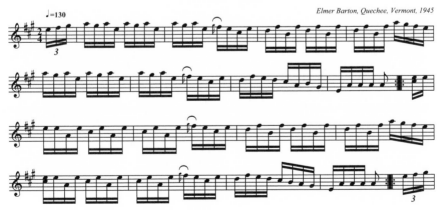

These core tunes are firmly planted in British, Scottish, and/or Irish traditions and were used to accompany dances in both rural and urban contexts. Their popularity was maintained by their use by musicians to accompany dances in salons and ballrooms in southern New England, by their inclusion in popular dance manuals and tune books that were distributed widely in New England, and by their stable role in local rural traditions, where musicians maintained the tunes that had been in their family repertoires for generations. Other popular early tunes with origins that have been more elusive include "The Girl I Left Behind Me," "Turkey in the Straw," or "Old Zip Coon," as well as a tune with even more tenuous ties to the British tradition that has taken on an American identity: "Arkansas Traveler."

One tune we find consistently among rural fiddlers from the early years of the twentieth century is "Darling Nellie Gray." Ohioan Benjamin Hanby wrote the song in 1856, and it was marketed in sheet music and broadside form during the second half of the nineteenth century. It was also found frequently in published song collections between 1890 and 1920. The tune quickly became a favorite in many New England communities and occasionally was preserved in manuscript form, as in this example from a book of dance tunes that belonged to an unidentified fiddler from Panton, Vermont.

Illus. 4.7. "Darling Nellie Gray" manuscript, c. 1915.

Illus. 4.8. "Darling Nellie Gray" sheet music.

Illus. 4.9. "Darling Nellie Gray" broadside.

J. H. Buck of East Bethel, Vermont, called "Darling Nellie Gray" this way in 1939[37]:

Darling Nellie Gray

J. H. Buck, East Bethel, Vermont, 1939

Oh the first young gent he will bal-ance to the right, And he'll swing with the Dar-ling Nel-lie

Gray. Now you lead to the next and you'll bal-ance once a - gain, And you'll swing with the Dar-ling Nel-lie

Gray. Oh you lead to the next and you'll bal-ance once a - gain, And you'll swing with the Dar-ling Nel-lie

Gray. Oh you lead to your own and you'll ne-ver be a - lone, Now you all swing your Dar-ling Nel-lie

Gray. Oh you'll pro-me-nade a - round, twice a - round, yes twice a - round, Oh you'll

pro-me-nade a - round, twice a - round. Now you'll pro-me-nade your own and you'll

nev-er be a - lone, While you all pro-me-nade twice a - round.

The first young gent he will balance to the right,
And he'll swing with the Darling Nellie Gray.
Now you lead to the next and you'll balance once again,
And you'll swing with the Darling Nellie Gray.
Oh you lead to the next and you'll balance once again,
And you'll swing with the Darling Nellie Gray.
Oh you lead to your own and you'll never be alone,
Now you all swing your Darling Nellie Gray.

Oh you'll promenade around, twice around, yes twice around,
Oh you'll promenade around, twice around.
Now you'll promenade your own and you'll never be alone,
While you all promenade twice around.

Other tunes connected to popular songs that gained popularity in the region include "Wabash Cannonball" and "Redwing." Some of the older traditional songs provided tunes for dances as well, including the "Lass of Mohea" for waltzes and "Margery Grey" for two-steps. In the early twentieth century other tunes to support the expanding dance styles that were becoming popular included "Flop Eared Mule," "Heel and Toe Polka," and "Silver and Gold." These tunes have remained standards for many instrumentalists tied to an "old-time" tradition throughout most of the century. While Franco-American performers shared a separate repertoire of dance tunes (primarily reels), some of their tunes became standards in the region, especially "Maple Sugar," "Joys of Quebec," "Gaspé Reel," and "St. Anne's Reel." Dot Brown of Bristol, Vermont, played "Gaspé Reel" this way in 1974.[38]

Gaspé Reel

Dot Brown, Bristol, Vermont, 1974

Performers maintained local and regional tunes that were part of their family or local community traditions, but they also expanded their repertoires with new tunes. Manuscript books from the eighteenth and nineteenth centuries provide ample evidence that repertoires included both traditional and local tunes. Interviews with fiddlers also often yield information on tunes they have created. In some cases the tunes represent variations on a traditional tune or even a simple renaming of a tune to identify it more clearly. A practice common to fiddlers is to name a tune for an individual or a location.[39]

STYLE

In New England the characteristic playing style of the nineteenth and early twentieth centuries was derived from the dominant Irish, Scottish, and English traditions found in many rural American communities. The regional tradition emerged with the increasing influence of Franco-American traditions on dance music, and the adoption of media transmitted and inspired music that was inserted into the local tradition. The cultural synthesis in the region has generated regional playing styles that are often referred to as New England, or Yankee, or "old-time New England" styles. While initially the character of the playing may have been governed by a fairly staid, unembellished style, this gradually changed during the twentieth century as a result of a constant interplay in repertoire and playing style between the dominant Anglo-Celtic and French-Canadian tunes,

Music in Rural New England Family and Community Life

styles, and instrumentation. The role of a developing national style cannot be ignored, though. The widespread attraction of the radio and the wide variety of musics that emanated from it and from the Victrola provided valuable oral tradition material for fiddlers in the region throughout the twentieth century. The stylistic influences outside of the community (throughout the airwaves) came from fiddlers from the south and the north: Canadian Don Messer is often cited as the most important source of influence for many fiddlers remembering the practices of the 1930s and 1940s.

Regional fiddlers maintained an old-time Yankee style characterized by a clear melodic line with a sparing use of double-stopping (compared to southern fiddling styles). Tunes were typically played at a moderate tempo and rhythmic punctuation was moderate as well; for many, it might be described as understated. The bowing style groups notes in twos and fours with little change in dynamics and emphasis, in contrast to the southern playing style more influenced by African American syncopation, which utilizes a "stylized anticipation of the beat" (Jabbour 1971: 254).

For many years the French-Canadian style of playing developed as a parallel tradition to the Anglo-Celtic New England styles. The little communities established by Franco-American settlers provided sites for these Canadian immigrants to reinforce the traditions of their homeland. Increasingly, fiddlers fused their styles as they came into contact with one another at dances and, later, festivals and fiddlers' contests and meetings. The French-Canadian style also drew from Anglo-Celtic dance music traditions, but it was identified especially by its use of the bow to add rhythmic emphasis. Many fiddlers further reinforced the rhythm with clogging.[40] While both styles shared tunes derived from Anglo-Celtic traditions, the French repertoire provided new tunes for dancers as well.

RELATIONSHIP BETWEEN TUNES AND DANCES

It is important to consider that the musicians' role in the dances affected the character and playing style of the music. Many fiddlers in the latter part of the twentieth century who have had the opportunity to perform in contest and festival fiddling sharply contrast solo fiddling with typical dance accompaniment. First of all, the regularity of rhythm and tempo was naturally of great concern to the instrumentalists, since the primary function of the music was to accompany dance. While an elastic meter was common in the singing traditions, especially in the lumbercamps and other casual performance-based environments, instrumental music rarely used this technique. More importantly, the pace of the music placed the dancers in greater control. While a fiddler may have been capable of playing a tune at a fast pace (and some of the field recordings of individual fiddlers at home demonstrate this), in the context of the dance, the pace was tempered. After playing "Fisher's Hornpipe" at a rapid pace, Elwin Corey of Fair Haven, Vermont, identified the contrasting contexts and the differing tempos:

Fisher's Hornpipe

Elwin Corey, Fair Haven, Vermont, 1985

You going to play it for dances, you want to slow it down, 'bout half that speed. I've always said if I'm going to play something for someone to listen to, for somebody's amusement, it ain't going to make no particular difference. But if I was to play it for somebody to dance, it has to be played slower than that. Back in those days they never played that music like that. Everybody danced to the dances in time to the music—no foolin' around. And if they didn't, the prompter stopped everything. If they didn't dance like he wanted them to dance, he stopped everything.[41]

While dance tunes can be identified by name and classified by meter and rhythmic phrasing, tunes were also changed to fit the needed meter for a dance formation. Similarly, the same tunes were used for different dances as the tunes became popular: reels in 2/4 or 4/4 were initially used to accompany contradances, but ultimately became popular for other dances as well. In addition to reels, jigs in 6/8 and (less often) 9/8, hornpipes in 4/4 and marches in 2/4 were all popular for accompanying contras. Popular specialty dance tunes included schottisches for step dancing, waltzes, and polkas.

FORM AND ITS RELATIONSHIP TO DANCES

There is regularity in the form of the fiddle tunes played for all of the dances, allowing the same song to be used for a variety of dances. The tunes are often played in two (symmetrical) sections (or strains) of eight measures each. The first section is followed by a cadence, and the second is generally at a higher pitch.[42] The result is an AABB structure that typically is repeated until a dance set is completed—or, in a contra, until all of the couples have taken a turn as the head couple. Sometimes medleys of tunes were used, presenting two or three tunes strung together. These sections (and their internal phrase structure) relate directly to the organization of the dances and dance steps. For example, in the tune "Hull's Victory," the following call sequence, danced in contra formation, was played and called by Bill Woodward of Bristol, New Hampshire in the 1940s from a transcription by Eloise Linscott.[43] (After giving dancers a line of directions, each figure can be distributed in one four-bar phrase of the tune.)

Music in Rural New England Family and Community Life

Hull's Victory

Right hand to your partner, left hand to your opposite
Balance four in a line (4 bars)
Turn your opposite with your left hand (4 bars)
Right hand back and balance four (4 bars)
Turn your partner in the center, in the center turn your partner (4 bars)
Down the center with your partner (4 bars)
Back and cast off (4 bars)
Right and left, right and left (4 bars)
Everyone right and left (4 bars)

In the quadrille, several tunes were played, sometimes with a break between them, and new steps were introduced for each tune. There were specific tunes associated with quadrilles, such as the popular "Black Cat," but other tunes were quickly adopted, including popular songs like "Buffalo Gals," "Little Brown Jug," "Turkey in the Straw," and "Golden Slippers."

In the "Black Cat Quadrille" played in 1939 by Ed Larkin of Chelsea, Vermont, the changes he uses for the first figure document the dance steps used and the variations called upon as the tune is repeated every 32 bars.[44]

Black Cat Quadrille

Ed Larkin, Chelsea, Vermont, 1939

Introduction
Address your partners (4 bars)
And your corners (4 bars)
The first couple right about face (4 bars)
All step in line (4 bars)

And sashay to the right (4 bars)
Sashay to the left (4 bars)
March, ladies to the right and gents to the left (8 bars)
All women sashay (4 bars)
Turn your partners twice in step (4 bars)
Promenade yours (8 bars)

And the ladies grand chain (8 bars)
Promenade yours (8 bars)
The next couple, right about face (4 bars)
First four cast in line (4 bars)
Sashay to the right (4 bars)
Sashay to the left (4 bars)

March, ladies to the right and gents to the left (8 bars)
All women sashay (4 bars)
Turn your partners twice in step (4 bars)
Promenade yours (8 bars)
And the ladies grand chain (8 bars)

Promenade yours (8 bars)
The next couple, right about face (4 bars)
Step in line (4 bars)
Sashay to the right (4 bars)
Sashay to the left (4 bars)
Now ladies to the right and gents to the left (8 bars)

Forwards and back eight (4 bars)
Turn your partners and right hand step (4 bars)
Promenade yours (8 bars)
The ladies grand chain (8 bars)
Promenade yours (8 bars)

The next couple right about face (4 bars)
First four step in line (4 bars)
And sashay to the right (4 bars)
Sashay to the left (4 bars)
etc.

TRANSMISSION

Fiddlers and other instrumentalists who provided accompaniment for dances
played traditional tunes that they learned in the context of their local commu-

nities. The opportunities for learning and sharing tunes were informal, like that of learning and sharing songs. While fiddlers assign some of their tunes to members of their family, they also learned tunes from other musicians (especially later, in the expanding geographic sphere that included dances and contests). Many fiddlers refer to other fiddlers at dances as sources for their tunes; as dance traditions widened geographically to include larger bands and different musicians, the repertoires became more diverse. Later they learned tunes from popular radio programs and recordings, as well as from printed sources.

At music festivals and contests today it is not unusual to see fiddlers (and other musicians) huddled together, their backs to the crowd, teaching each other new tunes. Young fiddlers today talk about going to a respected older fiddler to learn (or as they sometimes say, "get") their repertoire and style. Sometimes this occurs informally, although more formal lessons on the fiddle have replaced the informal learning environment for some.

The dance and dance music practices of northern New England were the results of influences that emerged from within local communities and established neighborhoods and from outside sources. At the inception of the social dance events, it has been suggested that kitchen dances were established as a mechanism to deal with a new, geographically defined social system founded by settlers when they arrived from villages in England. They moved from a tight-knit village context in England where dances took place occasionally to a looser context where they were living at some distance from one another; in order to maintain their connections, they established new social patterns (Groce n.d.: 22).

During the twentieth century, modernization that included easier travel both within the region and in and out of the region provided greater opportunities for sharing dance and dance music practices. The rural residents traveled more, relatives took the opportunity to move farther away and only returned to visit, and publications and media sources such as radio and commercial recordings were more readily available. It is also significant that musicians were taking dance jobs farther afield. The effect of these changes was an alteration in the social network that was initially established with settlement in the rural regions and then maintained in neighborhood dances and other social events.

Beginning in the early years of the twentieth century, dance promoters such as Henry Ford for American dance, and later in New England, Ralph Page, who was concerned with regional customs, actively sought opportunities for change in dance and music practices in the urban and rural landscapes. The new practices interfaced with and ultimately replaced many of the older customs in the region. As historians identified the contradance as the primary New England dance form and urban settlers sought to maintain this imagined tradition, the older, varied traditions that included a wide spectrum of dances and tunes remained hidden in the memories of some of the rural residents who were participants in the early kitchen junkets and community dances.

Appendix: Core Repertoires

A core repertoire for northern New England can be constructed for the period from 1850 to the mid-1940s using manuscript and fieldwork data. Sources for this list include nineteenth- and early-twentieth-century manuscripts and collections from Maine, Vermont, and New Hampshire, and field recordings from individuals and organizations in all three states. Field recordings of fiddlers in the 1970s and 1980s represent older performers who were playing tunes of their youth and tunes they designated as "old-time." For many in this later period, the tunes also represented a portion of their contemporary repertoire. Tunes identified in this sample fall into three broad categories: those that continued to be popular in the region from the mid-nineteenth century through the mid-twentieth (and later); those that were popular earlier on but little evidence of them remained after the first few decades of the twentieth century; and those that were adopted in the first few decades of the twentieth century and continued to be played throughout the century. The purpose of this list is to demonstrate that there are tunes that can be identified with the region over a considerable period. In addition, the character of the region can be characterized by the unique combination of Anglo-Irish, Franco-American, and American popular tunes that are consistently found in various social circumstances. This collection presents a representative sampling of sources that help to establish a clearer understanding of dominant tunes during a specific period in New England history.

Sources in Chronological Order

Cobb ms (c. 1850): Tunebook compiled by Charles M. Cobb, Woodstock, Vermont (Vermont Historical Society)

Daily ms (c. 1850): Tunebook compiled by S. [Samuel] Daily, Pittsburg, New Hampshire (Helen Hartness Flanders Ballad Collection)

Taggart ms (1915): Tunes compiled in a memoir by John A. Taggart, New Hampshire (New Hampshire Historical Society)

Panton ms (c. 1915): Tunebook by an unidentified transcriber, Panton, Vermont (Flanders Collection)

Dunham (1920s): Published collection by Mellie Dunham, Norway, Maine

Stewart (1930): Field recordings of John Stewart, Dorset, Vermont (Flanders Collection)

Girard (1932): Field recordings of Lucien Girard, Burlington, Vermont (Flanders Collection)

Ashford (1937): Field recordings of Henry Ashford, Grafton, Vermont (Flanders Collection)

Barton (1939): Field recordings of Elmer Barton, Quechee, Vermont (Flanders Collection)

Buck (1939): Field recordings of J. H. Buck, East Bethel, Vermont (Flanders Collection)

Larkin (1939): Field recordings of Edwin Larkin, Chelsea, Vermont (Flanders Collection)

Weeks (1939): Field recordings of Luther Weeks, Springfield, Vermont (Flanders Collection)

Cates (1941): Field recordings of Frank Cates, Rockland, Maine (Eloise Linscott Collection)

Dragon (1941): Field recordings of Daniel Dragon, Ripton, Vermont (Flanders Collection)

Farnham (1941): Field recordings of Herbert Farnham, Wardsoro, Vermont (Linscott Collection)

Robinson (1941): Field recordings of Roger Robinson, Bowdoinham, Maine (Linscott Collection]

Young (1941): Field recordings of Nathansel Young, Rockland, Maine, 1941 (Linscott Collection)

C. Barton (1942): Field recordings of Cyrus Barton, Cornish, New Hampshire (Flanders Collection]

Bedell (1942): Field recordings of George Bedell, Vershire, Vermont (Flanders Collection)

Gibbons (1942): Field recordings of Frank Gibbons, Surrey, Maine (Flanders Collection)

McKeage (1942): Field recordings of Robert McKeage, Pittsburg, New Hampshire (Flanders Collection)

Wass (1942): Field recordings of Harry Seymour Wass, Addison, Maine (Flanders Collection)

Wilson (1942): Field recordings of Bill Wilson, Pike, New Hampshire (Flanders Collection)

Earl (1958): Field recordings of Merritt Earl, Eden, Vermont (Flanders Collection)

CVFA 1 (1974): Field recordings of Champlain Valley Fiddlers' Association meetings, recorded in September and October 1974 (recorded by Kim Chambers; housed at Middlebury College)

Brown (1974): Field recordings of Dot Brown, Bristol, Vermont (recorded by Kim Chambers and Debra Conroy in 1974 and 1984, respectively; housed at Middlebury College)

Barrows (1978): Field recordings of Ted Barrows, Perkinsville, Vermont (recorded by Kim Chambers; housed at Middlebury College)

CVFA 2 (1984): Field recordings of Champlain Valley Fiddlers' Association meetings, recorded in March and April 1984 (recorded by Jennifer Post)

Stark (1984): Field recordings of Harry Stark, Cornwall, Vermont (recorded by Debra Conroy)

Corey (1985): Field recordings of Elwin Corey, Fair Haven, Vermont and Freeman Corey, Benson, Vermont (recorded by Jennifer Post)

Gove (1985): Field recordings of Ramon Gove, Warren, Vermont (recorded by Jennifer Post)

Grimes (1985): Field recordings of Ray Grimes, Lincoln, Vermont (recorded by Jennifer Post)

Neill (1985): Field recordings of Albert Neill, Warren, Vermont (recorded by Jennifer Post)

Brooks (1987): Field recordings of Leo Brooks, Pittsburg, New Hampshire (recorded by Jennifer Post)

Covill (1987): Field recordings of Clyde Covill, Pittsburg, New Hampshire (recorded by Jennifer Post)

Title	Appearance
Arkansas Traveler	Daily ms (c. 1850); Taggart ms (1915); Panton ms (c. 1915); Dunham (1920s); Weeks (1939); Barton (1939); C. Barton (1942); Gibbons (1942); Brown (1974); Stark (1984); Gove (1985)
Beau of Oak Hill	Cobb ms (c. 1850); Panton ms (c. 1915); Weeks (1939)
Black Velvet Waltz	CVFA 2 (1984); Stark (1984); Brooks (1987); Covill (1987)

Title	Appearance
Bonaparte Crossing the Alps	Panton ms (c. 1915); Weeks (1939)
Boston Fancy	Dunham (1920s); Young (1941); Bedell (1942); McKeage (1942); Neill (1985)
Caledonian March	Panton ms (c. 1915); Weeks (1939)
Chorus Jig	Daily ms (c. 1850); Taggart ms (1915); Panton ms (c. 1915); Dunham (1920s); Stewart (1930); Larkin (1939); Barton (1939); Cates (1941); McKeage (1942); Wass (1942); Gove (1985); Neill (1985)
College Hornpipe	Daily ms (c. 1850); Taggart ms (1915); Cates (1941); Robinson (1941); Wass (1942)
Coming through the Rye	Daily ms (c. 1850); Panton ms (c. 1915)
Darling Nellie Gray	Panton ms (c. 1915); Buck (1939); Cates (1941); Brown (1974); CVFA 1 (1974); CVFA 2 (1984); Stark (1984); Gove (1985); Neill (1985); Grimes (1985); Covill (1987)
Devil's Dream	Daily ms (c. 1850); Taggart ms (1915); Dunham (1920s); Girard (1932); Barton (1939); Buck (1939); Weeks (1939); Robinson (1941); Cates (1941); Farnham (1941); Gibbons (1942); Wass (1942); Wilson (1942); Brown (1974); Stark (1984); CVFA 2 (1984); Corey (1985); Brooks (1987)
Drunken Sailor	Daily ms (c. 1850); Farnham (1941)
Durang's Hornpipe	Daily ms (c. 1850); Taggart ms (1915); Dunham (1920s); Barton (1939); Stewart (1940); Cates (1941); Wass (1942); CVFA 1 (1974); Stark (1984); Corey (1985); Grimes (1985)
Fisher's Hornpipe	Daily ms (c. 1850); Taggart ms (1915); Dunham (1920s); Stewart (1930); Weeks (1939); Barton (1939); Buck (1939); Robinson (1941); Wilson (1942); Brown (1974); CVFA 1 (1974); Stark (1984); Corey (1985)
Flop Eared Mule	Girard (1932); CVFA 1 (1974); Brown (1974); CVFA 2 (1984); Corey (1985)
Flowers of Edinburgh	Panton ms (c. 1915); Barton (1939); Corey (1985)
Flowers of Michigan	Daily ms (c. 1850); Larkin (1939); Stark (1984)
Girl I Left Behind Me	Taggart ms (1915); Panton ms (c. 1915); Dunham (1920s); Stewart (1930); Weeks (1939); Larkin (1939); Barton (1939); Buck (1939); Cates (1941); Robinson (1941); Young (1941); Wilson (1942); C. Barton (1942); Gibbons (1942); Bedell (1942); Brown (1974); CVFA 1 (1974); CVFA 2 (1984); Corey (1985); Neill (1985)
Green Ribbon	Daily ms (c. 1850); Earl (1958)
Haste to the Wedding	Daily ms (c. 1850); Taggart ms (1915); Dunham (1920s); Weeks (1939); Farnham (1941); Brown (1974); CVFA 1 (1974); Stark (1984)
Heel and Toe Polka	Dunham (1920s); Cates (1941); CVFA 2 (1984)

Title	Appearance
Hull's Victory	Daily ms (c. 1850); Taggart ms (1915); Dunham (1920s); Weeks (1939); Larkin (1939); Barton (1939); Farnham (1941); Cates (1941); Robinson (1941); Corey (1985)
Irish Washerwoman	Daily ms (c. 1850); Taggart ms (1915); Panton ms (c. 1915); Dunham (1920s); Cates (1941); Young (1941); Robinson (1941); CVFA 1 (1974); Stark (1984); Corey (1985); Brooks (1987)
Joys of Quebec	Barton (1939); Brown (1974); CVFA 1 (1974); Stark (1984)
Lady of the Lake	Robinson (1941); Farnham (1941); CVFA 2 (1984)
Lady Walpole's Reel	Taggart ms (1915); Gibbons (1942)
Lamplighter's Hornpipe	Dunham (1920s); Weeks (1939); Robinson (1941); CVFA 1 (1974); Stark (1984); Brooks (1987)
Lannigan's Ball	Dunham (1920s); Weeks (1939)
Larry O'Gaff	Daily ms (c. 1850); Taggart ms (1915); C. Barton (1942); Gibbons (1942)
Liverpool Hornpipe	S. Daily ms (1850); Dunham (1920s); Barton (1940); Grant (1942)
Maple Sugar	CVFA 1 (1974); CVFA 2 (1984); Stark (1984); Brooks (1987); Covill (1987)
McDonald's Reel	Daily ms (c. 1850); Dunham (1920s)
Miss Brown's Reel	Daily ms (c. 1850); Taggart ms (1915); Cates (1941)
Miss MacLeod's Reel	Taggart ms (1915); Panton ms (c. 1915); Dunham (1920s); Cates (1941); Wass (1942); C. Barton (1942); Gibbons (1942); CVFA 2 (1984)
Money Musk	Daily ms (c. 1850), Taggart ms (1915), Larkin (1939); Stark (1984); Grimes (1985); Covill (1987)
Mountain Hornpipe	Panton ms (c. 1915); Dunham (1920s)
Old Zip Coon	Daily ms (c. 1850); Taggart ms (1915); Dunham (1920s); Farnham (1941); Cates (1941); Brown (1974); Neill (1985)
Opera Reel	Daily ms (c. 1850); Taggart ms (1915); Barton (1939); Robinson (1941)
Petronella (Patnella)	Daily ms (c. 1850); Weeks (1939); Barrows (1978); Stark (1984)
Pop Goes the Weasel	Daily ms (c. 1850); Taggart ms (1915); Panton ms (c. 1915); Dunham (1920s); Barton (1939); Larkin (1939); Young (1941); Cates (1941); Gibbons (1942); Wass (1942); Brown (1974); CVFA 2 (1984); Stark (1984); Neill (1985); Brooks (1987)
Portland Fancy	Taggart ms (1915); Dunham (1920s); Stewart (1930); Buck (1939); Weeks (1939); Cates (1941); Farnham (1941); Gibbons (1942); Wass (1942); Brown (1974); CVFA 1 (1974); CVFA 2 (1984); Stark (1984); Brooks (1987)

Title	Appearance
Portsmouth Hornpipe	Cobb ms (c. 1850); Daily ms (c. 1850)
Red Wing	Brown (1974); CVFA 1 (1974); CVFA 2 (1984)
Rickett's Hornpipe	Cobb ms (c. 1850); Daily ms (c. 1850); Grant (1942)
Rochester Schottische	Daily ms (c. 1850); Panton ms (c. 1915)
Rory O'More	Daily ms (c. 1850); Dunham (1920s)
Rustic Reel	Dunham (1920s); CVFA 2 (1984)
Sailor's Hornpipe	Dragon (1941); Wilson (1942)
Scotch Hornpipe	Daily ms (c. 1850); Cobb ms (c. 1850)
Silver and Gold	Brown (1974); CVFA 1 (1974); CVFA 2 (1984); Stark (1984); Brooks (1987)
Smash the Windows	Stark (1984); CVFA 2 (1984); Corey (1985); Brooks (1987)
Soldier's Joy	Daily ms (c. 1850); Taggart ms (1915); Panton ms (c. 1915); Dunham (1920s); Girard (1932); Ashford (1937); Buck (1939); Barton (1939); Robinson (1941); Cates (1941); Bedell (1942); C. Barton (1942); Gibbons (1942); CVFA 1 (1974); CVFA 2 (1984); Gove (1985); Neill (1985); Corey (1985); Covill (1987)
Soldier's Return	Daily ms (c. 1850); Cobb ms (c. 1850)
Speed the Plough	Daily ms (c. 1850); Taggart ms (1915); Dunham (1920s); Weeks (1939); Robinson (1941); Cates (1941); CVFA 1 (1974)
St. Anne's Reel	Brown (1974); CVFA 1 (1974)
St. Patrick's Day in the Morning	Panton ms (c. 1915); Weeks (1939); Barton (1939)
Steamboat Quickstep	Daily ms (c. 1850); Taggart ms (1915); Panton ms (c. 1915); Weeks (1939)
Steamboat Waltz	Daily ms (c. 1850); Dunham (1920s)
The Tempest	Daily ms (c. 1850); Taggart ms (1915); Panton ms (c. 1915); Dunham (1920s); Ashford (1937); Buck (1939); Gove (1985); Neill (1985)
Turkey in the Straw	Dunham (1920s); Barton (1939); Wass (1942); Brown (1974); Stark (1984); Grimes (1985)
Twin Sisters	Daily ms (c. 1850); Weeks (1939)
Wabash Cannonball	Bedell (1942); Brown (1974); Stark (1984); Gove (1985)
Wake Up Susan	Barton (1939); CVFA 2 (1984); Stark (1984)
White Cockade	Daily ms (c. 1850); Taggart ms (1915); Buck (1939); Cates (1941); Weeks (1939); CVFA 1 (1974); Stark (1984)
Woodchopper's Reel	Stark (1984); CVFA 2 (1984)
Wrecker's Daughter	Taggart ms (1915); Panton ms (c. 1915); Wass (1942)
Yankee Doodle	Panton ms (c. 1915); Buck (1939); Larkin (1939)

CHAPTER 5

The Social Landscape: Gendered Spaces

*I*n 1985 I sat with fiddler Ray Grimes in his home in Lincoln, Vermont. A man in his eighties, he had been well known in the region as a fiddler for local dances for many years. I first heard Ray at a meeting of the Champlain Valley Fiddlers' Association in the early 1980s. With his clear tone and confident playing, he stood out among the thirty or so players that gathered monthly to share dance tunes with one another. He was a reticent man, however, and when I went to his house to talk with him about his musical background he seemed uncomfortable at times. We sat in his living room, a table between us, and he responded—somewhat reluctantly—to my questions. His wife was present at the interview as well, although she remained in the kitchen, and the sound of dishes punctuated our conversation. When Ray had trouble remembering, she would insert the missing information. Her voice on my tapes is a weak sound in the background, but the content of her comments was always relevant to our discussions. And she freely offered information on her own musical background when I asked. Her place in the kitchen provides a contemporary illustration of the clearly delineated spatial spheres of women and men that we find throughout the nineteenth and early twentieth centuries in the region. This difference often provided separate experiences for women and men in their social lives, thereby creating gendered variations on the dominant forms of musical expression.

In fact, the scene at the Grimes's was played out again and again as I talked with other musicians in their homes. When I interviewed fiddlers (who were generally male), their accounts were frequently embellished by information offered by their wives. When I interviewed women alone to ask about music in their households, they offered information representing their independent point of view, yet when their husbands were present this seldom happened. Women stayed in the background, remaining silent or adding only briefly to the discussion.

In the late nineteenth and early twentieth centuries in northern New England, women and men, while sharing responsibilities in the home, also lived and worked in separate spheres. The social conventions that dictated these practices affected women's and men's cultural output, yielding forms of expression that can be delineated by gender. Even when women and men were in a shared space for a particular social occasion, their performance experiences often differed. Women and

113

men carried elements of their separate life experiences—expressions of their gendered identities—into social events throughout the period.

In this chapter I look at how music can be identified with specific forms of social behavior that negotiate gender and spatial relationships.[1] I explore the connection between space and place, and gender and music, and I seek cultural patterns that identify the region's gendered characteristics during the nineteenth and early twentieth centuries.

Social Spheres

Concepts related to private and public spheres, and the issue of distinct domains for women and men from which power and dependence have emerged are topics that have been defined, redefined, and widely debated during the last three decades. Scholars in many disciplines, including history, gender studies, sociology, and political science, have used these domains to look at social and cultural contexts during different historical periods.[2] While some researchers dismiss any public-private dichotomy that may emerge from scholarly study of gendered behaviors as contrived, this occurs especially when the model is applied cross-culturally, sometimes without regard to history. Some form of the model remains useful for many historians and social scientists as they attempt to better understand how society is structured and, especially, to describe social and cultural events in a historical context.

For a historical study of music in rural American social life during this specific time period, it is useful to explore aspects of the separation of domains. Any spheres that we document or design in this context, though, should be viewed on a continuum rather than in a binary form, for there are spaces that are more and less private or public in any individual's life. It is also valuable to look at spheres that are not *exclusive* of women or men but rather include interactions by all participants. Nancy Osterud in *Bonds of Community* addresses the subject of the role of participants in gendered "spheres" for nineteenth-century rural women in northern New York State: "Defined in relation to men rather than as distinct from them, rural women tried to transform the bonds of kinship and labor into sources of sharing and strength, renegotiating the terms of gender relations and modifying them in a more symmetrical and egalitarian direction" (Osterud 1991: 2).

Furthermore, historians have found that the social exchanges that took place among women and among men was constantly interspersed with interactions that took place *between* women and men (as well as among several generations, and among individuals from both inside and outside the family). This social interaction affected the gendered spaces of the household and community and created a sphere that cannot so easily be defined as public or private, or even placed on a continuum between them. The gendered social spheres, identified and described by Hansen for the eighteenth and nineteenth centuries in New England, allow for the inclusion of activities in which women and men interact in both public and private contexts. The social sphere "provided a meeting ground for men and women that enabled them to mingle with greater equality of circumstance and to act with greater freedom than in either the public or private worlds" (Hansen 1994: 1).

The socials where families and neighbors gathered to reinforce their family and community bonds combined activities (and musical repertoires) of both the public and the private spheres. Social life had an important impact on cultural expression. Hansen says of the private sphere:

> The social equally influenced the private. The parading of people in and out of households, making family business social business and creating social space out of a private home, effaced the physical barrier of the house and the arbitrary boundary constructed around the conjugal family. Visitors, gossipers, extended kin, and friends transformed household interactions into social relations. (Hansen 1994: 167)

This does not mean, though, that all of the roles within each sphere were equal—that women's and men's forms of expression were the same or that women and men had comparable opportunities in all areas.[3] In fact, it is the issue of inequality (and difference) that appears and reappears as we look at patterns in the cultural output of individuals, families, and communities in each social realm.

Social Spaces: Engendering in Space and Time

The household, neighborhood, school district, village or town, and occupational sphere were all realms that framed a community's structuring of social space in northern New England during the nineteenth and early twentieth centuries.[4] In the context of rural residents' lives, the household was central, especially for developing life patterns that were further reinforced in the neighborhood and occupational spheres. The engendering process that took place there, as in other nineteenth-century American cultures, was caught up in the business of everyday life. Lifestyle patterns for women and men provided clear models for distinct social behavior by women and men, as well as girls and boys. The patriarchal, hierarchical society in which women were expected to take responsibility for household maintenance implied behavior that acted as a constant model for their children in their everyday life patterns. Thus the engendering process began early and was reinforced constantly in the family context, especially on family farms, where other spheres of influence were relatively limited. Activities that revolved around family life, both inside and outside the home, were generally accessible only to a limited group. Participants knew each other well. Musical interaction occurred while women attended to household chores and while men were working or relaxing after work. Household laborers shared songs with members of the family along similar gendered lines.

Women and men experienced less socially restricted social spaces when they attended events that took place outside the household sphere. These gatherings frequently involved people who were not part of a single household or neighborhood; the participants did not necessarily know each other well, and the overall make-up of the group was not as consistent as the household social unit tended to be. Musical events outside the household sphere revolved around community and other civic activities. Groups gathered for a dance or a meeting, a holiday event or concert that sometimes included visiting performers. While there was a greater integration of women and men, and a greater diversity of activities and ideas, outside of the household sphere, this aspect of social life was directed largely by men, the primary participants as leaders and decision-makers.

Women and Men: Same Spaces, Separate Spheres

Local and regional music and dance culture was defined and maintained by women's and men's participation in events that took place in specific spaces at different times of the day, week, and year. The relationship between gender, culture, and sense of place becomes clear as we look at realms occupied by women and men, and the specific characteristics of their cultural output. While women and men lived, worked, and played in rural New England in many of the same spaces, sang many of the same songs, or danced and enjoyed instrumental music together, a closer look at their social behavior and the characteristics of the music that was performed offers evidence that each developed separate expressive styles resulting in part from their gendered experiences.

At monthly meetings of the Champlain Valley Fiddlers' Association in Vermont, members gather for five hours on a Sunday afternoon to share music, dance, and socialize. Held in a school gymnasium, public hall, or VFW hall, the event is especially enjoyed by older residents from throughout the Champlain Valley, who play old-time dance tunes, listen to their friends perform, waltz and step dance, and share stories and food together. While the room is always filled with laughter and conversation, the focus of the event is on the activities at the front of the room, first on the emcee who manages the event, then on the fiddlers who perform on stage, accompanied by piano, guitar, drums, and other instruments that might include accordion, mandolin, guitar, and electric bass. Each fiddler is given an opportunity to play three tunes for the audience, a standard established by the fiddlers' contest and associations that developed during the latter part of the twentieth century.[5]

What is immediately noticeable about the event is that the "stage" area is dominated by men: the emcee and nearly all of the musicians are men. While each meeting does include a few female fiddlers, the vast majority of them, and most of the backup musicians, are men (although it is not unusual to see a woman playing piano and/or accordion). At the event, women and men both have a relationship to the music. Women actively respond through dance, coaxing their chosen partners out onto the floor to demonstrate their dance skills to the room.[6] Male instrumentalists perform and prepare for performance near the stage, and in every corner of the hall. In the organization and the event as a whole, though, women and men work together to maintain old-time musical traditions in their community. Women hold positions behind the scenes; they take on organizational roles connected with association membership, fundraising, newsletter production, and preparing and selling refreshments.

Like this contemporary example, nineteenth- and early-twentieth-century women and men in northern New England shared spaces yet played distinct roles in social events in which music and dance played primary parts. These separate social roles are recorded at both household and community events. Altogether they present to the historian an elusive character that made up the local culture in many communities; their musical expression did not always relate directly to their physical spheres. In fact, we cannot easily assign distinct musical genres and performance practices to specific spaces. Instead, it is important to recognize that some spaces in the home had multiple roles and thus offered more than one type of environment for musical growth and interaction. Similarly, these spaces held song traditions that broadened over time and changed with the addition of new people (and new *functions*). What we see is a dichotomy that expressed families' and communities' changing lives, while at the same time reflecting women's and men's separation, but also their interaction.

While women and men shared private and public domains and interacted in social spheres, they were not always simultaneously in the same places. Their roles varied with different family and community responsibilities. Musically, we find a direct effect of these spatial practices. While women (and their music) dominated the kitchen during the daytime, men controlled the music performed there on a Saturday night, when families gathered for the local kitchen dances or men met for jam sessions. The parlor, on the other hand, was often used by men to relax in the evening and to share songs with their children, yet it was used by women in the afternoons for local work bees and other social gatherings where they sometimes sang songs and hymns.[7] The barn and other work spaces on the farm were shared by the entire family and neighbors during critical production times (haying, milking, corn husking), but were always dominated by men (who sometimes sang while they worked).[8]

Songs and tunes that women and men performed—and women's and men's distinct roles in the dances—expressed these gendered spaces, pointing to women's and men's separate place in the family, society, and community. When women sang alone or to their children in the kitchen during the day, their relationship to the music was largely functional; when men performed in the kitchen at dances or jam sessions, it was primarily for entertainment. And when fathers and their children gathered to sing in the parlor, mothers (sometimes) listened from the kitchen while completing their chores. Each participated in the musical event in a unique way, thereby developing separate patterns for music learning, remembering, and performing.

Music further reflects the multiple roles of space and gender in the churches and schools that were attended by both women and men, which also relied upon gendered approaches to performance related to social convention. In the nineteenth- and early-twentieth-century churches, women were participants, but it was the men who taught the songs, led the worship, and chose the repertoire. In the schools female teachers taught songs to children, but when a school was used for a social function like a box social followed by a dance, men dominated musically as fiddlers and callers, as they did in other community dance events. In the occupational spheres, especially in the lumbercamps, few women were present; therefore the music was dominated by men's repertoires and styles. The contact women had with the cultural expression in that domain was dependent on what men chose to bring home and share with the family.

The following table identifies clearly delineated roles and musical contributions by gender in specific spatial spheres during the late nineteenth and early twentieth centuries.

Space	Daytime	Evening
kitchen	women: ballads/popular songs	men: dance music
parlor	women: hymns, ballads	men: dance music, ballads/ popular songs families: ballads/popular songs
barn/farmland	men: ballads, ditties	
town hall, grange		men: ballads/dance music women: prepared songs/ piano
churches	women and men: hymns (men taught)	
schools	(primarily) women and children: game songs, play party songs	women and men: box socials; meetings (men were leaders)
work/lumbering		men: ballads/songs, dance tunes

We can characterize women's roles in the early period as more *passive* than those of men.[9] This behavior affected how they enriched their repertoires, and how they expressed themselves socially and musically, absorbing the environment around them rather than pursuing new sounds. In the contrasting roles of women and men during this period we see that, through their leadership and innovation in almost all of the social contexts that involved women and men together, it is the men who had the greatest opportunity for creative input. This is played out very clearly in the musical performance of the period.

When we look carefully at historical performance practice in the region, particularly at how songs were learned, remembered, and performed, evidence of the different opportunities for women and men and its effect on musical expression emerge again and again.

Sources of Songs and Tunes

The dichotomy between women's and men's music was affected by how songs and tunes were learned. Informal learning, at the heart of many musical traditions in this period, provided opportunities for developing musical styles across gender lines. Women and men, boys and girls learned songs in a number of social contexts. All broadened their repertoires by learning from repeated listening in a socially stable environment. Yet until the arrival of the radio in rural households, women seemed less in control of their learning opportunities.

Songs and tunes were learned in each social sphere, and the learning was regulated by established socialization and performance standards, in household, neighborhood, village, and occupational spheres. Some young women learned songs at home from their mothers or other women in a gendered social group such as a work bee. Others learned by listening in the *background* to their brothers or fathers singing songs they learned in the woods, or at neighborhood gatherings in which men had dominant roles. Children learned ballads and songs when they listened to the singing of hired hands who were temporary members of the household. The home environment fostered a more intimate learning atmosphere, yet there was relatively little time devoted specifically to learning songs and musical information was not accessible on a regular basis. Women learned songs at the will of others who came into their homes. Men, on the other hand, actively learned songs and tunes from social contact among other men in their occupational groups, casual gatherings during leisure time, social gatherings that included participants from the neighborhood or village, as well as family affairs. At these events they had the opportunity to choose the songs and to pursue the singers to learn a song.[10] The men's wider social sphere thus brought a broader spectrum of songs for them to choose from and more opportunities for developing their repertoires.

Even when they were in the larger community, social strictures kept women from gaining access to cultural information in the same way that men did. Their delineated roles, despite the appearance of the gender-integrated environment, gave women fewer opportunities for socialization outside of their family and neighborhood spheres and a more limited access to musical information.

How Songs Were Remembered

The songs and tunes that were important to individuals, families, and communities were held in the memories of singers and their listeners, recorded in notebooks, printed in songbooks, and performed on audio recordings. Women and men approached these practices in different ways. When collectors roamed the rural regions of northern New England or the southern Appalachians, they sought songs held in the memories of singers and passed orally within families and communities. The resulting historical recordings from Maine, New Hampshire, and Vermont demonstrate that both women and men had extraordinary repertoires of orally transmitted songs that they offered to collectors.[11] Men seemed to more readily hold songs in their memories; for years they had repeated performances of many of the songs in both public and private contexts. Florence Scott in Pittsburg, New Hampshire, said the following about her father, David Shatney, and his repertoire of songs: "He could reel songs right off one after the other. I've seen Dad sit down and sing all night and never sing the same song twice."[12] Women, on the other hand, more often wrote their songs down in copybooks or pasted printed copies of songs (clipped from newspapers or magazines) in old bound books. Some of the women that I interviewed showed me these books, saying the books reminded them of the old repertoire—the songs that they didn't want to forget. It is possible that women were more concerned with printed and media sources because they provided an opportunity to construct and be in control of a body of literature that impacted their cultural and social lives. In recent years, women—and men—cherish these books, which provided them with a tangible memory of their family traditions.

Women and Men: Differences in Performance Practice

In a typical instrumental ensemble to accompany a neighborhood dance or kitchen junket, the primary performer was a local fiddler (male) who was accompanied by a keyboard player (often a female relative or friend of the fiddler). In making the spatial arrangements for the event, one of the goals was to provide maximum dancing space in the kitchen, living room, and/or porch. The musicians, then, were at the edge of the room, and the fiddler (who was also often the caller) faced and interacted with the dancers, responding to their needs with music, calls, and good humor. The pianist faced the keyboard and responded only to the fiddler, providing the chords for the popular melodies that the dancers enjoyed.

Women and men's participation in musical performances reflected their social roles in the family and community. Through these musical practices and others, they further defined their places in the social group. Women's performance practices demonstrated a tendency to remain in the private sphere, even when expressing themselves outside of the home. In the dance ensemble, the women's keyboard playing acted as an underpinning for the instrumental music, providing the chordal framework for dance pieces. Similarly, their place in the family was often to provide a solid foundation for the home sphere, using their organizational and nurturing skills. When singing, women generally performed alone or before a small audience of family members. Similar to their physical stance in the dance ensemble, they often sang with their heads down or their backs to their listeners (usually their children) while they worked.

Northern New England men in the rural sphere used music regularly in their social lives in group singing and in instrumental ensembles. They performed in their occupational spheres, and in ensembles that were increasing in size, complexity, and popularity throughout the period of this study, including dance bands, military and, marching bands, and by the 1930s and 1940s, hillbilly groups. The nature of men's performance practice, though, is illustrated particularly well in their performances in the lumbercamps. Many men in the region spent several months each winter hauling logs out of the woods for lumber companies. Men who worked in the woods included unmarried young men, farmers, and itinerant workers. Music and dance took place during leisure time. The men faced their audience of other men, singing loudly in a loosely metered (parlando rubato) style, entertaining their peers with songs that used humor, sentimentalism, and other expressive techniques. Men challenged one another to sing and compose songs, play fiddle tunes, or dance, demonstrating and reinforcing socially sanctioned male behavior found less often among women: independence, self-confidence, and relative ease in the public performance sphere.[13]

REPERTOIRE, CONTENT, AND PERFORMANCE STYLE

While women and men shared music together, and their repertoires were similar, the social conventions that dictated specific functions, spaces, and time frameworks for their performances (as well as their respective acquisitions of songs) affected their repertoires, content, and performance styles. We can clearly see how women's and men's music differed by looking at their overall repertoires, what they chose to sing in a particular context, and their textual choices in songs, as well as their styles of singing.

Reviewing historical collections of songs from the region and discussing repertoire with older regional residents reveals correspondingly different repertoires that reflect their separate life experiences.[14] Ives has suggested that women held onto the older songs in their domestic sphere longer than men in the public sphere. He notes, for example, that most of the Child or classical ballads found in the Northeast have been collected from women (Ives 1978: 396). Yet an examination of regional repertoires collected from older residents between 1920 and 1960 by both Helen Hartness Flanders and Phillips Barry reveals that the number of Child ballads collected from women, while slightly larger, is not radically different from men's. Similarly, both women and men offered American or regional songs in nearly equal number (including songs on the subjects of war, murder, and even lumbering). While women and men sang a similar number of songs in these categories, the songs they sang were different. For example, among the Child ballads, women offered collectors more songs that were less frequently heard. These included the songs cited in chapter 2 that were rarely found outside of New England, such as "Willie of Winsbury" (Child 100), "The Bonnie House of Airlee" (Child 199), and "The Keach i' the Creel" (Child 281).

Examining the repertoires of individual singers helps to distinguish some of these differences. Elmer George and Myra George Daniels, a brother and sister from northern Vermont, each performed a number of songs recorded for collectors during the 1930s, 1940s, and 1950s. Sometimes they identified their songs as from the same sources; they even sing some songs together on historical recordings in the Flanders Ballad Collection. Although Myra Daniels sang some songs popular in the lumbercamps, and other songs learned from the same source as her brother, they share only 20 percent of their songs. Myra Daniels sang songs popular in the lumbercamp that she noted she had learned from her brother, but she also sang hymns and Child ballads that her brother did not sing for collectors. Similarly, Belle Luther Richards of northern New Hampshire, who had a broad

Illus. 5.1. Myra Daniels, Hardwick, Vermont, 1940s. Helen Hartness Flanders Ballad Collection.

Illus. 5.2. Elmer George, North Montpelier, Vermont, 1940s. Helen Hartness Flanders Ballad Collection.

repertoire of ballads, hymns, and popular songs, sang a large number of songs that were popular in the lumbercamps. Like many women whose families worked in the woods, she said she learned many of her songs from her brothers. Her repertoire also included religious songs, children's songs, and a few rare Child ballads. On the other hand, her brother, Sidney Luther, sang primarily American and British broadsides and American popular songs. We know of no Child ballads that he sang (while Belle sang twelve), and he sang very few religious songs.[15] There is little evidence that Daniels's or Richards's brothers sang songs that *they* taught *them*. In fact, we find few male singers who identify their sisters as sources of their songs.

When women and men do share specific songs, including many American regional songs such as the popular "Young Charlotte," "Margery Grey," "Lass of Mohea," and "Mary Wyatt," a closer look at their performances demonstrates different approaches to singing—actions that sometimes alter the meanings of the songs themselves. For example, the well-known lumbering ballad "The Jam on Gerry's Rock," in which a much-loved lumberman (often named Jack Monroe) is killed, has been a favorite throughout the region among both women and men for years. The lyrics for a version titled "Young Monroe" from a lumbering community in central Vermont were offered by Herbert Haley in 1932:

Young Monroe

O come all of you bold shanty boys wherever that you may be,
I hope you'll pay attention and listen now to me.
It being on Sunday morning as you will plainly hear
And the logs were piled up mountings high and they could not keep
    them clear.

And the boss he cries, "Turn out, brave boys, let your hearts survey no fear,
While breaking the jam at Gerry Rocks for Reganstown we'll steer."
O some of them were willing, while others they did hang back
For to work upon a Sunday they thought it was not right.

But six of those bold shanty boys who volunteered to go
To break the jam on Gerry Rocks with the foreman, Young Monroe.
They had not rolled off many logs 'til the boss to them did say,
"I'll have you fur to be on your guards, brave boys, for the jam will soon
    give way."

And scarcely had he spoken 'til the jam did break and go
And carried away those six brave youths and the foreman, Young Monroe.

Sad news to the shanty boys next day
In searching for their dead comrades for the river they did steer.
They found the bodies of four of them, to their sad grief and woe,
All cut and mangled on the beach lay the head of Young Monroe.

O we took him from his watery grave, brushed back his raven hair.
There was one fair form amongst them whose cries did rent the air.
'Twas the girl from Saginaw town whose wails and cries did rent the skies
For her true love who was drowned.

O we buried him respectfully, 'twas on the fourth of May.
Now come all of you bold shanty boys and for your comrade pray.
And engraved upon a hemlock tree which on the beach did grow
Was the day and date of the drowning of the foreman Young Monroe.

Mrs. Clarke, she was a widow woman and lived by the river bend
And her daughter she was a noble girl, likewise a riverman's friend.
And the wages of her own true love the boss to her did pay,
And a liberal subscription she received from the shanty boys next day.

And when she took the money thanked them everyone,
But it did not seem to be her lot to enjoy it very long
For less than three weeks after death called her for to go
And the last request she granted was to be buried by Young Monroe.

Now come all you bold shanty boys who wish to go and see.
There's a little mound on the river bend there grows a hemlock tree.
Where the shanty boys they cut those words, "Here lies two lovers low—
The noble girl, Clara, and the foreman, Young Monroe."[16]

From Howland, Maine, Sarah Lane provided a melody often used for this ballad.[17]

The Jam on Gerry's Rock

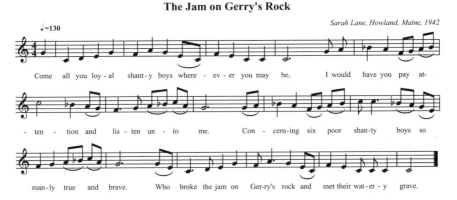

Her lyrics are also like many of the versions shared by men in the lumbercamps, although when she sings about finding the shanty boys, it differs slightly from the previously cited version. She sings:

> When the rest of these brave shanty boys these tidings came to hear,
> In search of their dead comrades, to the river they did steer.
> And among those reckless bodies, to their sad grief and woe
> All cut and mangled on the beach lay the form of John Monroe.

Scholars have theorized that there are two versions of this widely sung ballad, one in which "the form" of Jack Monroe is found "crushed and bleeding" on the beach and the other in which "the head of" Jack Monroe is found "cut" or "bruised" and "mangled" on the bank.[18] Although this song is connected to lumbering, both women and men sing it in almost equal proportion in historical collections. Yet it is rare to hear women sing the phrase about finding "the head of young Monroe." Some women refer to "the form of John Monroe," but an equal number sing "While crushed and bleeding near the bank was that of

Young Monroe," sometimes drawing out the word "that" as they sing. In some cases this appears to be a glossing of the phrase "the head of." Have the women chosen (consciously or subconsciously) to alter these words?

A similar tendency can be heard in women's interpretations of the American ballad "Josie Langmaid," about the brutal murder of a young girl in Suncook, New Hampshire. In the fullest versions of the song, Josie's body—with its head separated—is found in the woods. Many of the women who sing this song skip that verse altogether, while men more often include it.[19] Women's omission of especially gruesome details in "The Jam on Gerry's Rock" and "Josie Langmaid" in this region indicates values that they may have established and maintained in the household sphere.

Historical recordings reveal striking differences in how women and men approach creative development of songs. In the first place, few women are known as creators of original compositions found in local song traditions popular throughout the north country. In addition, many women sing less elaborate versions of songs and expand the texts and tunes of songs less frequently.

Examining the songs that invited the singer to actively develop them, we again see clear differences in women's and men's performances. In the regional singing tradition, songs were altered routinely, especially those that were identified with a local event (which were often adapted from another ballad) or those that invited a moralizing statement at the end. In addition, tall-tale songs, cumulative songs, and songs with nonsense refrains all invited the singer to make changes.

Cumulative songs such as "The Tree in the Wood" and tall-tale songs such as "The Derby Ram," while sung by both women and men, are found with greater elaboration by male singers. "The Tree in the Wood," in its well-known American form, accumulates a tree, limb, twig or branch, nest, egg, bird, and feather.

> On the hill there is a tree
> And the pretty tree and the curious tree
> And the tree is on the hill,
> And it stands there still, and forever will.
> Dee-ow and dee-ow and dee-ow, dee-ow.
>
> On that tree there is a limb
> And the pretty limb and the curious limb
> And the limb is on the tree,
> And it stands there still, and forever will.
> Dee-ow and dee-ow and dee-ow, dee-ow.[20]

In some local versions, however, singers accumulate as many as nine items, including an elephant, a boy, a cap, and a tassel, as sung by one man, and on the bird's feather another even included a couple. The women's versions of this song contain fewer items and do not show the same kind of invention. Similarly, all of the women's versions of "The Derby Ram" were shorter, and most maintained a specific lyrical formula. The men's versions, on the other hand, added a line or stanza to embellish the song. In the following example, the shorter version was sung by Laura Hooker Sessions in Vergennes, Vermont, in 1932, and B. L. Twitchell performed the longer version in Shaftsbury, Vermont.

The Derby Ram

As I was going to Derby
Upon a market day,
I saw the largest ram, sir,
That ever fed on hay.

Chorus:

Perhaps you don't believe me;
Perhaps you think I lie,
But just go down to Derby town
And see the same as I.

He had four feet to walk, sir,
He had four feet to stand,
And every foot he had, sir,
Covered an acre of land.

Chorus

The wool upon his back, sir,
It reached up to the sky,
And eagles built their nests there.
I heard the young ones cry.

Chorus

The horns upon his head, sir,
They reached up to the moon.
A man climbed up in January
And never came down 'til June.

Chorus

The Derby Ram

As I was going to Derby
Upon a market day,
I saw the largest ram, sir,
That ever was fed on hay.

Chorus:

To di ro di do do
To di ro di da
To di ro di do do
To di ro di da

He had four feet to walk, sir,
He had four feet to stand, sir,
And every foot he had, sir,
Covered an acre of land.

Chorus

The wool upon his back, sir,
It reached up to the sky,
And eagles built their nest there,
For heard their young ones cry.

Chorus

Heard their young ones cry, sir,
Heard their young ones cry, sir,
And eagles built their nest there,
For heard their young ones cry.

Chorus

The horns upon his head, sir,
They reached up to the moon.
A man climbed up in January
And he never came down 'til June

Chorus

And he never came down 'til June.
And he never came down 'til June.
A man climbed up in January
And he never came down 'til June.

Chorus

The wool upon his tail, sir,
I heard the weaver say,
Made three hundred yard of cloth
He wove it in a day.

Chorus

The butcher killed the ram, sir,
And drowned in the blood,
And the little boy that held the bowl
Was carried away in the flood.

Chorus[21]

The wool upon his tail, sir,
I heard the weaver say,
Made three hundred yards of cloth
For he wove it in a day.

Chorus

He wove it in a day, sir,
He wove it in a day, sir,
Made three hundred yards of cloth
For he wove it in a day.

Chorus

The butcher that killed this ram, sir,
Was drownded in the blood
And the little boy that held the bowl
Was carried away in the flood.

Chorus

Carried away in the flood, sir,
Carried away in the flood, sir,
And the little boy that held the bowl
Was carried away in the flood.

Chorus[22]

The women's direct manner of singing, with its simpler refrains, was clearly related to their placement in a domain in which there was neither time nor encouragement to embellish their songs. Women did not seek public approval for their songs (Ives 1978: 396) and apparently did not receive public encouragement for song elaboration.

The differences between women's and men's music are also clear when we look specifically at performance practice outside of the household sphere. Men regularly contributed and maintained songs connected to their occupations (or the occupations of friends), especially lumbering, and to support social contact within the community itself. In the lumbercamps men sang a broad spectrum of songs among their co-workers: popular songs, ballads, humorous, bawdy, and satirical songs. While some of these songs were also shared among friends and family members in the community, the style of performance was not always replicated as it moved into different venues. Typically men shared songs in an environment in which participants were challenged to entertain one another. In public performance contexts such as a town meeting, men could get away with simply "offering a song." This might include a ballad, a popular song from the turn of the twentieth century, or even a local song. Women interviewed for this study, on the other hand, remembered rehearsing before performances (at a public meeting, for example) and offered only popular songs learned from songbooks. Information on men's performance traditions outside of the household reveal they tended to put the older ballads aside to sing newer broadsides and locally created ballads and humorous popular songs (some of which were seldom found in women's repertoires) to suit their diverse social situations.

The Music

The many recordings of ballads and songs made by collectors during the first half of the twentieth century demonstrate that northern New England women's melodies were distinctly less embellished than men's. Men placed grace notes in a melody where women did not; when a woman graced a note, a man would draw out the ornament to create a glide or a more complex trill. Men invariably held notes longer for effect in singing. Men also more frequently placed passing notes between notes. Women performed songs at a tempo like the men's, yet more matter-of-factly, with little expression, keeping a steadier pulse and paying more attention to regular meter (i.e., using less rubato). This made the songs sound faster even when they weren't. Men often placed long pauses between phrases and at phrase endings. This is found less often in women's renditions of songs. While there are differences in singing style from region to region (especially from Vermont or New Hampshire to Maine), there are consistently similar characteristics of women's and men's singing, regardless of location. A closer look at this subject further reinforces the theory that the characteristics of women's and men's music relates directly to the differing social functions of their performances.[23]

The most easily identifiable differences between women's and men's musics appear when one studies families where songs were shared by parents and their children, and by brothers and sisters. When singers identify a parent or sibling as the source of a song, their performances reveal the close relationship. Yet comparative study of the material makes it increasingly clear that any individual singer's performance is gendered. For example, both Sidney Luther and his sister, Belle Luther Richards of Pittsburg, New Hampshire, sang versions of the ballad "Bold Kelly (The Irish Patriot)" for collectors in the early 1940s. Belle said that she learned the song from her brothers, and while the texts are similar, and the melodic contour is the same, the performances are markedly different.[24] Belle delivers her song maintaining the 6/8 rhythm throughout, pausing only briefly on the first note and the word "gazing." The tempo is steady, most of her syllables are assigned to single notes, and she does little to develop the melody.

Sid, on the other hand, sings in lyrical phrases. He opens with a florid—for a New Hampshire singer—descending line that refuses to be tied to a meter. The metrical instability continues throughout the song as he holds notes longer than Belle. He also "embellishes" many more syllables with added notes.

Illus. 5.3. Belle Luther Richards, Colebrook, New Hampshire, early 1940s. Helen Hartness Flanders Ballad Collection.

As I stood 'neath the shade of those lofty pines on India's burning shore,
A-listening to the tigers howl and the savage lions roar.
As I stood gazing on the scene that looked lonely, dark, and drear,
To me approaching from the woods an old man did appear.

Bold Kelly

Sidney Luther, Pittsburg, N.H., 1941

As I stood 'neath the shades of a lofty palm on India's burning shore,
A-listening to the tigers howl and the savage lions roar.
As I stood gazing on the scene, 'twas lonely, bleak, and bare,
On me approaching from the woods an old man's form drew near.

I looked at him inquiring, I saw it bathed in pain.
He said, "Kind sir, you doubt my word, but I'll tell you over again.
Before India's hot burning sand, my skin was fair as thine.
There's nothing but old Kelly's blood flows through these veins of mine.

"I lived down on the Shannon in the year of sixty-eight,
Me and my darling babes and wife on a English lord's estate,
Before that cruel war began that caused me to go
To fight for home and friends so dear 'mid this horrid Saxton foe.

"Before now had this young lord tried in vain to slay my life,
Revenged his cruel deeds upon my babes and loving wife.
He mangled their dead bodies with a curséd Saxton sword.
Cried he, 'Those Irish brats might live to serve an Irish lord!'

"At midnight in the mountains their bodies were borne to me
I swore by their dead bodies revenged I would be.
And to fulfill what I had sworn the consequence would be
That we should sail in the same ship for the Cape of Colony.

"When we arrived in Capetown, there appointed I was to be
Commander of the Army of the Cape of Colony.
One day as we were hunting alone all in the woods,
I drew my King's revenger, before that villain stood.

"'O draw that curséd sword of thine with which you killed my wife.
Defend thyself, base murderer, for a husband seeks your life.'
In vain he tried to shield my blows with all his coward's art,
But I soon drove my polished steel into that coward's heart.

"I flew into the mountains where I fear I'll end my life.
I would like to die in old Ireland and be buried by my wife.
I have now a gold locket which is all on earth I bear;
A shamrock brought from old Ireland and a lock of my father's hair."

"Rise up my good and honest friend, that big ship I command,
And it shall sail to bear us to our own dear native land."
And now down on the Shannon, in that consecrated ground,
The bones of this old patriot and his loved ones may be found.[25]

Other contrasting characteristics are found when examining the songs of Myra Daniels and her brother Elmer George of East Montpelier, Vermont. In "Polly" ("Polly Oliver," Laws N14), Myra and Elmer both sing the song at the same tempo and they both extend the value of notes (typically on the second beat of the measure).[26] Yet Elmer uses a wider melodic range, draws his notes out more frequently, and sings with greater emphasis on significant notes than his sister. Overall, Myra seems to maintain the metrical quality of the song more "effectively" than her brother. In fact, Elmer seems to throw the meter off by holding notes so frequently that it seems to move between 3/4 and 4/4.[27]

Polly

As Pol-ly lies a-mus-ing all a-lone in her bed, A whim-si-cal no-tion came in-to her head. Neith-er fa-ther nor mot-her can make me false prove, For I'll dress like a sol-dier and fol-low my love.

Polly

As Pol-ly lie a-mus-ing all a-lone in her bed, Some whims or false no-tions came in-to her head. "Neith-er fath-er nor moth-er shall e'er my faults prove, For I'll dress like a sol-dier and fol-low my love."

Polly (Myra Daniels)

As Polly lie a-musing all alone in her bed
A whimsical notion came into her head
"Neither father nor mother can make me false prove
For I'll dress like a soldier and follow my love."

So early next morning when Polly arose,
She dressed herself up in a suit of men's clothes
She went to the stable to the horses around
At length she found one could step over the ground.

[Two lines missing]

With a pair of brass pistols and a sword by her side
On her father's fast horse like a trooper did ride

She rode till she came to a town of renown
She brought her poor horse at the first of the sun
The first that came in was an English Lord Prue
And the next it was the capting whom Polly adored

Polly (Elmer George)

As Polly lie amusing alone in her bed
Some whims or false notions came into her head.
"Neither father nor mother shall e'er my faults prove
For I'll dress like a soldier and follow my love."

So early next morning when Polly arose
She dressed herself up in a suit of men's clothes.
She went to the stable, viewed the horses all round
And at length she found one could step over the ground.

She rode till she came to the town of renown.
She put up her horse at set of the sun.
She went to the barroom where the boys gathered all in;
She ordered for herself a good drink of good gin.

The first that came in was an English Lord Prude.
The next was the capting whom Polly adored.
She gave him a letter, a letter in hand
She said that she brought it from Polly his friend.

She gave him a letter, a letter in hand;
She said she had brought it from Polly his friend
And under the sealing a guinea was found.
It was meant for the house to drink Polly's health round.

As Polly being weary, she hung down her head.
She called for a candle to light her to bed.
"To bed," said the stranger, "I have a bed at my ease,
And you may lie with me, young man, if you please."

'Twas early next morning when Polly arose.
She dressed herself up in her own native clothes;
So gay in her attire, so fond in her love,
They thought 'twas an angel came down from above.

Now Polly is married; she lives at her ease.
She goes when she's a mind to and comes when she please.
She left her poor parents to weep and to mourn
And those who'd give thousands if Polly return.

She gave him a letter, a letter in hand;
She said she had brought it from Polly his friend.
And under the sealing a guinea was found
For the capting is the soldier to drink Polly's health round.

As Polly being weary she hung down her head
She called for a candle to light her to bed. to light her to bed
"To bed," said the capting, "I've a bed at my ease,
And you may lie with me, young man, if you please."

So, early next morning when Polly arose
She dressed herself up in her own native clothes
So gay in her attire, so fond in her love,
They thought she was an angel came down from above.

Now Polly is married and lives at her ease
She goes when she's a mind to, and comes when she please
She's left her poor parents to weep and to mourn
And there's those who'd give thousands for Polly's return.

Both older ballads and more contemporary popular songs were affected by the stylistic differences between women's and men's singing. A recording of versions of "Two Little Orphans" from a husband and wife of Menardo, Maine, further demonstrate the distinctions.[28] The song is about two young children whose parents are dead and who have come to a church to sleep. Mrs. Mayo's version is delivered with little expression, and she maintains a consistent tempo throughout most of the song.

Two Little Orphans

Vernon Mayo draws out the song by holding notes in nearly every measure, moving away from the original meter and giving the effect of an elastic tempo.

Two Little Orphans

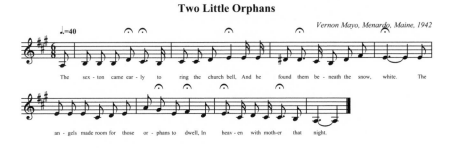

While listeners can hear clear differences between men and women in singing style by region even within northern New England, such distinctions are not as apparent among women from the same region. In Maine, singing was influenced by the more florid Irish style of delivery, an affect that was cultivated by men who worked in the lumbercamps and seldom heard in women's renditions of songs.[29] "Sir James the Rose" probably best illustrates men's embellished style in this context. Hanford Hayes of Staceyville, Maine, delivers his lines in long phrases, embellishing notes and extending their lengths to completely obscure the meter.[30]

Illus. 5.4. Hanford Hayes, Staceyville, Maine, 1940s.
Helen Hartness Flanders Ballad Collection.

Sir James the Rose

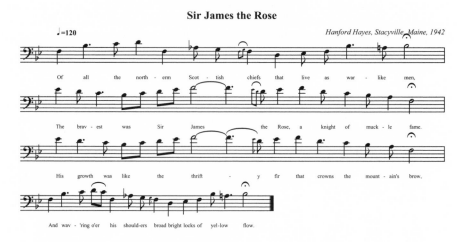

Edward Ives, in *Joe Scott: The Woodsman-Songmaker,* talks about the "traits of men's singing" in the lumbercamps, referring to their performance practice as "woods singing." In his description of this style he mentions "a 'harder' type of singing, with men putting tremendous pressure on their voices . . ." (Ives 1978:

384). Field recordings from the early years of the century *do* demonstrate that men sing with a stronger or fuller voice; the words and melody are drawn out. In contrast, women's voices are more inclined to be hesitant, thinner, and nasal. Women appear to be more concerned with the statement of the words, while men seem more conscious of an interrelationship between music and text. Ives points out, "We have the lovely paradox that the men's tradition of lumbercamp and public performance was involved with the serious business of leisure-time entertainment, while the women's tradition of domestic, in-the-family singing was often work oriented in that songs were sung to pass the time while one was spinning or sewing or cooking or looking after the children" (Ives 1978: 395–96).

The slower tempo or, especially, the free use of rubato in men's songs contrasts sharply with the women's delivery. Men had the "leisure" to develop their songs, while women did not. The fact that songs were sung while women were working could also be responsible for their seemingly faster tempo and more rhythmic pacing. The relative weakness of force in their voices, though, may partially be due to their lack of experience with public singing of any kind (including singing for a collector's microphone).

Access to Information/Knowledge

Cultural knowledge (specifically musical information) was transmitted in northern New England in families and communities that coexisted in relative isolation. Before the first few decades of the twentieth century, there were fewer opportunities for song sharing, learning and transmitting songs in unmodified forms (such as through the media), or personalizing and making songs and dance tunes part of a community's body of knowledge. Individual, family, and community experience created a musical culture that could be identified to a large extent as specific to that family, community, or region. Yet this communication of culture took place unevenly, for an individual's perception of place in the society was defined by social traditions that separated women and men and isolated women from certain experiences, and therefore from some forms of cultural knowledge.

Women's limited access to cultural knowledge in nineteenth- and early-twentieth-century northern New England affected their participation in cultural events, their overall cultural output, their role in family and community life, and their worldview and view of themselves in society. In interviews about their musical practices, many women said that they don't see any difference between women's and men's music. Yet a closer look reveals that many of the songs they sing *are* different, or are sung differently. When men or women are asked about the woman's consistent role as a pianist in an instrumental ensemble, as opposed to the leading role of fiddler, men are surprised by the question. Women typically respond by stating that their father or husband needed them to play backup for the fiddle, and they were simply doing what was expected of them.

While interaction between women and men played a role in framing a sense of place, ultimately the understanding that each individual carried forward resulted from how she used her experience within her own social sphere—what women carried forward was a more limited sphere of knowledge. Restricted access to musical information affected women's memories of their traditions and therefore what they had to pass on to other generations. A lumbering ballad sung by a father to her daughter will be filled with the expression common in the camps, yet when she sings that song in her family to her daughter, it will already have lost the expression, the free meter, the emphasis. The words may remain nearly the same, yet the ways of singing change.

CHAPTER 6

Family Song Traditions:
The Pierce-Spaulding Family of
North Shrewsbury, Vermont

The history of the Pierce-Spaulding family in North Shrewsbury (Northam) offers valuable data for better understanding the role that music played in family life in a rural Vermont community. The musical memories of one member, Marjorie Pierce, provide details on her family life and reveal some of the values she

Illus. 6.1.   Marjorie Pierce, North Shrewsbury, Vermont, 1983. Photo by Jonathan Sa'adah.

learned in the family environment. They also provide links to the regional repertoire and social practices that are found in historical data and oral testimonies in communities throughout northern New England. Marjorie's narrative illustrates how interconnected daily life and cultural expression were for many families during the early years of the twentieth century.

Marjorie's memories of the Pierce family traditions also illustrate an important relationship between individual and collective memory in the maintenance and recollection (and revival) of traditions. Marjorie's experiences were hers alone, yet her memories relied upon members of her family and community and were impacted by local and regional cultural and social history throughout the second half of the twentieth century. In many ways it is impossible to separate her story from that of her family, or to identify fully how her memories of her family life have been altered by personal experience.

I met Marjorie Pierce in 1984 when I was seeking information on New England musical traditions by talking to relatives of people who had been recorded by collectors connected to the Helen Hartness Flanders Collection. Her mother, Gertrude Spaulding Pierce, was visited by Flanders in the 1930s and recorded several family songs for the archive, including the Child ballad "Lord Bateman" (Child 53), British broadsides "The Half Hitch" (Laws N23) and "The Prince of Morocco" (or "The Lawyer Outwitted," Laws N18), the American ballad "Fair Charlotte" (Laws G17), and humorous songs "The True Story" and "The Fox and the Hare."[1] Marjorie was born in 1903 and was the second child in a family of five children. At the time she was living with her brothers in the family home, they ran the country store that was attached to it in the center of North Shrewsbury, Vermont (a town also known locally as Northam).

In the fall of that year I called to ask Marjorie if I might come down to talk with her about her mother's songs. She readily agreed and I visited with her on several occasions during the 1980s and early 1990s. I learned during my first visit that the Pierce family had lived in the Bridgewater–North Shrewsbury region of Vermont since the eighteenth century. Members of her family had worked in the home sphere, farmed, participated in the family business, traveled to war and returned, and moved away for education and/or work and come back. In fact, Marjorie had spent many years out of the state teaching in nearby Massachusetts before she returned in 1958 to help her father with the family store. Their home in North Shrewsbury held memories of family musical traditions that were all affected by the arrivals and departures of its various members. By the 1980s Marjorie had become the vehicle for her family's musical memories because of her lifelong interest in music, her devotion to her family, and her great respect for historical tradition.

Each time I arrived at the Pierce home, I was captivated by Marjorie's energy and the enthusiasm with which she recounted family and community traditions. Her home expressed these values too: the warm, open kitchen heated with a wood burning stove, the living room and parlor filled with family heirlooms that included her furniture, the braided rugs, an old Estey organ, and many family portraits. During my visits we made ourselves comfortable in one of the social spaces of the house: the living room, kitchen, or porch. On one occasion, Marjorie presented me with typewritten copies of some of the old songs her family knew. She sang family versions of some of the songs she remembered and reminisced about her mother, father, siblings, grandparents, uncles, and neighbors, all of whom played a role in shaping her musical memories. When I visited in the spring we moved to the glassed-in porch that sits at the back of the house. Marjorie had filled it with plants as soon as it was warm enough for them to survive outdoors. From the porch we looked onto a neatly kept yard divided by a brook and a charming bridge built by one of her brothers. This was balanced by the wooded, hilly backdrop and her flower and vegetable gardens.

The significance of family tradition to Marjorie can be seen in her precise and poignant memories of each family member, in her care for the ancestral home, in her treasured heirlooms, and in her sense of responsibility for the family store. Family traditions were also important to Marjorie's mother, with whom Marjorie spent so much time during her early years, and from whom she learned many of the songs that she recalled for me. She was eager to share memories of her mother's, extended family's, and community's traditions. She described herself as particularly interested in history and genealogy, and she made a special effort to remember the old songs. She discussed her practice of writing down her family songs:

> And then in later years I decided I would forget them and so I wrote them down and tried to recollect the tunes. And sometimes it was difficult to get started. Once I got started it was all right, but I knew at that time that my mother's songs—after Helen Hartness Flanders had been here—I knew that my mother's songs would be forgotten, and so I tried to write down quite a lot of them.[2]

Marjorie referred to notes that she kept to recall the words to some of her family songs, but the melodies and the events that framed each performance were embedded in her mind. The depth of detail that emerged during our conversations made it clear that she held onto memories of music in her family very carefully, and they had stayed with her throughout her life.

My discussions with Marjorie provided an opportunity for me to learn about some of the rural Vermont musical traditions and to see both how these traditions fit into a family's life and how an individual might be affected by this dynamic relationship. Marjorie depicts a multifaceted musical landscape in her descriptions of musical events in her family and community. What she finally offers is not just a view of the larger Pierce-Spaulding clan or the Bridgewater or North Shrewsbury community but her own definition of what music means to her. Her immediate and extended family worked hard and played little, yet Marjorie carries fond memories of the times when music was an important source of entertainment for all generations in her home and community.

Marjorie's narrative also reinforces some of what we have observed about gendered spaces and performance practice. The Pierce-Spaulding family exemplifies household practices and cultural expressions that combined learned and gendered behaviors for children. She reveals that there were social expectations that could be delineated by gender, but that many cooperative relationships in the farming and village-oriented Pierce family were governed more by necessity.

Marjorie's mother, Gertrude Spaulding Pierce, was from West Bridgewater, Vermont. Her mother's parents, Joseph Kennedy Spaulding and Sarah Aiken Spaulding, lived in West Bridgewater at the junction of Routes 4 and 100 in a large house where they farmed and ran a grocery store. Marjorie's maternal grandfather was the postmaster of West Bridgewater for forty years. Ties to the West Bridgewater family were strong when Marjorie was young. Although the Pierces lived in Shrewsbury, Marjorie and her older sister, Marion, were born at their grandparent's home, where their mother returned to give birth to her first two children. They also visited their mother's family frequently, especially during holiday times. Sometimes her mother drove a one-horse wagon or sleigh over the mountain alone with the children to visit her sisters.

Marjorie's mother was engaged with household tasks, chores connected with the farm, and responsibilities in the family store throughout her adult life. Marjorie talked repeatedly about her mother's involvement in farm work, washing the sap buckets after sugaring, mopping the hardwood kitchen floor, skimming the milk, making and shaping butter, and washing the dishes. Music played an important role in alleviating the pressures of these all-encompassing responsibilities.

> We had a neighbor, Avis Poore, who lived in the little old-fashioned cottage next door that burned around 1957–58. And she asked my mother once why she sang so much, and my mother said: "Well, when you're singing, you can't think." In other words, my mother had a lot of problems in the way of work and responsibility. She had responsibility for the home. She had five children to bring up and wash and iron for. And in those days, we washed by hand with the old tubs, you know. Bring the tubs into the kitchen, get a big pail and fill the tubs with water, and then the rinsing water, and go through the ringer, put the liquid bluing in the rinse water, and go through all these motions, and then hang the clothes out on the line. And that was almost an all-day job if you have five children.[3]

The kitchen was the central room in the farmhouse for her mother, because it was where most of her household obligations were completed. And it was largely in this space that Marjorie, her sister, Marion, and their mother shared their family musical traditions. Marjorie's memories of this period (1908–1909) were vivid.

> Well, when I was a small child, probably five–six years old, my mother used to sing, and she also used to whistle while she was doing her work. And she sang songs that she had learned from her father, my grandfather, Joseph Kennedy Spaulding, who had a store in West Bridgewater, Vermont. And he was quite a singer, along with his brother, Hosea Spaulding, who played the fiddle. And they used to get together evenings and sing. And it was said that they could sing until two o'clock in the morning and never repeat a song!
>
> And naturally my mother learned many songs from her father and then when she married and came to this town of Shrewsbury to live, and she

started to raise a family. During her work she would sing to pass away the time while she was doing her dishes or baking or skimming the milk pans—she had big pans of milk with cream on the top and she would skim the cream from the milk pans—we made butter in those days—and all that time she would be whistling or singing. And I had an older sister, about two years older than I am, and we loved to be entertained by our mother. And I remember so well that in our kitchen we had a big woodbox behind the cookstove, and it was a very nice woodbox. It was painted sort of a cream color with a red trim and a nice wooden red top. And quite large. And when my mother was mopping, my sister and I would get up on top of the woodbox and then we would plead with our mother to sing to us. And our favorite song was called "Cabbage and Meat," but of course she sang lots of other songs that she'd learned from her father.[4]

Cabbage and Meat

Marjorie Pierce, N. Shrewsbury, Vermont, 1984

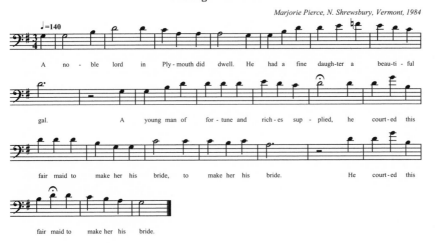

A noble lord in Plymouth did dwell
He had a fine daughter, a beautiful gal
A young man of fortune, and riches supplied
He courted this fair maid to make her his bride
To make her his bride
He courted this fair maid to make her his bride

He courted her long and he gained her love
At length this fair maiden intend him to prove
From the time that she owned him, she fairly denied
She told him right off, she'd not be his bride
She'd not be his bride
She told him right off, she'd not be his bride

Then he said, "Straight home I will steer,"
And many an oath under her he did swear
He swore he would wed the first woman he see
If she was as mean as a beggar could be
As a beggar could be
If she was as mean as a beggar could be

She ordered her servants this man to delay
Her rings and her jewels she soon laid away
She dressed herself in the worst rags she could find
She looked like the devil before and behind
Before and behind
She looked like the devil before and behind.

When Marjorie talked about her mother entertaining her while she worked, she was as often referring to a recitation as a song. "My mother also recited poems; Marion and I would sit: 'Mother, tell us about the ride of Jennie McNeal.'"[5] During my first visit she referred briefly to this ballad, but later she discussed the poem in greater detail: "'The Ride of Jenny McNeal'... was one of my sister's and my favorites. Only it was very long and my mother was rather reluctant to start it because she had so much work to do it would take a long time to stay in one room and recite it. But we just loved to hear it . . . Oh, I thought that was the most thrilling thing, you know."[6]

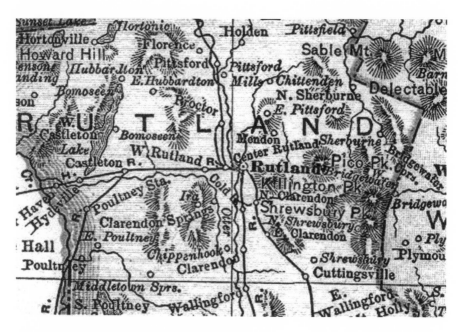

Illus. 6.2.   1895 map of Rutland, Vermont, region.

Music in Rural New England Family and Community Life

I asked her how her mother performed the piece and she described her delivery as "dramatic." Her mother would recite the poem in a chant-like voice while the children sat on the woodbox behind the stove: "Dozens and dozens of times we'd ask for that. And sometimes she'd start it and then wouldn't finish. She'd say: 'I can't finish this now. I have other things to do.'"[7]

She gave me a newsprint copy of this poem and I asked her how close it was to her mother's version. She said, "That's practically the same thing. Oh, there may be a few words different, but if so, I can't remember them."

The Ride of Jennie McNeal
By Will Carleton

Paul Revere was a rider bold —
Well has his valorous deed been told;
Sheridan's ride was a glorious one —
Often it has been dwelt upon;
But why should men do all the deeds
On which the love of a patriot feeds?
Harken to me, while I reveal
The dashing ride of Jennie McNeal.
On a spot as pretty as might be found
In the dangerous length of the neutral Ground,
In a cottage cozy, and all their own,
She and her Mother lived alone.
Safe were the two, with their frugal store,
From all of the many who passed their door;
For Jennie's mother was strange to fears,
And Jennie was large for fifteen years;
With vim her eyes were glistening,
Her hair was the hue of a blackbird's wing;
And while the friends who knew her well
The sweetness of her heart could tell,
A gun that hung on the kitchen-wall
Looked solemnly quick to heed her call;
And they who were evil-minded knew
Her nerve was strong and her aim was true.
So all kind words and acts did deal
To generous, black-eyed Jennie McNeal.

One night, when the sun had crept to bed,
And rain-clouds linger'd overhead,
And sent their surly drops for proof
To drum a tune on the cottage roof,
Close after a knock on the outer door
There entered a dozen dragoons or more.
Their red coats, stain'd by the muddy road,
That they were British soldiers show'd;
The captain his hostess bent to greet,
Saying, "Madame, please give us a bit to eat;
We will pay you well, and, if may be,
This bright eyed girl for pouring our tea;
Then we must dash ten miles ahead,

To catch a rebel colonel abed.
He is visiting home, as doth appear;
We will make his pleasure cost him dear."
And they fell on the hasty supper with zeal,
Close-watched the while by Jennie McNeal.

For the gray-haired colonel they hover'd near
Had been her true friend, kind and dear;
And oft, in her younger days, had he
Right proudly perch'd her upon his knee,
And told her stories many a one
Concerning the French war lately done.
And oft together the two friends were,
And many the arts he had taught to her;
She had hunted by his fatherly side,
He had shown her how to fence and ride;
And once had said,"The time may be,
Your skill and courage may stand by me."
So sorrow for him she could but feel,
Brave, grateful-hearted Jennie McNeal.

With never a thought or a moment more,
Bare-headed she slipp'd from the cottage door,
Ran out where the horses were left to feed,
Unhitch'd and mounted the captain's steed,
And down the hilly and rock-strewn way
She urged the fiery horse of gray.
Around her slender and cloakless form
Patter'd and moan'd the ceaseless storm;
Secure and tight a gloveless hand
Grasped the reins with stern command;
And full and black her long hair streamed,
Whenever the ragged lightning gleamed.
And on she rush'd for the colonel's weal,
Brave, lioness-hearted Jennie McNeal.

Hark! from the hills, a moment mute,
Came a clatter of hoofs in hot pursuit;

And a cry from the foremost trooper said,
"Halt! or your blood be on your head";

She heeded it not, and not in vain
She lashed the horse with the bridle rein.
So into the night the gray horse strode;
His shoes hew'd fire from the rocky road;
And the high-born courage that never dies
Flashed from his riders coal-black eyes.
The pebbles flew from the fearful race;
The raindrops grasped at her glowing face.
"On, on, brave beast!" with loud appeal
Cried eager, resolute Jennie McNeal.
"Halt!" once more came the voice of dread;
"Halt!" or your blood be on your head!"
Then, no one answering to the calls,
Sped after her a volley of balls.
They pass'd her in her rapid flight,
They screamed to her left, they screamed to her
    right;
But, rushing still o'er the slippery track,
She sent no token of answer back,
Except a silvery laughter-peal,
Brave, merry-hearted Jenny McNeal.

So on she rush'd, at her own good will,
Through wood and valley, o'er plain and hill;
The gray horse did his duty well,
Till all at once he stumbled and fell,
Himself escaping the nets of harm,
But flinging the girl with a broken arm.
Still undismay'd by the numbing pain,
She clung to the horses bridle-rein
And gently bidding him to stand,
Petted him with her able hand;
Then sprung again to the saddle bow,
And shouted,"One more trial now!"
As if ashamed of the heedless fall,
He gathered his strength once more for all,
And, galloping down a hillside steep,
Gain'd on the troopers at every leap;
No more the high-bred steed did reel,
But ran his best for Jennie McNeal.

They were a furlong behind, or more,
When the girl burst through the colonel's door,
Her poor arm helpless hanging with pain,
And she all drabbl'd and drenched with rain,
But her cheeks as red as fire-brands are,
And her eyes as bright as a blazing star,
And shouted, "Quick! be quick, I say!
They come! they come! Away! away!"
Then sunk on the rude white floor of deal,
Poor, brave, exhausted Jennie McNeal.

The startled colonel sprung, and press'd
The wife and children to his breast,
And turned away from his fireside bright,
And glided into the stormy night;
Then soon and safely made his way
To where the patriot army lay.
But first he bent in the dim firelight,
And kiss'd the forehead broad and white,
And bless'd the girl who had ridden so well
To keep him out of a prison cell.
The girl roused up at the martial din,
Just as the troopers came rushing in,
And laugh'd, even in the midst of a moan,
Saying, "Good sirs, your bird has flown.
'Tis I who have scared him from his nest;
So deal with me now as you see best."
But the grand young captain bow'd, and said,
"Never you hold a moment's dread.
Of womankind I must crown you queen;
So brave a girl I have never seen.
Wear this gold ring as your valor's due;
And when peace comes I will come for you."
But Jennie's face an arch smile wore,
As she said, "There's a lad in Putnam's corps,
Who told me the same, long time ago;
You two would never agree, I know.
I promised my love to be as true as steel,"
Said good, sure-hearted Jennie McNeal

Illus. 6.3. "The Ride of Jennie McNeal."

In addition to "The Ride of Jennie McNeal," her favorite poems included "Johnny Sands," "The Three Little Kittens," "The Two Kittens," and "The Blackberry Girl." In fact, several of the recitations that Marjorie referred to were sung in other parts of northern New England during the same period. "Johnny Sands" (Laws Q3) was a popular British broadside ballad, and "The Blackberry Girl," referenced earlier, was for some a sentimental "parlor" song. Like other families, the Pierces did not distinguish much between occasions when singing took place and when poetry was recited: "I was more interested in the words, you know, entranced by stories. I liked to have stories told. We didn't have playthings the way children have today, you know. And toys. Why, we had paper dolls, and we would feed the chickens. We didn't have all these toys that children have today to amuse us."[8]

She laughed and laughed when she recalled the lines of some of the ballads, like "Billy Grimes the Drover,"[9] which her mother recited, or "Learning McFadden to Waltz," which she sang. In Marjorie's family, her mother was the storyteller. While our conversation might stray from her mother's songs to reveal other sources for Marjorie's musical domain, it always seemed to return to those stories she most enjoyed.

> Well, of course we always wanted our mother to sing the "Cabbage and Meat" song, that was our very, very favorite. But I liked "Fair Charlotte"; I was quite thrilled with poor Charlotte freezing to death. And that was supposed to happen down near Ludlow, but there are many different places that have been claimed as the scene where Charlotte froze to death. But that was very touching, you know. And we liked those old stories.[10]

In 1932, Marjorie's mother and her friend Mrs. Elwin Burditt sang fragments of their versions of "Fair Charlotte" for Helen Hartness Flanders. Gertrude Spaulding Pierce's version was sung with a somewhat loose rhythmic structure.[11] Remembering her mother's singing, Marjorie sang her version and submitted a typewritten copy of the song to Helen Hartness Flanders in 1953.

Fair Charlotte

Marjorie Pierce, N. Shrewsbury, Vermont, 1984

Young Charlotte dwelt on the mountainside
In a lone and dreary spot.
No dwellings there for three miles round
Except her father's cot.

And yet on many a winter's eve
Young swains would gather there
For her father kept a social board,
And Charlotte she was fair.

Her father loved to see her dressed
Fine as a city belle
For she was the only child he had
And he loved his daughter well.

At a village inn fifteen miles off
There's a merry ball tonight.
The air without is freezing cold,
But the hearts are warm and light.

'Twas New Year's Eve, the sun went down
And she sat with a restless eye
As along the frosty window panes
The merry sleighs passed by.

"Why sit there with a restless air?"
When a well-known voice she heard—
Then dashing up to her father's door
Young Charlie's sleigh appears.

"Now Charlotte dear," her mother said,
"This blanket 'round you fold
For 'tis a fearful night abroad
And you'll take your death a'cold."

"Oh no, oh no," fair Charlotte said,
And she laughed like a gypsy queen,
"For to ride in garments muffled up
I never will be seen.

My silken coat is quite enough
'Tis lined you know throughout.
Besides I have a silken shawl
To wrap my face about."

With gloves and bonnet being on,
She jumped into the sleigh
Away they glide o'er the mountainside
And over the hills away.

There is music in the sound of bells.
What a crash the runners make!
The air without is freezing cold
Which caused the sleigh to creak.

With muffled faces silently
Five cold long miles were past
When Charles in these feeble words
Their silence broke at last.

"Such a night as this I never knew—
My reins I scarce can hold."
And Charlotte said in a feeble voice,
"I am exceeding cold."

Then he cracked the whip and urged his steed
Much faster than before
Until another five long miles
In silence they rode o'er.

"How fast," said Charles, "the freezing air
Is gathering on my brow."
And Charlotte said in a feeble voice,
"I'm growing warmer now."

Then o'er the hills in the frosty air
All by the cold starlight
Until at length the village inn
And ballroom were in sight.

They reached the inn and Charles sprang out
And gave his hand to her.
"Why sit she there like a monument
That has no power to stir?"

He called her once, he called her twice,
But she answered not a word.
He called for her hand again and again,
But still she never stirred.

He took her hand in his, O God!
It was as cold as stone.
He tore the mantle from her face
And the pale stars on her shone.

Then quick into the lighted hall
Her lifeless form he bore.
Fair Charlotte was a frozen corpse
And words spoke never more.

Then he sat himself down by her side
And the bitter tears did flow.
Said he, "My young intended bride
I never more shall know."

Then he put his arm around her waist
And kissed her marble brow,
And his thoughts went back to where she said,
"I'm growing warmer now."

Then he carried her out into the sleigh
And with her he drove home.
And when he reached her father's door,
Oh how her parents mourned.

They mourned the loss of their daughter dear,
And Charles mourned in the gloom
Until at length his heart did break
And they slumbered in one tomb.[12]

In 1984, Marjorie laughed and said to me after singing part of the song: "We loved 'Fair Charlotte' because my grandmother said she knew a woman who knew a woman who was in the hall when she was brought in."[13]

"Fair Charlotte" was one of many late-nineteenth and early-twentieth-century ballads that traveled among the participants in this active musical tradition: families and neighbors, collectors and publishers, poets and scholars all played roles in its development. A particularly interesting example of these contributions to this song is the scholar Phillips Barry's 1937 broadside version. Replicating the nineteenth-century practice of publishers who identified popular songs and poems for mass printing, Barry redistributed this ballad during a period of time when the genre was waning in popularity. Marjorie accepted the story of Fair Charlotte, which she probably knew was constructed by poet Seba Smith, into her own personal narrative, using the same inclusiveness that she applied to all of the songs that framed her own history.

The songs Marjorie learned from her mother actually represented her relationships with different people in their household, extended family, and larger community. Thus, her songs have associations with both people and contexts in these spheres. They represent the web of contacts that bind family traditions together and demonstrate the variety of musics that make up an individual's repertoire. Yet there remains an assigned ownership of songs within the family sphere that is demonstrated by Marjorie's association of specific songs with particular people. This ownership is elusive, though, and may even be imagined through the memories her mother shared with her daughter. Before singing "The Sailor Boy," she identified it as her grandfather's song. I then asked her if her mother knew it as well.

MP: Oh yes! Oh yes. I presume that my grandfather knew a lot of songs that she didn't know.

JP: And you spent time with him? You remember him?

MP: Well, we used to go there Christmas or Thanksgiving and then during the summer we'd sometimes go over and stay a week, something like that.

YOUNG CHARLOTTE,

or,

A CORPSE GOING TO A BALL!

THE incident, from which the following ballad is woven, was given in the papers three or four years ago as *a fact*. It was stated, that a young lady in the country, while riding some distance to a ball on New Year's evening, actually froze to death.

YOUNG Charlotte lived by the mountain side,
  A wild and lonely spot;
No dwelling there, for three miles round,
  Except her father's cot;

And yet on many a winter's eve
  Young swains were gather'd there,
For her father kept a social board,
  And she was very fair.

Her father loved to see her dress'd
  As prim as a city belle,
For she was all the child he had,
  And he loved his daughter well.

'Tis New Year's eve—the sun is down—
  Why looks her restless eye
So long from the frosty window forth,
  As the merry sleighs go by?

At the village inn, fifteen miles off,
  Is a merry ball to-night—
The piercing air is cold as death,
  But her heart is warm and light;

And brightly beams her laughing eye,
  As a well-known voice she hears;
And dashing up to the cottage door
  Her Charley's sleigh appears.

"Now daughter dear," her mother cried,
  "This blanket round you fold,
"For 'tis a dreadful night abroad,
  "You'll catch your death a-cold."

"O nay, O nay," fair Charlotte said,
  And she laugh'd like a gipsy queen,
"To ride with blankets muffled up
  "I never could be seen—

"My silken cloak is quite enough;
  "You know 'tis lined throughout;
"And then I have a silken shawl
  "To tie my neck about."

Her bonnet and her gloves are on,
  She jumps into the sleigh;
And swift they ride by the mountain side,
  And over the hills away.

There's life in the sound of the merry bells,
  As over the hills they go;
But a creaking wail the runners make,
  As they bite the frozen snow.

How long the bleak and lonely way!
  How keen the wind does blow!
The stars did never shine so cold—
  How creaks the frozen snow!

With muffled faces, silently,
  Five cold, long miles they've pass'd,
And Charles, with these few frozen words,
  The silence broke at last—

"Such night as this I never saw—
  "The reins I scarce can hold;"
And Charlotte, shivering, faintly said,
  "I am exceeding cold."

He crack'd his whip, and urged his steed
  More swiftly than before,
And now five other dreary miles
  In silence are pass'd o'er—

"How fast," said Charles, "the freezing ice
  "Is gathering on my brow;"
But Charlotte said, with feebler tone,
  "I'm growing warmer now."

And on they went through the frosty air
  And the glittering, cold star-light;
And now at last the village inn
  And the ball-room are in sight.

They reach the door, and Charles jumps out,
  And holds his hand to her—
Why sits she like a monument,
  That hath no power to stir?

He call'd her once—he call'd her twice—
  She answer'd not a word;
He ask'd her for her hand again,
  But still she never stirr'd—

He took her hand in his—O God!
  'Twas cold and hard as stone;
He tore the mantle from her face;
  The cold stars on her shone—

Then quickly to the lighted hall
  Her voiceless form he bore—
His Charlotte was a stiffen'd corse,
  And word spake never more!

                    SEBA SMITH.

The Rower, II, 225. Printed for Phillips Barry, May, 1937. The Powell Printing Company, Cambridge, Massachusetts.

Illus. 6.4. "Fair Charlotte," Phillips Barry broadside.

JP: This was in West Bridgewater?

MP: Yes. But of course, I think I remember him more by pictures. I think I was too young to really remember him. I remember my grandmother, but I think I remember him, but I think it's because I've seen pictures. I think that's it. This is called "The Sailor Boy."

The Sailor Boy

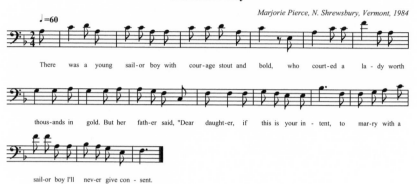

Marjorie Pierce, N. Shrewsbury, Vermont, 1984

There was a young sailor boy with courage stout and bold,
Who courted a lady worth thousands of gold.
But her father said "Dear daughter, if this is your intent
To marry with a sailor boy I'll never give consent.

Here's twelve thousand pounds unto you I will give,
And this shall be your portion so long as you live.
My blessing you shall have and your fortune I will make,
Provided this young sailor boy you never will forsake."

She wrote her love a letter though not very long
To just let him know her old father's intent.
"But my mind it is sincere and my heart it shall prove true
For there's none in this world I can care for but you."

Said he, "My dearest Polly if you I can't obtain,
I'll cross the wide ocean and go unto Spain.
And some crafty project that I'm trying out to try,
To deceive your old father or else I must die."

He bought him a robe in splendor did appear,
Disguised like a prince to Morocco did steer.
With a star upon his breast went to see his love again,
The old man he was well pleased with the young prince of Spain.

He said "Noble prince, if you can agree
To marry with my daughter your bride she shall be."

"With all my whole heart," this young sailor boy did say,
"If she will consent we will married be today."

So then to the church they were hurried with speed,
The old man gave up his daughter, his daughter indeed.
While the full flowing bowl went so merrily around,
The old man paid off his daughter the twelve thousand pounds.

This caused the old man for to caper and to prance,
To think how his daughter got married to a prince.
The old man he did rejoice with exceeding great joy,
To think how he cheated that little sailor boy.

Then up sets this young sailor boy, saying "Don't you know me?
I am the young sailor boy you once turned away,
But since I have outwitted you and crafted in your life,
I've twelve thousand pounds and a beautiful wife."

"Go to the devil," the old man he did reply.
"You've robbed me of my daughter, my money, and my pride.
If I had once mistrusted that this had been your plot,
Not a farthing of my money would you ever got.

"Depart from my house and take it long with you,
My curses they shall follow you wherever you go.
Depart from my house and take it long with you
My curses they shall follow you wherever you go."

JP: So your mother sang it. She sang it like that?

MP: More or less. She had more of a lilt. Some of these were sung with a lilt, and others were sung very solemnly.

Marjorie discussed the sources of the songs she knew, and she also talked about what she ascertained from her mother about the environment in which her mother learned her songs. I asked her whether her mother talked about any of the songs before she sang them.

Well, she'd tell where she learned them and she told about people who used to come to her father's house and play musical instruments; or how her father used to sing with his brothers in the evening. They didn't have much entertainment; they didn't have a radio even, so my grandfather's brother would come and they would sing, I suppose and while away the time.
    This was sung by [my grandfather] J. K. Spaulding to his daughter Gertrude . . . And the name of it is "The True Story."

The True Story

Marjorie Pierce, N. Shrewsbury, Vermont, 1984

As I went out a hunt-ing all on a sum-mer's day, the trees were all in blos-som the flowers were fresh and gay, gay. The flowers were fresh and gay.

As I went out a hunting
All on a summer's day
The trees were all in blossom
The flowers were fresh and gay, gay
The flowers were fresh and gay

I took my gun upon my back
A-hunting I did go
I followed a herd of deer all day
And I tracked them in the snow, snow
And I track them in the snow

I followed them around the hill
And under water went
To kill the fattest one there was
It was my sole intent, tent
It was my sole intent.

When I was under water
Ten thousand feet or more
I fired off my pistols
And like cannons they did roar, roar
And like cannons they did roar

I fired off my pistols
By chance I did kill one
The rest they stuck their bristles up
And at me they did come, come
And at me they did come

Their horns were soft as velvet
And long as a ship's mast
Quicker than the lightning
They through my body passed, passed
They through my body passed

My body was a riddle
That bull frogs might swing through

And when I came to shore again
My naked sword I drew, drew
My naked sword I drew[15]

Marjorie's Uncle Hosea—her grandfather Spaulding's brother—was also an important family source for songs and especially musical memories. Marjorie discussed her contact with him as a very young child but also carried memories of him through her mother. She referred to him over and over in our conversations about music, although she remembered only one of his songs: "Another song I remember was sung by my Uncle Hosea Spaulding—my great uncle—my grandfather's brother—who lived in the little cottage upon the hill, and as a very small child I went up there and he would play the fiddle and sing. The only real song I remember hearing him sing was about the frog."[14]

The Frog Song

Marjorie Pierce, N. Shrewsbury, Vermont, 1984

♪ =144

There was a frog lived in a well with a rink stum bud-dy me ki-mo. And if he's not gone he

lives there still and a rink stum bud-dy me ki-mo. Ki-mo ka-ro built a si-ro ki-mo ri-ro ki-ro.

Rink stum fom-ma did-dle lul-la bud-dy rook and a rink stum bud-dy me ki-mo.

There was a frog lived in a well,
And a rink stum buddy me kimo.
And if he's not gone he lives there still,
And a rink stum buddy me ki-mo.

Kimo riro built a siro
Kimo riro kimo
Rink stum fomma diddle lulla buddy rook
And a rink stum buddy me ki-mo.

Said he "Miss Mouse, will you have me?"
And a rink stum buddy me kimo.
Said she, "Kind sir, I will agree,"
And a rink stum buddy me ki-mo.

Marjorie's father, Willie Pierce, and his family were longtime Shrewsbury residents. In fact, her paternal grandmother, Demaris Aldrich Pierce, was a descendant of one of the original settlers of the community. "My father was a Shrewsbury man. He lived on a farm his father owned. There was a little cheese factory [Northam Cheese Factory] owned by my great uncle. And my father learned to make cheese there. He then went to a West Bridgewater factory to make cheese. It was in West Bridgewater that he met my mother."[16]

After he was married, her father and grandfather continued to farm until 1918, when her father bought the North Shrewsbury store. At that time the family moved from the farm to the home that Marjorie still lived in. According to Marjorie, her father was often busy, yet he sometimes relaxed in the evening by singing songs and accompanying himself on his guitar. He also liked to dance and taught Marion and Marjorie to waltz.

> Well, my father, he wasn't any musician, but he did have a guitar and he used to play the guitar some. And there were two or three different old tunes that he sang. But they wouldn't be so old as some of these I just told about. The only one I remember was "Daisy."

> > Daisy, Daisy, give me your answer true
> > I'm half crazy over the love of you.
> > Cannot be a stylish marriage
> > I can't afford a carriage
> > But we'll look neat, upon the seat
> > Of a bicycle built for two.[17]

Other memories of music from her father's side of the family came from her grandfather, Edwin Pierce. Her grandfather's experiences in the Civil War made a strong impact on the family.

> Well, my father's father was Edwin Pierce, and he was born and brought up in Shrewsbury, Vermont, and he lived in this town and he was a volunteer, and he went to the Civil War and was in the Battle of Gettysburg and Pickett's Charge, which was a terrible, terrible conflict. And he never talked about it too much when he came home, but I know—I learned from my aunt—a few little details about the war. And one was that when he came home from the war he must have come up through Cuttingsville, which is in the village in our town. He must have come home by train, and when they walked from Cuttingsville up to his home in North Shrewsbury, which would be a distance of four miles, and he was actually exhausted by the trip evidently—I know they said that when he reached the house—they didn't know he was coming—when he reached the house he opened the door and fell in flat on his face. He was so exhausted. And of course the family was very surprised and happy to see him return.

> And one other little incident I remember is that we used to ask him about the Battle of Gettysburg and he said that there was a fearful battle and that he was crouched behind a stone wall—I think it was near what history books call the Peach Orchard—and the opposing army was marching up in closed ranks and with a cannon, and when they got to a certain distance away they fired. The cannon went off and the air was filled with smoke and the bullets were coming in all directions, and we asked him if he wasn't afraid and if he

didn't want to run—and he said yes, he wanted to run, but he was too proud. And when the smoke cleared away he looked down to his friend and companion who was beside him—his name was Billy Carnes—and he had a bullet in his forehead.[18]

Marjorie has vivid memories of her grandfather singing in the evening when they lived up on the farm. In fact, her slow and gentle renderings of his songs seemed to be the most carefully executed of all those she sang for me. She appeared to be recreating the moment—the song and its context—rather than simply delivering a song from her memory.

I recall, up on the farm, going into the apartment where my grandparents lived—we lived on one side of the house and my grandparents had an apartment on the other side—and I remember him sitting in the rocking chair in the evening after work was done, and he would be singing more or less to himself. He sang only two songs that I remember. One was "Tenting Tonight."

Tent-ing to - night, tent-ing to - night, tent-ing on the old camp - ground.

Tenting tonight, tenting tonight
Tenting on the old camp ground

Dying tonight, dying tonight
Dying on the old campground.

And the other song I remember that was his favorite was "Beulah Land."

Beulah Land

Marjorie Pierce, N. Shrewsbury, Vermont, 1984

I see the land of corn and wine
And all its joys they will be mine
There dawns again one blissful day
When earth's dark cares have passed away.

Oh Beulah land, fair Beulah land—

JP: He used to rock and sing?

MP: He would rock in the old Massachusetts rocking chair, yes.

JP: Did you sit and listen to him?

MP: Oh, I would be sitting very quietly and listening, perhaps behind his back. He didn't hear me or know I was there.[19]

Marjorie's narrative demonstrates the diverse musical styles that were part of household traditions in the early years of the twentieth century. While Flanders's initial collection of songs from her family (nearly all of them Child and Laws ballads) created an impression that music in families like Marjorie's was limited to the "old songs," the interviews reveal a considerably more diverse repertoire. A variety of musical genres was represented, including locally created songs, religious songs, and a wide repertoire of American songs popular between the 1890s and the 1930s. Like many other families in northern New England, the Pierce and Spaulding families did not always differentiate among these song types, although Marjorie indicated to me that she became aware of these categories—especially the placing of a higher value on older songs—through her contact with Flanders. Our discussion shows that the Pierce family context for singing older and more recent songs was the same.

MP: I have this little song about "Two Little Girls in Blue." It's not such an old song, but it's a song that my mother used to sing. Although I think it dates more recently.

JP: When did she sing this song?

MP: Oh, probably 1908 or 1909, along in there.

JP: And again, while she was working?

MP: Oh, always, always. Or in the evening, when we had nothing else to amuse ourselves, or it was too cold to go outdoors, we would beg her to sing.

JP: So you would sit around in the living room?

MP: Oh yes. Yes. Do you want to hear the "Two Little Girls in Blue?" I've forgotten the tune of everything except the chorus, and I'm not sure that my mother knew anything but the chorus tune, because I think she recited the verse. A rather sad little item.

> *(Spoken.)*
> An old man gazed at a photograph
> On a locket he'd worn for years
> His nephew asked him the reason why
> That picture should cause him tears.
> Come listen, he said, and I'll tell you, lad
> A story that's old, but true
> Your father and I at a school one day
> Met two little girls in blue

Two Little Girls in Blue

Marjorie Pierce, N. Shrewsbury, Vermont, 1984

Two lit-tle girls in blue, lad. Two lit-tle girls in blue. They were sis-ters, we were broth-ers and learned to love the two. And one lit-tle girl in blue, lad, won your fath-er's heart. Be-came your moth-er I mar-ried the oth-er but we have drift-ed a - part.

(Chorus.)
Two little girls in blue, lad
Two little girls in blue
They were sisters, we were brothers
And learned to love the two
And one little girl in blue, lad
Won your father's heart
Became your mother I married the other
But we have drifted apart.

That picture was one of those girls he said
To me she was once a wife
I thought her unfaithful, we quarreled, lad
And parted that night for life.
A fancy of jealousy wronged a heart
A heart that was good and true
For no better girls ever lived than they
Those two little girls in blue.

Two little girls in blue, lad
Two little girls in blue
They were sisters, we were brothers
And learned to love the two
And one little girl in blue, lad
Won your father's heart
Became your mother, I married the other
But we have drifted apart.[20]

Marjorie's information also reinforces our understanding of the importance of printed sources in family repertoires. As noted earlier, when early-twentieth-century collectors looked exclusively for songs passed orally in families, they were contributing an incomplete view of the sources for songs and dance tunes popular during that time. Narratives of local residents like Marjorie contribute to our knowledge today that songs defined as family or community songs were *not* all

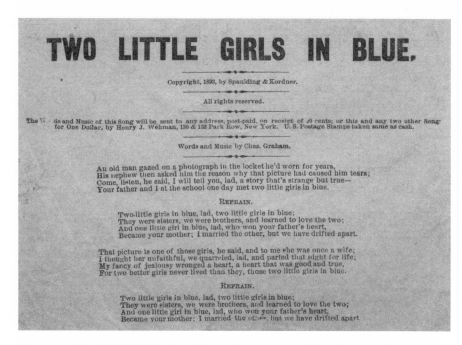

Illus. 6.5. "Two Little Girls in Blue," from a four-page pamphlet of songs belonging to Marjorie Pierce.

learned orally, nor did they all come from within a family sphere. The repertoire that each individual took away from an experience in a household or community, even during the nineteenth and early twentieth centuries, resulted not only from experiences with relatives and friends but also from contact with printed media such as sheet music, magazines, and newspapers with weekly song entries; the radio and the Victrola; and traveling musicians.

Marjorie and I talked about songs her family knew that were learned from printed song collections, including hymnbooks and songsters. She mentioned titles such as "The Faded Coat of Blue," "The Rose of Tralee," "They Never Told a Lie," "The Spanish Cavalier," and "The Orphan Children."[21] At times she differentiated between songs she knew were valued by Flanders and other collectors, and those that were transmitted primarily in printed form. At other times, these songs were simply part of her mother's repertoire. I asked her about other songs that she sang in the family:

> I can tell you about a song that my mother used to sing, and it's about fishing—some fishermen. And of course she heard that when she was a young girl. This song was sung by a man by the name Aswell Maxham, and he was the brother of Uncle Hosea's wife, Susan. He used to be a campaign singer and was doorkeeper at the House of Representatives in Washington. He sang this song about fishermen once at the North Shrewsbury (Northam) church at a concert he was giving. This song is entitled: "They Never Told a Lie."

They Never Told a Lie

Marjorie Pierce, N. Shrewsbury, Vermont, 1984

Two wily fishermen they went forth
To the sparkling stream where fish are caught
For they oft told of things they'd done
The times they'd fish and the fish they'd won.
For there never was a fisherman but knew the spot
The times, the place that fish were caught
But they never told a lie,

They never told a lie
They were Sunday school scholars every one
And they followed in the steps of Washington
But they never told a lie.

They fished all day in the red hot sun
The number they caught it was not one
And homeward stopped at a market shop
And out of the icebox they bought alot
Just to show their friends what they had caught
But they never said a word about what they bought
But they never told a lie.

Their friends flocked 'round expectantly
A wonderful mess of fish to see
But as each one gazed they held their nose
But what was the matter do you suppose
For they didn't smell as sweet as fresh fish ought
For it must have been a week since they'd been caught
But they never told a lie,

They never told a lie
They were Sunday school scholars every one
And they followed in the steps of Washington
And they never told a lie.[22]

When Marjorie was fourteen, right after her family left the farm to move to the store, she went to Rutland to go to high school. During her first year there, she lived with her aunt and her Uncle Clyde (her mother's brother) and was exposed to another style of music.

> Then it was routine duty on Sunday afternoons, we'd walk up the railroad tracks and we'd have to go bird hunting. And then when we came back from the bird walk, then we had to sit down in the living room, and my uncle would open up the big Victrola and he would play classical music, and he would explain: "Now this is *Aida*." This is the story of so-and-so, and this is John McCormack and he will sing "Kathleen Mavourneen," or a song like that. But most of the music was classical. I can't think of all the names now. And then he would tell the stories of the operas and we would have to listen. And so he was very musically inclined, and he liked music the way my mother did. This is one of the songs that he enjoyed singing, and it's called "The Old Refrain."[23]

The Old Refrain

Marjorie Pierce, N. Shrewsbury, Vermont, 1984

I often think of home dee-oo-lee-ay.
When I am all alone and far away.
I sing an old refrain dee-oo-lee-ay.
For it recalls to me a bygone day.
It takes me back again to meadows fair
Where sunlight's golden rays beam everywhere.
My childhood joys again come back to me
My mother's face in fancy too I see.
It was my mother taught me how to sing
And to that memory my heart will cling.
I'm never sad and 'lone while on my way
As long as I can sing dee-oo-lee-ay

The years have passed and gone dee-oo-lee-ay
And though my heart is young, my head is gray
Yet still the echoes ring dee-oo-lee-ay
And dear old memories forever stay.
My song can bring me visions full of light
And sweetest dreams throughout the darkest night

Of all that life can give that song is best
I'll take it with me when I go to rest.
And when at last my journey here is o'er
'Twill ring more joyfully than e'er before
For up to heaven I will take my way
The angels too will sing dee-oo-lee-ay

I asked Marjorie if her mother had ever sung "The Old Refrain," or if it was the kind of song she would sing, and she responded: "No, it sounds like his type—he was very sentimental."

Marjorie and I talked several times about game songs she knew as a child, but she had some difficulty recalling them. She did report that games were played at school and were also popular at other times when children and young teenagers gathered together, especially at socials. I asked her if she knew the song "The Needle's Eye."

Oh yes! Those were games we played at socials, I think. We used to have socials at different homes and we'd play "Jacob and Rachel," "Drop the Handkerchief," and—oh, I do recall "London Bridge"! Yes, we did play that. You're bringing back all these memories.

> (Spoken.)
> The needle's eye it does supply
> The thread that runs so truly
> It has caught many a smiling one
> And now it has caught you.[24]

Marjorie's information on socials was specific to her community, yet it also provided connections to similar traditions in communities in other parts of northern New England. I asked her to describe a "social":

MP: What is a social? Well, in our town of Shrewsbury, a social was held usually at somebody's home—somebody would offer to open their home—mostly some of the younger people would gather together in the evening, and they would talk and chat, and then they'd decide to play some games, and then they would have refreshments. Sometimes the person whose house was being opened up would furnish refreshments. Or more often, each family would bring something like a cake or some sandwiches or what have you.

JP: So the people that came to the social were neighbors—

MP: All neighbors, yes. And some of them would come by horse and buggy or horse and sleigh. But a lot of them, right, around in this little area, would walk. I remember that there was a party down on the Cold River Road about a mile from here. And it would be eight or ten people all walked together down to the party and then they would all walk back.[25]

Marjorie identified kitchen dances as separate from the socials. She reported that in the North Shrewsbury area, kitchen dances were only held once or twice each winter: "Dances would be held in the winter—but you could have a social anytime, you know." Marjorie's family did not take part in these social functions as often as they did occasions in which singing was the primary or secondary activity to the occasion. Her narrative also exemplifies the timing of the transition in this specific community from family and neighborhood to town and region for social dancing.

> I remember only one kitchen dance, and I probably wasn't more than four years old. It was at a farmhouse, and my mother and father attended, and they put me upon the table in the corner of the room so I wouldn't be in the way, and I looked down upon all these wonderful dancers. I thought it was so interesting. But I didn't take part myself. And then, at the Grange hall they had entertainment, the townspeople attended and had entertainments and had square dancing. And they must have had some local callers, I don't recollect who they were.[26]

Public (and semipublic) buildings such as the Grange, the local church, and the schoolhouse held other events where families sometimes shared music learned at home from popular literature such as songbooks. The aesthetic values for these performances clearly differed from those that took place in the home sphere. When they were very young, Marjorie and her sister were taught songs by their mother so that they could perform at these gatherings.

> My mother would teach my sister and me a song. And when we were about—oh, perhaps seven, eight, nine, ten years old—she would teach us from some sheet music, or some Christmas songs, and we would sing at Christmas programs, or at Grange meetings, or at Modern Woodman meetings, when there were programs . . . I remember at the Modern Woodman— my father was a Modern Woodman, sort of an insurance company—and there was a Modern Woodman meeting at the Grange hall out at Shrewsbury Center. And my sister and I sang a silly little song:
>
> > My Papa was a Woodman
> > What a pity yours is not
> > For all the Woodmen are so kind and true
> > They were so good when Papa died
> > And all of them have got
> > A great big heart for little ones like you.

And of course we had Christmas programs at the Northam church. All the families collected and had their Christmas at the church. They didn't have Christmas in the homes in those days. The families took all the presents to the church, and we had a big Christmas tree reaching to the roof, and there would be a program that the schoolteacher had arranged, and we would have the younger ones—the scholars would sit in the front row and they would recite and sing and have duets—and then there would be older people who sat in the chorus and sang. And we sang Christmas songs. I don't really remember what those Christmas songs were. Just Christmas hymns, I imagine.

And when I was too young to go to school, and couldn't sit in the front row with the schoolchildren, I sat in the back with my grandma, my grandma Pierce. And after the program we heard a shout and a tramping and—outdoors on the steps—he said, "Oh ho ho ho!" and bells were jingling and this door was flown open and Santa Claus came striding down the aisle, and he'd say, "Oh ho ho! Merry Christmas! And this is a heavy bag I'm carrying!" And I was frightened. Oh, I was really frightened. And I sat beside Grandma, who was a little woman all dressed in black. And my father was probably standing in the back, because the men had to stand in the back, there weren't enough seats for everybody. My mother was probably in the choir. So I got up close to Grandma and was so frightened. And she said, "Don't be afraid, Margery, it's just Uncle Warner."[27]

The social sphere for residents of this somewhat isolated community was limited because of its location. The landscape during the winter, for example, made it difficult to travel more than a few miles.

When I was young, we had all dirt roads and we didn't have any snowplows. The snow was shoveled by the men in town, or we had an old snow roller to pack the roads. And we didn't move around as much as people do now. I rarely went to Cuttingsville, which is four miles away. I did go occasionally to the center with the town hall for a few events; we had oyster suppers and harvest suppers, things like that.

I asked about the music at community events of this type:

MP: Well, there were two girls in town who were called the belles of Shrewsbury and they always sang, and of course we had graduation exercises where we had music, or group music.

JP: Now, these songs were different from the songs your mother sang, though?

MP: Yes, yes. They would be more modern, if you think 1929 is modern. But these are not modern songs that you have here [referring to her typed texts of "The Half Hitch," "Lord Bateman," "Fair Charlotte," etc.]. These are 1890s songs, you know, it's quite a difference.[28]

The memories that Marjorie recounted during the 1980s and early 1990s represent her experience as an individual, yet they provide insight into her family tradition as well. Marjorie's values were established in her family and reinforced by her mother, especially. They grew over time, though, to be altered by those of a collecting and media community that identified certain songs and song types as more significant than others. At times Marjorie referenced songs that showed this shaping force in her values (what she thought I would be interested in, what she valued in her later years, all based on those songs Flanders and other historians valued; Flanders played an important role in Marjorie's desire to maintain what had become a historical tradition of family singing). Her narrative demonstrates that she participated in the practice of singing more passively than her mother and members of her mother's generation. Yet it is because of Marjorie's active remembering and desire to hold on to traditions that we have access to her contextual information on family and community practices in the early twentieth century.

The musical traditions that Marjorie remembers are not actively performed in families. Yet Marjorie's recollection of details of musical events and occasions provides clear information about the role that music and song played in her family's life during the early years of this century. While songs played different roles in the lives of various members of her family, for Marjorie, songs were probably most important as a source of the family narrative.

> **JP:** You talked about the kinds of songs that your various relatives sang, and you talked about Uncle Clyde's songs being sentimental. Can you characterize the kinds of songs that your mother and your grandfather sang?

> **MP:** I think they were just folk songs and most of them had stories. And I think these folk songs—most of them—probably came from England or Scotland, because my mother's background is Scotch Irish. My father's background is English and Dutch. But I think they're just telling little stories, as "Margery Grey" tells a story, you see. And they just pick them up, and it takes the place of reading a book. It's like reading a book. You pick up a book and it has one type of story and another song has a different type of story. Sometimes there's a happy ending, and often there's a sad ending.

> **JP:** So people that sang those kinds of songs really were storytellers in a way.

> **MP:** I think so. They're what you call folk songs. That's what folk songs are, in my opinion. Just stories.[29]

Appendix: Family Songs and Recitations Mentioned by Marjorie in Interviews between 1984 and 1990

Song	Source
Beulah Land	paternal grandfather
Billy Boy	mother
Billy Grimes the Drover (recitation)	mother
The Blackberry Girl (recitation)	mother
Bright Alfanata	mother
Bringing in the Sheaves	
Cabbage and Meat (The Half Hitch)	mother
Charley	
Daisy (Daisy Bell)	father
The Faded Coat of Blue	paternal grandfather
Fair Charlotte	mother
The Fox and the Hare	mother/grandfather
The Frog	maternal uncle
The Gypsy's Warning (recitation)	mother
I'll Remember You	
Johnny Sands (recitation)	mother
Just Before the Battle Mother	paternal grandfather
Learning McFadden to Waltz	
London Bridge	socials
Lord Bateman	mother
Love, in My Prayers	
Margery Gray	mother
My Papa Was a Woodman	mother
The Needle's Eye	socials
O My Darling Clementine	mother
Old Dan Tucker	
The Old Refrain	maternal uncle
The Orphan Children	
The Ride of Jenny McNeil (recitation)	mother
The Rose of Tralee	
The Sailor Boy	mother
The Spanish Cavalier	
There Is a Tavern in the Town	mother
They Never Told a Lie	
Two [Three] Little Kittens (recitation)	mother
Two Little Girls in Blue	mother
Uncle Ned	
Uncle Tascus and the Dead (recitation)	
We're Tenting Tonight	paternal grandfather
When the Roll Is Called Up Yonder	
Whispering Hope	sheet music
The Young Counselor	mother

CHAPTER 7

Reconstructing Community Traditions

*I*f you drive through Pittsburg today, you seem to pass quickly through New Hampshire's northernmost town. However, Pittsburg is geographically large compared to other northern New England towns; its 364 square miles accounts for 4 percent of the land in New Hampshire, yet less than one percent of the population resides there (867 residents in 2000). Among the northern New England communities, Pittsburg and the nearby towns of Stewartstown, Clarksville, and Colebrook are especially valuable sites for exploring music in community life during earlier decades.[1] Many social, cultural, and economic changes that took place in other parts of New England reached the Pittsburg area much later partly because of its distance from the urban centers of Concord, New Hampshire; Portland, Maine; Boston, Massachusetts; and Burlington, Vermont. Ultimately, however, changes did affect Pittsburg, and it began to look like other small northern New England towns. Many of its unique characteristics are now hidden in the memories of people who were young in the earlier years of the twentieth century.

Fieldwork that took place in the region occurred during several key periods.[2] In the 1930s Robert Pike interviewed some of the older lumbermen who had worked at Connecticut Lake, men still actively singing songs popular in the lumbercamps during the nineteenth and early twentieth centuries.[3] Also in that decade Helen Hartness Flanders recorded a number of songs from a man who had grown up in Pittsburg and was living in Charlestown, New Hampshire, near her home in Springfield, Vermont. In the early 1940s Marguerite Olney recorded several hundred songs for the Flanders Ballad Collection from both women and men who remembered the songs popular in the northernmost communities of New Hampshire. In the late 1980s I traveled to the region to conduct a series of interviews with relatives of the performers recorded in the 1930s and 1940s, and I found others as well who were especially active in musical traditions during the early years of the century.

This field research over a sixty-year period shows the effects of the social, cultural, and economic changes that occurred in the area from the nineteenth to the mid- to late twentieth centuries, as the region became less independent. Until the 1920s, Pittsburg and the surrounding communities depended primarily on

Illus. 7.1. Northern New Hampshire barn.

farming and lumbering for their wellbeing. While local geography and kinship ties framed the characters of the neighborhoods, they began to break down when connections to land and family were altered by the impact of regional and national changes. Today neighborhood schoolhouses are gone, replaced by a single regional school; the churches, grange halls, and stores that served as gathering places are weathered, and many are bare. Businesses cater to visitors who travel to the region to snowmobile in the winter, hunt in the fall, and fish or hike in the summer. The tourist industry plays a huge role in the local economy, replacing a lifestyle that once included self-sufficient farmers, lumbermen, and other individuals who contributed to local industry.

The town of Pittsburg today combines elements of the old and the new. Some of the long-term residents still recall events of the past in that community and continue their cultural practices in the yearly Old Home Day celebration, occasional jam sessions, and senior citizen's gatherings where instrumental ensembles fronted by a local fiddler are popular. Fiddlers, both young and old, also reinforce connections to the past by attending nearby old-time fiddlers' competitions, such as the annual Stark Old-Time Fiddlers' Contest, which began in the early 1970s.

The old songs of singers from the local communities—referenced throughout this study—are seldom heard in the homes that once regularly held neighborhood sings. Today people struggle to recall lines or verses of ballads, popular songs, and hymns. Yet they smile as they remember the singers and the way the songs were sung, their stories, and the social times they accompanied.

Relatively equal time was once given to singing and dance music traditions in Pittsburg and its surrounding towns. Families and neighbors gathered in both

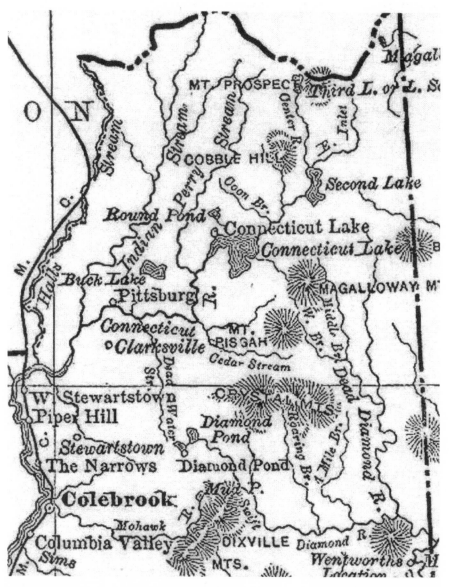

Illus. 7.2. Pittsburg region, 1895, N. H. map.

organized and casual meetings of friends to share their music. Community residents recall a broad spectrum of songs and dance tunes with little concern for category. When residents talk about music and dance practices of the earlier years of the century, they return again and again to certain songs and contexts for dancing, each time expressing similar recollections about their community. These common memories bind peoples together through their shared community history.

Songs

Songs in the Pittsburg region in many ways typify the northern New England repertoire. Many of the older ballads, popular songs, and hymns noted throughout this study are well represented in family and community repertoires; nineteenth- and early-twentieth-century sentimental songs and Anglo-American ballads with fantastic, tragic, humorous, and historical subjects were sung in families and neighborhoods for generations. Descriptions of songs and hymns and their functions in everyday life are vivid, often because the traditions were practiced well into the twentieth century.

Interviews with residents during the 1980s demonstrate how linked their local traditions were with some of the broader regional practices. I spoke several times with Marcia Dingman, a woman in her eighties whose family was actively involved in both singing and dancing in and around Pittsburg. I asked her whether her family sat around in the evening to sing.

> **MD:** Yes, oh my goodness yes. We did it in my own home, Mother's home. And after I got married it was a common occurrence. We used to have these kitchen junkets. Not all the time every night, but once in a while, as I said before. And then a lot of times some of the neighbors would come in and we'd all get together and sing.

> **JP:** What songs would you sing?

> **MD:** Well, most always we'd sing "Margery Grey" or "When You and I Were Young, Maggie." And then "Golden Slippers" was a familiar song. Whatever happened to be in our minds, you know, them old-timers' songs. Oh yes, we used to have that a lot. Used to come to my place—ten or twelve people every little while.

> **JP:** Did you all sing together? Or did one person sing a song and then another?

> **MD:** No, some knew it and we'd sing together. If they didn't know they'd wait until we got another one . . . If they didn't have a good voice they'd sing just the same, it didn't matter . . . Oh yes, you know years ago we didn't have television, we didn't have radio, so we couldn't have all those things, we had to make our own entertainment. And we used to do it really good. We loved to do it; we enjoyed it.[4]

A diverse repertoire is also documented in several handwritten collections of songs. Marcia's sister, Avis, kept a notebook of old songs that she passed down to her own daughter. The schoolbook was deeply yellowed when I had an opportunity to take a look at it in the late 1980s. Without a cover, undated, and missing the first twenty-three pages, the book nevertheless held sixty songs that comprised a broad selection of ballads, hymns, and popular songs drawn from the nineteenth and twentieth centuries. They ranged from the early-twentieth-century evangelical hymns "Jesus Goes with Me," "In the Garden," and "Nothing Between" to the

American ballad "Margery Grey," from country songs such as Vernon Dalhart's "Sinking of the Great Titanic" (1928), Ernest Tubb's "Walking the Floor Over You" (1941), and cowboy song "Great Grand Dad," to the British ballads "The Butcher Boy," "Will the Weaver," and "Tailor and the Chest." Also significant was "Seven Long Years," as preserved by this mother of three daughters:

Seven Long Years

1.

For seven long years I've been married
I wished I had lived an old maid
My eyes seen nothing but trouble
My husband won't work at his trade.

2.

He told me before we were married
He would dress me all stylish and gay
And in the evening of summer
He would take me to a ball or a play.

3.

He told me before we were married
He would never leave me alone
And in the evening at summer
When his day's work was done he'd come home.

4.

Now ladies get up in the morning
She would wash and toil all day
And in the evening at summer
She would put the dishes away.

5.

Oh take me back to my mammy,
As quick as ever you can,
A young girl never sees trouble
Until she's tied up to a man.

6.

Take warning, take warning young ladies,
Take warning, take warning by me,
And when you go to get married,
Just leave the drunkard be.[5]

Discussions with Avis Terrill Shatney's daughters, sister, and brother provided information about how much of her musical community's repertoire this book represents. These discussions indicate that while it is not a comprehensive collection, it is representative of the wide-ranging traditions shared in this region.

Musical experiences in the family revolved around several significant areas of influence: her husband, David, who often spent winters in the lumbercamps, her sisters, who helped to maintain connections to family traditions, and the radio, an important source for new songs. The ever-widening musical community was constantly contributing to their repertoire. Other sources for music not represented in this manuscript were the dances that, I learned in my interviews, were especially important to this family.

A closer look at the communities in this region, though, demonstrates a particular concern for connecting songs with location and a valuing of locally created songs even into the late twentieth century. Data from fieldwork in the 1930s, 1940s, and 1980s in Pittsburg and nearby communities shows that specific songs seem universally to hold the sentiments of long-term residents in the once tightly knit communities that comprised this region, connected during the last 150 years by family and proximity as well as common memory. The songs offered to collectors were connected to the local landscape in different ways. Some were adopted from other traditions and "reassigned" to the local landscape. Others were products of residents who generated new songs that in many ways acted as social commentary for the community.

Local, and even localized, songs have received a mixed reception in the scholarly community. Their characteristic referencing of the local landscape separates them from the ballads and songs that were canonized in the nineteenth and twentieth centuries by Child, Laws, and Coffin. In his 1980 study on English folk poetry, Roger Renwick explored local songs in the British Isles, comparing them to the more widely known ballads and songs. Local songs, while sharing some characteristics with these songs, are set apart from them especially because they are generally *not* popular over a wide geographic region; many have maintained an existence exclusively in print; they have seldom lasted for a long time in a community's repertoire; and their topics are not often generalized but rather quite specific. Renwick elaborates: "The topics of such songs . . . are real places, peoples, and events within the sphere of experience ready at hand, their dominant functions at the level of the community . . . [They are] referential in their treatment of a known (or at least knowable) world, and conative in that they call for the audience to take a responsive stance toward the real topic" (Renwick 1980:117–18). It is just these qualities—the referential nature of the songs, the opportunity for a continuing discourse with local history that they provide, and a clear demonstration of the significance of the community in maintaining them—that were reinforced in my discussions with residents in this region.

Adopted Songs

Among the songs once popular in Pittsburg, "Margery Grey" may be the one referred to most frequently by members of the older generation. The ballad tells the story of a woman, Margery, and her baby, who were lost in the woods on their way home from visiting a friend. Despite her knowledge of the land around her, Margery is unable to find her way home. When her husband returns at the end of the day to an empty house, a community-wide search for his wife and child begins. Days later, Margery's baby dies, and she wanders in the wilderness through the spring and summer and into the fall. One day she arrives in Charlestown, New Hampshire.

> Wondering glances fell upon her, women veiled the modest eyes,
> As they slowly ventured near her, drawn by pitying surprise.
> "It's some crazy one," they whispered. Back her tangled hair she tossed.
> "Oh, kind friends, take pity on me, for I am not mad, but lost."
>
> Then she told her piteous story, in a vague desponded way,
> And with cold white lips she murmurs, "Take me home to Robert Gray."
> "But the river," says they, pondering, "How crossed you to its eastern side?
> How crossed you those rapid waters, deep its channel is and wide?"
>
> But she said she had not crossed it in her strange erratic course.
> She had wandered so far northward 'til she'd reached its fountain source.
> Down the dark Canadian forest and then blindly roaming on,
> Through the wild New Hampshire valley, her bewildered feet had gone.[6]

Even today, many Pittsburg residents feel that Margery (or Margaret as many call her there) began her journey in their community. Some trace her path from Back Lake in town (near the Connecticut River) up *above* the Connecticut Lakes (Third Lake) where she could cross into New Hampshire without traversing the rapid waters.

When the three daughters of Avis Terrill Shatney met with me in 1988 to talk about some of the locally popular songs, inevitably they brought up this one. The subsequent discussion demonstrated the participants' connectedness to the characters, the landscape, and the sense of history that were contained in the ballad and its performance. At the time it was as if they were discussing a tragedy that had actually occurred at one time in their community.

FS: That was a true story. That was a true story, Margery Grey.

JP: Where did that take place?

BP: In Back Lake. Right up in Back Lake.[7]

FC: She got lost that mornin'. She went way up into Canada and come down on the New Hampshire side. They found her in—way down in the middle of the state—Charlestown. She came out there.

FS: But she'd lost the baby. Oh yeah, she'd buried it. She thought she'd marked the place in the woods where she buried the baby. But—

BP: It was up far enough so she stepped across Connecticut Lake.

FC: Yeah and that's Third Lake. Right across. That's Third Lake. That's when she didn't know, you know—

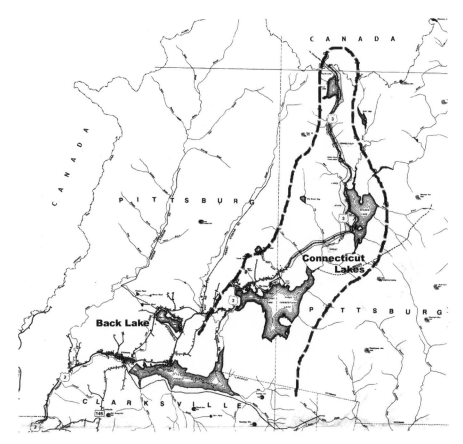

Illus. 7.3. The approximate route some believe Margery Grey took during her ordeal.

FS: When that Willard and I was painting the borderline up there to the State Park, we stepped acrost that same place.

The last statement, spoken quietly by Florence Shatney Scott, was followed by a long silence shared by all three women.

The social role the story of "Margery Grey" played in this community was demonstrated when another resident, who was recalling her mother's songs said:

She never sang "Margery Grey" too much. She knew it, and this always amused me. She said that song made her a little nervous. It irritated because, she said, if she'd a done as she was told—meaning Margery Grey—and stayed where she belonged, this wouldn't have happened, so I suppose that she felt bad that it did happen and this was her reaction to it, because I've heard her say that so many times.[8]

The song "Margery Grey," sung throughout northern New England for over one hundred years, was actually written by poet Julia Dorr in the nineteenth century.[9]

There is some historical evidence that her poem was based on fact; there were news stories during the 1860s that reported on a young couple in the Springfield, Vermont, region who had an experience very much like the one recounted by Dorr.[10] In Pittsburg, however, people came to believe that the event was part of their own local history.

Altogether, many people in the area communicate a deep respect for Margery Gray, for the song, and for the individuals who could "stand up under it" and sing all its twenty-five verses. Residents adopted "Margery Grey" because it held an imagined association with their physical landscape; they made a connection to the story through common life experience as residents of a rural and somewhat isolated region. Men who worked in the woods as trappers, guides, and lumbermen knew how easy it was to get lost in the woods; laborers who worked in the lumbercamps said that hearing the song drove men to tears as they thought about their wives and children at home. Helen Hartness Flanders recorded Orlon Merrill, who grew up in the Connecticut Lakes district of Pittsburg and worked as a trapper, guide, lumberman, and carpenter. She described her experience recording him in a 1931 letter to Phillips Barry:

> Yesterday I went about a mile into New Hampshire across the river, to get from a "guide, trapper, hunter, lumberman and the like" his tune to the ballad "Margaret Gray"... It was a thrilling experience to hear this lumberman sing with difficulty the parts where the mother wanders with the dead baby for three days, passing the fires the settlers had made in looking for her, seeing even the footprints of her husband near the dead ashes. The man explained that, in his work, *he* knew what it was to be lost, to miss the gashed trees, to throw the stick in the water to learn the direction it was flowing.[11]

As was the situation with "Young Charlotte," referred to by Marjorie Pierce of North Shrewsbury, Vermont, there can be a firm belief that a song's characters did live in the region, and singers and their audience find ways of connecting them to their local history.

"Josie Langmaid" or "The Suncook Town Tragedy," referred to earlier in this study, is an example of a song about a documented event that occurred in a different part of New Hampshire but was sung during a period of time in the Pittsburg region. While no more than a few lines have been recovered from Pittsburg, several respondents referred to the song and its local popularity. Clyde Covill remembered his mother singing the song; another resident remembered a friend, Willie Danforth, singing the song. When I asked one of the Shatney sisters about the song and recited the first few lines—*Twas in the morning very cool / when Josie started for her school / many a day these woods she passed / little did she know this time would be her last*—she immediately connected it with the ballad of "Mary Phagan" ("Little Mary Fagan"), a song that was written after a Georgia murder in 1913:[12] "That makes me think of a ballad—'Mary Pagan's Love Song' is the name of it.... Grammy Terrill used to sing that to us."[13]

Mary Pagan

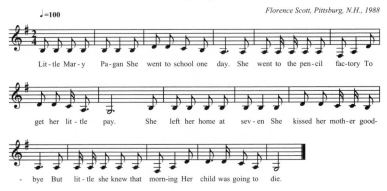

Florence Scott, Pittsburg, N.H., 1988

Little Mary Pagan
She went to school one day.
She went to the pencil factory
To get her little pay.

She left her home at seven
She kissed her mother goodbye
But little she knew that morning
Her child was going to die.

And then a fellow met her,
With a brutal heart you know.
He smiled and said "Little Mary,
You will go home no more."

He crept along behind her
'Til he came to the pencil room.
He smiled and said, "Little Mary,
You've met your fatal doom."

And then there came the watchman
And when he turned the key,
A way down in the basement
Pretty Mary he could see.

He called for a policeman
Their names I do not know.
They came to the pencil factory
And told him he must go.

Her mother sits a weeping,
She weeps and mourns all day.
She prays to meet her baby
In a better world someday.

Well-known songs were also altered to fit the region. In Charlestown, New Hampshire, near Lancaster, the song "Lancaster Jail" ("It's Hard Times in Lancaster Jail") provides an example of a song that was adapted by a singer and his community. Patterned after a ballad from late-eighteenth or early-nineteenth-century England, this song has often been adapted and has been found in many regions of the United States. The local singer of this version worked in the lumbercamps and learned many of his songs in the Colebrook area. He retains many of the words of the widely known song, but he localizes it with names of people he (or the singer) had come in contact with, thus also connecting it to the local satirical song tradition.

Lancaster Jail

A prisoner's fate let me tell you is hard,
The doors they are locked and the sills they are barred;
With bolts and with bars they will make you secure,
Damn 'em to hell and they can't do no more.
And it's hard times in Lancaster Jail
And it's hard times, I say.

The food that you have is a loaf of brown bread
As hard as a rock and as heavy as lead;
Or a pint of bean soup, and your meat it is stale,
You're bound to go hungry in Lancaster jail.

Oh the bed that you have is the dirty old rugs
And when you lie down you're all eat up with bugs
For the bugs they swear they'll never give bail;
And you're bound to go lousy in Lancaster jail.

There is old Colby, a very rich man,
He spends all his time in loafing around;
Your boots he will rob and your clothes he will sell;
Get drunk on the money—O damn him to hell!
And it's hard time; it's hard times in Lancaster Jail.

Now there is young Reilly, he's a dirty Maine crew,
He looked at his men as he's looking them through;
To Lancaster Jail he will send you to dwell
And for one pint of whiskey he would send you to Hell
And it's hard time, it's hard times in Lancaster Jail.

Now to conclude and finish my song,
I hope that I've sung nothing that's wrong;
May the stars and the stripes together prevail
To hell with Old Colby and Lancaster Jail
And it's hard times.[14]

In northern Vermont there is a similar version of this song, "Newport Jail," writ-ten by a man from Lowell.[15] Examples of other versions found throughout the United States include "Hard Times in Mount Holly Jail," "Hard Times in San Quen-tin Jail," "Hard Times in Cryderville Jail," and "Hard Times in Durham's Old Jail."[16]

It was also common in the lumbercamps to adopt songs recounting tragedies that singers and their audiences could easily identify with. Many Pittsburg resi-dents in the nineteenth and early twentieth centuries worked in the camps and maintained (and identified with) songs such as "The Jam on Gerry's Rock," "Peter Amberley," "Guy Reed," and others. "Guy Reed" contains a detailed description of the local landscape and the work conditions in the woods. As Clyde Covill was at-tempting to remember "The Jam on Gerry's Rock" for me, the song that emerged instead was "Guy Reed." He sang a fragment that his uncle, Orlon Merrill, knew.

Guy Reed

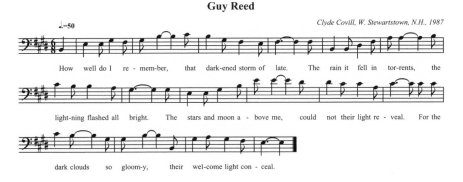

How well do I remember that darkened storm of late.
The rain it fell in torrents, the lightning flashed all bright.
The stars and moon above me could not their light reveal.
For the dark clouds so gloomy, their welcome light conceal.

This young man and his companions where the waters they do roam
Was breaking in the landings on the Androscoggin shore.
They picked the face on one of them from bottom to the top.
Full thirty feet this landing had, a perpendicular drop.

To work the face much longer, 'twould be a foolish part.
A jar so slight, you see, it might this landing start.

Landing, you know. Big landings, logs piled way up. Where they cut 'em in the winter, you know, and make a yard, you know, they call a yard. Then they put in gin pole, they used to call 'em, to hold 'em back so that they could put in some more logs, see. So when you took them out they would start rolling! But they had 'em all scaled before that took place, then they rolled away into the river, some of 'em. My father used to be on what they called the long log drive. I think he drove twenty-one springs. They used to drive on the high water in the spring.[17]

Local Tragedies

Songs recounting actual events that occurred in the community were also locally known and maintained, continuing the collective memory of individuals and events and expressing a common understanding of their sense of place. The process of remembering songs of local tragedies provides information on the context for song creation as well as the relationships among the ballads that residents established.

One example is "The Dudley Willis Song," remembered by Clyde Covill in fragmentary form.

The songs that Father knew, I suppose, most of them was local. I suppose they were. They generally made up songs about—now one of them was about a fellow by the name of Dudley Willis. He got killed on a load of logs, he fell off and the wheels run over him—caused his death . . . I knew his father and mother. I didn't know Dudley Willis though. He was older than me, I believe. His father and mother lived right beside of my grandparents—up in the Connecticut Lake country.[18]

Dudley Willis

Clyde Covill, W. Stewartstown, N.H., 1988

It was in the month of July
In the year of eighty-five,
When this accident happened
It took away a precious life.

It was on a load of lumber
Being carried off to mill.
If you people do not remember,
'Twas at the foot of the Lyford Hill.[19]

Clyde referred to this song several times during our conversations and sang this fragment for me each time. Others in the community remembered and discussed the Willis family, and at least one person in the region recalled that there was a song about the accident, but no one else was able to contribute to its completion.

"The Four Cousins," found in local manuscripts and remembered by many in the community today, preserves the details of a drowning accident that took place on Moose Pond in the nineteenth century. As recorded by Robert Pike, a man named Stonewall Jackson introduced it this way:

> This is called "Moose Pond Song" or sometimes "The Song of the Four Cousins." Moose Pond lies at the height of land between Indian Stream and Back Lake. In the winter of 1853, four young men, Ransom and George Sawyer and Smith and Ben Currier, went there to haul logs with oxen. From the tracks in the snow, it was deduced that one boy had fallen through the ice with the oxen, and the others were drownded while trying to rescue him. (Pike 1959: 185–86)

The 1942 performance by Ed Day exhibits a fluid meter throughout, holding the first two words of each bar to identify it loosely in a 3/4 meter. He finishes the song by speaking the last two words, a practice commonly found in the lumbercamps.

The Four Cousins

Ye blooming youths I pray give ear,
An awful story you shall hear,
'Twas of four cousins and their fate
Their circumstances I'll relate.

In the next lines, their names I'll pen,
Ransom, George, Smith, and Benjamin
Two taken from each family,
Such a case as this you'll seldom see.

In eighteen hundred fifty-three
They left their homes no more to see

To get some timber as we find
Return at night was their design.

Night coming on, their parents hear
No tidings of their children dear,
It filled their minds with grief and woe
In search of them they then did go.

They rallied all the neighbors 'round
To see if these children could be found
They went unto the pond that night,
And there they stayed until daylight.

'Twas early next morning they did start
With tearful eyes and aching heart.
They searched until the spot they found
Where these four cousins all were found.

They took them out and carried them home,
And then conveyed them to the tomb,
Their bodies all lie in one grave,
Their spirits gone to God who gave.

And now may this a warning be
To all mankind as well as me.
To raise to God a prayer each breath,
That we may be prepared for death.

For when our Saviour was on earth
He spoke concerning the new birth.
He says, there's one thing doth remain,
A sinner must be born again.[20]

Two additional verses provided by the Shallow family in 1941 include a message to the families before the last two verses:

Now the Currier's loss is great
He must submit unto his fate,
And neither murmur or complain
For what is his loss is their gain.

And Mr. Sawyer, he must be
Contented with his destiny
Remembering he must also die
And pass from life to eternity.[21]

Like "Josie Langmaid" and "The Murder of Sarah Vail," which were discussed in chapter 2, this ballad exhibits many of the characteristics of obituary ballads, including the come-all-ye opening and the carefully narrated details of the event followed by a homiletic statement, the use of iambic tetrameter, and an AABB rhyme scheme.[22]

Pittsburg is also home to other songs that express individual and community relationships, both to the physical landscape and to the social organization. All of these songs help to maintain local history in the region and provide links between landscape, community, and cultural expression. While the relationship among these elements is often made through references to individuals, we find the values of many of the local residents in these expressions.

Robert Pike recorded a version of locally created "Bright Eyed Etta Lee" in the 1930s.[23] Fifty years later, Clyde Covill, in his eighty-eighth year, helped renew his connections to family, the land, and the community of his youth in Pittsburg as he remembered this song for me. His lyrics and recollections of Etta Lee include geographical references, personal information, and genuine delight in the memory of an individual with whom his family had contact. His narrative communicates a sense of the importance of the song in expressing the sentiments of his family and framing his memory of the local landscape.

Illus. 7.4.   Clyde Covill at the Coos County Nursing Home, West Stewartstown, New Hampshire, 1988. Photo by author.

Remembered by many in the community, Etta Lee lived in the nineteenth and early twentieth centuries just below Indian Stream. Covill said, "I know where she lived 'cause I've seen her. I've seen Etta Lee. My mother used to be a might jealous of my father and Etta Lee. She was much older, but Father used to chum with her some. I don't think it was anything serious, but that's why I remember it." He struggles to remember the song, recalling the following lines on his own:

Bright-Eyed Etta Lee

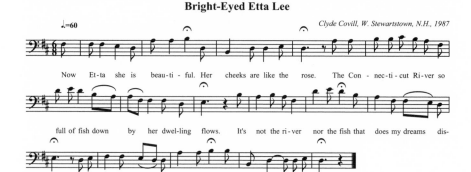

Now Etta she is beautiful,
Her cheeks are like the rose.
The Connecticut River so full of fish
Down by her dwelling flows. [Laughs.]
It's not the river nor the fish
That has my dreams disturbed.
I expect someday to make my wife
That bright-eyed Etta Lee. [Laughs.]

He then begins the song again, referring to Pittsburg resident Abe Washburn's lyrics, recorded by Marguerite Olney in 1941.[24] Note that the second verse of the Washburn version does not begin with "Now Etta she is beautiful, her cheeks are like the rose" but with "Oh Pittsburg, you are beautiful, as everybody knows."

In the golden vale of Pittsburg,
Down by the Connecticut stream,
There lived a maid who holds my heart
And haunts me like a dream;
At night my rest she does disturb,
My mind is never free,
And wishing her to be my bride,
That bright-eyed Etta Lee.

[Laughs.] I can remember her, but she was an old woman when I knew her.

Oh, Pittsburg, you are beautiful,
As everybody knows,

The Connecticut River so full of fish
Down by her dwelling flows;
It's not the river nor the fish,
That dwells so on my mind,
Nor with the town of Pittsburg,
I haven't any fault to find.

My father used to sing that, so it comes handy to me.

The one I loved is fairer
Than all other female kind,
Her skin is whiter than the foam
That floats on the silvery tide,
Her eyes they sparkle like the sun
That glitters on the sea,
And cheeks that make the red rose pale
That bright-eyed Etta Lee.

[Laughs.] I remember. She wasn't very bright-eyed when I remember. But she was a good-looking woman. Oh, yes.

Was I the governor of the State,
Or Pittsburg at my command,
Or was I William McKinerly
The man that rules this land;
I'd give up my role of office
To the people under me,
I'd give her all my fighting ships,
That's on the briny sea,
A beggar would go to bed,
Wake up content and free,
If by his side all for my bride,
I'd find fair Etta Lee.

So fare you well my Etta, dear,
No more for you I'll moan,
But while there's breath in my heart,
'Twill be for you alone,
Most night and day for you I'll pray,
No matter where I be,
At the hour of death my dying breath
Will murmur, Etta Lee.

[Laughs.] Ain't that good? Yeah, Etta Lee.

The song also sometimes blurs the relationship between Etta Lee and the geographical landscape, allowing those singing to simultaneously express their adoration for the individual, their land, and the town of Pittsburg. It is unusual to see direct references to the landscape in songs shared between the British Isles and the United States; the landscape is constantly changing as the song moves from location to location. It is only in some of the American songs, such as the lumbering ballads, and in the local songs that this connection to the literal or symbolic landscape emerges, reinforced by local singers and those remembering the old songs of their community.

Social Commentary Songs

Social commentary songs from the region evaluated or remarked on people, focusing especially on an individual's conduct in a community. These songs were sung in small gatherings of friends (sometimes just two or three) in a well-defined community, such as an occupational group or a neighborhood. Characteristically, such songs in northern New England are satirical. Their local orientation and individual focus kept most of them from remaining in community repertoires for more than one or two generations, and today such songs are generally found only in fragmentary form.

One man from Stewartstown Hollow was in his ninetieth year when he sang fragments of a song he said he and a friend had created. The song, sung to the tune of "Ta ra ra boom di aye," recalled an incident that took place at the local school involving what was probably an illicit relationship between one of their friends and a young woman. It provided social commentary on this behavior as well as satirical characterization of the young man. This song was referenced by at least one other respondent living in the region, although he was unable to remember any of the lines.

Clyde Covill recollected that there were two women that used to make up songs; one, he remembered, was Ida Daily:

> She made up one song about Wyman Huggins. I can't remember, probably . . . you're not familiar with that. They used the tune of a lot of other old songs when they was making up songs. You know, they would, naturally. Yeah. Wyman Huggins, he used to, uh, used to make buckets, wooden buckets. They always sold good. He had a regular way he could turn 'em out, you know. The staves, you know, was rounded. Round. And, he put 'em together, of course, and made a bucket . . . . His name was Wyman, but they called him Wym. [Laughs.] Wym Huggins.

> > Now Wym, don't be dis'pointed,
> > For you've done nothing wrong,
> > And we've been two whole hours,
> > Composing up this song.

> > And if you'd had more timber,
> > More tubs you'd made to sell . . .

I can't remember the whole of it now. You probably wouldn't of heard of that.[25]

The largest group of social commentary songs in Pittsburg and the neighboring communities grew out of the lumbercamp tradition. The writers distinguished themselves within a community of men in a camp with their display of poetic, musical, and (in some cases) performance ability. Edward Ives in his studies of song-makers in Maine and the Maritimes identifies and discusses local satires directed at individuals or groups in the lumbercamps.[26] Throughout the Northeast at that time, woodsmen like Larry Gorman were involved in "songing" people—making up "satirical or invective verses about people he worked for or with" (Ives 1978: 365). In Pittsburg, this tradition was carried into the community, where the songing took place in a variety of environments.

Social commentary songs that were sung in communities outside the lumbercamp have been harder to find because they were created and maintained in isolated neighborhoods or towns and did not have features that encouraged others to adopt or adapt them even in nearby towns. In "The Bear Rock Song" (sometimes called "The Rocky Road to Diamond"), a local song from Stewartstown Hollow (a village that borders Pittsburg), an entire road of families is described and satirized. Marcia Dingman recited and described several verses for me in 1987.[27]

> There's a road that leads to Diamond
> And a crooked road we see
> And the people live upon it
> And this song will prove to be

And then it starts on this lady, she's a widow, talks about that. Then he goes to the next farm and he's a farmer, but he's a boocher, call him Boocher Brown. Says he's got a stock of cattle and he tries to make them pay:

> But I think that rum and whisky
> Has a full and only sway.

Then there's another one about Bill Placey, he got two boys and one of them's working on a farm. Then we go to another neighbor—

> Now we'll stop to Abraham Covill's
> They say Abraham's on a booze,
> You'll find him in the bedroom,
> On his back you'll see him snooze.

> Mamie's dancing in her shirttail
> While Ernest trots his feet
> And the dog lies in the corner
> Watching Mamie's two bare feet.

Bill Hook, who was living on the Diamond Pond Road in the 1980s, said he knew the creator of this local satire; he confessed that he also played a role in making up some of the verses. He offered additional verses and the melody of the song:[28]

Illus. 7.5. Bill Hook, Stewartson Hollow, New Hampshire, 1987.
Photo by author.

The Rocky Road to Diamond

Bill Hook, Stewartstown Hollow, N.H., 1987

♩=130

There's a road that leads to Dia-mond and a crook-ed road you'll see. And the peo-ple that live on it are as crook-ed as can be. First we'll call on wi-dow Cum-mings she's an or-chard and a farm, and Clint Hur-ley works up-on it and things go just to a charm.

> There's a road that leads to Diamond,
> And a crooked road you'll see.
> And the people that live on it,
> Are as crooked as can be.

Music in Rural New England Family and Community Life

First we'll call on Widow Cummings,
She's an orchard and a farm;
And Clint Hurley works upon it
And things go just to a charm.

Quite a worker is the widow,
And she tries to make ends meet.
But I've heard before next winter,
She'll be turned out in the street.
Up steps Clint the gentle father
Takes the widow by the arm,
He will feed her hungry children
And he'll keep them all from harm.

Next we'll call on Charley Carleton
Take to look at his household.
He's a wife, a precious jewel,
So this man been oft times told.
He is working in a millyard,
For Pearl Knapp not far away.
And it is Bill Placey's pleasure
To go there and stay all day.

Next we'll call on William Placey,
Take a look at Guy and Fay.
Guy he's workin' on a farm,
For Pearl Knapp not far away.
But now Pearl is gettin' jealous
Of that great good-natured chap.
And I think it is a wonder,
That he does not break his neck.

Now we'll go a little further
They say Abraham's on a booze
You look in upon the window
On his back you'll see him snooze
Mamie's dancin' in her shirttails
While that Ernest trots his feet
And the dog lies in the corner watching
Watching Mamie's two bare feet

Now we'll go a little further
And we'll call on William Brown.
He's a great good-natured fellow
And they call him "Boocher Brown."
He's a man workin'——
A good man I do declare.

But the way that boocher using it
Would make a preacher swear.

Now we'll climb the hills to Franklin,
Frank Meheurin's on the hill.
You can plainly see by this time
Things in Bear Rock don't stand still.
For the geese, the pigs, the chickens,
Have the kitchen for a pen.
Now I think this truthful story,
I will now bring to an end.

While the "Bear Rock Song" is well known in the region, the local satirical song most residents refer to is "The Old Dan Day Song." This was true also in the 1930s when Robert Pike was collecting songs.[29] In this social commentary song, Dan Day is criticized for his heavy drinking:

There lives an old man in Pittsburg here,
Who sometimes drinks rum and sometimes beer,
Or a little cold water when rum ain't near.

Every night when he goes to bed,
He places a bottle under his head;
And in the morning when he awakes
A jolly good dram this old man takes.

I wish to God that time would come
When old Dan Day won't drink no rum;
But you might as well wish for the day of his death
For he'll drink rum as long as he draws breath.

Robert Pike heard this song in the 1930s, and in the 1980s many people remembered lines from this song, especially the refrain. They talked about their relationship to Dan Day, and to members of the Day family, and they discussed whether the songmaker went too far in satirizing them.[30]

"The Old Dan Day Song" and "The Bear Rock Song" have existed for several generations in a very limited geographical sphere. People living in nearby towns have little more than a cursory knowledge of the songs, unless they are related to the Day family or had lived up near Diamond Pond, where the Bear Rock Road is located.

Local songs demonstrate the desire for people in communities to keep alive memories of certain events or figures. The surviving ballads depicting tragedies and murders may be representative of the many accidents and tragedies that took place in communities over several generations. Colorful individuals were remembered in local songs. Ways of life were recounted; lumbering life, especially, is described in great detail in songs created locally in northern New Hampshire. Local songs recognize and celebrate shared experience among relatives, neighbors, friends, or work partners.

Music in Rural New England Family and Community Life

Generally, local songs keep alive the circumstances that an individual or a group of people choose to recall. They clearly express a concern for the individual in daily circumstances: names are stated in these songs with regularity. They express the importance of humor in daily life, especially in the occupational sphere, as in this example from Abe Washburn of Pittsburg:

The Bulldog Song

There was an old farmer who lived on Clarksville Hill
He raised a pack of bulldogs, his neighbors' blood to spill
He raised a great big Charley, the fiercest of them all
He'd get a chance to steal a sheep, he would eat it wool and all.

Laddle le do a dang laddle le fol da do a daddy
Laddle le do a dang laddle le fol da do a day

He had another son and George it is his name
He's got lots of money, but git it if you can.
He walks about the street, and he thinks he's mighty smart,
If he cannot bite you, he'll snap his teeth and bark.

He has another son, and his name it is Dan,
He thinks to himself that he is quite a man.
He's always looking 'round to see what he can find
And if he gets a chance, he'll steal every time.

He has another son and his name it is John,
He thinks that he can do nothing that is wrong.
He'll run all over the country for a job sawing wood,
He'll beat Bill at sawing by lying if he could.

He has an only daughter, Palmyry is her name
I think that her character is just about the same

She married George Chapple down by the river side
'Twould've been a blessing to him if he'd in his cradle died.

It's lie and dishonesty this old man always was,
His Maker's name profaned, he regarded not His laws.
No more from the peddler's cart the barley will prolong
Old Lull has done his peddling, because he's dead and gone.

Now to conclude and finish, I'm going to end my song.
I hope that I have said, sung, nor done nothing that is wrong;
But if that they should hear of this, that make a terrible brawl
And to make my escape I should have to climb the wall. [31]

Hymns

In the Pittsburg area hymns were sung by individuals at home, neighborhood social occasions, and religious meetings, including camp meetings. Residents that I
interviewed rarely remembered titles or lyrics of hymns they once sang, although
they referenced hymn singing in discussions about music in social life frequently.
The hymn singing in the region is representative of some of the practices found in
the wider northern New England region. As in other areas, there were times set
aside specifically for singing hymns, but there were also many occasions when religious and secular music were performed at the same event. When I asked a man
who grew up in the center of Stewartstown Hollow whether his family sang together when he was growing up, he responded: "Oh yeah. That was one of Dad's
requests in the evening—we used to have to make most of our own fun back in
those days anyway. 'Course I was born and brought up on a farm up beside the Old
North Hill Church. And pretty often he'd say, 'Well Alice, you get on the piano and
play a few hymns.'"[32]

Hymn singing as well as church services took place in various locations. While
some neighborhoods had a nearby church building, others did not have such easy
access to church. Several people spoke of services held in homes, and in at least
one neighborhood the schoolhouse served as a church. Katherine Fogg recalled
her mother's singing:

> My mother sang, always sang. So I don't remember when I didn't hear sing-
> ing around the home. And she used to sing a lot of hymns, because of
> course back in her younger days, and even after she was first married and all,
> this was one of the things that people spent a lot of time at—they didn't
> have a church in our area, but our schoolhouse . . . was used as a meeting
> place. And the ministers from Pittsburg or Colebrook or Stewartstown
> would come up there and hold meetings and I don't know, she just always
> sang all these old hymns that they sang at their meetings. And I think per-
> haps I remember her singing more hymns than I do these other old ballads,
> although she knew a lot of songs.[33]

Illus. 7.6.   North Hill Church, Stewartstown Hollow, New Hampshire.

Another regional resident, Belle Richards, recorded a number of hymns during the 1940s that she identified with her family. In a 1945 interview she said:

> I'll tell you the way it is about these hymns. I don't know where I got them all, but I know that my father used to sing all that I ever sung, and so I think I must have got them mostly from him. My mother used to sing some, but she weren't much of a hand to sing. But she did sing hymns. She sung "Sunbright Clime" and "The Lord Will Provide," and she had others. One she used to sing was "Let Me Go to My Mother."[34]

Homes were also used for organized as well as informal religious meetings. Several elderly residents remembered weekly meetings in nearby homes where their hymn singing was accompanied by fiddle, piano, or organ. Belle Richards regularly held Sunday school classes for neighborhood children in her Stewartstown Hollow home. "She played the organ. And on a Sunday you'd see sometimes, oh I seen as high as fifteen, twenty kids there around the organ and singing while she played. All hymns. On Sunday it had to be hymns, nothing else."[35]

The music she presented was influenced by revival repertoires transmitted at local camp meetings and in hymn books. Many of the hymns Belle sang for Marguerite Olney in 1945 were performed slowly and deliberately, even expectantly. She recorded "O Thou in Whose Presence" in 1945.

O Thou in Whose Presence

Belle Luther Richards, Colebrook, N.H., 1945

O thou in whose presence my soul takes delight,
On whom in affliction I call.
My comfort by day and my song in the night,
My hope, my salvation, my all.

Oh why should I wander an alien from thee,
Or cry in the desert for bread?
Thy foes will rejoice when my sorrows they see
And smile at the tears I have shed. [36]

Belle also recorded versions of the well-known revival hymns "Land of Rest,"
"Come Oh My Soul to Calvary," and "Bower of Prayer." In her performance of
"Alas and Did My Savior Bleed" ("At the Cross"), she sings the Ralph E. Hudson
tune and refrain from the late nineteenth century; this is a revival version of a
hymn first popularized by Isaac Watts in the eighteenth century.[37]

Alas and Did My Savior Bleed

Belle Luther Richards, Colebrook, N.H., 1945

Illus. 7.7. Belle and Frank Richards in Stewartstown Hollow, New Hampshire, c. 1945. Helen Hartness Flanders Ballad Collection.

Alas and did my Savior bleed,
And did my Savior die?
Did he devote that sacred head,
For such a worm as I?
At the cross, at the cross, where I first saw the light,
And the burden of my heart rolled away;
It was there by faith I received my sight,
And now I am happy all the day.

The region also appears to have been a site for a Christian sect that the local residents referred to as the "Black Stockings" or "Christ's Followers."[38] Several people I interviewed were members or had relatives that had been members. One resident described the practices:

Reconstructing Community Traditions   195

The ministers traveled in twos, based on Christ's sending disciples in twos. Members wear no ornaments, the women wear their hair long (they don't believe in cutting their hair) and they don't intend to wear anything "showy." The women mostly wear black stockings, although I have seen some women wearing gray ones. Members stick closely to the Biblical statement that women do not make public prayers . . . Meetings were held by two ministers in people's homes or a town hall. They believe that a church is a group of people, not a building.[39]

Clyde Covill described the meetings in his neighborhood:

People used to meet so often in places. Religious meetings as a rule. And they never turned a religious meeting into a dance, you know. He wasn't the only one, Grandfather wasn't the only one that had meetings like that. But I think of him because we knew all about it. We were just young, very young, you know. It was on that farm . . . that was called the Covill farm. Grandfather's house was big enough to hold quite a service in, and that's the way with lots of others.[40]

I asked Clyde what the name of the group was, and he said: "No special name, they was all called Christians. Them that believed in the Lord."

At another time we spoke about other hymn singing in his family. He said, "Mother knew all the hymns, a lot of 'em. Father knew some of 'em too, but Mother was way ahead of him on that. She used to play the church organs." I asked Clyde for the name of some of her hymns, and he had trouble remembering the titles: "Oh, I just can't think of 'em . . . think of a lot of them they used to play. I haven't even got a hymnbook here with me. Seems as if we had a hymn book we used to call *The Golden Sheaf.*"

He was probably referring to *The Golden Sheaf: A Collection of Choice Hymns and Songs Especially Designed for Tent and Revival Meetings, Prayer and Social Services,* published first in Boston in 1898 by the Advent Christian Church. It begins with two hymns that immediately connect rural singers to the landscape: "Harvest Fields" and "Sowing for the Harvest." Familiar nineteenth-century evangelical hymns and tunes include "Throw Out the Life Line" (1888), "Leaning on the Everlasting Arms" (1887), and "God Be with You 'Till We Meet Again" (1880). Yet the collection is especially characterized by hymns that provide more tenuous links that simply recall some of those familiar nineteenth century titles and lyrics, such as "Just as I Am without One Plea" (with a new melody and added refrain), and hymns that use the formulaic language of the eighteenth- and nineteenth-century hymnists, such as "Will You Go?" (a composite of "There's a Land of Pure Delight," "Will You Come," "Life's Railway to Heaven," and others) and "The General Roll Call" (combining a shape-note title, lyrics related to the refrain of "When the Roll Is Called Up Yonder"). Clearly published for a wide range of uses, it provides a "modern" example of the developing hymnody, responding to a local landscape by providing referential material using diverse musical and theological strains.

The hymnody in the region, then, was informed by neighborhood religious gatherings, camp meetings, and other revival practices. Contextual information on religious singing in this area was especially difficult to compile. By the 1980s, few people could discuss family or community practices that involved hymn singing, and there were few examples of the integration of hymns with secular ballads and songs at the local neighborhood sings. While Belle Richards's repertoire of hymns was large, and some people had heard her sing these hymns, hymn singing for her seemed to relate more to religious education. As an otherwise reclusive individual, there was no apparent connection between hymns and sociability.

Dance Music

We used to have dances at the neighbors'. First they'd be at one neighbor's, then the next . . . There was a neighbor that lived near to us; the man's name was John Marsh. And they used to have quite a lot of 'em down there, because he had a big house—place where they could dance . . . Rob McKeage played the violin. And then in some [homes] they had an organ and somebody would play that.[41]

In the towns of Pittsburg, Colebrook, Clarksville, and Stewartstown, neighbors gathered together often, congregating in each other's homes for kitchen dances where the music played by a fiddler was characterized with the same stylistic flexibility found in the local singing traditions. Residents remember attending dances in neighborhood houses, yet in the same period, some only went to public venues for dances: town halls, granges, and dance halls (sometimes a converted space in a barn). In the late 1980s, many older residents recounted both the social experience of the kitchen dances, which continued into the 1940s, and the social and musical environment at the town halls. Their memories of these practices are based not only on their own experiences, but also those of their parents and friends.

Local customs in the region were transformed as musical and social practices from outside the community were adopted and people began to go to community dances attended by an ever-widening group of participants. Ultimately the character of the events changed; those in homes were moved to locations that could accommodate larger ensembles and bigger crowds. Today the dances are only held in public buildings and are attended by a broad spectrum of participants.

We have little information on nineteenth-century regional fiddlers and their music. A manuscript book of dance tunes belonging to the Daily (or Dailey) family of Pittsburg provides a glimpse of the repertoire of several fiddlers, and some of the calls, for an undefined mid- to late-nineteenth-century social community.[42] During my interviews, several people referred to the Daily family and their contributions to the Pittsburg community. Tunes in this manuscript (as noted also in chapter 4) are drawn largely from an Anglo-Celtic repertoire with a wide range of titles that range from "Hulls Victory," "The Flowers of Michigan," and "Money Musk" to "The Drunken Sailor," "Dixie," and "Pop Goes the Weasel."

Illus. 7.8. Daily ms., Pittsburg, New Hampshire.

There are also several hymns interspersed with the tunes. Many of the dance tunes also include the changes, as in "Money Musk," in the above excerpt from the manuscript book. The notation style within the volume indicates that at least three different musicians contributed to its contents.

Other information on nineteenth-century dance music was provided by individuals whose family memories included parents, grandparents, and great-grandparents who participated in dance music practices as performers on fiddle and organ. Their narrative data indicates an active tradition that involved both women (primarily on keyboard) and men as performers.

The twentieth-century recordings and narrative data from residents of the region provide information on social and musical practices in many of the towns in this northernmost area of New Hampshire. Their discussions revolved around fiddlers and other musicians, the repertoires, and the social contexts for dancing. While they were able to provide limited information on playing style, their mediated performances offered a glimpse of the practices of the past.

FIDDLERS

If you ask older area residents about the fiddlers at neighborhood and community dances before the mid-twentieth century, typically just a few names are raised. The fiddlers that played at dances were local musicians, and many of them performed in various social environments, including homes and public and private dance halls. Marcia Dingman remembered some of the fiddlers and the neighborhood events:

> And we used to have dances at our homes and we'd pick up a violin player— our neighbor's or somewhere. Now that Guy Haynes . . . he used to be the violin player. He'd come to our house and we'd have a nice little dance. We'd clean everything out of the kitchen except the stove and had a dance and had a good time. Most always there was neighbors that went. We had an organ or piano and I'd play the chords. I made pretty good music. And then this Clyde Covill, he was good at it, really good. And, let me see, there used to be an old man when we was in Pittsburg; that was before I ever married. He was a violin player, boy he was good. And he used to go to neighbors' homes once in a while and we would play. Didn't go into no big halls, just had entertainment for families, you know. And he'd play the violin and I'd play chords with him. That was a long time ago 'cause that was before I was ever married.[43]

I asked if she was referring to Robert McKeage, and she said, "Yes! He's one of the men that used to play violin."

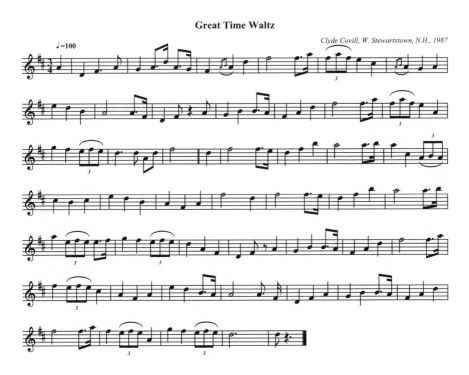

Great Time Waltz

Clyde Covill, W. Stewartstown, N.H., 1987

Robert McKeage, born in the mid-1860s, traveled throughout the region to accompany dances. His granddaughters characterize his movement as focused largely on the opportunities to play at dances.

[He] used to live out in Kidderville. Back then they used to have kitchen junkets and he used to go around and play for them. And our Aunt Christie [his sister] used to play the organ most of the time. She would play that when he played the fiddle. And they used to sing old, old songs. I can't remember. Well, one I can remember the most was "My Darling Nellie Gray," I remember that.[44]

In fact, nearly every person I spoke with about dances mentioned Robert McKeage. Most remembered that when he played he was accompanied either by his sister or daughter on piano or organ. Only occasionally did other instrumentalists contribute to the ensemble. He was a professional musician in this region and was paid for his services even at the junkets. Clyde Covill remembered him well. In one of our conversations, he said, "Old Bob McKeage was the chief fiddler around here for a long time." Clyde was having trouble with his memory on the first day I talked with him about McKeage, but he took out his violin, and after struggling with several tunes, he played a lilting waltz with great care.

As Clyde finished, he said, "It's 'Great Time,' that's a good waltz. That used to be one of old Bob McKeage's favorite waltzes."[45]

As his granddaughters noted, Robert McKeage lived in Kidderville during a period, but there was a time when he lived in Pittsburg as well. According to the Pittsburg town records, he was born in Canada; his father was originally from Quebec and his mother from Northern Ireland. He was married in 1888 to Jennie Crawford. Robert McKeage's brother Will also lived in Pittsburg. Clyde also remembered going to dances that McKeage played at before Clyde himself "took up the violin." He marked the Pittsburg area that McKeage played in as "the Connecticut Lakes country." One place he described was the old Covill farm: "The old original Covill farm—Father's people—they had a house big enough to dance in. And what made it one room, they closed off double doors 'cause they didn't use it all the time, you know. Then when they had a dance, they'd open all them doors and you had a long room for it—it was a pretty good one."[46]

Katherine Fogg of Pittsburg remembered McKeage from the dances in her neighborhood.

Now Rob McKeage . . . he could sure play the violin and call the changes. My uncle built a house on the place above here, and he didn't have it finished inside and I never could figure out why he built it on this property above here that didn't belong to him, so it was on skids so he knew he was going to be moving it. Well, some of the young people around said, "I should think you would have a dance there." Well, they kind of talked him into it. But he didn't get anything out of this, he did it for the enjoyment of having the people around and hearing the music. And every Saturday night they had a dance there for a long time, and he'd get Rob McKeage to play. Oh, sometimes my mother played the organ with Rob. Rob would play the violin and call the changes. I've seen him get onto the floor and dance to finish off the string. Because if they lacked someone, he'd get up there and dance with them and play and call his changes.[47]

I asked another long-time Pittsburg resident about his tunes, and she remembered two in particular: "Portland Fancy" and "Boston Fancy." Robert McKeage played his version of "Boston Fancy"—calling his own changes—for Marguerite Olney in 1942.[48]

Boston Fancy

Another fiddler highly regarded in the community came from a generation that followed Robert McKeage's. Born in 1906, Leo Brooks learned his music in his family; his father and uncle played the fiddle, and his mother the organ and piano. His family recollections include memories his relatives passed on to him; they played at kitchen junkets, at dance halls, and informally at home. Their repertoire included old New England tunes as well as popular songs.

> My father, he used to play violin; I learned to play from him over there at that old place [the house he grew up in]. They had all gone to Grange one night—his brother and my mother—went up to the Grange in Pittsburg— kind of a cold night. He set out in the kitchen in the chair that we kept by the stove there, played the fiddle. He showed me how to play "School Days." I learned to play that. That's where I started.

School Days

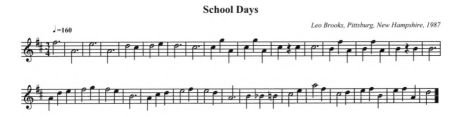

Leo began playing professionally with a group of friends when he was barely in his teens, emulating the dance orchestras that were forming in various communities. He and several friends, including Willie Hawes, another locally recognized fiddler, established a band in around 1918 and played first at a camp at Back Lake. The musical world that Leo Brooks recalled for me revolved around dance music,

Illus. 7.9.   Leo Brooks, Pittsburg, 1987. Photo by author.

performed primarily at public establishments. While his parents played for and attended kitchen dances and other home-based socials, he remembered playing at the Grange halls in Colebrook, East Colebrook, and Pittsburg, and the town halls, theaters, and dance halls in Kidderville, Stewartstown, Pittsburg, and other communities. "We played all around this northern country." I asked him if he remembered his parents singing at home when he was young, and he said: "No, I never heard 'em."

The Canadian fiddler Don Messer had an important influence on Leo Brooks and some of his friends: "Oh I played a lot of them Don Messer tunes. He had one, 'Silver and Gold,' and 'Buckwheat Batter,' 'Rippling Water Jig.' I got a book here with some of 'em."[49]

Buckwheat Batter

Leo shows the influence of his experience as an accompanist for dances but also as a soloist. He was a traveler; he spoke a great deal about his journeys to Quebec, Vermont, and Maine for regional contests and dances. This is illustrated in his stylized version of "Buckwheat Batter," and his performance of the Don Messer tune "Rippling Water Jig," using an irregular ("crooked") meter that was relatively rare among old-time New England fiddlers.[50] Dance music adapted to the changing interests and tastes of musicians and listeners, which by the mid-twentieth century revolved around dance orchestras and hillbilly bands.

Rippling Water Jig

Many community members remembered the dance orchestras that were established in the 1930s and 1940s to provide music for dances in the local halls. Doc Converse's Hillbilly Band had ten to fifteen members who accompanied dances in the local halls on fiddle, guitar, horn, piano, drums, accordion, and harmonica. I talked with Clyde about Doc Converse and the Hillbilly Band on several occasions, and he revealed their tightly controlled organization and repertoire.

JP: Did you used to play with the Hillbilly Band?

CC: Yes! I did. Doc Converse was the manager. Called the Hillbilly Band. I just went with them, just for the fun of it. And I used to go up to see him quite often, anyway. He could play pretty good himself.

JP: He played fiddle?

CC: Yes, he played violin. I play fiddle, but he played the violin. [Laughs.]

JP: What's the difference, to you?

CC: There isn't any, just in the style you're playing.

JP: So, in the Hillbilly Band, did they play by note?

CC: No, they didn't play by note. No. They probably could, a lot of 'em, but that wasn't it. In the old Hillbilly Band we had, well, mostly all old-timers. Pieces we'd play, old-timers, you know. Converse picked 'em out himself.

JP: What were some of the tunes you played?

CC: Well, we played, of course, a lot of the diddly-diddly pieces and then there was sometimes at the end of a square dance, you know, you'd play another little piece on, like "Way Down Upon the Swanee River"—they'd come in with that, right after playing a fast piece, see. They'd be playing all them old fiddling pieces and then they'd come right off with . . . with that one.[51]

From the different reports about the membership of this group, it is likely that it varied in size and composition during the many years it provided music for Pittsburg and the surrounding communities. The group changed with the availability of musicians and instruments while stimulating the growth of other ensembles as well. They played for town meeting dances and at dances at the grange halls and town halls in Pittsburg, Colebrook, and the neighboring communities of Stewartstown Hollow, East Colebrook, and Kidderville.

At the Town Hall, well, they had an orchestra. Leo Brooks, he had an orchestra. He used to play a lot to the dances. When I lived down East Colebrook, after we sold the farm we bought a place down to Kidderville, it was a hall upstairs, it was a store downstairs, and we finished that off into a place to live and we run dances for a while upstairs. And Leo Brooks used to play, then Gerald Young, his orchestra we used to have there.[52]

The enthusiasm for social dancing and the active dance orchestra movement encouraged musicians to travel for performances, and many dancers by the 1930s and 1940s traveled to attend dances in nearby communities as well—Clarksville and Stewartstown Hollow, West Stewartstown, Kidderville, East Colebrook, and Colebrook.

REPERTOIRES

The repertoire of dances and their tunes offered by residents from their memories of the old times helps to identify this region's unique character. The particularly high regard for the fiddlers of the past, the Quebec landscape just a few miles north that was a source of tunes and playing styles, and the music transmitted through the radio and available on commercial recordings all provided repertoires that were a unique combination of the old-time Anglo-Celtic and French-

Canadian tunes and the popular song tunes learned from the radio. In addition, play-party songs played a significant role at dances as well. Due to its population and isolation, the region depended on a relatively limited group of fiddlers and other musicians to provide dance music, which maintained a consistent repertoire that was valued by many of its residents.

One characteristic of the region in the twentieth century was the use of songs in dance tunes; many people referred to group singing during dances. While "Darling Nellie Grey" and "Wabash Cannonball" were popular there, as in many rural areas, other popular tunes for dances ranged from locally popular songs to late-nineteenth and early-twentieth-century songs popularized through the media.

Florence Scott remembered some of the dance tunes her family enjoyed before the 1940s when they held weekly dances in their home:

Every time that we ever lived in a house that was big enough, Saturday night we'd have an old time dance! 'Course then we used to sing old time waltzes: "Alice Blue Gown" and "The Waltz You Save for Me." And then we'd have—they call 'em square dances now—we called 'em quadrilles then! "Soldier's Joy," "Boston Fancy," but we used to have a lot of galops, a lot of 'em call it polkas now—but it's two different dances.

> Left foot, right foot
> Any foot at' all
> Sally lost a bustle
> Coming home from the ball[53]

When I asked Marcia Dingman whether they danced the "Boston Fancy" at the neighborhood dances she had been describing, she answered:

Yes, they used to dance that. That was a plain dance, that's what called the changes; someone out of the bunch. I don't know whether we was doing it right or not, we never had a real caller. The neighbors would do it, you know, who happened to be there, that's all. I know one that was a real common song to dance by: "Turkey in the Straw." And then "Golden Slippers," that was another one we could dance very good. And one "Beautiful Ohio," I think that was one of the tunes. And let me see. They used to play that "Old Black Joe," we used to dance to that. That made a pretty good quickstep.

And then they used to play—I don't remember the tune they'd go by but—and don't know as I know the name of the dance "Duck for the Oyster": "And that for the clam and that for the holey old tin pan." And had to have two, four, six, eight people and one couple at a time would go into the middle and then they'd back up and they'd go back and they'd say "Duck for the oyster" and we'd go bow to the next couple and then we'd back up and they'd say "Duck for the clam." We'd go bow to them again, and they'd say "Duck for the hole in the old tin pan." And then people'd hold their hands apart and we'd go between 'em. And the next couple'd do the same thing. We been all four people. It was really fun; it was kind of cute too.[54]

Clyde Covill mentioned the locally popular song "The Little Mohea" as a tune source for dances, then asked me if I knew the song about "Margaret Grey": "We used to play it for a two-step."[55]

Margaret Gray

Clyde Covill, W. Stewartstown, N.H., 1987

PLAY-PARTY GAMES

Older members of the regional communities, including Pittsburg, Stewartstown Hollow, and Colebrook, also describe play-party games, such as "Go In and Out the Window" and "On the Green Carpet," that adults and teenagers took part in, dancing from room to room in the large farmhouses. Dr. Brooks, who grew up in Stewartstown Hollow, described these occasions:

> We used to have a bunch of places, they were really good singers, and years and years ago, oh my heavens, sixty years ago, we used to have to make our own fun mostly. And they had maybe once a week or once in two weeks they'd go to somebody's home. Now if they came here fifty people, they'd all join hands and go out through this room and out through the kitchen and back through here. And then there'd be one woman planted here and one man planted there, and those old songs. Ray Placey used to do all the singin' and in the song would be what you're supposed to do. If there was a man over there he'd pick a woman out of the group . . . and part of the song would say, "and kiss her and send her away" then she'd get back in the line. I think it always would start:
>
> > On the green carpet here we stand,
> > Take your true love by the hand,
> > Take the one that you love best,
> > Will be the one that you profess.
>
> And then another one we would be singing was—this was when someone was pulling somebody out of the ring—another part would be:
>
> > It's a hard one, it's a hard one
> > For you, young man,

You promised to marry her six months ago,
But stick to your bargain, or out you go.

'Course Ray would have a few drinks in him and that would make him sing all the better.[56]

This was echoed by Ardes Haynes of Pittsburg, who remembered a similar practice, with lyrics that added to the festive quality of the events:

They didn't have music [instruments] at those parties lots of times. It was just somebody'd start singin' a song, everybody'd take up whether they could sing or not. And sing along. And they'd form a great big ring and go round and round. And sometimes if a house could go around through the living room, and another room, and the kitchen, and so on, they'd go from room to room, have a ring, and they'd be couples stop every which way and when that they'd sing it and come right, they'd kiss their partner and the one that had been there would go back in the ring. And then the one that was there could choose another one.

On the green carpet here we stand
Take your true love by the hand
Take the one that you profess
To be the one that you like best.

Oh what a good, good choice you've made
You've got the old woman instead of the maid
Her nose as long as thick as a knife
And they're all laughing at your old wife.

[Laughs.] Part of that was a parody to the regular song, but that's the way they used to sing it quite a lot. [57]

Remembering the Musical Practices

The process of recollecting songs, tunes, and environments for dancing provided opportunities for individuals to discuss the characteristics and the maintenance of musical traditions. In earlier times, residents looked to individuals in the community to preserve music and dance traditions through both organized and impromptu events.

For some people in northern New England, dance culture and singing traditions were quite separate. And in Pittsburg, this was true as well. Leo Brooks talked about his focus on fiddle playing and had a difficult time discussing songs. Rob McKeage's granddaughters remembered his fiddling and dance tunes, but their memories of songs in their family were hazy. For some, though, memories of dance tunes and dances blurred the relationship between instrumental music and singing because events often included both. During a discussion about dance music with Marcia Dingman of Stark, New Hampshire, I asked her if she ever waltzed to "The Little Mohee." She responded with references not to experiences at dances, but instead showed her association of this piece with various songs that were connected to memories of music in everyday life.

> I used to know that. We used to sing that. And another song, "Young Charlotte," we used to sing that. And then what was the name of that other one that we used to sing, and my daughter still remembers. She says "Mama, you was walking through the woods sometimes." But years ago, we didn't know lullabies, we would sing whatever happened. Gosh, what's that song the child died in? "Letter Edged in Black." And of course that isn't a very good song to sing as a baby's lullaby . . . Another old-timer is "The Old Arm Chair." My mother used to sing that many, many times, too.[58]

Memories of some songs reminded Clyde Covill of people in his household, neighborhood, and occupational sphere who were important to him and his family. His recollections also provide information on the creation and transmission of local, regional, and Anglo-Celtic songs—and how the household played a role in song transmission. We discussed the local "Dudley Willis Song":

CC: I used to know the women that made up them songs too. A lot of 'em.

JP: One of them was named Ida Daily?

CC: Yes, that's one of 'em. I knew Ida Daily. I was a small boy though, when that I remember her. She was a distant relative of my father, the Dailys were, you know.
  Now another has come to my mind that used to make up songs like that: Clarence Wheeler. He was in that, well, call it gang if you want to, it weren't a gang, but he was in with that category.

JP: And what did he do? He made up songs—

CC: Yes, and he sung songs that some of the women had a hand in makin' up, you know. Some of them songs were pretty good.

JP: Can you tell me what they were about?

CC: Most of them about lumbering and generally an accident happened. They'd get a song together about it.

JP: But the accidents, were they like log jams—

CC: Yes, yes, log rollin' and landings. They used to haul logs in, you know, all winter long—

JP: And there were accidents that happened in the process of doing that?

CC: Yes. Clearin' out landings, once in a while, a fella get caught by the log comin' off of it—and kill him. Not too much. But they'd make up a song about it. That was Ida Daily, and I knew of the other woman that used to be with her, used to do the same thing.

As he tried to remember another local song about an accident in the woods, he said:

> What was that song now, he got killed in a log jam—he got drownded too. The landing give way and down it went and put 'im right into the water, you know, and of course he drownded. Couldn't get out, there was so many logs there. I know what part of the song was. Just a little piece of it.
>
> They rolled those logs so carefully from off his mangled form
> The birds were singing sweetly, the sun shone bright and warm
> Brave hearts looked down to see him could not their grief command
> And bring tears drop from their eyes and fell into the sand.
>
> That's one of the old songs they used to sing. Hope it'll come to me. I wished that I had set them down.[59]

The song he remembered was a verse of "Guy Reed." Three other verses of this song, known in his family and popular in woods, emerged on another occasion when he was attempting to remember a different woods song.

Another time I asked Clyde about "The Flying Cloud," a broadside ballad song sung throughout the north country, and from his response I learned about how new songs came into a household:

> Oh, "The Flying Cloud," well, mother didn't sing that, but Willis J. Danforth, that lived—just a neighbor with us, he used to sing that. Yes, I've heard him sing it lots of times. [Sings.] "The *Flying Cloud* was as good a ship as ever sailed the sea." That's the way I think it starts in. I remember the tune that we always sung by "The Flying Cloud." 'Course it's been so long since I heard the whole of it that I don't know. But this Mr. Danforth used to sing it and I know it would take him half the night to sing it. [Laughs.] He lived in Pittsburg, I think, all of his life.
>
> And after his wife was dead and one thing or another, he used to come over and get up Father's woodpile . . . you know, for the winter. And he had a pair of horses and all of that. That's back in the old days, and we used to get him to sing them songs, you know. We had another man that used to be in charge of a lot of woodsmen. His name was Burt Inglesall. And he says, "Now you boys will have to do somethin' today (he was, of course, the boss, you know, he was 'bout half jokin', 'cause he knew 'em all) and don't you get Willie to singing 'The Flying Cloud' all day either." [Laughs.]

About Willis Danforth, Clyde said to me, "Boy I wished I knew the songs he used to know. He used to sing 'em evenings there, in my home, while he was boarding at the time. We liked Willie awfully well."[60]

Songs with similar lyrical and melodic structures were also adopted and sometimes fused, as with Clyde's melodic and lyrical blending of "Jam on Gerry's Rock" and "Guy Reed." Similarly, two other songs in the American tradition popular in the Pittsburg area, "Lass of Mohee" (also known locally as "Little Mohee" or

"Lassie Mohee") and "The Chipperwash Stream" (also known as "The Chickelord Stream") were sometimes confused.[61] The "Lass of Mohee" was widely popular throughout the United States for its story as well as its tune, and it was recorded in the Pittsburg region in the 1930s, 1940s, and 1980s. "The Chipperwash Stream," on the other hand, is not as well known. Both share a similar opening stanza:

The Little Mohee

As I was out walking one morning in spring
With a fond recreation to wile time away;
As I sat amusing myself on the grass
It is whom should I spy but a fair Indian lass.

The Chipperwash Stream

As I was out walking one morning in spring,
To hear the birds whistle and the nightingale sing.
I spied a fair damsel all alone in the rain,
She was bleaching her linens on the Chipperwash Stream.

They share also the story of two strangers meeting, a proposal that they establish a relationship, and a resolution that benefits each party (although their outcomes are quite different). Both songs, sung in the region, are set in waltz-time, and the similarity of the two often caused their confusion when I spoke with residents. Flora Campbell began singing her version of "The Little Mohee" using the tune of "The Chickelord Stream," not settling on the right tune until the second verse. What was especially interesting, though, was the opportunity to compare the melodies of the songs that were recalled in the 1940s and the 1980s. The relationship of Maude Covill's version of "Chipperwash Stream" to Flora Campbell's is clear, yet her melody for "Little Mohee" also shares similar contours and rhythmic phrasing. What it illustrated is the complex interweaving of two songs connected by individuals and their communities to generate new tunes. The process that we have recorded during a short period in the region's history had been taking place, of course, for generations.

Chipperwash Stream

Maude Covill, Pittsburg, N.H., 1941

Music in Rural New England Family and Community Life

Chickelord Stream

Flora Campbell, Stark, N.H., 1988

Little Mohee

Flora Campbell, Stark, N.H., 1988

Reconstructing the Community

Information from collectors who traveled in the region during the first half of the twentieth century helps us to reconstruct musical traditions. The reconstruction of some of the musical traditions in this region shows a community that reflects the changing interests and needs of its residents, and this community's impact on cultural expression. It is difficult to find individual and community musical practices in the Pittsburg region unaffected by earlier collectors and their published collections. Nor can we strip away the influence popular music has had on this community during the last one hundred years.

Collectors who moved through the region, the literature published and disseminated in the community, musical practices adopted from mainstream traditions, and the influx of tourists *do* affect how residents view and express themselves today. Yet, earlier in the century, when other communities modeled musical practices on urban traditions that brought singing out of a private sphere and encouraged public performance, the song tradition in Pittsburg remained largely in the household and neighborhood.

Throughout the period individual musicians were identified by the community and invited again and again to perform at socials or public dances. There was support for singers with new songs to bring to a gathering, and for those who made up songs. There was admiration for singers who knew a lot of songs, and fiddlers with a wide repertoire of tunes. The memory of songs and dances demonstrates a desire to recall and to celebrate common experiences among relatives or neighbors or friends or work partners.

Residents' discussions about the songs and dance tunes that were important to them help us to understand the specific character of this rural singing tradition. We learn about families engaged in farm-based practices, where songs were shared among family members, neighbors, and coworkers. Their descriptions of get-togethers or socials also show that proximity and relationship were important for participants in social gatherings. Work and play were intertwined in the lives of the people in this community. Today the music connected to community traditions of the nineteenth and early twentieth centuries is heard in some homes on cassettes, CDs, and videotapes, and at public events where local musicians play fiddle, guitar, accordion, and drums to accompany old-time dances. The local songs, the British ballads, even the popular songs of the earlier years of the century are offered only as memories. Active singing has been replaced by active listening to country songs and other popular genres.

These discussions provide evidence that song repertoires were broad, with little separation of songs or tunes by the genres devised by scholars. An exception to this was in hymn singing. When I asked Clyde if they sang songs that were not hymns at some of the religious gatherings at his home, he responded: "No, no, no . . . They wouldn't be doing that . . . They wouldn't stand for to have a song mixed up with a song that was wicked. That didn't sound good."[62]

Aesthetic standards described in narratives include a concern for vocal quality; those who sang well, and loudly, were asked to sing again and again. Clyde described his parents: "They both could sing quite good. I thought, anyway. Not just 'cause they was my father and mother, but the company we used to have used to think so too!"[63]

There was also a great deal of support for singers with new songs to bring to a gathering. Furthermore, there was admiration for singers who had a lot of songs, and for those who made up songs. My discussions with residents about songs made up in their communities ("The Dan Day Song" and "Etta Lee," for example) were particularly valuable because we have so little information on local songs in the region that had a life outside of the lumbering tradition.

From Clyde we learn too that, unlike many regions in northern New England, women were valued as singers in Pittsburg. In fact, women played a role in song creation and transmission that is closer to Maritime traditions (where women are recognized as singers and song makers more often than in New England).

The songs most valued by communities in the Pittsburg region exhibited a high degree of sentimentalism, morality, and satire. This includes songs that were adopted and created, representing influences from popular, traditional, and local song traditions.

Some of the residents also demonstrated that they identified individuals with specific songs and tunes, and that this music contributed to their (and the community's) sense of place. Some of the songs, especially the local songs, show the desire for people in the community to keep memories alive of specific events or people and to celebrate common experiences among relatives, neighbors, friends, or work partners.

Residents' narratives confirm that the very active singing tradition in the community depended upon shared community values and practices that were confined to relatively private spaces: the household, neighborhood, and occupational spheres. As the geographical and social gaps between families, generations, neighbors, and communities widened, the traditions began to break down. And as Clyde Covill said: "It just wore away. First we knew it was getting . . . fainter and fainter . . . and finally it didn't take place."[64]

Appendix: Songs and Tunes from the Pittsburg Region

When we consider the contributions of information from relatives of singers who remember songs performed in their families, along with the repertoires offered at the request of collectors in the 1930s and 1940s, we find a broader repertoire of songs represented for the period. Sources on musical repertoires in the Pittsburg region including manuscript data and fieldwork from the 1930s through the 1980s.

Title	Performance title	Source (last name first)	Date
Abide with Me	Abide with Me	Day family (Katherine Fogg)	1987
About Jesus Christ Who Died for Sinners	About Jesus Christ Who Died for Sinners	Robie Alice	1940s
Adieu to Cold Winter	Adieu to Cold Winter	Luther Sidney	1941
	Adieu to Cold Winter	Richards Belle Luther	1942
A-Growing	Daily Growing	Richards Belle Luther	1942
	Young but He's Daily A-Growing	Shatney Floyd	1987
Alas and Did My Savior Bleed	Alas and Did My Savior Bleed	Richards Belle Luther	1945
Alice Blue Gown	Alice Blue Gown	Richards Belle Luther (G. Richards)	1987
	Alice Blue Gown	Shatney family (Florence Scott)	1987
Almond Coach	Almond Coach	Richards Belle Luther	1945
Answer	Answer	Rowell Mrs. (Katherine Fogg)	1987
Auld Soldier	Sailor and the Soldier	Hawes L. A.	1941
	Sailor and the Soldier	Luther Sidney	1941
Backwoodsman	Teamster's Lament	Luther Sidney	1941
Baggage Coach Ahead	Baggage Coach Ahead	Day family (Katherine Fogg)	1987
Bailiff's Daughter of Islington	Bailiff's Daughter	Richards Belle Luther	1941
Banks of Brandywine	Banks of Brandywine	Richards Belle Luther	1943
Banks of Caledonia	Caledonia	Luther Sidney	1942
Banks of Claudy	Banks of Claudy	Luther Sidney	1941
Banks of Dundee	On the Banks of the Sweet Dundee	Day Edwin	1942
	Banks of Sweet Dundee	Hawes Fred Mrs.	1941
	Banks of the Sweet Dundee	Luther Sidney	1941
	Banks of the Sweet Dundee	Robie Alice	1940s

215

Songs and Tunes—(*continued*)

Title	Performance title	Source (*last name first*)	Date
Bold Pedlar and Robin Hood	Bold Robin Hood and the Pedlar	Richards Belle Luther	1941
Bold Princess Royal	Bold Princess Royal	Luther Sidney	1942
Bold Privateer	Soldier	Richards Belle Luther	1942
Bonaparte on St. Helena's Shore	Bonaparte on St. Helena's Shore	Richards Belle Luther	1943
Bonny Laboring Boy	Bonny Laboring Boy	Hawes L. A.	1941
Bonnie Lassie's Answer	Bonnie Lass's Answer	Richards Belle Luther	1943
Bonny Barbara Allen	Barbara Allen	Day family (Katherine Fogg)	1987
	Barbara Allen	Hook Bill	1987
	Barbara Allen	Merrill Orlon	1932
	Barbara Allen	Reynolds Maynard	1941
	Barbara Allen	Richards Belle Luther	1941
Bonny Black Bess	Bonny Black Bess	Luther Sidney	1941
Bonny Blue Handkerchief	Bonny Blue Handkerchief	Jackson George A.	1943
Bonny Laboring Boy	Bonny Laboring Boy	Day Edwin	1942
	Bonny Laboring Boy	Luther Sidney	1941
Boston Burglar	Boston Burglar	Shatney Floyd	1987
Botany Bay	Botany Bay	Hawes L. A.	1941
Bower of Prayer	Bower	Richards Belle Luther	1945
Braes of Yarrow	Dewy Dells of Yarrow	Richards Belle Luther	1941
Bramble Briar	Constant Farmer's Son	Robie Alice	1941
Brave Wolfe	General Wolfe	Richards Belle Luther	1942
Brennan on the Moor	Brennan on the Moor	Luther Sidney	1941
Bright-Eyed Etta Lee	Bright-Eyed Etta Lee	Dingman Marcia	1987
	Bright-Eyed Etta Lee	Covill Clyde	1987
	Bright-Eyed Etta Lee	Richards Gerard	1987
	Bright-Eyed Etta Lee	Washburn Abe	1941
Broad Is the Road	Broad Is the Road	Richards Belle Luther	1945
Bulldog Song	Bulldog Song	Washburn Abe	1941

217

Songs and Tunes—(*continued*)

Title	Performance title	Source (*last name first*)	Date
Crafty Farmer	Yorkshire Boy	Day Edwin	1941
	Crafty Farmer	Merrill Orlon	1931
Cuckoo	Cuckoo	Luther Sidney	1941
	Cuckoo	Washburn Abe	1942
Cumberland Crew	Cumberland Crew	Luther Sidney	1941
Curfew Shall Not Ring Tonight	Curfew Shall Not Ring Tonight	Haynes Ardes	1987
Darling Nellie Grey	My Darling Nellie Grey	Shatney Floyd	1987
Daemon Lover	House Carpenter	Covill family (Clyde)	1987
	House Carpenter	Luther Sidney	1942
	House Carpenter	Merrill Orlon	1931
	House Carpenter	Reynolds Maynard	1941
	House Carpenter	Richards Belle Luther	1942
	Young Turtle Dove	Robie Alice	1941
Daisy Dean	Daisy Dean	Richards Belle Luther	1942
Dark-Eyed Sailor	Dark-Eyed Sailor	Luther Sidney	1941
	Dark-Eyed Sailor	Reynolds Maynard	1941
	Dark-Eyed Sailor	Richards Belle Luther	1941
Daughter of Old England	Daughter of Old England	Amey Clark	1942
David and Bathsheba	David and Bathsheba	Richards Belle Luther	1943
Death of Floyd Collins	Death of Floyd Collins	Amey Clark	1942
	Death of Floyd Collins	Shatney family (Florence Scott)	1987
Deer Island down the Bay	Deer Island down the Bay	Covill Clyde	1987
	Deer Island down the Bay	Jackson George A.	1943
Deserter	Deserter	Richards Belle Luther	1942
	Soldier Boy	Robie Alice	1942
Devil He Did Appear	Devil He Did Appear	Richards Belle Luther	1943
Diamonds of Derry	Diamonds of Derry	Richards Belle Luther	1942
Dirty Old Cook and the Lousy Cookee	Dirty Old Cook and the Lousy Cookee	Hook Bill	1987
	Dirty Old Cook and the Lousy Cookee	Shatney family (Florence Scott)	1987

Disguised Sailor	Rich Merchant	Richards Frank	1942
Down at the Old Cherry Orchard	Down at the Old Cherry Orchard	Covill Clyde	1988
Down by the Shannon Side	Down by the Shannon Side	Hawes L. A.	1941
Down on Dixie's Isle	Down on Dixie's Isle	Washburn Abe	1942
Dreary Scenes of Winter	Dreary Scenes of Winter	Richards Belle Luther	1942
Drive on Sandy Stream	Fire at Sandy Stream Camp	Merrill Orlon	1931
	Fire on Sandy Stream	Richards Belle Luther	1942
Drop the Handkerchief	Drop the Handkerchief	Haynes Ardes	1987
Drowsy Sleeper	Silver Dagger	Luther Sidney	1945
	Silver Dagger	Richards Belle Luther	1942
	Silver Dagger	Robie Alice	1942
Drummer Boy of Waterloo	Drummer Boy of Waterloo	Richards Belle Luther	1943
Drunkard's Doom	Drunkard's Doom	Richards Frank	1943
Drunkard's Wife	Drunkard's Wife	Richards Belle Luther	1943
Drunken Captain	Drunken Captain	Washburn Abe	1941
Duck for the Oyster	Duck for the Oyster	Dingman Marcia	1987
Dudley Willis	Dudley Willis	Covill Clyde	1988
Dying Brother	Dying Brother	Richards Belle Luther	1942
Dying Californian	Dying Californian	Reynolds Maynard	1942
	Dying Californian	Richards Belle Luther	1942
Dying Cowboy	Dying Cowboy	Shatney Floyd	1987
Dying Ranger	On the Banks of the Potomac	Day Edwin	1941
	Dying Soldier	Hawes Fred	1941
Eden Home	Eden Home	Day family (Katherine Fogg)	1987
Edwin and Mary	Edwin and Mary	Hawes Fred Mrs.	1941
	Edwin and Mary	Luther Sidney	1941
Effie the Maid of the Mill	Effie the Maid of the Mill	Richards Belle Luther	1943
Elfin Knight	I Want You to Plant Me an Acre of Corn	Reynolds Maynard	1942
	Cambric Shirt	Richards Belle Luther	1941

Songs and Tunes—*(continued)*

Title	Performance title	Source *(last name first)*	Date
Emigrant's Farewell	Emigrant's Farewell	Richards Belle Luther	1943
Engineer's Child	Engineer's Child	Dingman Marcia	1987
Englishman's Dream	Englishman's Dream	Luther Sidney	1942
Erin's Green Shore	Erin's Green Shore	Richards Belle Luther	1943
Erin's Lovely Home	Erin's Lovely Home	Robie Alice	1941
Exile of Erin	Exile of Erin	Richards Belle Luther	1943
Exile's Lament	Exile's Lament	Richards Belle Luther	1943
Face on the Barroom Wall	Face on the Barroom Wall	Robie Alice (daughter)	1987
Fair Fanny Moore	Fair Fanny Moore	Luther Sidney	1942
Fallen Leaves	Fallen Leaves	Richards Belle Luther	1943
False Flora	Fields and Green Bushes	Richards Belle Luther	1941
Famed Waterloo	Famed Waterloo	Jackson George A.	1943
Famous Flower of Serving Men	Famous Flower of Serving Men	Richards Belle Luther	1942
Farewell Charming Nancy	Jimmie and Nancy	Luther Sidney	1941
Farewell Dear Rosanna	Rosanna	Richards Belle Luther	1942
Farmer and the Shanty Boy	Farmer and the Shanty Boy	Merrill Orlon	1931
Farnsworth's Camp	Farnsworth's Camp	Hawes L. A.	1942
Fatal Snowstorm	O Cruel Was My Father	Merrill Orlon	1931
Fatal Wedding	Wedding Bells	Hook Bill	1987
Female Warrior	Female Warrior	Richards Belle Luther	1943
Fight On You Bold American Boys	Fight On You Bold American Boys	Richards Belle Luther	1943
Flat River Side	Flat River Side	Shatney Floyd	1987
Flying Cloud	Flying Cloud	Covill Clyde	1987
	Flying Cloud	Danforth Willis (Katherine Fogg)	1987
	Flying Cloud	Washburn Abe	1941
Foot of the Mountain Brow	At the Foot of the Mountain Brow	Covill Clyde	1987
	Maid of the Mountain Brow	Danforth Willis (Katherine Fogg)	1987
	Maid of the Mountain Brow	Richards Belle Luther	1942

Title	Recorded as	Singer	Year
For Twenty-One Years	For Twenty-One Years	Covill Clyde	1987
Former Picture	Former Picture	Luther Sidney	1941
Four Cousins	Four Cousins	Covill Maude	1941
	Four Cousins	Day Edwin	1942
	Four Cousins	Rowell Mrs. (Katherine Fogg)	1987
	Four Cousins	Shallow Lizzie (Katherine Fogg)	1987
Frog and the Mouse	Frog in the Well	Richards Belle Luther	1942
Fuller and Warren	Fuller and Warren	Richards Belle Luther	1942
	Fuller and Warren	Shatney David	1942
	Fuller and Warren	Washburn Abe	1942
	Henry Orrison	Covill Clyde	1987
Gallant Brigantine	Gallant Brigantine	Luther Sidney	1941
	Henry Orrison	Merrill Orlon	1931
	Streets of Derry	Luther Sidney	1941
Gallows	Gallows	Merrill Orlon	1931
	Gallows Tree	Richards Belle Luther	1942
	Gallows Tree	Robie Alice	1941
Garden Hymn	Garden Hymn	Richards Belle Luther	1945
Gay Spanish Maid	Gay Spanish Maid	Merrill Orlon	1931
	Gay Spanish Maid	Reynolds Maynard	1942
	Gay Spanish Maid	Richards Belle Luther	1943
Gentle Laura	Gentle Laura	Richards Belle Luther	1943
Geordie	Life of Geordie	Richards Belle Luther	1943
George Aloe and the Sweepstake	Coast of Barbary	Richards Belle Luther	1942
Go In and Out the Window	Go In and Out the Window	Richards Belle Luther	1941
Golden Slippers	Golden Slippers	Haynes Ardes	1987
Golden Wedding Day	Golden Wedding Day	Dingman Marcia	1987
Gospel Train	Gospel Train	Covill family (Clyde)	1987
	Old Arm Chair	Richards Belle Luther	1943
Grandmother's Old Arm Chair	Grandmother's Old Arm Chair	Dingman Marcia	1987
	Grandmother's Old Arm Chair	Hook family (Haynes)	1987

Songs and Tunes—*(continued)*

Title	Performance title	Source *(last name first)*	Date
Great Speckled Bird	On the Wings of a Great White Bird	Richards Belle Luther	1987
Green Grow the Rushes	Green Grow the Rushes	Luther Sidney	1945
Green Grows the Laurel	Green Grows the Laurel	Richards Belle Luther	1943
Green Mossy Banks of the Lea	Green Mossy Banks of the Lea	Luther Sidney	1942
	Green Mossy Banks of the Lea	Richards Belle Luther	1943
Guy Reed	Guy Reed	Covill Clyde	1987
	Guy Reed	Merrill Orlon	1931
		Richards Belle Luther	1942
Gypsy Laddie	Gypsy Davey	Covill family (Clyde)	1987
Gypsy's Warning	Gypsy's Warning	Rowell Mrs. (Katherine Fogg)	1987
	Gypsy's Warning	Day Edwin	1941
Hebrew Daniel	Hebrew Daniel	Richards Belle Luther	1941
	Hebrew Daniel	Day Edwin	1942
Heights of Alma	Heights of Alma	Merrill Orlon	1931
Henry K Sawyer	Henry K Sawyer	Luther Sidney	1941
High Low Jack and the Game	High Low Jack and the Game	Richards Belle Luther	1942
Highland Chief	Highland Chief	McKeage Robert	1942
Highland Fling	Highland Fling	Richards Belle Luther	1942
Highlands of Eden	Highlands of Eden	Jackson George A.	1943
Hills of Glenshee	Hills of Glenshee	Hawes L. A.	1941
Hoist Up the Flag	Old Civil War Song	Richards Frank	1942
Holly Twig	Old Bachelor	Haynes Ardes	1987
I Brought Back What I Borrowed	I Brought Back What I Borrowed	Richards Belle Luther	1945
I Saw a Weary Pilgrim	I Saw a Weary Pilgrim	Richards Belle Luther	1945
I Was Once Far Away from the Savior	I Was Once Far Away from the Savior	Day family (Katherine Fogg)	1987
If I'm Poor I'm a Gentleman Still	If I'm Poor I'm a Gentleman Still	Robie Alice (daughter)	1987
If Jack Were Only Here	If Jack Were Only Here	Hawes L. A.	1941
I'm Going to Be Married Next Monday Morn	I'm Going to Be Married Next Monday Morn	Luther Sidney	1942
In the Days of '49	Days of '49		

Songs and Tunes—(continued)

Title	Performance title	Source (last name first)	Date
Jam on Gerry's Rock (continued)	Gerry's Rock	Luther Sidney	1943
	Gerry's Rock	Merrill Orlon	1931
	Jam on Gerry's Rock	Richards Belle Luther	1942
	Jam on Gary's Rock	Scott Florence	1987
	Jam on Gerry's Rock	Shatney David	1942
	Jam on Gary's Rocks	Shatney Floyd	1987
James Bird	James Bird	Luther Sidney	1941
James Ervin	James Osgood	Richards Belle Luther	1943
James MacDonald	Young James	Luther Sidney	1941
Janie of the Moor	Janie of the Moor	Richards Belle Luther	1943
Jealous Lover	Fair Florella	Merrill Orlon	1931
Jeanno and Jennette	Jeanno and Jennette	Richards Belle Luther	1943
Jimmie Murphy	Jimmie Murphy	Richards Belle Luther	1943
John Riley I	George Reilly	Hawes L. A.	1941
	George Reilly	Luther Sidney	1941
	George Reilly	Richards Belle Luther	1943
John Ross	John Ross	Richards Belle Luther	1942
	John Ross	Washburn Abe	1942
John Singleton	John Singleton	Richards Belle Luther	1943
	John Singleton	Richards Frank	1943
Johnny German	Johnny German	Robie Alice	1941
Johnny More	Young Johnny More	Luther Sidney	1942
	Young Johnny More	Richards Belle Luther	1943
Johnny the Sailor	Green Bed	Richards Belle Luther	1942
Johnny's a False Young Man	Johnny's a False Young Man	Richards Belle Luther	1943
Jolly Roving Tar	Jolly Roving Tar	Richards Belle Luther	1941
Jordan's Stormy Banks	Jordan's Stormy Banks	Richards Belle Luther	1945
Kate and Her Horns	Kate and Her Horns	Richards Belle Luther	1942

Songs and Tunes—(*continued*)

Title	Performance title	Source (*last name first*)	Date
Little Mohea (*continued*)	Lass of Mohea	Robie Alice	1941
	Little Mohee	Shatney Floyd	1988
Little Musgrave and Lady Barnard	Lord Banner	Covill Clyde	1987
	Lord Banner	Covill Maude	1941
	Lord Banner	Merrill Orlon	1931
Logan's Lament	Logan's Lament	Day Edwin	1942
London Trooper	Trooper	Richards Belle Luther	1942
Londonderry Air	Londonderry Air	Richards Belle Luther (G. Richards)	1987
Lord Lovel	Lord Lovel	Richards Belle Luther	1943
Lord Thomas and Fair Eleanor	Brown Girl	Robie Alice	1942
Lost Jimmie Whalen	Lost Jimmie Whalen	Luther Sidney	1941
	Lost Jimmie Whalen	Richards Belle Luther	1941
Love of God Shave	Lather and Shave	Luther Sidney	1941
Lovely Sally	Lovely Sally	Richards Belle Luther	1942
Lovely Willie	Lovely Jimmy	Covill Clyde	1987
	Lovely Jimmie	Merrill Orlon	1931
Lumberer	Lumberer	Luther Sidney	1941
	Lumberer	Richards Belle Luther	1943
Lumberjack Song	Lumberjack Song	Shatney Floyd	1987
Lumberman's Life	Lumberman's Life	Luther Sidney	1945
Maid Freed from the Gallows	Maid Freed from the Gallows	Merrill Orlon	1931
Maid of Sweet Garthene	Maid of Loggin's Green	Richards Belle Luther	1942
Maid Only Nineteen Years Old	Girl Only Nineteen Years	Old Richards Belle Luther	1942
	Maid Only Nineteen Years Old	Robie Alice	1941
Mantle So Green	Plains of Waterloo	Richards Belle Luther	1942
	Her Mantle of Green	Rowell Mrs. (Katherine Fogg)	1987
Margaret Gray	Margery Grey	Covill family (Clyde)	1987
	Margery Grey	Dingman Marcia	1987

Index entry	Title	Singer	Year
	Margery Grey	Gould Ida	1987
	Margery Grey	Haynes Ardes	1987
	Margery Grey	Hook Bill	1987
	Margaret Gray	Merrill Orlon	1931
	Margaret Grey	Reynolds Maynard	1941
	Margery Grey	Richards Belle Luther (G. Richards)	1987
	Margery Grey	Robie Alice (daughter)	1987
	Margery Grey	Shatney Floyd	1987
Mary Acklin	Mary Ackland	Reynolds Maynard	1942
	Mary Ackland	Richards Belle Luther	1943
Mary Ann	Mary Ann	Richards Belle Luther	1942
Mary of the Wild Moor	Mary of the Wild Moor	Day family (Katherine Fogg)	1987
	Mary of the Wild Moor	Reynolds Maynard	1941
May I Sleep in Your Barn Tonight Mister	May I Sleep in Your Barn Tonight Mister	Richards Belle Luther (G. Richards)	1987
McClellan	McClellan	Richards Belle Luther	1945
Molly Bawn	Shooting of the Swan	Luther Sidney	1941
Molly McCarthy	Molly McCarthy	Jackson George A.	1943
Morrissey and the Russian	Morrissey and the Russian	Richards Belle Luther	1943
Mother Parting with Her Son	Mother Parting with Her Son	Richards Belle Luther	1943
Mother the Queen of My Heart	Mother the Queen of My Heart	Shatney Floyd	1987
Murder of Edward Mathews	Murder of Edward Mathews	Robie Alice	1942
My Bonnie Black Bess II	Bonnie Black Bess	Luther Sidney	1941
	Bonnie Black Bess	Richards Belle Luther	1943
My California Boy	My California Boy	Richards Belle Luther	1943
My Jesus I Love Thee	My Jesus I Love Thee	Richards Belle Luther	1945
My Soul Takes Delight	O Thou in Whose Presence	Richards Belle Luther	1945
Nancy II	Smutty Logger	Luther Sidney	1941
	Gay Gold Chain	Reynolds Maynard	1941
	Smutty Logger	Robie Alice	1941

Songs and Tunes—(continued)

Title	Performance title	Source (last name first)	Date
Napoleon's Song	Napoleon on the Isle of St. Helena	Richards Belle Luther	1942
Napoleon's Song (continued)	Bonaparte	Robie Alice	1941
Needle's Eye	Needle's Eye	Reynolds Maynard	1942
Nell of Naragansett Bay	Nell of Narragansett Bay	Day family (Katherine Fogg)	1987
	Nell of Narragansett Bay	Luther Sidney	1941
Never to Come Back Anymore	Never to Come Back Anymore	Richards Belle Luther	1945
No Irish Wanted Here	No Irish Wanted Here	Richards Belle Luther	1943
No Sir	Spanish Lady	Hawes L. A.	1943
Northwest Carry	Wood's Song	Shatney David	1942
O Come Let Us Sing	O Come Let Us Sing	Richards Belle Luther	1945
Oh Dear What Can the Matter Be	What Can the Matter Be	Richards Belle Luther	1943
Old Bachelor	I Am a Stern Old Bachelor	Deschene Florence S.	1942
Old Black Joe	Old Black Joe	Dingman Marcia	1987
Old Dan Day Song	Old Dan Day Song	Covill family (Clyde)	1987
	Old Dan Day Song	Dingman Marcia	1987
Old Elm Tree	Old Elm Tree	Richards Belle Luther	1943
Old Grey Bonnet	Old Grey Bonnet	Covill family (Clyde)	1987
Old Maid's Complaint	Old Maid's Petition	Deschene Florence S.	1942
Old New Hampshire Home	Old New Hampshire Home	Day family (Katherine Fogg)	1987
	Old New Hampshire Home	Rowell Mrs. (Katherine Fogg)	1987
Old Oak Tree	Old Oak Tree	Covill Maude	1941
	Old Oak Tree	Day Edwin	1942
	Old Oak Tree	Luther Sidney	1941
Old Oaken Bucket	Old Oaken Bucket	Haynes Ardes	1987
Old Rugged Cross	Old Rugged Cross	Dingman Marcia	1987
Old Wooden Rocker	Old Wooden Rocker	Shatney Floyd	1987
On the Chippewa Stream	On the Chippewa Stream	Covill family (Clyde)	1987
On the Green Carpet	On the Green Carpet	Haynes Ardes	1987

Once More A-Lumbering Go	A-Lumbering We Will Go	Luther Sidney	1945
One Pound of Tow	Pound of Tow	Luther Sidney	1941
Paisley Officer	Young Henry Went to Mary	Covill Maude	1941
	In Bonny Scotland	Luther Sidney	1945
	India's Burning Sands	Merrill Orlon	1931
	On India's Burning Sands	Richards Belle Luther	1942
Papa's Letter	Papa's Letter	Haynes Ardes	1987
Paper of Pins	Paper of Pins	Floyd Shatney	1987
Pat O'Brien	Pat O'Brien	Merrill Orlon	1931
	Pat O'Brien	Robie Alice	1941
Patrick Sheehan	Patrick Shayen	Merrill Orlon	1932
	Patrick Shayen	Richards Belle Luther	1943
Paul Jones	Paul Jones	Richards Belle Luther	1942
Pensive Dove	Dove	Richards Belle Luther	1945
Peter Amberley	Peter Anderbell	Day family (Katherine Fogg)	1987
	Peter Anderbell	Hook Bill	1987
	Peter Ambery	Hurlbut Alden	1942
	Peter Emery	Merrill Orlon	1931
	Peter Anderson	Reynolds Maynard	1941
	Peter Emberly	Richards Frank	1942
	Peter Emberly	Washburn Abe	1941
Plain Golden Band	Plain Golden Band	Covill Clyde	1987
	Plain Golden Band	Day Edwin	1941
	Plain Golden Band	Fogg Katherine	1987
	Plain Golden Band	Richards Belle Luther	1941
	Plain Golden Band	Rowell Mrs. (Katherine Fogg)	1987
Plain Quadrille	Plain Quadrille	McKeage Robert	1942
Plains of Waterloo	William Smith	Merrill Orlon	1931
Poor Man	Poor Man	Covill Julia	1941

Title	Performance title	Source (last name first)	Date
Poor Pussy	Poor Pussy	Haynes Ardes	1987
Preacher and the Bear	Preacher and the Bear	Peabody Arthur	1954
Pride of Glencoe	Pride of Glencoe	Richards Belle Luther	1943
Put on Your Old Red Bonnet	Put on Your Old Red Bonnet	Covill Clyde	1987
Put Your Hats On	Put Your Hats On	Haynes Ardes	1987
Queenstown Mourner	Queenstown Mourner	Richards Belle Luther	1942
Red River Valley	Red River Valley	Shatney family (Florence Scott)	1987
Red Wing	Red Wing	Haynes Ardes	1987
Red Wing	Red Wing	Hook Bill	1987
Rich Old Miser	Old Miser	Richards Belle Luther	1942
Rifle Boys	Rifle Boys	Luther Sidney	1941
Riley's Farewell	Reilly the Fisherman	Brown George	1945
	Will Reilly the Fisherman	Luther Sidney	1942
Rinordine	Mountains of Pomeroy	Richards Belle Luther	1942
Ripest Apples	Ripest Apples Soon Will Grow Rotten	Richards Belle Luther	1943
Roaring Cannons	Roaring Cannons	Richards Belle Luther	1945
Robin Hood and the Pedlar	Robin Hood and the Pedlar	Richards Belle Luther	1941
Rock of Ages	Rock of Ages	Shallow Lizzie (Katherine Fogg)	1987
Rock that Is Higher than I	Rock that Is Higher than I	Shallow Lizzie (Katherine Fogg)	1987
Roll On Silver Moon	Roll On Silver Moon	Hillard Marie	1942
Rolling Stone	Wisconsin Emigrant's Song	Washburn Abe	1942
Sailor and the Tailor	Sailor and the Tailor	Dingman Marcia	1987
Sailor Boy	Sailor Boy	Hawes Bert	1942
Sailor's Grave	Sailor's Grave	Richards Belle Luther	1943
Sally Monroe	Sally Monroe	Richards Belle Luther	1942
Saucy Sailor	Saucy Sailor	Covill Maude	1941
Saucy Sailor	Saucy Sailor	Richards Belle Luther	1942
Scolding Wife	Scolding Wife	Day Edwin	1942

Songs and Tunes—(continued)

Title	Performance title	Source (last name first)	Date
Texas Ranger	Texas Ranger	Amey Clark	1942
Texas Ranger (continued)	Texas Ranger	Hawes Fred Mrs.	1941
	Texas Rangers	Luther Sidney	1945
	Texas Rangers	Richards Belle Luther	1943
	Texas Rangers	Washburn Abe	1941
This the End of Our Sinning	This the End of Our Sinning	Richards Belle Luther	1943
Thomas Clifford	Belvidere	Richards Belle Luther	1942
Tragedy of Edward Matthews	Tragedy of Edward Matthews	Robie Alice	1941
Tree in the Wood	Tree in the Wood	Amey Clark	1942
	Tree in the Wood	Hall John	1943
True Lover's Discussion	True Lover's Discussion	Luther Sidney	1941
	Orthodox Lie	Robie Alice	1941
True Story	Tune the Old Cow Died On	Dingman Marcia	1987
Tune the Old Cow Died On	Three Black Crows	Robie Alice	1941
Twa Corbies	Box on Her Head	Day Edwin	1941
Undaunted Female	Box on Her Head	Haynes Ardes	1987
	Box on Her Head	Reynolds Maynard (Hunter)	1987
	Apprentice Girl	Robie Alice	1940s
Van Dieman's Land	Van Dieman's Land	Richards Belle Luther	1942
Wabash Cannonball	Wabash Cannonball	Dingman Marcia	1987
Waltz Me Around Again Willie	Waltz Me Around Again Willie	Dingman Marcia	1987
Wanderers of Maine	Wanderers of Maine	Smith Ruby M.	1987
Way Down on Dixie's Isle	Way Down on Dixie's Isle	Richards Belle Luther	1942
Way Up in Old Vermont	Way Up in Old Vermont	Robie Alice	1941
We Are Coming Sister Mary	We Are Coming Sister Mary	Comstock Mrs.	1941
	We Are Coming Sister Mary	Richards Belle Luther	1943
	Banks of Albany	Luther Sidney	1942
Wexford Girl	On the Banks of Albany	Richards Belle Luther	1942

Songs and Tunes—(continued)

Title	Performance title	Source (last name first)	Date
Willie the Sailor Boy	Willie the Sailor Boy	Reynolds Maynard	1941
Willie's on the Dark Blue Sea	Willie's on the Dark Blue Sea	Richards Belle Luther	1943
Woman Is So Enticing	Woman Is So Enticing	Richards Belle Luther	1943
Woodsman's Alphabet	Lumberman's Alphabet	Dingman Marcia	1987
	Woodsman's Alphabet	Merrill Orlon	1931
	Woodsman's Alphabet	Richards Belle Luther	1943
	A Is the Axe to Cut Down the Pine	Robie Alice	1941
	Woodsman's Alphabet Song	Scott Florence	1987
	Lumberman's Alphabet	Shatney Floyd	1987
Young Albion	Young Albion	Robie Alice	1941
Young Beichan	Lord Bateman	Covill family (Clyde)	1987
	Lord Bateman	Merrill Orlon	1931
	Lord Bakeman	Richards Belle Luther	1943
	Lord Bateman	Covill Maude	1941
Young Charlotte	Young Sharlotte	Dingman Marcia	1987
	Young Charlotte	Merrill Orlon	1931
	Young Charlotte	Robie Alice (Fogg)	1987
	Young Charlotte	Rowell Mrs. (Katherine Fogg)	1987
	Young Charlotte	Shallow Lizzie (Katherine Fogg)	1987
	Young Charlotte	Smith Ruby M.	1957
Young Man Who Couldn't Hoe Corn	Young Man Who Couldn't Hoe Corn	Richards Belle Luther	1942
Young Strongbow	Young Strongbow	Day family (Katherine Fogg)	1987
	Young Strongbow	Merrill Orlon	1932
	Young Strongbow	Richards Belle Luther	1941

CHAPTER 8

Conclusion: Landscape and Memory

*A*t a fiddlers' contest held on farmland in rural northern New Hampshire during the summer of 2002, the performance platform was draped with American flags. The event began with the raising of the American, New Hampshire, and town (150 residents) flags, accompanied by a lone fiddler's rendition of the "Star-Spangled Banner." Following the Pledge of Allegiance, the gathered group of several hundred sang other patriotic songs. The contemporary political climate and the nationalism that pervaded the first fifteen minutes of the event contrasted sharply with participants' apparent concern during the competition itself that they maintain a level of historical and regional accuracy in repertoire and playing style connected especially to northern New England. In order to participate, fiddlers agreed to play only tunes derived from an Anglo-American repertoire that, while identified as ranging from the Canadian Maritimes to the South, focused clearly upon old-time New England, Down East or Maritime, and Franco-American performance practices—those styles that have characterized northern New England playing for over one hundred years.[1] The struggle between the personal, political, and economic pull of national and global influences and the desire to maintain or revive a local or regional form had a significant impact on musicians' and listeners' aesthetic (and economic) concerns.

We find a related pattern in the contemporary singing traditions in the region. While most of the ballads and popular songs that were commonly found in the late nineteenth and early twentieth centuries are no longer actively performed in families and neighborhoods, as noted in chapter 1, they are occasionally heard in historical concerts and revival traditions that have adapted and adopted the early practices. Using Anglo-American frameworks, and strategies that involve reconstruction, parody, and new creation, contemporary singer-songwriters from Vermont, New Hampshire, and Maine navigate local and regional, as well as national and international, styles and expressions to generate voices that maintain at least some connection to the northern New England landscape. They are both consciously and unconsciously involved in continuing social and musical traditions that they learned in their families, in song and tune books, or through the media. For some, there is a deliberate effort to maintain or revive selected aspects of a tradition that they believe ended during the first few decades of the twentieth century.[2] At the same time, many are reaching out to a national and global audience that has been deeply affected by the music industry in recent decades.

The revival and reconstruction of instrumental and vocal musics in northern New England (as well as other regions of the United States) has generated new and modified forms of expression. The process of revival is connected to identity that for some remains rooted in the geographic sphere, and a musical landscape that contains carefully selected elements of the past: dance tunes, playing style, song forms, and generalized subject matter. What performers and historians are not always willing to accept is that the concern for reviving sounds, practices, lyrics, and values—and for maintaining a sense of place in historical context—is not that different from the energy and values that drove the growth and development of music in the region in the period between 1870 and 1940. The social and musical practices and the aesthetic concerns of the late nineteenth and early twentieth centuries are the result of individual and community responses to local, regional, and national influences.

Some of the outward social characteristics in the northern New England communities have changed—the towns and neighborhoods, both physically and socially, seem very different places to its older residents. During the period of intense song collecting in Maine, New Hampshire, and Vermont from 1920 to 1960, the songs and tunes gathered by Flanders, Olney, Barry, Eckstorm, Linscott, and others were identified with an "older" way of life; some designated the music as "endangered" and saw their role as preservers of a tradition. During the last two decades of the twentieth century, most of my interviews were with older residents in their seventies and eighties; many expressed discomfort with the multitude of social and geographic changes that had taken place since the 1940s. When I asked them to remember traditions of the past, they often focused on its recent transformation. They complained about changes in musical style, tempo, and other aspects of performance practice while glorifying the sounds and memories of the past. I asked an older couple in central Vermont about dance traditions when they were young, and they immediately began to talk about the "old fashioned" dances, contrasting them with dancing today: "I think that people today don't know enough to dance by the music. And they don't dance with the music. You get 'em on the floor for a waltz and they'll go around there and knock you over and everything else. When I learned to waltz you could carry a dish on your head."[3]

The older singing traditions today for the elderly residents serve as sources for remembering the "old times." On several occasions I asked Clyde Covill about the widely known song "The House Carpenter" ("The Daemon Lover"), a song about a love triangle that involved a sailor, or the devil, depending on how you "read" the tale. A popular ballad in many households in North America, I knew that Clyde's uncle and mother used to sing it. Each time I asked him about the song, he responded with isolated verses that he struggled to connect together. Two verses connected to loss seemed to emerge most readily from his memory, especially the verse in which the woman realizes that she has lost a way of life by leaving her home and family. Clyde said to me on one occasion: "She was sorrowing, you know. Crying, I suppose." After singing a verse or two, there was a long pause, then he sang:

The House Carpenter

Clyde Covill, W. Stewartstown, N.H., 1987

Oh it's nei - ther for your gold that I weep; It's nei - ther for your store. It's

all for the sake of that dar-ling lit - tle babe, Which I ne - ver shall see a - ny more.

And she wept most bitterly.

Oh it's neither for your gold that I weep
It's neither for your store
It's all for the sake of that darling little babe
Which I never shall see any more.

I used to like to hear them old timers sing. Oh, they could sing it so nice. It almost brings tears to my eyes, because I used to like the whole [lot] of 'em . . . Oh, if I get into it a little or something on some of those old songs like that. But I've got nobody to back me up now. I used to have Father and Mother. 'Cause they both knew all them old songs. And Will Danforth, Willis Danforth, he knew all them old songs . . . Will were a good singer. And he sung loud. [Laughs.] I mean quite loud, you know.[4]

Clyde looked to the "old-timers," as he called them, for entertainment and to maintain the practices of a musical tradition that his family and community valued. Most importantly, he recognized that it was their social network, where singing was enjoyed, that enabled the continuation of the tradition for so long. Clyde connected its absence with the "breakdown" of the communal practice.

What Clyde refers to, of course, is loss—and in many ways it is loss that performers dwell on and draw on to frame their new forms of expression in each generation. In northern New England, what has been lost are the specific songs and tunes built using familiar formulaic patterns, but also an environment that includes the musicians and their families: the landscape and the community that is concerned with economic health, social and spiritual wellbeing, personal expression, and creative opportunity. The process of remembering, constructing, and reconstructing was part of the tradition. It was motivated by the settlers that moved in and brought ideas from other locations and families, community members who built music on their memory of a tradition, relatives that moved away and came back with new songs or tunes, collectors that sought specific styles and reinforced their role in the community for a brief time, or even the media and the music industry that have framed and frozen ideas for the residents since the late nineteenth century.

Traditions in dance music and song today demonstrate both continuity and change in repertoire, performance style, and social practice. When we seek to trace a continuous tradition from the historical practices of the nineteenth and early twentieth centuries to contemporary performances we observe in the region, we find that the path is indirect. Like the indirect reflection of the physical and social landscape we found in the song repertoires of the nineteenth and early twentieth centuries, performers and listeners have imagined their historical traditions in relation to a number of factors from both inside and outside the local culture (including commercial and scholarly intrusion). The revivalism that has been put into play connects to the older traditions, sometimes obliquely: singers find themselves performing using aesthetic values connected to the old traditions, but they have reached this place through the mainstream music sphere, rather than through consciously imitating the music of their forebears (as they, and the scholarly community, perceived their relatives did).

Scholars use historical data—primary and secondary sources—to inform their understanding of the place of music in social and historical context. The historical data helps to reconstruct community traditions. At the same time, members of the communities themselves are involved in a process of revival and reconstruction that is informed by personal experience, community memory (lore), and scholarly and commercial contributions, often from people outside the community. For a full understanding of northern New England music, consideration of the collaborative role of the individual and the community, as well as the performer and her supporters, is essential. Also significant are the roles of collectors, publications, the recording industry, festival organizers, and the tourist industry in framing local, regional, and national knowledge about and appreciation for their practices. There are times—because of the influence of these external elements—that the music of northern New England sounds and looks like many other rural regions in the United States. But the turn of phrase, the musical repertoire and playing style, the specific references to place as it relates to musical pieces and events, and the land itself that feeds the cultural, social, and economic character of the region all reinforce the importance of continuing to identify this specific place—for the historian, but especially for the residents and their kin, whose memories of the landscape have played a significant role in their cultural expression.

In Springfield, Vermont, I spoke with a woman about music in her family and community during the early years of the twentieth century. At first I struggled to get her to remember the songs and dance tunes; she had difficulty isolating specific musical activities and identifying performers and performances. During her reflection on this, she recognized the integrated role that music played in everyday life, and showed that music was at the heart of the wellbeing of her family and community:

> I guess it just was part of living. And people used to entertain themselves so much more than they do now. And evenings were taken up with singing, and card playing, and parties. The neighborhood where I was brought up, my husband and I bought the farm with my father. We used to have kitchen dances through the winter and such times and there was a girl about my age that played the organ, and her father played the violin, and we used to have such good times dancing; my father and mother, my brothers.[5]

Appendix

Music in Rural New England Family and Community Life, 1870–1940

The songs and tunes that were popular in rural northern communities were drawn from a wide repertoire of music that residents accessed in different social spaces. They were shared in families and extended households, neighborhoods, and villages or towns. The contexts for songs ranged from the kitchen, where mothers sang to their children, to parlors, where songs were shared by families and close neighbors, to local grange halls and town halls, where communities gathered for meetings that were sometimes followed by musical events. Singers were not concerned about song categories but enjoyed the entertainment that the songs and their stories provided. Dances also took place in homes and community buildings, and they—along with the songs—served an important function in providing regular social networking among family and friends.

The following is a representative selection of songs and tunes drawn from the repertoires of northern New England residents between 1870 and 1940; many are referred to in the preceding text. The songs and tunes are drawn primarily from the Helen Hartness Flanders Collection, recorded between 1930 and 1965, and field recordings made in New Hampshire and Vermont during the 1970s, 1980s, and early 1990s that document traditions dating to before the middle of the twentieth century.

1. "Arise My Soul Arise," Lena Bourne Fish, East Jaffrey, New Hampshire
2. "The Backwoodsman," Judson Carver, West Jonesport, Maine
3. "The Bower" ("Bower of Prayer"), Belle Luther Richards, Colebrook, New Hampshire
4. "Cabbage and Meat" ("The Half Hitch"), Marjorie Pierce, North Shrewsbury, Vermont
5. "Charming Mohee" ("The Lass of Mohea"), Alonzo Lewis, York, Maine
6. "The Chipperwash Stream" ("The Chippewa Girl"), Maude Covill, Pittsburg, New Hampshire
7. "Durang's Hornpipe," Bill Wilson, Pike, New Hampshire
8. "The Female Smuggler," Charles Finnemore, Bridgewater, Maine
9. "The Flying Cloud," Jack McNally, Stacyville, Maine
10. "The Garden Hymn, "Belle Luther Richards, Colebrook and Pittsburg, New Hampshire
11. "The Girl I Left Behind Me," Mellie Dunham, Norway, Maine
12. "Guy Reed," Charles Finnemore, Bridgewater, Maine
13. "I'm Sitting on the Stile Mary," ("Lament of the Irish Emigrant"), Clyde Covill, West Stewartstown, New Hampshire
14. "In the Garden" (fiddle tune), Clyde Covill, Pittsburgh, New Hampshire
15. "The Jolly Sailor," ("The Sailor and the Tailor"), George A. Jackson, Columbia, New Hampshire
16. "Jones' Paring Bee," Walter Titus, Johnson, Vermont

17. "Josie Langmaid," Josiah Kennison, Bennington, Vermont
18. "Lord Banner," Clyde Covill, Pittsburg, New Hampshire
19. "Margaret Gray," Maynard Reynolds, Pittsburg, New Hampshire
20. "Money Musk," S. Daily ms., Pittsburg, New Hampshire
21. "The Old Maid and the Burglar," Flora Campbell, Stark, New Hampshire
22. "The Orphan Children," Marjorie Pierce, North Shrewsbury, Vermont
23. "Paper of Pins," Floyd and Bea Shatney, Groveton, New Hampshire
24. "Peter Emberley," Mrs. W. H. Smith, Houlton, Maine
25. "Petronella," Mr. Allen, Reading, Vermont
26. "Portland Fancy," Luther Weeks, Springfield, Vermont, and Harry Stark, Cornwall, Vermont
27. "Sir James the Rose," Hanford Hayes, Staceyville, Maine
28. "There's No One to Welcome Me Home," Elmer George, East Calais, Vermont
29. "The Tod and the Sow," Murchie Harvey, Houlton, Maine
30. "Woodmen's Song" ("Lumberman's Alphabet"), Edward Dragon, Ripton, Vermont

1.

Arise My Soul Arise

Lena Bourne Fish, E. Jaffrey, N.H., 1945

Arise my soul, arise, shake off my guilty fears.
The bleeding sacrifice in my behalf appears.
Before His throne my Savior stands.
My name is written on His hands;
My name is written on His hands.

He ever lives above, for me to intercede;
His all-redeeming love, His precious blood to plead.
His blood atoned for all our race,
And sprinkles now the throne of grace;
And sprinkles now the throne of grace.

Five bleeding wounds he bears, received on Calvary.
They pour effectual prayers and strongly plead for me.
"Forgive him, oh forgive," they cry.
"Nor let that ransomed sinner die."
"Nor let that ransomed sinner die."

My God is reconciled, His pardoning voice I hear.
He owns me for His child, I can no longer fear.
With confidence I now draw night,
And "Father Abba, Father," cry.
And "Father Abba, Father," cry.

"Arise My Soul Arise," sung by Lena Bourne Fish of East Jaffrey, New Hampshire, was recorded by Marguerite Olney on September 13, 1945. Lena Bourne Fish said about the hymn: "Used to hear my people sing it and used to hear it sung in church."

2.

The Backwoodsman

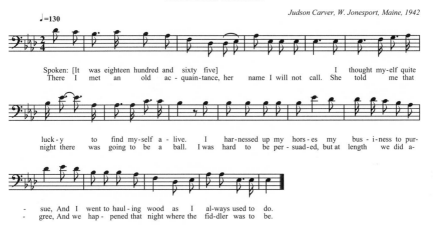

Judson Carver, W. Jonesport, Maine, 1942

It was eighteen hundred and sixty-five
I thought myself quite lucky to find myself alive.
I harnessed up my horses, my business to pursue,
And I went to hauling wood as I always used to do.

There I met an old acquaintance, her name I will not call.
She told me that night there was going to be a ball.
I was hard to be persuaded, but at length we did agree,
And we happened that night where the fiddler was to be.

There were four and twenty of us got on the floor to dance,
Twelve of them was pretty girls as could be picked in France.
The fiddler being willing and his arm being stout and strong,
Played "The Grounds of Old Ireland" for four hours long.

Now the day star has risen, boys, we've all danced enough.
Let's take a half an hour in gathering cash for cuff.
We'll go home to our plow, boys, we'll fiddle and we'll sing,
But I never will be caught in such a darn scrape again.

Now, come all of ye old women who tell the news about;
You needn't go to lying, for it's bad enough without.
Come all you old women who was kicking up a fuss;
You have done the likes before, only a darn sight worse.

"The Backwoodsman" (Laws C19), sung by Judson Carver of West Jonesport, Maine, was recorded by Marguerite Olney on August 20, 1942. This song was also known as "The Green Mountain Boys" and was recorded in New Hampshire by Jonathan Moses, Orford (1939), and in Vermont by Paul Lorette, Manchester Center (1930); Elmer George, North Montpelier (1935); Josiah Kennison, Townsend (1939); and Asa Davis, Milton (1939).

3.

The Bower

Belle Richards, Colebrook, N.H., 1945

To leave my dear friends, and with neighbors to part,
And go from my home, it affects not my heart,
Like the thought of absenting myself for a day
From that blest retreat where I've chosen to pray,
Where I've chosen to pray.

It was under the shadows of that pleasant grove
That Jesus my Savior, my guilt did remove.
Presenting Himself as the only true way
Of life and salvation and taught me to pray,
And taught me to pray.

How sweet were the zephyrs perfumed with the pine,
The ivy, the balsam, and sweet eglantine;
But sweeter, far sweeter, superlative were
The joys that I tasted in answer to prayer,
In answer to prayer.

The early shrill notes of a loved nightingale
That dwelt in my bower, I observed as my bell,
To call me to duty, while birds in the air
Sing anthems of praises while I went to prayer,
While I went to prayer.

For Jesus, my Savior, oft deigns me to meet,
And blessed with His presence my humble retreat
Oft filled me with rapture and blessedness there,
Inditing, in heaven's own language, my prayer,
Own language my prayer.

Dear bower, I must leave thee and bid thee adieu,
And pay my devotions in parts that are new,
Well knowing my Savior resides everywhere,
And will all places give answer to prayer,
Give answer to prayer.

"The Bower" ("The Bower of Prayer"), sung by Belle Luther Richards of Colebrook and Pittsburg, New Hampshire, was recorded by Marguerite Olney on September 24, 1945.

4.

Cabbage and Meat

A noble lord in Plymouth did dwell
He had a fine daughter, a beautiful gal
A young man of fortune, and riches supplied
He courted this fair maid to make her his bride
To make her his bride
He courted this fair maid to make her his bride

Appendix

He courted her long and he gained her love
At length this fair maiden intend him to prove
From the time that she owned him, she fairly denied
She told him right off, she'd not be his bride
She'd not be his bride
She told him right off, she'd not be his bride

Then he said, "Straight home I will steer,"
And many an oath under her he did swear
He swore he would wed the first woman he see
If she was as mean as a beggar could be
As a beggar could be
If she was as mean as a beggar could be

She ordered her servants this man to delay
Her rings and her jewels she soon laid away
She dressed herself in the worst rags she could find
She looked like the devil before and behind
Before and behind
She looked like the devil before and behind.

She clapped her hands on the chimney back
She crocked her face all over so black
Then down the road she flew like a witch
With her petticoats heisted upon the half hitch
Upon the half hitch
With her petticoats heisted upon the half hitch

Soon this young man come riding along
She stumbled before him she scarcely could stand
With her old shoes on her feet all tread off askew
He soon overtook her and said, "Who be you?"
And said, "Who be you?"
He soon overtook her and said, "Who be you?"

(Spoken.) "I'm a woman, I s'pose."

This answer grieved him much to the heart
He wished from his very life he might part
Then he wished that he had been buried
And then he did ask her and if she was married
And if she was married
And then he did ask her and if she was married

(Spoken.) "No, I ain't."

This answer suited him much like the rest
It lay very heavy and hard on his breast
He found by his oath he must make her his bride
And then he did ask her behind him to ride
Behind him to ride
And then he did ask her behind him to ride

Appendix

(Spoken.) "Your horse'll throw me, I know he will."

"O no, O no, my horse he will not."
So on behind him a-straddle she got
His heart it did fail him. He dare not go home
For his parents would say, "I'm surely undone.
I'm surely undone."
For his parents would say, "I'm surely undone."

So to a neighbor with whom he was great
The truth of the story he dared to relate
He said, "Here with my neighbor you may tarry
And in a few days, with you I will marry
With you I will marry
And in a few days, with you I will marry."

(Spoken.) "You won't, I know you won't."

He vowed that he would and straight home he did go
He acquainted his father and mother also
Of what had befallen him, how he had sworn
His parents said to him, "For that don't you mourn.
For that don't you mourn."
His parents said to him, "For that don't you mourn."

"Don't break your vows but bring home your girl
We'll fix her up, and she'll do very well."
The day was appointed, they invited the guests
And then they intended the bride for to dress
The bride for to dress
And then they intended the bride for to dress

(Spoken.) "Be married in my old clothes, I s'pose."

Married they were and sat down to eat
With her hands she clawed out the cabbage and meat
The pudding it burned her fingers so bad
She licked 'em, she wiped 'em along on her rags
Along on her rags
She licked 'em, she wiped 'em along on her rags.

Hotter than ever, she at it again
Soon they did laugh 'til their sides were in pain
Soon they did say, "My jewel, my bride
Come sit yourself down by your true lover's side
By your true lover's side
Come sit yourself down by your true lover's side."

(Spoken.) "Sit in the corner, I s'pose, where I used to."

Some were glad and very much pleased
Others were sorry and very much grieved
They asked them to bed the truth to decide

Appendix

And then they invited both bridegroom and bride
Both bridegroom and bride
And then they invited both bridegroom and bride

(Spoken.) "Give me a light and I'll go alone."

They gave her a light, what could she want more
And showed her the way up to the chamber door

(Spoken.) "Husband, when you hear my old shoe go 'klonk'
    then you may come."

Up in the chamber she went klonking about
His parents said to him, "What you think she's about?"
"O mother, O mother, say not one word
Not one bit of comfort to me this world can afford.
This world can afford.
Not one bit of comfort to me this world can afford."

At length they heard her old shoe go klonk
They gave him a light and bade him go along
"I choose to go in the dark," he said,
"For I very well know the way to my bed.
The way to my bed.
For I very well know the way to my bed."

He jumped into bed, his back to his bride
She rolled and she tumbled from side unto side
She rolled and she tumbled, the bed it did squeak
He said unto her, "Why can't you lie still?"
Why can't you lie still?"
And he said unto her, "Why can't you lie still?"

(Spoken.) "I want a light to unpin my clothes."

He ordered a light her clothes to unpin
Behold she was dressed in the finest of things
When he turned over her face to behold
It was fairer to him than silver or gold
Than silver or gold
It was fairer to him than silver or gold

Up they got and a frolic they had
Many a heart it was merry and glad
They looked like two flowers just springing from bloom
With many fair lasses who wished them much joy.
Who wished them much joy.
With many fair lasses who wished them much joy.

"Cabbage and Meat," more commonly known as "The Half Hitch" (Laws N 23), was sung by Marjorie Pierce in North Shrewsbury, Vermont. It was recorded by the author in a 1986 interview. Helen Hartness Flanders also recorded Marjorie Pierce's mother singing this song in 1932 and 1943, and she published a transcription of these performances in her 1953 publication *Ballads Migrant in New England* (New York: Farrar, Straus, and Young).

Charming Mohee

Alonzo Lewis, York, Maine, 1947

As I went out walk-ing one morn-ing in May, In sweet re - cre - a - tion to while time a - way, As I sat a -mus -ing my - self on the grass, But who should I spy but this fair In - dian lass.

As I went out walking one morning in May,
In sweet recreation to while time away,
As I sat amusing myself on the grass,
But who should I spy but this fair Indian lass.

She came along beside me, and taking my hand
Saying, "You are a stranger and in a strange land,
And if you will follow, you're welcome to come
And dwell in my cottage that I call my home."

O the sun was fast sinking far o'er the blue sea
As I wandered alone with my charming Mohee
Together we wandered, together did roam
Till we come to her cot in the cocoanut grove.

Then this kind expression she made unto me:
"If you will consent, sir, to stay here with me
And go no more roaming upon the salt sea,
I'll teach you the language of the lass of Mohee."

Said I, "My pretty fair one, that never can be
For I have a sweetheart in my own coun-ter-ee,
And I'll not forsake her for I know she loves me
And her heart is as true as the charming Mohee."

It was early one morning, one morning in May,
I to my pretty fair one those words I did say:
"It is now I must leave you, so farewell my dear,
My ship sails are spreading and home I must steer."

O the last time I saw her she stood on the Strand
And when my boat passed her, she waved me her hand
Saying, "When you have landed to the girl that you love,
Think of charming Mohee in the cocoanut grove."

But when I had landed on my own native shore
My friends and relations gather 'round me once more,

Appendix

I gazed all around me, not one could I see
That is fit to compare with my charming Mohee.

And the girl that I trusted proved untrue to me
I'll turn my course backward across the blue sea
I'll turn my course backward, from this land I'll flee
Spend the rest of my days with my charming Mohee.

"The Charming Mohee" or "The Charming Lass of Mohee" ("The Little Mohee"); (Laws H8), sung by Mr. Alonzo Lewis of York, Maine, was recorded by Marguerite Olney on September 22, 1947. Known throughout the northern New England region, this song was recorded in Vermont by E. C. Green, Springfield (1931); Josiah Kennison, Townsend (1932); Elmer George (1938); Myra Daniels (1939); Ida Coburn, Waterville (1942); Asa Davis, Milton (1943); William Thompson, Canaan (1943); Walter Titus, Johnson (1954); Ellen Hoadley, Johnson (1954); and Merritt Earl, Eden (1958); in New Hampshire by Maynard Reynolds, Pittsburg (1942); Lena Bourne Fish (1943); Florence Scott, Pittsburg (1987); Floyd Shatney, W. Stewartstown (1987); Clyde Covill, Pittsburg (1987); and Flora Campbell, Stark (1988); and in Maine by Chandler Moore, Bingham (1905; see Eckstorm 1927: 230–32); Perley Quigg, Island Falls (1940); Mrs. W. H. Smith, Houlton (1940); Eugene Leech, Surry (1942); Jack McNally, Stacyville (1942); and Oliver Jenness, York (1947).

6.

Chipperwash Stream

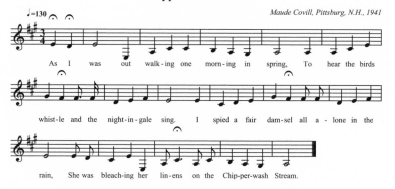

As I was out walking one morning in spring,
To hear the birds whistle and the nightingale sing.
I spied a fair damsel all alone in the rain,
She was bleaching her linens on the Chipperwash Stream.

I walked up to her and made a low bow
And what I said to her I will tell you now.
"For six months and better my mind's been on thee,
Let's go and get married, that's if you will agree."

"To marry, to marry, I'm afraid I'm too young
Besides all you young men have a false flattering tongue.
My daddy and mummy quite angry would be,
If I were to marry to a rover like thee."

I turned away from her, knowing well what to say.
"I wish you a good man, whoe'er he may be.
The day it is cloudy and I think it will rain."
We shook hands and then parted on the Chipperwash Stream.

"Come back, love, come back, love, you have quite won my heart.
Here is my right hand that we never shall part.
No we never shall part, love, 'til the day that we die.
We will always live happy on the brig, you and I."

"Since the last words you've spoken, you are quite out of time;
Since the last words you've spoken, I have changed my mind.
I think it far better, single to remain.
You go wed some other on the Chipperwash Stream."

Some marry for riches, get a bold saucy maid.
Some marry for beauty—a thing that soon fades.
But if ever I marry, 'til the day that I die,
The girl that proves constant is the darling for I.

"Chipperwash Stream," known also as "Chippewa Stream" or "Chippewa Girl," was sung by
Maude Covill of Pittsburg, New Hampshire. It was recorded by Marguerite Olney on September 5, 1941. A nearly identical version was remembered by Andrew Hawes, another Pittsburg resident, in 1941. In 1988, Flora Campbell, a North Country resident who grew up in
the region, sang a fragment of this song using the "Chickelord Stream" melody.

Chickelord Stream

Flora Campbell, Stark, N.H., 1987

Oh as I was out a-walk-ing one morn-ing in Spring To hear the birds whis-tle and the night-en-gale sing; I spied a pret-ty fair maid all dressed up in green She was wash-ing her gar-ments in the Chick-e-lord Stream.

Durang's Hornpipe

Bill Wilson, Pike, N.H., 1942

"Durang's Hornpipe," played by Bill Wilson, was recorded on July 17, 1942, in Pike, New Hampshire, by Marguerite Olney for the Helen Hartness Flanders Ballad Collection. This tune was also recorded in Dorset (1930), Quechee (1940), and Lincoln (1985), Vermont, and in Rockland and Addison, Maine (1940s).

8.

The Female Smuggler

Charles Finnemore, Bridgewater, Maine, 1941

Come listen awhile and you soon shall hear,
By the raging seas lived a maiden fair;
Her father followed a smuggling trade
Like a war-like hero, like a war-like hero,
That never was afraid.

In seamen's clothing young Jane did go,
Just like a sailor from top to toe,
In her belt two daggers prepared for war,
Went the female smuggler, went the female smuggler
That never feared a scar.

She had not sailed far from the land
When death's dark sail put her to a stand,
"Those saucy pirates," young Jane did cry,
Said the female smuggler sayed the female smuggler,
"We'll conquer, boys, or die."

Then close alongside those two vessels came
"Cheer up," said Jane, "Boys, we'll board the same,
We'll take our chances to rise or fall,"
Said the female smuggler, said the female smuggler,
"I never feared a ball."

We beat those pirates and took their store
And soon returned to Old England's shore;
Like a gay young dandy she marched along,
This young female smuggler, this young female smuggler
And sweetly sung a song.

She had not traveled far on the shore
Till she was met by the Commodore
"Stand and deliver or you shall fall."
But the female smuggler, but the female smuggler
Said "I never feared a ball."

"What do you mean," said the Commodore.
"I mean to fight for my father's poor,"
She drew a dagger and ran him through.
This young female smuggler, this young female smuggler.
Then to her father flew.

But she was followed by the blockade,
In iron strong they put this fair maid;
The day that she was to be tried,
This young female smuggler, this young female smuggler
Was dressed like a bride.

The Commodore against her did appear,
His health restored and from danger cleared
And when he saw to his great surprise
It was a female smuggler, it was a female smuggler
That fought him in disguise.

The Commodore to the jury said
"My heart won't let me persecute this maid
Pardon, I ask on my bended knee;
She's a valiant maiden, she is a valiant maiden
So pardon if you please.

"Why do you pardon?" said a gentleman,
"To make her my bride now it is my plan
And I'll live happy forevermore
With my female smuggler, with my female smuggler,"
Then said the Commodore.

"The Female Smuggler," sung by Charles Finnemore of Bridgewater, Maine, was recorded by Marguerite Olney on September 30, 1941.

9.

The Flying Cloud

My name is Edward Holland, as you may understand.
I belong to the county Watersford, in Erin's happy land.
When I was young and in my prime beauty did on me smile.
My parents doted on me, I being their only child.

My father bound me to a trade, in Waterford's old town.
He bound me to a cooper there by the name of William Brown.
I served my master faithfully for eighteen months or more,
'Til I shipped on board of the *Ocean Queen* bound for Bermuda's shore.

I wasn't long in that fine town 'til I met with Captain More.
Commander of the *Flying Cloud,* a native of Trymore.
He kindly saluted me and asked me if I'd go
On a slavage voyage to Africa where the sugar cane does grow.

I gave consent to go with him and we sailed off the next day.
With eighteen hundred of those blacks from their native isles we bore.
With eighteen hundred of those blacks we sailed off the next day
And it would been better for those poor souls, they were dead and in their grave,
For the fever and plague it came on board and swept one half away.
We dragged the dead bodies on deck and threw them in the sea.

And in a short time after we reached Bermuda shore.
We sold them to the planters there to be slaves forevermore.
For to haul the tea and cotton fields beneath the burning sun,
For to lead a poor and wretched life, till their career was done.

And when our money it was all gone, we went to sea again.
And Captain Morse he come on deck and said to all his men,
"There is gold and plenty to be had if you will come with me,
We'll rise a lofty pirate flag, and scour the Spanish sea."

We all agreed but five young men, we ordered them to land.
Two of them they were Boston boys, two more from Newfoundland.
The other was an Irishman belonging to Trymore,
And I wish to God I'd joined those men and stayed with them on shore.

We robbed and plundered many a ship down on the Spanish Main.
We caused many a widow and orphan child in sorrow to remain.
We caused their men to walk the plank, we gave them a watery grave,
It was a saying the captain had: "The dead man tells no tales."

Now chased we were by many a ship, by the liners and frigates, too.
They fired their hot shells *[hanchans]* after us, the cannons roared so loud.
But all in vain, none on the Main could catch a *Flying Cloud*.

'Til the British Man of War sailed out, her dungeon hove in view.
She fired a shot acrost our bow, a signal to heave to.
We paid her back no answer but flew before the wind.
When a chain ball cut our main mast up and soon we fell behind.

Then we cleared our decks for action as they ranged up long-side.
And soon acrost our quarter-deck there flowed a crimson tide.
We fought till Captain Morse was slain and eighty of his men,
When a bombshell shot our ship on fire, we were forced to surrender then.

Then I was quickly taken, bound down in iron chains.
For robbing and plundering merchant ships down on the Spanish Main.
It was strong drink and bad company that made a wretch of me,
So all young men a-warning take and shun bad company.

So fare you well you green shady bowers and the girl I left behind.
Whose voice like music to my ears did ringing in my mind.
Whose voice like music to my ears I ne'er shall see no more.
I shall never press her ruby lips or squeeze her lily white hand.
But I must die a scornful death in a strange and foreign land.

"The Flying Cloud," sung by Jack McNally of Stacyville, Maine, was recorded by Marguerite Olney on August 28, 1942. This song, popular in the woods, was also sung in Maine by Jerry Desmond, Island Falls (1940); Dale Potter, Kingman (1940); and Asa Brown, Carthage (1938); in New Hampshire by Abe Washburn, Pittsburg (1941); and Lena Bourne Fish, East Jaffrey (1940); and in Vermont by O. G. Sparks, Weston.

The Garden Hymn

Belle Richards, Colebrook, N.H., 1945

The Lord into his garden came,
The spices yield a rich perfume,
The lilies grow and thrive,
The lilies grow and thrive.

We make the dry and barren ground
Bring springs of water to abound,
And fruitful soil become,
And fruitful soil become.

Refreshing showers of grace divine
When Jesus dies to every vine
And makes the world His own,
And makes the world His own.

The desert blossom's like the rose,
When Jesus conquers all His foes,
And bids the world rejoice,
And bids the world rejoice.

"The Garden Hymn," sung by Belle Luther Richards of Colebrook and Pittsburg, New Hampshire, was recorded by Marguerite Olney on September 23, 1945. Belle Richards introduced it as "a hymn my father used to sing."

The Girl I Left Behind Me

Mellie Dunham, Norway, Maine, 1926

"The Girl I Left Behind Me" was published by Mellie Dunham's 1928 collection, *Fiddlin' Dance Tunes Composed, Selected, and Played by Mellie Dunham, Maine's Champion Fiddler* (New York: Carl Fisher). This tune was also recorded in Maine in the towns of Rockland (1941), Surry (1942), and Searsport (1946); in Vermont in Chelsea (1939), Vershire (1942), Benson (1985), and Warren (1985); and in New Hampshire in Cornish (1942).

12.

Guy Reed

Charles Finnemore, Bridgewater, Maine, 1942

How well do I remember that dark and stormy night
The rain it fell in torrents, the lightning flashed so bright.
The star and moon above me could not their light reveal
For the dark clouds so gloomy did their welcome light reveal.

The post brought me a letter, I hastened to pursue.
'Twas written by a friend of mine, that brought me startling news,
For well I knew a fine young man, as ever you did see,
Who in one instant had been hurled into Eternity.

Appendix

This young man and his companions where the waters they do roam
Were breaking in the landings on the Androscoggin shore.
They picked the face on one of them from bottom to the top
Full thirty feet this landing had, a perpendicular drop.

To work the face much longer, 'twould be a foolish part,
A jar so slight, you see it might this lofty landing start
There were a few among them did volunteer to go
And roll a log from o'er the top to start the logs below.

This young man, he among them, with heart so strong and brave,
Not thinking e'er the setting sun, held be straightened for the grave,
Not thinking Death's dark cruel hands so soon might lay him low
To leave behind the ones he loved, in sorrow, grief and woe.

At this log they quickly started—the landing creaked below
And on it spread unto the verge, but would no further go.
This young man he approached the verge, the verge of landing high,
While all his pals with pallid cheeks and trembling limbs stood by.

Up came a shout of warning, to warn him of his fate.
Just for a moment he did pause—he seemed to hesitate.
He rolled this log just half way o'er and the landing broke like glass
And quick as thought he disappeared into the rolling mass.

They rolled those logs so carefully from off his mangled form.
The birds were singing sweetly, the sun shone clear and warm.
Brave men knelt down beside him, could not their grief command,
Unbidding tears burst from their eyes and fell into the sand.

Tenderly they bore him and laid him on the green
Beneath a shady tree that grew near yon purling stream.
The sparkling bubbling waters a-speeding o'er his bed
Seemed to whisper gently, a farewell to the dead.

This young man's name was Guy Reed—his age was twenty-three
He was killed in September in the town known as Riley,
In the little town of Byron, was laid beneath the earth.
He lays beside his kindred near the spot that gave him birth.

His remains they were buried by the Order of KP
A funeral more attended you seldom-ever see.
His brothers of the order, as they marched two by two,
On to the casket a spray let fall—a token of adieu.

His mother she died early when he was but a child.
They laid her down to slumber near a forest fair and wild.
A brother and a sister is sleeping by her side
In a quiet country churchyard near the river's dancing tide.

His casket was decorated with roses sweet and fair,
His pillow too, with every hue of flowers bright and fair,
The church and yard was crowded with people young and old
Once more to look upon that face once fair, in death now pale and cold

His poor old aged father is stricken now with grief.
All joys of earthly pleasure could bring him no relief,
For untold gold and silver, position, wealth in store.
Sunny skies and music sweet, will not the dead restore.

The cuckoo and the sparrow, the sunshine and the rain,
The robin and the swallow in the spring will come again,
But the one you love so dearly you n'er will see more
'Till yon cross death's dark valley to that bright celestial shore.

"Guy Reed," sung by Charles Finnemore of Bridgewater, Maine, on August 30, 1942. He said
that he learned the song from his son, Stanley Finnemore, who learned it when working in
the woods. This song was also recorded by Alton Irish of Island Falls, Maine (1940), Orlon
Merrill of Charlestown, New Hampshire (1931), and Clyde Covill of Pittsburg, New Hampshire (1987).

13.

I'm Sitting on the Stile Mary

I'm sitting on the stile, Mary.
Where we sat side by side.
On that bright May morning.
Long ago when first you were my bride.

Oh the grass was waving fresh and green
And the larks sang out on high
And the bloom was on your cheeks, Mary,
And the love light was in your eyes.

'Tis but a step down yonder lane,
And the little church stands there.
The place where we were wed, Mary
I can see the spire from here.

But the graveyard lies between, Mary
And my steps might break your rest
They have laid you down to rest, Mary,
With a baby on your breast.

"I'm Sitting on the Stile, Mary," is also widely known as "The Lament of the Irish Emigrant." This version, sung by Clyde Covill in West Stewartstown, New Hampshire, was recorded by the author on May 5, 1988. The lyrics of this nineteenth-century song are attributed to Helen Selina Sheridan (Lady Dufferin) (1807–1867). "The Lament of the Irish Emigrant" was also sung by Lena Bourne Fish of East Jaffrey, New Hampshire, in 1945.

14.

In the Garden

Clyde Covill, W. Stewartstown, N.H., 1988

"In the Garden," played on the fiddle by Clyde Covill of Pittsburg, New Hampshire, recorded in West Stewartstown by the author on September 29, 1988. Clyde accompanied hymns on the fiddle during family and neighborhood gatherings.

15.

The Jolly Sailor

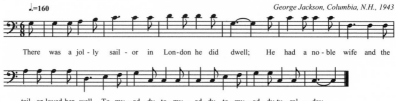

George Jackson, Columbia, N.H., 1943

There was a jol-ly sail-or in Lon-don he did dwell; He had a no-ble wife and the
tail-or loved her well. To-my-ad-dy, to-my - ad-dy, to-my - ad-dy-tu-ral - day.

There was a jolly sailor in London did dwell;
He had a noble wife and the tailor loved her well.
To-my-addy, to-my-addy, to-my-addy-tural-day.

She says, "My jolly sailor, my husband's gone to sea
And all this dreary night you can lay along with me."
To-my-addy, to-my-addy, to-my-addy-tural-day.

They hadn't been to bed over an hour, two or more
Before they was awakened by a knocking at the door.
To-my-addy, to-my-addy, to-my-addy-tural-day.

"Oh, where can I hide; it's where can I creep?"
"O here's my husband's chest, here by the bedside!
And there you can creep and there you can hide."
To-my-addy, to-my-addy, to-my-addy-tural-day.

She jumped out of bed and she unlocked the door
And there stood the sailor with seven sailors more.
To-my-addy, to-my-addy, to-my-addy-tural-day.

"I've come not to rob you nor break you of your rest,
But I'm bound for the sea and I'm after my chest."
To-my-addy, to-my-addy, to-my-addy-tural-day.

They mounted the stairs, some seven sailors strong,
They picked up the chest and they carried it along.
To-my-addy, to-my-addy, to-my-addy-tural-day.

The chest was so heavy that they had to stop and rest
And says one to the other, "What the devil's in the chest?"
To-my-addy, to-my-addy, to-my-addy-tural-day.

They opened the chest with never a call
And there stood the tailor—a pig in the stall.
To-my-addy, to-my-addy, to-my-addy-tural-day.

"It's now I have got you; I'll take you to sea,
I'll take you to China and trade you for tea."
To-my-addy, to-my-addy, to-my-addy-tural-day.

"It's now I have got you; I'll take you to sea,
If I don't wallop you, may the devil wallop me!"
To-my-addy, to-my-addy, to-my-addy-tural-day.

"The Jolly Sailor," also known as "The Sailor and the Tailor" (Laws Q8), sung by George A. Jackson of Columbia, New Hampshire, was recorded by Marguerite Olney on July 18, 1943. This song was also recorded in Vermont by Elmer George, North Montpelier (1934); Eugene Hall, Ludlow (1933); and in Maine by Oliver Jenness, York (1948). The song was remembered, and recited, by Marcia Dingman in Stark, New Hampshire, in 1987.

Jones' Paring Bee

Walter Titus, Johnson, Vermont, 1954

Oh Susan Jane do you re-mem-ber, Down to Jones' par-in' bee; When I took you and your broth-er, A-long with Sal-ly Green and me. Tu-ra lu-ra lu-ra li-dle lu-ra lu-ra lu-ra lee. Oh what fun we had to-geth-er, Down to Jones' par-in' bee.

> Oh Susan Jane do you remember
> Down to Jones' parin' bee,
> When I took you and your brother,
> Along with Sally Greer and me.
>
> Tura lura lura lidle lura lura lura lee
> Oh what fun we had together
> Down to Jones' parin' bee.
>
> Yes, Josiah, I remember
> 'Twas in winter time, you know,
> As we wandered along the highway
> Then we'd go up through the snow

"Jones' Parin' Bee," sung by Walter Titus of Johnson, Vermont, was recorded on November 17, 1954, for the Helen Hartness Flanders Ballad Collection. About this piece, Titus said: "A parin' bee is where neighbors of years ago used to congregate at some particular farmhouse and pare apples. There would be some parin' with parin' machines, other would be parin' with knives, others would be stringin' with twine string and a darning needle and then they'd hang the apples up to dry. That was what we used to call a parin' bee."

17

Josie Langmaid

Josiah Kennison, Bennington, Vermont, 1930

'Twas on the morn-ing ver-y clear, When Jos-ie start-ed for her school, For man-y the time these woods she passed But lit-tle thought this time her last.

'Twas on a morning very clear,
When Josie started for her school.
For many a time these woods she passed,
But little thought this time her last.

As Josie passed the lonely spot,
The monster by her clothing caught.
Then in the woods he took his flight,
And there in secret, took her life.

Her father watched with tender care,
Hoping his daughter would appear,
But as the night, it did draw near,
His darling child did not appear.

The anxious father and the son,
All through the woods in search begun,
And found at last to his surprise,
His murdered child before his eyes.

Her head was from her body tore,
Her clothes were in a crimson gore,
And marks upon her body show,
Some skillful hand had dealt the blow.

Her father fell upon her breast,
Crying, "Is my daughter Josie dead?"
And there in anguish he did moan,
'Til he was taken to his home.

The one that did this wretched deed,
Was Joe LePage, chopper by trade;
For many a time outrage had made,
And took the life of three fair maids.

Now LePage your work is done,
And you like Tatro must be hung.
And we will all example take,
'Til crime shall cease the Granite State.

"Josie Langmaid" or "The Suncook Town Tragedy" (Laws F21) was sung by Josiah Kennison of Bennington, Vermont, on November 27, 1942. Other Vermont recordings include Mabel Tatro, Springfield (1930), whose relatives knew the characters in this New Hampshire tragedy; Elmer Barton of Quechee (1940); Alice Dodge Titus and her son Walter Titus, Johnson (1954); Lena Eldred Rich and Bertha Eldred, Belvidere (1958); in New Hampshire it was recorded by Jonathan Moses, Orford (1939).

18

Lord Banner

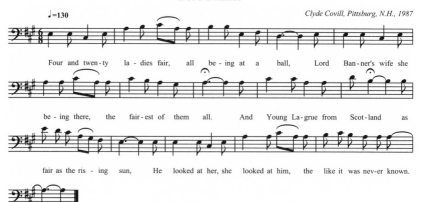

Clyde Covill, Pittsburg, N.H., 1987

♩=130

Four and twen-ty la - dies fair, all be - ing at a ball, Lord Ban-ner's wife she be - ing there, the fair - est of them all. And Young La-grue from Scot-land as fair as the ris - ing sun, He looked at her, she looked at him, the like it was nev-er known.

Four and twenty ladies fair, all being at a ball,
Lord Banner's wife being there, the fairest of them all.
And young LaGrue from Scotland as fair as the rising sun,
He looked at her, she looked at him, the like it was never known.

"Oh will, oh will you take a ride, oh will you take a ride?
You shall have servants to wait on you, and a fair lady by your side."
"Oh no, oh no, I dare not do it, oh no, for all of my life.
For by the ring on your third finger, you are Lord Banner's wife."

"What if I am Lord Banner's wife? Lord Banner he's not at home.
He's gone o'er to Henry Thorne's, to take care of young Henry Thorne."
One of his servants a being there, which heard this all that was done,
He swore his master would hear of this, before the next rising sun.

He ran 'til he came to the river's side and he ploughed to his breast and swam;
He swam 'til he came to the other side and he took to his heels and ran.
He ran 'til he came to the castle there; so loud he rapped at the door.
And who was there so ready as Lord Banner to let him in.

"Oh is there any of my towers down nor any of my towers three,
Or has there anything happened unto my fair lady?"
"Oh no, there's none of your towers down, and there none of your towers three,
But Young Lagrue from Scotland is in bed with your fair lady."

"If this be a lie you tell to me, which I suppose it to be,
I will rig a gallows and hanged you shall be."
"If this be a lie I tell to you, which you suppose it to be,
You need not rig a gallows, but hang me on a tree."

And he called by one of his merry, merry men, by one, by two, by three,
Saying, "We will ride over to old Scotland this fair couple for to see."
"What's this I hear so loud and in my ear that sounds so loud and drear?
It is Lord Banner's bugle, and he will soon be here!"

"Lie still, lie still and keep me warm and keep me from the cold,
It's only Lord Banner's shepherd boy a driving the sheep to the fold."
They huddled and they cuddled; they both fell fast asleep,
And when they awoke in the morning, Lord Banner, he stood at their feet.

"How do you like my blankets fine, and how do you like my sheets?
And how do you like that fair maid that lies in your arms asleep?"
"Quite well I like your blankets fine, quite well I like your sheets,
But I like this fair maid better that lies in my arms asleep."

"Rise up, rise up, put on your clothes as quick as ever you can;
I'll never have it said in old Scotland that I fought with a naked man."
"Oh no, oh no, I dare not do it, not for all of my life
For by your side you have two broadswords, while I have nary a knife."

"What if I have two broadswords, they cost me deep in purse.
You shall have the very best one, and I will take the worst.
And you may strike the very first blow and strike it like a man,
And I will strike the second blow and I'll kill you if I can.

Young Lagrue he struck the very first blow, that wounded Lord Banner sore,
Lord Banner struck the second blow and laid him in his gore.
Then he took his fair lady by the lily-white hand and he gave her kisses three,
Saying "Which of the two do you love the best, this Young Lagrue or me?"

"Quite well I like your rosy cheeks, quite well I like your chin,
But I'd ten times rather have Young Lagrue than you or all of your kin."
He grabbed her by the hair of the head and he split her head in two;
She sank upon her bended knees by the side of Young Lagrue.

Then he put the heel of the sword to the floor and the point unto his breast,
Saying, "Was there ever three lovers more easily laid at rest?
Go dig my grave, go dig my grave, go dig it both wide and deep,
And place my fair lady by my side and Young Lagrue at my feet."

This version of "Lord Banner" ("Little Musgrave and Lady Barnard," Child 81) includes the first three verses sung by Clyde Covill of Pittsburg, recorded in West Stewartstown by the author on June 19, 1987, followed by eleven verses sung by his uncle Orlon Merrill, who remembered this ballad in 1931. Clyde sang fragments of this ballad on several occasions, ultimately reconstructing seven or eight verses. Both his uncle and his mother (Maude Covill) recorded the song for Helen Hartness Flanders and Marguerite Olney, and their versions were published in *Ancient Ballads Traditionally Sung in New England*. Clyde's version, fifty years after his mother's recording and sixty years after his uncle's, was very similar, both lyrically and melodically. Many other recordings of this widely known song were made in Maine, New Hampshire, and Vermont between 1930 and 1965.

19

Margaret Gray

Maynard Reynolds, Pittsburg, N.H., 1941

Fair the cabin walls were gleaming in the sunbeam golden glow,
'Twas a lovely April morning, just a hundred years ago.
When upon that humble threshold sat the young wife, Margaret Gray,
With her fond blue eyes a gleaming down the lonely forest way.

In her arms her laughing baby with its father's dark hair played.
As he lingered there beside them, leaning on his trusty spade.
"I am going to the wheat lot," with a smile, says Robert Gray,
"Would you be too lonely, Margaret, should I leave you all the day?"

Then she smiled a cheerful answer ere she spoke a single word.
And the tones of her replying were as sweet as songs of birds.
Then she says, "I'll take the baby and go stay with Anna Brown,
You must meet me there, dear Robert, ere the sun has quite gone down."

Thus they parted straight and steady, all day long he labored on,
Spading up the fertile acres of the stubborn forest won.
Until lengthy shadows warned him that the sun was in the west,
Down the woodland aisle he hastened, whispering, "Now for home and rest!"

But when he had reached the clearing, from his friend a mile away,
Neither wife nor child were waiting there to welcome Robert Gray.
"She is safe at home," says Anna, "for she went an hour ago."
"It is strange I did not meet her," came his answer quick and low.

Back he turned for night was falling, and the path he scarce could see.
Here and there his feet were guided onward by some deep gashed tree.
'Til at length he reached the cabin, dark and desolate it stood;
Cold the hearth and rayless windows in their stillest solitude.

With a murmur, prayer, a shudder, and a sob of anguish wild,
Back he hastened to the forest calling on his wife and child.
Soon the scattered settlers gathered from their clearing far and near,
And the solemn words resounded with their voices ringing clear.

Torches gleamed and fires were kindled and the horns, long pealed, rang out.
While the startled echoes answered to the hardy woodmen shout.
But in vain their sad endeavors night by night and day by day,
But no signs or token found they of the child or Margaret Gray.

Woe, ah woe, to pretty Margaret with her baby on her arm,
As she slowly ventured homeward, fearing nothing that could harm.
With a lip and brow untroubled and a heart at utter rest,
Through the dim woods she went singing with her darling at her breast.

But when paused in sudden terror gazed around in blank dismay,
Where were all those white scarred hemlocks pointing out the lonely way?
God of mercy she had wandered from the pathway—not a tree
Giving mute and kindly warning could her straining vision see.

Twilight deepened into darkness and the stars came out on high.
All was silent in the evening save the owl's low brooding cry.
'Round about her in the midnight stealthily the shadows crept,
And the baby upon her bosom closed its timid eyes and slept.

Hark a shout, and in the distance she could see the torches gleam.
But, alas, she could not reach them, they would vanish like a dream.
Then another shout, another, she would shriek and sob in vain,
Rushing wildly to the place she could never, never gain.

Morning came and with the sunbeams hope and courage rose once more.
Surely ere another nightfall her long wanderings would be o'er.
Then she soothed her wailing baby and went faint for the want of food.
She would gather nuts and acorns that she found within the wood.

Ah, the days so long and dreary, oh the nights more dreary still.
More than once she heard the sounding of the horn from hill to hill.
More than once some smoldering fire in some shading nook she found.
And she knew her husband's footstep close beside it on the ground.

Dawned the fourth relentless morning rose the sun's unpitying eye,
Looked upon the haggard mother watched to see the baby die.
All day long its plaintive mourning wrang the heart of Margaret Gray,
All night long her bosom cradled a palled thing of clay.

Three more days she bore it with her on her rough and toilsome way,
'Til across its marble beauty stole the plague spot of decay.
Then she knew that she must leave it in the wilderness to sleep,
Where the prowling wild beast only watch above its grave to keep.

Down, with grief, she set beside it, oh, how long she never knew.
And the tales her mother taught her of her dear old Father true.
When the skies were brass above her and the earth was cold and dim
And from all her prayers and pleadings brought no answer down from Him.

Up she rose and tramped forward through the forest far and wide,
'Til the mayflowers bloomed and perished, and the sweet June roses died.
Sometime from her dreary pathway wolves and black bear turned away,
But not once did human faces bless the sight of Margaret Gray.

Soon July and August brought her fruit and berries by the store.
Soon the goldenrod and aster said that summer was no more.
Soon the maples and the birches donned their leaves of green and gold.
Soon the birds was hastening southward and the days were growing cold.

One chilly morning in October when the woods were brown and bare,
Through the streets of aging Charlestown, with the wild bewildered air,
Strolled a gaunt and pallid woman with disheveled locks of brown,
Oe'r her naked breast and shoulders in the wind was streaming down.

Wondering glances fell upon her, women veiled the modest eye,
As they slowly ventured near her, drawn by pitying surprise.
"'Tis some crazy one," they whispered, back her tangled hair she tossed,
"Oh, kind friends, take pity on me, for I am not mad, but lost."

Then she told her pitiful story in a vague despondent way,
And with cold white lips she murmured, "Take me home to Robert Gray."
"But the river," said they, pondered, "how crossed you to its eastern side?
How crossed you those rapid waters, deep the channel is and wide."

But she said she had not crossed it in her desolated course.
She had wandered so far northward 'til she'd reached the fountain source.
Through the dark Canadian forest and then blindly roaming on,
Down the wild New Hampshire valley her bewildered feet had gone.

Oh the joy bells sweet there were ringing on the frosty autumn air.
Oh the boats across the waters how they leaped the tale to bear.
On that wondrous glorious sunset of the blest October day,
When the weary wife was folded in the arms of Robert Gray.

"Margaret Gray" or "Margery Gray" was widely known in Vermont and New Hampshire.
One of the most complete versions of this ballad, sung by Maynard Reynolds, Pittsburg,
New Hampshire, was recorded by Marguerite Olney on September 5, 1941. It was also re-
membered in New Hampshire by Orlon Merrill, Charlestown (1931), and in Vermont by
Bertha Chapin, Colchester (1955), and Asa Davis, Milton (1940).

20.

Money Musk

S. Daily ms., Pittsburg, N.H., c. 1850

This version of "Money Musk" was entered into the mid- to late-nineteenth-century S.
Daily manuscript book from Pittsburg, New Hampshire. Also recorded in Vermont by Ed
Larkin, Chelsea (1939), Harry Stark, Cornwall (1984), and Ray Grimes, Lincoln (1985).

21

Old Maid and the Burglar

Flora Campbell, Stark, N.H., 1988

I'll sing you a song of a burg-lar boy Who came to rob a house.

Think-ing at night that all was right He crept in a still as a mouse.

I'll sing you a song of a burglar boy
Who came to rob a house.
Thinking at night that all was right
He crept in as still as a mouse.

He looked all around for a place to hide,
A place for to cover his head.
Thinking at night that all was right
He crept in on under the bed.

And under the bed the burglar crept
And he huddled next to the wall.
He did not know 'twas an old maid's room,
Or he would not have gone in there at all.

About nine o'clock the old maid came in
A-saying "How tired I am."
Thinking at night that all was right,
She forgot to look under her bed.

She took out her teeth, laid them on the stand,
And the hair from the top of her head.
The burglar had about seventy shakes
As he looked out from under the bed.

While under the bed the burglar cracked
He looked like a total wreck.
The old woman being wide awake
She grabbed him by the neck.

She did not holler nor screech for help
But took him as still as a clam.
Saying "Thank the good Lord, my prayers been heard,
And at last I have found me a man."

From the bureau drawer a gun she took
And unto the burglar she said,
"Now if you do not marry me,
I will blow off the top of your head."

The burglar looked all around the room
He looked for a place to scoot.
He looked at her eyes, her nose, and her mouth
And he said "Well for God's sake shoot!"

"The Old Maid the Burglar," sung by Flora Campbell, was recorded by the author in Stark, New Hampshire, on May 6, 1988. This song was known to members of her family, including her sisters, Florence Scott and Beulah Parks. They heard their father sing it to them, especially in the evenings after dinner: "My dad kept us in wool stockins and mittens and hats and everything, all winter long. He just loved to knit. After he'd get home from work at night he would start knitting and—right after supper he'd always lay down on the floor—he'd smoke a pipe—he'd lay down on the floor and he'd have that pipe going, and my sister Beulah would lay on one side of him and I on the other and he'd start singing" (interview with Florence Scott, Pittsburg, New Hampshire, June 15, 1987). Also recorded by Horatio Luce, Pomfret, Vermont (1931), and Oliver Jenness, York, Maine (1941).

22.

The Orphan Children

Marjorie Pierce, N. Shrewsbury, Vermont, 1984

The marriage rite was over, I turned my face aside;
To keep the guests from seeing the tears I could not hide.
I wreathed my face in smiling, and led my little brother
To greet my father's chosen, but I could not call her mother.

She was a fair young creature with mild and gentle air;
With blue eyes soft and loving and sunny silken hair.
I knew my father gave her the love he bore another,
But if she were an angel, I could never call her mother.

Last night I heard her singing a song I used to love.
And every word was hallowed by her who sings above.
It grieved my heart to hear it, and the tears I could not smother.
For every word was hallowed by the voice of my dear mother.

They have taken mother's picture from its accustomed place.
And hung beside my father's a younger, fairer face.
They have made the dear old chamber the boudoir of another.
But I shall ne'er forget thee, my own, my angel mother.

My father in the sunshine of happy days come.
May half forget the shadow that darkened our old home
His heart no more is lonely, but I and little brother.
Must still be orphan child, God can give us but one mother.

"The Orphan Children," sung by Marjorie Pierce, was recorded by the author in North Shrewsbury, Vermont, on October 2, 1984.

23.

Paper of Pins

♩.=110

Floyd and Bea Shatney, Groveton, N.H., 1987

Oh   mad-am I'll give you a   pa-per of pins, For   that's the way that   love be-gins; If

you will mar-ry   me, me, me, If   you will mar-ry   me.

Floyd:
Oh madam I'll give you a paper of pins,
For that's the way that love begins;
If you will marry me, me, me,
If you will marry me.

Bea:
Oh I'll not accept your paper of pins,
For that's the way that love begins;
And I'll not marry you, you, you,
And you'll not marry me.

Floyd:
Oh madam I'll give you a dress of red,
Bound all around with golden thread;
If you will marry me, me, me,
If you will marry me.

Bea:
Oh I'll not accept your dress of red,
Bound all around with golden thread;
And I'll not marry you, you, you,
And you'll not marry me.

Floyd:
Oh madam I'll give you a coach of six,
With all the little horses as black as pitch.
If you will marry me, me, me,
If you will marry me.

Bea:
I'll not accept your coach of six,
With all the little horses as black as pitch.
And I'll not marry you, you, you,
And you'll not marry me.

Floyd:
Oh madam I'll give you the key to my heart,
If you and I may never part.
If you will marry me, me, me,
If you will marry me.

Bea:
I'll not accept the key to your heart,
That you and I may never part.
And I'll not marry you, you, you,
And you'll not marry me.

Floyd:
Oh madam I'll give you the key to my chest,
That you may have money at your bequest.
If you will marry me, me, me,
If you will marry me.

Bea:
Oh I will accept the key to your chest,
That I may have money at my bequest.
And I will marry you, you, you,
And you will marry me.

Floyd:
Ha ha ha ha, I plan to keep
My money you want, and you don't want me.
And I'll not marry you, you, you,
And you'll not marry me.

"The Paper of Pins," sung by Floyd and Bea Shatney of Groveton, New Hampshire, was recorded by the author in 1987. This dialogue song was popular throughout New England and was recorded by quite a few singers in Maine, New Hampshire, and Vermont between 1930 and the late 1980s.

Peter Emberley

Mrs. W. H. Smith, Houlton, Maine, 1940

My name is Peter Emberley as you may understand.
I belong to Prince Edward's Island, down by the ocean strand.
In eighteen hundred and eighty, when flowers were pleasant to view,
I left my own dear native land, my fortune to pursue.

I landed in New Brunswick, that lumbering country;
I hired to work in the lumberwoods on the northwest Miramichi;
I hired for to cut the spruce logs down.
It was loading spruce logs on the yard, I received my deathly wound.

There's danger in the ocean, where the waves roll mountains high;
There's danger in the battlefields, where the angry bullets fly;
There's danger in the lumberwoods where death lies lurking there,
And I have fallen a victim to that most deadly snare.

I know my lot seems very hard since fate has proved severe,
But faithful death is waiting there, I have no other fear.
Since God will relieve my deathly pains and liberate me soon,
And I shall sleep that long, long sleep called, "slumber in the tomb."

Here's adieu unto my father. 'Twas him who sent me here.
I thought it very hard of him, his treatments were severe.
It does not do to press a boy or try to keep him down.
It's sure to drive him from his home when he is far too young.

Here's adieu unto my dearest friend, I mean my mother dear.
She reared her boy who fell as soon as he left her tender care.
It's little did my mother think when she sang lullaby,
What strange lands I would travel through or what death I might die.

Here's adieu unto my younger friends, the Island girls so true.
Long may they live to increase the Isle where first my breath I drew.
While in some foreign country my mouldering bones will lay,
To wait the Saviour's coming to the Resurrection Day.

"Peter Emberly," sung by Mrs. W. H. Smith of Houlton, Maine, was recorded by Helen Hartness Flanders on 23 September 1940. Known also to many other residents of the region, the song has been recorded in Maine by Hanford Hayes, Stacyville (1940); Perley Quigg, Island Falls (1940); Annie Tate Moore, Ellsworth Falls (1941); Jack McNally, Stacyville (1942); and Mary Jones, Sherman Mills (1942); in New Hampshire by George Brown, Tamworth; Orlon Merrill, Charlestown (1931); James Rattery, Walpole (1939); Abe Washburn, Colebrook (1941); Garret Hurlburt, Clarksville (1942); Maynard Reynolds, Pittsburg (1941); and Belle Luther Richards, Colebrook (1942); and in Vermont by Henry Ashford, Groton (1937); and John Henry Curtis, Rockingham (1939).

25.

Patronella

ms. of Mr. Allen, Reading, Vermont, 1930

"Patronella" (more commonly known as "Petronella"), played on the fiddle by Mr. Allen of Reading, Vermont, was recorded in manuscript form by George Brown in 1930.

26.

Portland Fancy

Luther Weeks, Springfield, Vermont, 1932

Portland Fancy

Harry Stark, Cornwall, Vermont, 1984

"Portland Fancy," widely known in northern New England, is represented here by two Vermont recordings: Luther Weeks, Springfield, recorded in 1932, and Harry Stark, Cornwall, recorded by Debra Conroy in 1984. It was also recorded in Dorset (1930) and Bethel (1939), Vermont; Rockland (1941), Surry (1942), and Addison (1942), Maine; and in Pittsburg, New Hampshire (1987).

Sir James the Rose

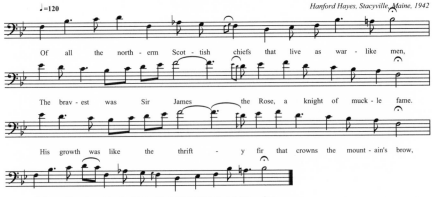

Of all the north-ern Scot-tish chiefs that live as war-like men,

The brav-est was Sir James the Rose, a knight of muck-le fame.

His growth was like the thrift - y fir that crowns the mount-ain's brow,

And wav-'ring o'er his should-ers broad bright locks of yel-low flow.

Of all the northern Scottish chiefs that live as warlike men,
The bravest was Sir James, the Rose, a knight of muckle fame.
His growth was like the thrifty fir that crowns the mountain's brow
And wavering o'er his shoulders broad, bright locks of yellow flow.

Three years he fought on bloody fields against their English king.
Scarce two and twenty summers yet this fearless youth had seen.
It was fair Mathildy that he loved, that girl with beauty rare,
And Margaret on the Scottish throne with her could not compare.

Long he had wooed, long she'd refused, it seemed with scorn and pride.
But after all confessed her love; her faithful words, denied.
"My father was born a cruel lord, this passion does approve.
He bids me wed Sir John a Grame, and leave the one I love.

"My father's will I must fulfill, which puts me to a stand
Some fair maid in her beauty bloom may bless you with her hand."
"Are those the vows, Mathildy dear," Sir James, the Rose, did say,
"And would Mathildy wed the Grame when she's sworn to be my bride?"

"I only spoke to try thy love. I'll ne'er wed man but thee.
The grave shall be my bridal bed ere Grame my husband be.
You take this kiss, fair youth," she said, "in witness of my love,
May every plague down on me fall the day I break my vows."

Ere they had met and there embraced, down by a shady grove,
It was on a bank beside a burn a blooming shelltree stood.
Concealed beneath the undie wood to hear what they might say,
A brother to Sir John the Grame and there concealed he lay.

Ere they did part the sun was set at haste he then replied,
"Return, return, you beardless youth," he loud insulting cries.
"O it's of my brother's slight love rests softly on your arm."
Three paces back the youth retired to save himself from harm.

Then turned around the beardless youth and quick his sword he drew.
And through his enemy's crashing blows, his sharp-edged weapon drew.
Grame staggered back. He reeled and fell, a lifeless lump of clay.
"So falls my foes," said valiant Rose, and straightly walked away.

Through the green woods he then did go till he reached Lord Bohan's Hall
And at Mathildy's window stood and thus began to call:
"Art thou asleep, Mathildy dear? Awake, my love, awake.
Your own true lover calls on you a long farewell to take.

"For I have slain fair Donald Grame. His blood is on my sword.
And distant are my faithful men, they can't assist their lord.
To the Isle of Skye, I must awa' where my twa brothers abide.
I'll raise the gallyants of that Isle, they'll combat on my side."

"Don't do so," the maid replied, "with me 'til morning stay,
For dark and rainy is the night and dangerous is the way."
"All night I'll watch you in my park my little page I'll send;
He'll run and raise the Rose's clan, their master to defend."

She laid him down beneath the bush and rolled him in his plaid.
At a distance stood the weeping maid; a-weeping for her love.
O'er hills and dales, the page he ran, till lonely in the glen,
'Twas there he met Sir John the Grame, and twenty of his men.

"Where art thou going, my little page? What tidings dost thou bring?"
"I'm running to raise the Rose's clan, their master to defend.
For he has slain fair Donald Grame. His blood is on his sword.
And distant are his faithful men, they can't assist their lord."

"Tell me where he is, my little page, and I will thee well reward."
"He sleeps now in Lord Bohan's Hall. Mathildy, she's his guard."
He spurred his horse at a furious gait and galloped o'er the lea.
Until he reached Lord Bohan's Hall, at the dawning of the day.

Without the gate, Mathildy stood, to whom the Grame replied,
"Saw ye Sir James, the Rose, last night, or did he pass this way?"
"Last day at noon fair James, the Rose, I seen him passing by.
He was mounted on a milk-white steed, and forward fast did fly.

"He's in Edinborotown now by this time, if man and horse proves good."
"Your page now lies who said he was a-sleeping in the wood."
She wrung her hands and tore her hair, saying, "Rose, thou art betrayed,
Thou art betrayed all by those means, I was sure you would be saved."

The hero heard a well-known voice; this valiant knight awoke,
Oh, he awoke and drew his sword as this brave band appeared.
"So you have slain my brother dear; his blood as dew did shine.
And by the rising of the sun your blood shall flow or mine."

"You speak the truth," the youth replies, "That deeds can prove the man.
Stand by your men and hand to hand, you'll see our valiant stand."
"If boasting words a coward hide, it is my sword you fear,
It's seen the day on Flodden's Field when you sneaked in the rear."

"Oh, at him, men, and cut him down, oh, cut him down in twain.
Five thousand pounds onto the man who leaves him on the plain."
Four of his men—the bravest four—fell down before that sword,
But still they scorned that mean revenge, and sought the cowardly Lord.

Till cowardly behind him stole the Grame, and wound him in the side.
Out gushing came his purple gore, and all his garments dyed.
But ne'er of his sword did he quit the grip nor fell he to the ground
Till through his enemy's heart his steel had pierced a fatal wound.

Grame staggered back. He reeled and fell, a lifeless lump of clay
Whilst down beside him sank the Rose that fainting, dying lay.
O when Mathildy seen him fall, "O spare his life," she cried,
"Lord Bohan's daughter begs his life. She shall not be denied."

The hero heard a well-known voice and raised his death-closed eyes
And fixed them on the weeping maid, and faintly this replies,
"In vain, Mathildy, you beg my life. By death's, it's been denied;
My race is run. Good-bye, my love." He closed his eyes and died.

She drew his sword from his left side with frantic hands, she drew.
"I come, I come, brave Rose," she cried, "I'm going to follow you."
She leaned the hilt upon the ground and pressed her snow-white breast;
Laid down upon her lover's face and endless went to rest.

So come all indulging parents, by this warning take
And never encourage your children dear their sacred vows to break.

"Sir James the Rose" (Child 1882–98: no. 213), sung by Hanford Hayes of Staceyville, Maine,
was recorded on May 5, 1942. This ballad was also sung by Charles Finnemore of Bridgewater, Maine (1941).

28.

There's No One to Welcome Me Home

Elmer George, N. Montpelier, Vermont, 1939

By the twi - light I wan-der a - lone all a - lone, A - way from the old house of
joy. It is fath - er-less, moth-er - less, sad - ly I roam, And there's no one to
wel-come me home. There's no one to wel-come me home, There is no one to

wel-come me home. For dead are the dear ones I left far be - hind, And there's

no one to wel-come me home.

By the twilight I wander alone all alone,
Away from the old house of joy.
It is fatherless, motherless, sadly I roam,
And there's no one to welcome me home.

There's no one to welcome me home,
There is no one to welcome me home.
For dead are the dear ones I left far behind,
And there's no one to welcome me home.

My mother stood onto the Liverpool dock
With her apron held up to her eyes.
And there the ships slowly moved out from the bank,
It was then that she bade me goodbye.

"My boy you are going far away, far away,
And your dear face I'll never see more.
But when you return to your own native shore,
There'll be no one to welcome you home.

"There'll be no one to welcome you home,
There'll be no one to welcome you home,
For dead will be the dear ones you have left far behind,
And there'd be no one to welcome you home."

"There's No One to Welcome Me Home," sung by Elmer George, East Calais, Vermont, was recorded by Helen Hartness Flanders on November 11, 1939. This song was first published in 1869 by M. H. McChesney.

29.

Tod and the Sow

Murchie Harvey, Houlton, Maine, 1942

♩.=90

Oh I used to dress well, and I cut a fine swell With a fine beav-er hat on me head. Oh

sev-eral fine suits and both five dol-lar boots And a good-look-ing chap, they all said. Un-

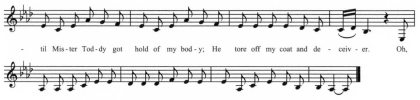

til Mis - ter Tod - dy got hold of my bod - y; He tore off my coat and de - ceiv - er. Oh,

then Jack a - rous - es and tore up my trous - ers And kicked in the crown of my beav - er.

Oh I used to dress well, and I cut a fine swell
With a fine beaver hat on me head.
Oh several fine suits and both five dollar boots
And a good-looking chap, they all said.
Until Mr. Toddy got hold of my body;
He tore off my coat and deceiver.
Oh, then Jack arouses and tore up my trousers
And kicked in the crown of my beaver.

Oh it was a dark night, and the people all tight,
And my money all spent for grog then.
I'd no place to go to bed, in my woe,
So that night I slept in the hog pen.
The old sow was pleased; she snuggled and sneezed;
She tangled her toes in my hair;
She grunted and cried, and fondly replied
And told me to move if I dare.

Next morning so early, I rose up so surly,
I found myself covered with dirt.
She'd done up my hat; it both greasy and fat,
And chewed the tail off 'n me shirt.
'Twixt tod and the sow, they've ruined me now;
But I'll tell you just what I will do:
I'll go to the west and I'll do my darn best,
And I'll muster up a little crew.

And back I will come, with four gallons of rum,
And my fingernails pointed with steam;
I'll murder old toddy and bury his body
[Spoken.] And make the old sow scream.

"The Tod and the Sow," sung by Murchie Harvey of Houlton, Maine, was recorded by Marguerite Olney on August 30, 1942.

30

Woodsman's Alphabet

Edward Dragon, Ripton, Vermont, 1938

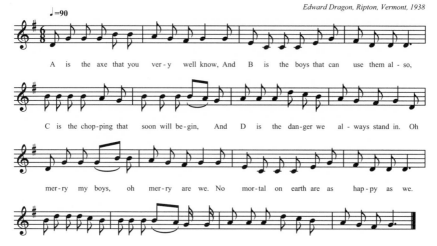

A is the axe that you very well know, And B is the boys that can use them al-so,

C is the chop-ping that soon will be-gin, And D is the dan-ger we al-ways stand in. Oh

mer-ry my boys, oh mer-ry are we. No mor-tal on earth are as hap-py as we.

Hi der-ry, ho der-ry, hi der-ry down, When the shant-y men's well and there's noth-ing goes wrong.

A is the axe that you very well know
And B is the boys that can use them also
C is the chopping that soon will begin
And D is the danger we always stand in.

Chorus:
Oh merry my boys, oh merry are we
No mortal on earth are as happy as we
Hi derry, ho derry, hi derry down
When the shantymen's well and there's nothing goes wrong.

E is the echo that rings through the woods
And F is the foreman the boss of the gang
G is the grindstone so swiftly will smooth
And H is the handle so slippery and smooth.

I is the iron we mark our spruce with
J is the joefle the boy of the ring
K is the keen edge our axes will keep
And L is the lice that keeps you from sleep.

M is the moss we stuff our camps with
N is the needle we sew our pants with
O is the owl that hoots out at night
And P is the pine that we always fall right.

Q is the quarrel we do not allow
R is the river we draw our logs through
S is the sled so stout and so strong
And T is the team that we draw them along.

U is the use we put our teams to
V is the is valley we build our roads through
W's the woods that we leave in the spring
And now you have heard all I'm going for to sing.

"The Woodmen's Song" or the "Lumberman's Alphabet," sung by Edward Dragon of Ripton, Vermont, was recorded by Helen Hartness Flanders on August 9, 1938. This widely sung piece was recorded in Vermont by Ellen Sullivan, Springfield (1933); Elmer George, East Calais (1939 and 1948); Harriet Eldred Eldredge, Hardwick (1958); and Merritt Earl, Eden (1958); in Maine by Ella M. Patterson, Hampden Highlands (1926); Frank E. Cram, Monmouth (1926); and Hanford Hayes, Stacyville (1942); and in New Hampshire by Orlon Merrill, Charlestown (1931); and Belle Richards, Colebrook (1943).

Notes

Preface (pp. ix–xiv)

1. Helen Hartness Flanders and George Brown, *Vermont Folk Songs and Ballads* (Brattleboro: Stephen Daye Press, 1930 and 1931); Helen Hartness Flanders et al., *The New Green Mountain Songster: Traditional Folksongs of Vermont* (New Haven: Yale University Press, 1939); Helen Hartness Flanders and Marguerite Olney, *Ballads Migrant in New England* (New York: Farrar, Straus, and Young, 1953); and Helen Hartness Flanders et al., *Ancient Ballads Traditionally Sung in New England* (Philadelphia: University of Pennsylvania, 1960–65). Other titles related to the collection include Helen Hartness Flanders, ed., *A Garland of Green Mountain Song* (Northfield, Vt.: Vermont Commission on Country Life, 1934), a collection of twenty-four ballads and songs with piano accompaniment by Helen Norfleet; Helen Hartness Flanders, ed. *Country Songs of Vermont* (New York, G. Schirmer, 1937), a second collection of twenty-four ballads and songs with piano accompaniment by Helen Norfleet; Helen Hartness Flanders, ed., *Vermont Chap Book: Being a Garland of Ten Folk Ballads* (Middlebury, Vt.: Middlebury College Press, 1941), and *Eight Traditional British-American Ballads from Helen Hartness Flanders Collection, Middlebury College, Middlebury, Vermont,* New England folksong series, no. 1, LP recording (Middlebury: Middlebury College, 1953), with program notes by Marguerite Olney.

2. Frances James Child, *The English and Scottish Popular Ballads* (Boston and New York: Houghton, Mifflin and Co., 1882–1898).

3. G. Malcolm Laws, *American Balladry from British Broadsides: A Guide for Students and Collectors of Traditional Song* (Philadelphia: American Folklore Society, 1957), and *Native American Balladry: A Descriptive Study and a Bibliographical Syllabus* (Philadelphia: American Folklore Society, 1950).

4. Fanny Hardy Eckstorm and Mary Winslow Smyth, *Minstrelsy of Maine: Folk-Songs and Ballads of the Woods and the Coast* (New York: Houghton Mifflin, 1927).

5. Phillips Barry, Fanny Hardy Eckstorm, and Mary Winslow Smyth, *British Ballads from Maine: The Development of Popular Songs with Texts and Airs* (New Haven: Yale University Press, 1929).

6. Phillips Barry, *The Maine Woods Songster* (Cambridge, Mass.: The Powell Printing Company, 1939).

7. Eloise Hubbard Linscott, *Folk Songs of Old New England* (New York: Macmillan, 1939).

8. Elizabeth Burchenal, *American Country Dances: Twenty-eight Contra Dances Largely from the New England States* (New York: G. Schirmer, 1918). This is the first volume in a series that included dances with piano accompaniment drawn from the United States and Europe.

9. Edith B. Sturgis, *Songs from the Hills of Vermont: Sung by James and Mary Atwood and Aunt Jenny Knapp* (New York: G. Schirmer, 1919).

10. Roland Palmer Gray, *Songs and Ballads of the Maine Lumberjacks with Other Songs from Maine* (Cambridge: Harvard University Press, 1924).

11. Robert Pike, "Folk Songs from Pittsburg, New Hampshire," *Journal of American Folklore* 48:190 (1935): 337–351. This was followed by two books characterizing the occupational and cultural lives of the region, which included many of the same songs (*Spiked Boots* and *Tall Trees, Tough Men*). Benjamin Botkin also devoted a chapter to ballads and songs in his 1947 collection, drawn from previously published material including the work of Linscott, Flanders, Barry, and Sturgis: Benjamin A. Botkin, ed., *A Treasury of New England Folklore: Stories, Ballads, and Traditions of the Yankee People* (New York: Crown Publishers, 1947).

12. Edward D. Ives, *Folksongs from Maine,* Northeast Folklore 7 (Orono: Northeast Folklore Society, 1966). The journal *Northeast Folklore* was restarted and renamed in 1960 in the tradition of the Barry-Eckstorm *Bulletin of the Folk-Song Society of the Northeast,* which had ceased publication when Barry died in 1937. Also see *Larry Gorman: The Man Who Made the Songs* (Bloomington: University of Indiana, 1964), *Lawrence Doyle: The Farmer Poet of Prince Edward Island,* Maine Studies No. 92 (Orono, Maine: University Press, 1972), and *Joe Scott: The Woodsman-Songmaker* (Urbana: University of Illinois, 1978).

13. Michael Pickering, *Village Song and Culture* (London: Croom Helm, 1983); Georgina Boyes, *The Imagined Village: Culture, Ideology and the English Folk Revival* (Manchester: Manchester University Press, 1993); Ruth Finnegan, *The Hidden Musicians* (Cambridge: Cambridge University Press, 1989); Roger Renwick, *English Folk Poetry: Structure and Meaning* (Philadelphia: University of Pennsylvania Press, 1980); Martin Stokes, *Ethnicity, Identity, and Music: The Musical Construction of Place* (Oxford: Berg, 1997); Barbara Allen and Thomas J. Schlereth, eds., *Sense of Place: American Regional Cultures* (Lexington: University Press of Kentucky, 1990); Gerald L. Pocius, *A Place to Belong: Community Order and Everyday Space in Calvert, Newfoundland* (Athens: University of Georgia Press, 1991); Kent C. Ryden, *Mapping the Invisible Landscape: Folklore, Writing, and the Sense of Place* (Iowa City: University of Iowa Press, 1993); Thomas C. Hubka, "Farm Family Mutuality: The Mid-Nineteenth-Century Maine Farm Neighborhood," in Peter Benes, ed., *The Farm,* The Dublin Seminar for New England Folklife Annual Proceedings, 1986 (Boston: Boston University), 13–23; Karen V. Hansen, *A Very Social Time: Crafting Community in Antebellum New England* (Berkeley: University of California Press, 1994); Stephen A. Marini, "Evangelical Hymns and Popular Belief," in Peter Benes, ed., *New England Music: The Public Sphere, 1600–1900* (Boston: Boston University, 1996), 117–126; and Joseph. A. Conforti, *Imagining New England: Explorations of Regional Identity from the Pilgrims to the Mid-twentieth Century* (Chapel Hill: University of North Carolina, 2001).

1. Introduction: The Geographic and Social Landscape (pp. 1–15)

1. Sung by Margaret MacArthur of Marlboro, Vermont, on *An Almanac of New England Farm Songs.* She selected verses from those sung by George Churchill of Brandon, Vermont in 1934.

2. This song is attributed to poet John G. Saxe in the nineteenth-century collection by Baker and Perkins, *The Tabernacle,* 35.

3. Ramon Gove, interview by author, Warren, Vermont, March 1984.

4. The tune and attached verses were notated by George Brown from the singing of Guy

Blood of Grafton, Vermont, September 1930. Additional lyrics were submitted to the Helen Hartness Flanders Ballad Collection by Mrs. Fred Blood of Chester, Vermont.

5. Several stories of Robin Hood's adventures recorded in song have been found in northern New England, including "The Bold Pedlar and Robin Hood," "Robin Hood and the Bishop," and this one, "Robin Hood Rescuing the Three Squires" (Child 140).

6. "Bold Robin Hood" as sung by Charles Finnemore of Bridgewater, Maine, in 1942. Twenty-one verses of this ballad were recorded by Helen Hartness Flanders and Marguerite Olney and published in *Ballads Migrant in New England* (69–72) and *Ancient Ballads* (111–15).

7. Freeman Corey, interview by author, Benson, Vermont, 11 May 1985.

8. Hubka categorizes these cooperative activities in the following way: work sharing (labor exchange, animal or tool exchange); health care (assistance in sickness, birth, death); education (district schools); artisan skills; disaster relief (sudden death, fire); celebrations and assemblies (sings and huskings); building construction; road maintenance; information sharing and other socializing (Hubka 1988: 15).

9. The local customary calendar included seasonal activities such as apple paring, haying, corn husking, hops gathering, sugaring, sheep shearing, and barn raising. These events encouraged oyster suppers, box parties, ice cream socials, other socials, and kitchen dances.

10. Sung by Walter Titus of Johnson, Vermont, and recorded in 1954 for the Flanders Collection, Middlebury College.

11. Freeman Corey, Sr., interview by author, Benson, Vermont, 11 May 1985.

12. Unfortunately, the "improvement" that the Vermont Commission sought was focused more on the population than on the quality of life. Recent studies on this commission have established that it was linked to a Eugenics Survey of Vermont (1925–1936): "Its purpose was to conduct eugenical studies of Vermont families and communities and publicize its findings to support a broad range of social reforms in the state, particularly in the areas of child welfare, education, and charities and corrections." See Nancy L. Gallagher. *Breeding Better Vermonters: The Eugenics Project in the Green Mountain State* (Hanover, N.H.: University Press of New England, 1999).

13. Northern New England communities lagged behind the southern regions sometimes because of their relative poverty (and insufficient access to electricity), geographic distance from urban centers, and poor roads.

2. The Musical Landscape: Singing Traditions (pp. 16–59)

1. See the collections of Helen Hartness Flanders (Middlebury College), Eloise Linscott (Library of Congress, Washington, D.C.), Phillips Barry (Houghton Library, Harvard University), and Fanny Eckstorm (University of Maine, Orono). While these collectors included some songs derived from other sources, they represent them as a very small proportion of the material typical of the regional repertoire.

2. Janet Blunt's collection of songs and dance tunes was used by Pickering to frame his critical study of the role of music in Adderbury, North Oxfordshire.

3. Elizabeth Vaara, interview by author, Middlebury, Vermont, 13 June 1989.

4. Clyde Covill, interview by author, Stewartstown, New Hampshire, 13 September 1988.

5. Ardes Haynes, interview by author, Pittsburg, New Hampshire, 18 June 1987.

6. Katherine Fogg, interview by author, Pittsburg, New Hampshire, 1987.

7. Ardes Haynes, interview by author, Pittsburg, New Hampshire, 18 June 1987.

8. Thelma Neill, interview by author, Warren, Vermont, 3 October 1985.

9. "The Auld Soldier," as recorded and transcribed by Helen Hartness Flanders in Springfield, Vermont, in September 1931.

> There was an auld soldier an' he had a wooden leg.
> He had no terbaccy, nor terbaccy could he beg.
> There was another soldier, as cunnin' as a fox,
> An he allus had terbaccy in his auld terbaccy box.
>
> Said the first auld soldier, "Won't you give me a chew?"
> Said the second auld soldier, "Shoot me dead if I do.
> Shtop yer drink' whisky. Go te pilin' up yer rocks,
> An' ye'll allus have terbaccy in yer auld terbaccy box."

10. Marjorie Pierce, interview by author, N. Shrewsbury, Vermont, 1 December 1984.

11. Gerard Richards, interview by author, Pittsburg, New Hampshire, 20 June 1987. He also recalled his grandmother inside the house playing the organ, singing hymns or popular songs quietly to herself.

> She'd get by the organ and she'd play for hours and sing. She had a memory like you wouldn't believe. I think if she heard a song once or twice at the most, she could sing it, both tune and words.

12. Most of the women I spoke to recalled working alongside their mothers, while men remembered working with their fathers. Yet there are also examples of girls who worked with their father on the farm and sometimes the woods.

13. Fanny Hardy Eckstorm reports that traditional shanties were also popular in the lumbercamps, although they were sung for entertainment only, not to regulate work (1927: 235).

14. See chapter 3 for more on this subject.

15. From song notes by Helen Hartness Flanders.

16. Lena Bourne Fish, East Jaffrey, New Hampshire. From song notes by Helen Hartness Flanders.

17. Myra Daniels, East Calais and Hardwick, Vermont. From song notes by Helen Hartness Flanders.

18. Moore contributed six songs to Phillips Barry's collection in 1936.

19. This from recordings made in Maine, New Hampshire, and Vermont primarily by Helen Hartness Flanders, Alan Lomax, and Marguerite Olney but also by Phillips Barry, Eloise Linscott, and Fanny Hardy Eckstorm. The sample includes 397 songs (235 titles and 186 singers) among them British and American ballads, hymns, nineteenth- and early-twentieth-century popular songs, and children's songs. The breakdown of the sample is as follows:

father	84	in-laws	8	public gathering	2
mother	81	uncle	8	sister	2
woods	61	aunt	4	school	2
grandmother	28	husband	4	wife	2
neighbors/friends	25	grandparents	3	blind singer	1
brother/s	17	great grandmother	3	boarder	1
grandfather	17	old resident	3	book	1
parents	12	soldier	3	boy	1
itinerant	8	cousin	2	church	1

hired girl	1	prayer meeting	1	traveling circus	1
hired man	1	relatives	1	young lady	1
Irish singers	1	stepmother	1		
man on train	1	teacher	1		

20. This may be a function of the types of songs that were collected from the individuals in the sample. The ballads and songs sought by collectors were not often transmitted in school songbooks or hymnals.

21. Manuscript letter to Flanders Ballad Collection, Margaret Shipman, 1932.

22. Letter of 1932 to Helen Hartness Flanders from Ida B. Morgan of Jeffersonville, Vermont. The lyrics to "Uncle Hall's Barn" from Ida Morgan follow:

> O, Dr. Hall he built a barn,
> He built it near some brakes,
> And for the want of pins,
> He drove in nutcakes.
>
> He had an orchard large,
> And made cider for to sell,
> And the water he put into it,
> Would dreen a common well.

23. In songs like "King William and Lady Margaret" or "Captain Wedderburn's Courtship."

24. In songs like "The Jam on Gerry's Rock" or "Peter Emberley."

25. Such as "The Needle's Eye" or "Green Gravel."

26. The scholars that established and maintained these categories, Francis James Child (Child 1882) and G. Malcolm Laws (Laws 1957; Laws 1964), published their research in sources that have become standard resource works for folklore and folksong scholars. Even today scholars generally recognize three types of Anglo-American ballads, despite controversies behind the methods for classification.

27. Francis James Child, a nineteenth-century Harvard professor, gathered and organized ballads by narrative type and clustered them into 305 titles with corresponding numbers. Child's numbering system became the standard for identifying many songs found in families and communities with Anglo-American roots, for about half of the songs identified by Child were brought to the United States by settlers in the seventeenth through the nineteenth centuries.

28. Cecil Sharp and Maud Karpeles (his assistant) collected songs in the southern Appalachians between 1916 and 1918. His collection from that period, *English Folk Songs from the Southern Appalachians,* was published posthumously in 1932. In New England the most influential collector was Phillips Barry. His collecting took place largely in the northern New England states beginning in 1903 and ending with his death in 1927. His collection, *British Ballads from Maine* (with Fannie Eckstorm and Mary W. Smyth) was published in 1929.

29. "The Outlandish Knight," sung by Jonathan Moses of Orford, New Hampshire, on 4 July 1942. Recorded by Marguerite Olney.

30. "Lord Bateman," sung by Lena Rich of Belvidere, Vermont, on 18 November 1954. Recorded by Marguerite Olney.

31. Sung by Hattie E. Smith of Springfield, Maine, 2 September 1942. Recorded by Marguerite Olney.

32. The traditional ballads also continued to be popular during the folksong revival movements of the 1930s and 1960s and are still well known especially among urban residents today.

33. Sung by Thomas Edward Nelson, Union Hills, New Brunswick, Maine, 28 September 1928. Cited in Barry 1929: 73–74; see also Flanders 1960–65: vol. 1, 224–25.

34. Broadsides sung in American homes and communities were collected, classified, and numbered by G. Malcolm Laws in the mid-twentieth century. Laws divided the songs into several broad topics: love, war, crime, sailors and the sea, and humor (see Laws 1957).

35. Sung by Charles Finnemore, Bridgewater, Maine, on 30 September 1941. Recorded by Marguerite Olney.

36. Sung by Belle Luther Richards, Colebrook, New Hampshire, 16 July 1943. Recorded by Marguerite Olney.

37. At least seventeen versions of this song were collected in Maine, Vermont, and New Hampshire between 1920 and 1960. Collectors included Eloise Linscott, Helen Hartness Flanders and Marguerite Olney, Fannie Hardy Eckstorm, and Phillips Barry.

38. Seven versions in the Flanders Collection.

39. Sung by J. E. Shepard, Baltimore, Vermont, in May 1933 and May 1939, transcribed by Elizabeth Flanders and Marguerite Olney and published in *The New Green Mountain Songster*, 36–37.

40. See Laws, 1950. Laws classified American ballads (which he calls Native American ballads) according to story types including war, cowboys and pioneers, lumberjacks, sailors and the sea, criminals and outlaws, murder, and tragedies and disasters.

41. While lumbering ballads related directly to lumbering accidents and other events in the camps, the repertoires of lumberers presented in the camps were actually quite broad and these songs represent a small fraction of those songs sung in there.

42. Asa Davis, Milton, Vermont, contributed this ballad to the Flanders Collection, 25 July 1943. Another typical opening line is "Come all you jolly shanty boys, wherever you may be / I would have you give attention and listen now to me" (Belle Richards, Pittsburg, New Hampshire, contributed this ballad to the Flanders Collection, 16 September 1942).

43. Taken down in 1916 "from the recitation of a lumberjack." Gray 1924: 22.

44. Albert Howard, Orford, New Hampshire, formerly of Blue Hill, Maine, 18 November 1942. Recorded by Marguerite Olney.

45. Sung by Richard Smith of Menardo, Maine, 1 September 1942. Recorded by Marguerite Olney.

46. See especially Fanny Hardy Eckstorm in *Minstrelsy of Maine: Folk-Songs and Ballads of the Woods and the Coast* (1927); Phillips Barry and Fanny Hardy Eckstorm in issues of *The Bulletin of the Folksong Society of the Northeast* (1930–1937); and Edward (Sandy) Ives in *Joe Scott: The Woodsman-Songmaker* (1978).

47. See Eckstorm 1927: 54–61 for two Maine versions of this song, which was well known in the Midwestern camps as well.

48. Sung by Lena Bourne Fish of East Jaffrey, New Hampshire, 9 May 1940. Recorded by Marguerite Olney.

49. Sung by Arthur Walker of Littleton, Maine, 30 August 1942. Recorded by Marguerite Olney. Also sung by Alex Neddeau, Lyndon Center, Vermont, 4 July 1942.

50. A few of these include "An Elegy on the Loss of a Little Boy in the Woods" (Daniel Sanders, Grafton, New Hampshire, 1820); "The Manchester Tragedy! Or the Death of Jonas L. Parker" [by murder]; "Lines Composed by William Ramsdell on the Death of Three Brothers" [by drowning] (Hooksett Falls, New Hampshire, 1845); "The Palmyra Moose-hunt" (John Harvey, Palmyra, Maine, 1841); "Lines Composed on the Abduction and Cruel Murder of Miss Sarah H. Furber" (Lucy A. Hall, Nottingham, New Hampshire, 1848); "The Waterville Tragedy: Lines on the Murder of Edward Mathews" (V. P. Coolidge, Waterville, Maine, 1848), Sung to the tune of "Mary's Dream"; "Last words of Peter Williams and

Abraham Cox" [execution for murder] (Auburn, Maine, 1858) sung to the tune of "Old Ironsides"; "The Nashua Fire" (Byron De Wolfe, Nashua, New Hampshire, 1870); "The Terrible Disaster on the Central Vermont Railroad" (Alexander B. Beard, W. Manchester, New Hampshire, 1887); "The Drowning Accident at Lake Massabesic" (Alexander B. Beard W. Manchester, New Hampshire, 1888); "In Memory of Schooner Brave: Which was lost May 4th, 1893 on Newburyport Beach, with all on board. She was commanded by Capt. J. W. Lane, with crew of three men, Mr. Norton, Fred Thompson and Sumner Stinson, all of Deer Isle, Maine" (George H. Eaton, Newburyport, Maine, 1893); The Cocheco Mill Fire (Dover, New Hampshire, 1907); "The Great Bangor Fire" (John F. Young, Old Town, Maine, 1911).

51. A. Tolin, Chester, Vermont (originally of Maine), contributed this ballad to the Flanders Collection in 1934. It was originally recorded and transcribed by Flanders and published by Flanders and Barry in *The New Green Mountain Songster,* 221–22.

52. See Coffin 1925, chapter 1 for a discussion of these characteristics.

53. Remembered by eighty-eight-year-old Alice Dodge Titus and her son Walter Titus of Johnson, Vermont, 17 November 1954, in the Flanders Collection.

54. Clyde Covill, interview by author, West Stewartstown, New Hampshire, 7 July 1987.

55. Sung by Hattie Eldredge Eldred, Hardwick, Vermont, 24 October 1958. A shorter version of this song with a similar melody was sung by Cordelia Cerasoli in Barre, Vermont, 28 November 1984, and recorded by the author.

56. Elwin Corey, Fair Haven, Vermont, interview by author, 7 February 1985.

57. Myra Daniels, Hardwick, Vermont, on 1 July 1954 for the Flanders Collection.

58. Sung by Annie Pollard, Baltimore, Vermont, 8 December 1939.

59. Sung by Jonathan Moses, Orford, New Hampshire, 10 July 1943. Recorded by Helen Hartness Flanders.

60. David Kane, Searsport, Maine, 8 June 1941. Recorded by Marguerite Olney for the Flanders Ballad Collection.

61. A. B. Cheney, Dorset, Vermont, 1930. Recorded by Helen Hartness Flanders, lyrics published in Flanders, *Vermont Folk Songs and Ballads,* 34.

62. Mrs. Grace Pettingill of South Royalton, Vermont, sang "Green Carpet" for the Flanders Collection on August 14, 1945.

63. Sung by Sadie Syphers Harvey, Monticello, Maine, on 8 May 1942 for the Flanders Collection. Another version was contributed by Myrtle E. Covey of West Brattleboro, Vermont, on 11 April 1932:

> The needle's eye it runs so high
> The thread it runs so true
> It had caught many a smiling lass
> And now it has caught you
> And now it has caught you
> It has caught many a smiling lass
> And now it has caught you.

64. Sung by Minnie Dillon Crane, Cornish, New Hampshire, formerly of Windsor, Vermont, on 21 November 1930. Recorded by Helen Hartness Flanders.

65. Sung by Mrs. Grace Pettingill, South Royalton, Vermont, for the Flanders Collection, 14 August 1945.

66. Sung by Mrs. Lyndon Beardslee, Barnet, Vermont, for the Flanders Collection, 28 August 1944.

67. Cordelia Cerasoli, interview by author, Barre, Vermont, 28 November 1984.

3. Religious Singing (pp. 60–75)

1. Katherine Fogg, interview by author, Pittsburg, New Hampshire, 5 June 1987.

2. See *The American Vocalist* (1849) for an example of a collection that played this dual role. By the late nineteenth century, this practice was common.

3. Charles M. Cobb, journal manuscript, 1849–50, Montpelier, Vermont: Vermont Historical Society Collection.

4. See Deacon 1991 for a study of this popular singing-school book in Maine and Vermont.

5. See Mansfield 1849.

6. Data on music in these mid-nineteenth- to early-twentieth-century rural households indicate that the shape-note hymnody popular in other regions of the United States did not play a significant role here.

7. Lena Bourne Fish, E. Jaffrey, New Hampshire, was recorded for the Flanders Collection, 27 August 1943.

8. This version by Lena Bourne Fish, E. Jaffrey, New Hampshire, was recorded for the Flanders Collection, 13 September 1945. For comparison, see the shape note version in White, *The Sacred Harp* (1869), 312, using the following melody:

9. Gene Staples, Dixfield, Maine, interviewed by Eloise Linscott, 17 November 1941.

10. Black's lyrics:

> When the trumpet of the Lord shall sound, and time shall be no more,
> And the morning breaks, eternal, bright and fair;
> When the saved of earth shall gather over on the other shore,
> And the roll is called up yonder, I'll be there.

> *Chorus:*
> When the roll is called up yonder,
> When the roll is called up yonder,
> When the roll is called up yonder,
> When the roll is called up yonder I'll be there.

> On that bright and cloudless morning when the dead in Christ shall rise,
> And the glory of His resurrection share;
> When His chosen ones shall gather to their home beyond the skies,
> And the roll is called up yonder, I'll be there.

> Let us labor for the Master from the dawn till setting sun,
> Let us talk of all His wondrous love and care;
> Then when all of life is over, and our work on earth is done,
> And the roll is called up yonder, I'll be there.

11. Ora Knapp, manuscript in the Flanders Collection, dated 16 September 1940.

12. Ida Morgan, manuscript in the Flanders Collection, dated 6 June 1931.

13. Sung by Margaret Shipman, Vergennes, Vermont, 16 November 1939, for the Flanders Collection.

14. Sung by Ella Doten, North Calais, Vermont, in 1933 for the Flanders Collection.

15. Joshua Himes, *Millennial Harp: Designed for the Meetings on the Second Coming of Christ: Three Parts in One Volume*, improved ed., Boston, 1846.

16. Ray Grimes, interview by author, Lincoln, Vermont, 4 October 1985.

17. Mrs. Ray Grimes, interview by author, Lincoln, Vermont, 4 October 1985.

18. Thelma Neill, interview by author, Warren, Vermont, 3 October 1985.

19. Katherine Fogg, interview by author, 15 June 1987, Pittsburg, N.H.

4. The Musical Landscape: Social Dance Music (pp. 75–112)

1. Typically these fiddlers' rules require that performers play three tunes in three genre categories: a slow traditional tune, a waltz, and a fast traditional tune. There are clear stylistic and melodic restrictions that serve to maintain an old-time style both regionally and nationally. See Blaustein 1975 for further information on this subject.

2. Freeman Corey Sr., interview by author, Benson, Vermont, 11 May 1985.

3. See Howe 1862 and James E. Morrison, *Twenty-Four Early American Country Dances, Cotillions and Reels for the Year 1976* (Country Dance and Song Society, 1976).

4. An exception to this is the work of Eloise Linscott, who has provided detailed field data and interpretation of historical and contemporary (1930s) dance traditions (Linscott 1939: 57–120). Others who worked to document dance traditions in the region in the early period include revivalists Ralph Page and Newton Tolman.

5. By the nineteenth century, though, the expanding dance repertoires, increased access to musical instruments, growing popularity of ensemble playing in military and other marching bands (especially during the Civil War), and growth of local dance bands were impacting many communities.

6. Elwin Corey, interview by author, Fair Haven, Vermont, 7 February 1985.

7. Thelma and Albert Neill, interview by author, Warren, Vermont, 3 October 1985.

8. From an interview noted in "Pastimes to Remember" by Martha B. Alt in Hidden and Ulitz 1976: 40–41.

9. Thelma and Albert Neill, interview by author, Warren, Vermont, 3 October 1985.

10. Lois Greeley, interview by author, Springfield, Vermont, 9 February 1989.

11. The kitchen dance was known throughout northern New England by a number of names including kitchen junket, junket, tunk, kitchen hop, and kitchen breakdown, as well as social, party, or frolic.

12. Food and drink varied, ranging from liquor to hard cider to coffee, and repertoire and dance styles likely varied as well (given the variations we know exist today, it is likely a wide range of styles was represented).

13. Elwin Corey, interview by author, Fair Haven, Vermont, 7 February 1985.

14. Albert Neill, interview by author, Warren, Vermont, 7 February 1985.

15. Ardes Haynes, interview by author, Pittsburg, New Hampshire, 8 June 1987.

16. Julie Beaudoin, interview by Fletcher Fischer for Vermont Public Television, 1985.

17. This was also reported as a practice when a musician from within the community became well known or was in particular demand for a performance.

18. Roy Clark, interview by author, Bristol, Vermont, 6 February 1984.

19. "The original Densmore Band existed as early as 1850 with Orange and Artemus Greene Densmore as two of its founders. By 1860 fourteen-year-old Charles A. Densmore, a son of Orange, was also playing with the group. Eventually, Charles became the Band's conductor, and for many years the orchestra played in Chelsea and surrounding towns.

Charles L. Densmore, the younger son of Charles A. Densmore, was also a musician who played both the clarinet and bass violin" (Chelsea Historical Society, 1984: 129).

20. Elwin Corey, interview by author, Fair Haven, Vermont, 7 February 1985

21. Ibid.

22. *English Dancing Master* (1651), its title later modified to *The Dancing Master,* edited by Henry Playford (John's nephew) and later by John Young. There were seventeen editions between 1652 and 1728.

23. This is to be distinguished from the *contradanse anglaise,* which indicated longways dancing.

24. See, for example, Washburn n.d. .

25. In the nineteenth century, this was led by American inventor Elias Howe, whose dance manuals and tune collections were published beginning in the 1840s (See Howe 1862 and Howe 1882 for examples of the dance manuals). H. G. Washburn published *The Ballroom Manual of Contra Dances and Social Cotillons with Remarks on Quadrilles and Spanish Dance* in 1863 in Belfast, Maine. In the twentieth century, Elizabeth Burchenal published *American Country Dances: Twenty-eight Contra-dances Largely from the New England States* in 1918; Henry Ford and Benjamin Lovett published "*Good Morning": After a Sleep of Twenty-five Years, Old-fashioned Dancing is Being Revived by Mr. and Mrs. Henry Ford* in 1925, with another edition entitled "*Good Morning": Music, Calls, and Directions for Old-time Dancing* published in 1941.

26. Variations include establishing active and inactive couples by alternating women and men at various intervals to generate a wide variety of combinations of interactive relationships.

27. Elias Howe says, "Sets are formed similar to cotillons with eight couples instead of four" (Howe 1862: 22).

28. As called by Edson Cole of Freedom, New Hampshire, and recorded by Eloise Linscott (Linscott 1939: 71–72).

29. As called by Ed Larkin of Chelsea, Vermont, and recorded by Helen Hartness Flanders and Alan Lomax in November 1939.

30. Step dancing by European Americans was sometimes combined with the step dances of African Americans, as well as the individual step dances of other immigrant groups. This ultimately generated a syncretic dance tradition that today dominates public perception of this genre.

31. And because so few people refer to tunes by name, and because names of tunes (sometimes variations of a more well-known tune) were adopted in conjunction with each era, we can only infer some of the practices based on those twentieth-century practices that are documented more completely.

32. Mike Pelletier of Old Town, Maine, as cited in Doty 1985: 85.

33. Philippe Lemay of Manchester, New Hampshire, as cited in Doty 1985: 30.

34. See the appendix of this chapter for a list of core tunes as identified by performers.

35. See Kate Van Winkle Keller and Ralph Sweet 1976, 24.

36. See John Adams Taggart "Recollection of a Busy Life." Typescript ms. New Hampshire Historical Society, 1915.

37. As called by J. H. Buck, E. Bethel, Vermont and recorded by Helen Hartness Flanders and Alan Lomax in November 1939.

38. Dot Brown, interview by Kim Chambers, Bristol, Vermont, 30 September 1974.

39. For example, John Taggart, fiddler from Sharon, New Hampshire named tunes "John A's Hornpipe" and "Sharon City." The S. Daily manuscript includes a tune called "Jess's Reel."

40. In contrast, in the southern United States, fiddlers use considerably more chording: the bowing is harsher, and rhythmic bowing with syncopation is employed.

41. Elwin Corey, interview by author, Fair Haven, Vermont, 7 February 1985.

42. "Devil's Dream" is an example of a tune in which this order is reversed; it starts with the higher-pitch phrase.

43. Eloise Linscott, *Folksongs of Old New England,* 1939, 86.

44. Played by Ed Larkin, Chelsea, Vermont, and recorded 8 November 1939.

5. The Social Landscape: Gendered Spaces (pp. 113–38)

1. While most research on access to knowledge deals with women in the work force and knowledge that yields power in society (or the loss of power due to the lack of knowledge), it is important to recognize that cultural knowledge plays a role in this process as well.

2. Some of the recent research on this subject can be found in Fahey 1995, Hansen 1994, Moore 1983, Ryan 1981.

3. Or that women and men's forms and styles of expression were the same.

4. See Pocius 1991: 61 for a discussion of the structuring of space in Calvert, Newfoundland.

5. See the discussion of fiddlers' associations in Blaustein 1975.

6. In a group of elderly people (sixty is very young among this group), women dominate the floor; they perform with greater numbers and more energy.

7. The parlor of the mid-19th century "served two fairly distinct functions, family rituals and social (or semipublic) activities. Private family rituals held in the parlor reinforced ideas of family solidarity, continuity, and patriarchy. The social aspect of the parlor encompassed female hegemony, entertainment of friends, and the display of feminine accomplishments" (McMurry 1988: 141).

8. There is little evidence that women who worked alongside men doing outdoor chores also sang. Those who talk about this type of cooperative work speak more about listening and learning songs at these times.

9. Despite greater freedom for women during the twentieth century, culturally they remained passive participants, drawing on media sources, especially the radio, for their entertainment.

10. Women talk about pursuing other women but not men, for songs.

11. A significant number of women offered substantial repertoires, including Susie Carr Young in Maine, Belle Richards and Lena Bourne Fish in New Hampshire, Ellen Sullivan in Vermont, all of whom were recorded by Phillips Barry and Helen Hartness Flanders in the 1930s and 1940s. The accuracy of this information remains in question, though—were some songs not recorded because women didn't have the kind of repertoires the collectors were seeking?

12. Florence Scott, interview with author, Stark, New Hampshire, 6 May 1988.

13. The *place* for these songs, and their specific characteristics *as they were sung in that context,* was the lumbercamp. Sung elsewhere, the songs might take on a different meaning. Data indicates that bawdy songs were not be sung at home when women and/or children were around; a woman singing a song learned from her father might sing it differently for a child or to pass the time while working.

14. Information on repertoires has been gathered from early field recordings, interviews, manuscripts, and local histories housed in the collections of Eloise Linscott, Phillips Barry, and Helen Hartness Flanders. It is important to note that these collections suffer from a low representation of American popular music, which was widely sung in the same

homes in this region. There is no indication, though, that the lack of representation of American music differed between women and men.

15. Information on Belle's and Sid's repertoires is taken from songs recorded for the Helen Hartness Flanders Ballad Collection and from recent interviews with relatives who recalled their music.

16. Sung by Herbert Haley, Cuttingsville, Vermont, 7 August 1932. Recorded by Helen Hartness Flanders.

17. Sung by Sarah A. Lane, Howland, Maine, 2 September 1942. Recorded by Marguerite Olney.

18. See Eckstorm, *Minstrelsy of Maine*, 176–98.

19. Olive Burt, however, points out that "In my search for murder ballads I have often found the most rewarding sources to be gentle, mother ladies . . . Margaret Masters . . . supplied me with one of my most gruesome ballads, 'The Ashland Tragedy,' which she learned as a child from her father . . ." (Burt 1958: 57).

20. Sung by Clark Amey, Pittsburg, New Hampshire, 25 April 1943, recorded by Marguerite Olney.

21. The Laura Hooker sessions, Vergennes, Vermont, were sent to the Flanders Collection in March 1932.

22. Recorded on 14 September 1930 by George Brown in Shaftsbury, Vermont, from the singing of B. L. Twitchell.

23. Many of the historical recordings of northern New England singers held in collections in Maine, New Hampshire, Vermont, and Massachusetts have been stored with little contextual information. While it is sometimes difficult to use these sources to inform research on musical performance in social context, the historical recordings do provide concrete data on singing styles. The number of recordings of the same songs and the representation of many relatives among singers in the collections provides an excellent opportunity to explore the singing styles of women and men, and especially to compile information on differences in their performance practices.

24. Sung by Belle Luther Richards in Colebrook, New Hampshire, 16 September 1942. Recorded by Marguerite Olney. About the song Belle said: "I used to hear my brothers sing it."

25. Sung by Sidney Luther, Pittsburg, New Hampshire, 18 November 1941.

26. "Polly" ("Polly Oliver") was performed by Myra Daniels for Helen Hartness Flanders in 1932.

27. Many singers performed with a flexible meter, indicating that meter wasn't as relevant as lyrical content. Discussion of this as a factor is for the purpose of comparison; many men sang with little apparent regard for meter.

28. "Two Little Orphans" sung by Mr. and Mrs. Vernon Mayo, Menardo, Maine, 1 September 1942. Helen Hartness Flanders Ballad Collection.

29. The source of the song among women and men had obvious effects on how it was sung, and historical recordings also demonstrate that there tends to be less embellishment in a song that a woman has learned from her mother than in one she learned from her father or brother.

30. Recorded by Helen Hartness Flanders on 9 May 1942.

6. Family Song Traditions: The Pierce-Spaulding Family of North Shrewsbury, Vermont (pp. 139–67)

An earlier version of this chapter was published by *Northeast Folklore* (vol. 30, 1995).

1. "The Half Hitch" was recorded by Flanders in 1932 and published in *Ballads Migrant in New England* (33–37) and *Ancient Ballads Traditionally Sung in New England* (vol. 1, 266–70); "The Sailor Boy" was recorded in 1932 and the text was published in *The New Green Mountain Songster* (39–40); "Lord Bateman" was recorded in 1932 and was published in *Ancient Ballads Traditionally Sung in New England* (vol. 2, 39–43); "The True Story" was published in *A Garland of Green Mountain Song* (32–33); "The Young Counselor" was published in *Country Songs of Vermont* (46–47).

2. Marjorie Pierce, interview by author, N. Shrewsbury, Vermont, 16 April 1985.

3. Ibid.

4. Marjorie Pierce, interview by author, N. Shrewsbury, Vermont, 1986.

5. Marjorie Pierce, interview by author, N. Shrewsbury, Vermont, September 1984.

6. Marjorie Pierce, interview by author, N. Shrewsbury, Vermont, 2 October 1984.

7. Ibid.

8. Ibid.

9. This song was recorded in 1945 from the singing of Agnes Shepard Torp in Weathersfield, Vermont.

10. Marjorie Pierce, interview by author, N. Shrewsbury, Vermont, 1985.

11. Sung by Gertrude Spaulding Pierce, N. Shrewsbury, Vermont, 14 July 1932. Recorded by Helen Hartness Flanders.

12. Submitted to Helen Hartness Flanders by Marjorie Pierce in 1953 as a version known to both of her parents.

13. Marjorie Pierce, interview by author, N. Shrewsbury, Vermont, September 1984.

14. Marjorie Pierce, interview by author, N. Shrewsbury, Vermont, 2 October 1984.

15. Marjorie Pierce, interview by author, N. Shrewsbury, Vermont, 2 October 1984.

16. Marjorie Pierce, interview by author, N. Shrewsbury, Vermont, September 1984.

17. Marjorie Pierce, interview by author, N. Shrewsbury, Vermont, 2 October 1984.

18. Marjorie Pierce, interview by author, N. Shrewsbury, Vermont, 1 December 1984.

19. Marjorie Pierce, interview by author, N. Shrewsbury, Vermont, 1986.

20. Marjorie Pierce, interview by author, N. Shrewsbury, Vermont, 2 October 1984.

21. Some of these songs are found in collections popular during the late nineteenth century, including *Wehman's Collection, Heart Songs,* and *Franklin Square Song Collection.* The Pierces owned the first two. Other books in the family collection included *Maxham's Melodies: Songs, Sacred and Secular* and *Favorite Radio Hymns of Edward McHugh.* A collection of cowboy songs was signed at the top with her mother's name.

22. Marjorie Pierce, interview by author, N. Shrewsbury, Vermont, 2 October 1984.

23. Marjorie Pierce, interview by author, N. Shrewsbury, Vermont, 1 December 1984.

24. Marjorie Pierce, interview by author, N. Shrewsbury, Vermont, 2 October 1984.

25. Marjorie Pierce, interview by author, N. Shrewsbury, Vermont, 1986.

26. Ibid.

27. Marjorie Pierce, interview by author, N. Shrewsbury, Vermont, 2 October 1984.

28. Marjorie Pierce, interview by author, N. Shrewsbury, Vermont, 1986.

29. Marjorie Pierce, interview by author, N. Shrewsbury, Vermont, 16 April 1985.

7. Reconstructing Community Traditions (pp. 168–234)

An earlier version of this chapter was published in August 2003 by the Elphinstone Institute, Aberdeen, Scotland.

1. Pittsburg is interesting also because of its proximity to Canada and the invisible border that provided opportunities for residents to move back and forth between the two countries, both literally and through the airwaves.

2. The region for residents today includes the towns of Pittsburg, Colebrook, Stewartstown Hollow, Clarksville, Stark, Groveton, and Kidderville. This regional affiliation emerged historically as family members moved—temporarily or permanently—to these (relatively) nearby communities.

3. See Pike 1935, 1959, and 1967 for documentation of his work in this region.

4. Marcia Dingman, interview by author, Stark, New Hampshire, August 13, 1987.

5. Avis Terrill Shatney, ms., n.d., Pittsburg, New Hampshire.

6. Sung by Orlon Merrill of Charlestown, New Hampshire, originally of Pittsburg. Recorded by Helen Hartness Flanders in 1930.

7. Back Lake is right in the center of Pittsburg; the Connecticut Lakes are just above the town.

8. Katherine Fogg, interview by author, Pittsburg, New Hampshire, 15 June 1987.

9. See Dorr, 1872, 59.

10. An 1865 story in the *Vermont Record, Brattleboro* apparently inspired Dorr.

11. Letter from Helen Hartness Flanders to Phillips Barry, 3 February 1931.

12. Known most commonly as "Little Mary Phagan." A recent discussion of the history of this ballad can be found in McNeil 1988: 72–75. Brown 1952: vol. 4, p. 295 includes a melody to accompany one of the six versions he includes in his collection of North Carolina ballads.

13. Florence Scott, interview by author, Stark, New Hampshire, 8 May 1988.

14. Sung by George Jackson, Columbia, New Hampshire, 18 July 1943. Recorded by Marguerite Olney.

15. Sung by Lester (Jack) Hoadley of Johnson, Vermont; M. Olney, collector, 8 October 1953.

> Oh, I went down to Newport one Fourth of July.
> I got at the liquor and got pretty high,
> Fell in with Stub Stannard and went on a sail
> And we both marched down to Newport Jail.
> Hard times—Newport Jail,
> And it's hard times they say.

16. See Pike 1935: 339–40 for a similar version. See also Halpert 1951: 66–67, Lomax and Lomax 1934: 138–43, and Belden and Hudson 1952: 419–20.

17. Clyde Covill, interview by author, 13 August 1987. "Guy Reed" was written by Joe Scott, a singer-songwriter of the Maine woods who wrote songs during the late nineteenth and early twentieth centuries. Flanders published Orlon Merrill's version of this ballad in *The New Green Mountain Songster*, 55–56. See Ives 1978: 140–77 for more on "Guy Reed."

18. Clyde Covill, interview by author, West Stewartstown, New Hampshire, 13 September 1988. One resident said that it was Clyde Covill's uncle that was driving the wagon when he was killed.

19. Clyde Covill, interview by author, Pittsburg, New Hampshire, 1988.

20. Sung by Edwin Day, Colebrook, New Hampshire, 18 April 1942. Recorded by Marguerite Olney.

21. From Mrs. Elizabeth Shallow, Pittsburg, New Hampshire, 8 December 1941, in the Helen Hartness Flanders Ballad Collection.

22. Mark Coffin (1975: 15–16, 156–57) discusses Pike's version of this ballad.

23. Printed in Pike 1935 and Pike 1959: 171–72 from the singing of "Stonewall Jackson."

24. Sung by Abe Washburn, Colebrook, New Hampshire, 12 November 1941. Recorded by Marguerite Olney.

25. Clyde Covill, interview by author, 24 September 1987.

26. See Ives, 1964, Ives, 1978; see also Szwed 1970.

27. Marcia Dingman, interview by author, Stark, New Hampshire, 13 August 1987.

28. Bill Hook, interview by author, Stewartstown Hollow, New Hampshire, 24 September 1987.

29. See Pike 1935. As an introduction to the local songs, he says, "I start with the most popular one of all; even the ladies of Pittsburg know it, though they discreetly omit some stanzas when they sing it. It is called Old Dan Day. Dan Day was the most notorious inhabitant of Pittsburg and much addicted to the cup that cheers. Anecdotes about him are many and remarkable—as the one concerning his drunken remark when he was informed that his wife had given birth to triplets" (337). One man I interviewed in 1987 said this about Dan Day: "Old Dan Day is quite a celebrity in Pittsburg. He often said that to his knowledge he was the only one that beat the Almighty. He made three Days in one night and never took his shirt off; I guess that's how they figured he beat the Almighty."

30. In another verse, for example:

> He had another and her name was Jane,
> I think that her character is deeply stained;
> With old Doctor Robbins she used to lay
> When her husband was far away.

31. Sung by Abe Washburn, Colebrook, New Hampshire, 21 November 1941, and recorded with the following note by Marguerite Olney: "This was about a family named Carl Stanton who used to live in Clarksville, New Hampshire."

32. Dr. Randall Brooks, interview by author, Colebrook, New Hampshire, 30 September 1988.

33. Katherine Fogg, interview by author, Pittsburg, New Hampshire, 15 June 1987.

34. Belle Richards, interview by Marguerite Olney, Colebrook, New Hampshire, 24 September 1945.

35. Gerard Richards, interview by author, Pittsburg, New Hampshire, 20 June 1987.

36. Sung by Belle Richards, Pittsburg, New Hampshire, and recorded in 1945.

37. Hudson's version of "Alas and Did My Savior Bleed" draws its refrain from "To the Sweet Sunny South," a song popular in the nineteenth century.

38. Members of this sect are also known by the names "Two-by-Twos" or "Cooneyites."

39. Ardes Haynes, interview by author, Pittsburg, New Hampshire, 18 June 1987.

40. Clyde Covill, interview by author, Stewartstown, New Hampshire, 5 May 1988.

41. Ida Gould, interview by author, Stewartstown Hollow, New Hampshire, 12 August 1987.

42. The leatherbound manuscript book has the name "S. Daily" on the cover and is signed in the back by Rosette Dailey. The dance music appears to include transcriptions and notes from at least three different contributors. Samuel Dailey died in 1887 at age seventy-two. Rosette Dailey was married in 1872 at age eighteen and died in 1873 of typhoid (Pittsburg town records.)

43. Marcia Dingman, interview by author, Stark, New Hampshire, 13 August 1987.

44. Evelyn Stebbins and Leora Hartlen, interview by author, Colebrook, New Hampshire, 24 September 1987.

45. Clyde Covill, interview by author, West Stewartstown, New Hampshire, 19 June 1987.

46. Clyde Covill, interview by author, West Stewartstown, New Hampshire, 13 September 1988.

47. Katherine Fogg, interview by author, Pittsburg, New Hampshire, 15 June 1987.

48. "Boston Fancy" performed by Robert McKeage, Colebrook, New Hampshire, 1942. Recorded by Marguerite Olney.

49. Leo Brooks, interview by author, Pittsburg, New Hampshire, 18 July 1987.

50. Ibid.

51. Clyde Covill, interview by author, W. Stewartstown, New Hampshire, 24 September 1987.

52. Ida Gould, interview by author, Stewartstown Hollow, New Hampshire, 12 August 1987.

53. Florence Scott and Flora Campbell, interview by author, Stark, New Hampshire, 6 May 1988.

54. Marcia Dingman, interview by author, Stark, New Hampshire, 13 August 1987.

55. Clyde Covill, interview by author, West Stewartstown, New Hampshire, 19 June 1987.

56. "And I remember when I was a kid growin' up—his father, old Bill Placey—when we used to have country telephones, he used to call Becky Williams—and of course everybody would take the phone down and listen to the conversation. And old Bill used to call Becky Williams and sing to her." (Dr. Randall Brooks, interview by author, Colebrook, New Hampshire, 30 September 1988).

57. Ardes Haynes, interview by author, Pittsburg, New Hampshire, 8 June 1987.

58. Marcia Dingman, interview by author, Stark, New Hampshire, 13 August 1987.

59. Clyde Covill, interview by author, West Stewartstown, New Hampshire, 13 September 1988.

60. Clyde Covill, Interview by author, West Stewartstown, New Hampshire, 18 July 1987.

61. Both of these songs were identified by Laws in *Native American Balladry*. "The Chippewa Girl" (Laws H10) was identified as found in Michigan and Nova Scotia; "The Little Mohee" (Laws H8) has been found widely in the United States, and theories as to its origin have been discussed by a number of scholars, including Phillips Barry in *The New Green Mountain Songster*, 146.

62. Clyde Covill, interview by author, West Stewartstown, New Hampshire, 5 May 1988.

63. Clyde Covill, interview by author, West Stewartstown, New Hampshire, 19 June 1987

64. Clyde Covill, interview by author, West Stewartstown, New Hampshire, 5 May 1988.

8. *Conclusion: Landscape and Memory (pp. 235–38)*

1. Most of the fiddlers were from Vermont, New Hampshire, Quebec, New York, and Massachusetts.

2. In New England, there are a number of performers that move between ballads collected in the eighteenth and nineteenth centuries and songs of their own creation—most notable among them are Pete Sutherland and Margaret MacArthur in Vermont and Gordon Bok in Maine.

3. Albert Neill, interview by author, Warren, Vermont, 7 February 1985.

4. Clyde Covill, interview by author, W. Stewartstown, New Hampshire, 1987.

5. Lois Greeley, interview by author, Springfield, Vermont, 9 February 1989.

Bibliography

Aiken, Ruth, M. J., ed. 1983. *No Boughs on My Bonnet: The Journal of the Times of Barbara Copeland Wentworth of Cushing, Maine, 1811–1890*. Augusta, Maine: Maine Historic Preservation Commission.

Aldrich, Elizabeth. 1991. *From the Ballroom to Hell: Grace and Folly in Nineteenth-Century Dance*. Evanston: Northwestern University Press.

Allen, Barbara, and Thomas J. Schlereth. eds. 1990. *Sense of Place: American Regional Cultures*. Lexington: University Press of Kentucky.

Allen, Mildred E. 1980. *Reflections of Tinmouth: A Concise History*. N.p.: n.d.

Andrews, Lydia C. 1986. *Three Towns (Averill, Norton, Stanhope)*. Littleton, N.H.: Sherwin/ Dodge, 1986.

Anonymous. [1915]. Tunebook, Panton, Vt. Helen Hartness Flanders Ballad Collection.

Arsenault, Georges. 1980. *Complaintes acadiennes de I'lle-du-Prince-Édouard*. Montréal: Lemeac.

Ayers, Edward, et al. 1996. *All Over the Map: Rethinking American Regions*. Baltimore: Johns Hopkins University Press.

Baker, B. F., and W. O. Perkins. 1864. *The Tabernacle: A Collection of Hymn Tunes, Chants, Sentences, Motetts and Anthems, Adapted to Public and Private Worship, and to the Use of Choirs, Singing Schools, Musical Societies and Conventions*. Boston: Ticknor & Fields.

Barron, Hal S. 1984. *Those Who Stayed Behind: Rural Society in Nineteenth-Century New England*. Cambridge: Cambridge University Press.

Barry, Phillips. 1914. "The Transmission of Folk Song." *Journal of American Folklore* 27: 67–76.

Barry, Phillips, ed. 1939. *The Maine Woods Songster*. Cambridge, Mass.: Powell Printing.

Barry, Phillips, and Fanny Hardy Eckstorm. 1930–1937. *The Bulletin of the Folksong Society of the Northeast*, Vols. 1–12. Cambridge, Mass.: The Powell Printing Company.

Barry, Phillips, Fanny Hardy Eckstorm, and Mary Winslow Smyth. 1929. *British Ballads from Maine: The Development of Popular Songs with Texts and Airs*. New Haven: Yale University Press.

Bayard, Samuel. 1944. *Hill Country Tunes: Instrumental Folk Music of Southwestern Pennsylvania*. Philadelphia: American Folklore Society.

———. 1982. *Dance to the Fiddle, March to the Fife: Instrumental Folk Tunes in Pennsylvania*. University Park: The Pennsylvania State University Press.

Beck, Horace. 1956. "Folksong Affiliations of Maine." *Midwest Folklore* 6: 159–66.

Belden, H. M., and A. P. Hudson. 1952. The *Frank C. Brown Collection of North Carolina Folklore*. Durham: Duke University Press.

Bender, Jan, ed. 1991. *A History of the Town of Grand Isle*. Grand Isle, Vt.: Landside Press.

Bethke, Robert. 1981. *Adirondack Voices*. Urbana: University of Illinois.

Bishop, J. M. 1984. *New England Fiddles*. Video recording. Milton, Mass.: Media Generation.

Blaustein, Richard J. 1975. "Traditional Music and Social Change: The Old Time Fiddlers Association Movement in the United States." Ph.D. thesis, Indiana University.

Blum, Stephen, Philip V. Bohlman, and Daniel M. Neuman. 1991. *Ethnomusicology and Modern Music History.* Urbana: University of Illinois Press.

Bohlman, Philip. 1988. *The Study of Folk Music in the Modern World.* Bloomington: Indiana University Press.

Botkin, Benjamin A. 1947. *A Treasury of New England Folklore: Stories, Ballads, Traditions of the Yankee People.* New York: Crown.

Boyes, Georgina. 1993. *The Imagined Village: Culture, Ideology and the English Folk Revival.* Manchester: Manchester University Press.

Bronson, Bertrand H. 1976. *The Singing Tradition of Child's Popular Ballads.* Princeton: Princeton University Press.

Brookfield Historical Society. 1987. *History of Brookfield.* Brookfield Historical Society.

Brown, Frank. 1952. *The Frank C. Brown Collection of North Carolina Folklore.* Newman Ivey White, ed. Durham: Duke University Press.

Bruce, Dickson D. 1974. *And They All Sang Hallelujah: Plain-folk Camp-meeting Religion, 1800–1845.* Knoxville: University of Tennessee Press.

Brunvand, Jan Harold. 1996. *American Folklore: An Encyclopedia.* Garland Reference Library of the Humanities 1551. New York: Garland.

Buchan, David. 1972. *The Ballad and the Folk.* London: Routledge and Kegan Paul.

Burchenal, Elizabeth. 1918. *American Country-Dances, Volume 1: Twenty-eight Contra-dances Largely from the New England States.* New York: G. Schirmer.

Burman-Hall, Linda. 1984. "American Traditional Fiddling: Performance Contexts and Techniques." In *Performance Practice: Ethnomusicological Perspectives,* Gerard Behague, ed. Westport, Conn.: Greenwood, 149–221.

Burns, Thomas A. 1978. "Social Symbolism in a Rural Square Dance Event." *Southern Folklore Quarterly* 42: 295–328.

Burt, Olive. 1958. *American Murder Ballads and Their Stories.* New York: Oxford University Press.

Bushaway, Bob. 1982. *By Rite: Custom, Ceremony and Community in England, 1700–1800.* London: Junction.

Carter, N. F., and T. L. Fowler. 1976. *History of Pembroke, New Hampshire, 1730–1895.* Allenstown and Pembroke: Allenstown-Pembroke Bicentennial Committee, 1976.

Cazden, Norman. 1955. *Dances from the Woodland.* 2nd ed. Bridgeport, Conn.: N. Cazden.

Cazden, Norman, Herbert Haufrecht, and Norman Studer. 1982. *Folk Songs of the Catskills.* Albany: State University of New York Press.

Chambers, Kimberley. 1975. "Traditional Fiddling in Northern Vermont." B.A. thesis, Middlebury College.

Chase, Gilbert. 1987. *America's Music: From the Pilgrims to the Present.* 3rd ed. Urbana: University of Illinois Press.

Chelsea Historical Society. 1984. *A History of Chelsea, Vermont, 1784–1984.* Chelsea: Chelsea Historical Society, Northlight Studio Press.

Child, Frances James. 1882–1898. *The English and Scottish Popular Ballads.* Boston: Houghton Mifflin.

Christeson, R. P. 1973. *The Old-Time Fiddler's Repertory.* Columbia: University of Missouri Press.

Cobb, Charles M. 1849–1850. Journal manuscript. Montpelier: Vermont Historical Society Collection.

Coffin, Mark Tristram. 1975. *American Narrative Obituary Verse and Native American Balladry.* Norwood, Penn.: Norwood Editions.

Coffin, Tristram Potter. 1977. *The British Traditional Ballad in North America.* Rev. ed., with a supplement by Roger DeV. Renwick. Austin: University of Texas Press.

Cohen, Marcie. 1985. "The Journals of Joshua Whitman, 1809–1811: An Analysis of Pre-Industrial Community in Rural Maine." M.A. thesis, William and Mary College.

Conforti, Joseph A. 2001. *Imagining New England: Explorations of Regional Identity from the Pilgrims to the Mid-twentieth Century.* Chapel Hill: University of North Carolina.

Conroy, Deborah. 1984. "Old Time Fiddling in the Context of the Champlain Valley Fiddlers." B.A. thesis, Middlebury College.

Cooke, Peter. 1986. *The Fiddle Tradition of the Shetland Isles.* Cambridge: Cambridge University Press.

Cox, Gordon. 1980. *Folk Music in a Newfoundland Outport.* Ottawa: National Museums of Canada.

———. 1983. "I've Changed from That Type of Life to Another: Some Individual Responses to Social Change by Singers in a Newfoundland Outport." *Folk Music Journal* 4(4): 385–400.

Crawford, Richard. 2001. *America's Musical Life: A History.* New York: W. W. Norton.

Daily, S. [1850]. Tunebook. Manuscript. Pittsburg, N.H. Helen Hartness Flanders Ballad Collection.

Damon, S. Foster. 1952. "The History of Square Dancing." *Proceedings of the American Antiquarian Society* 62(1): 63–98.

Darrett, B. Rutnam. 1986. "Assessing the Little Communities of Early America." *William and Mary Quarterly* 43(2): 163–78.

Deacon, David. 1991. "D. H. Mansfield and The American Vocalist." M.A. thesis, University of North Carolina at Chapel Hill.

Dorr, Julia C. R. 1872. *Poems.* Philadelphia: J. B. Lippincott.

Doty, C. Stewart. 1985. *The First Franco-Americans: New England Life Histories from the Federal Writers' Project, 1938–1939.* Orono: University of Maine at Orono.

Downey, James C. 1965. "Revivalism, the Gospel Songs and Social Reform." *Ethnomusicology* 9(2): 115–25

Dunham, Mellie. 1926. *Mellie Dunham's 50 Fiddlin' Dance Tunes.* New York: Carl Fisher.

Dunn, Ginnette. 1980. *The Fellowship of Song: Popular Singing Traditions in East Suffolk.* London: Croom Helm.

Eckstorm, Fanny Hardy, and Mary Winslow Smyth. 1927. *Minstrelsy of Maine: Folk-Songs and Ballads of the Woods and the Coast.* New York: Houghton Mifflin.

Emery, Edwin. 1987. *History of Sanford, Maine, 1661–1900.* Sanford: Harland H. Eastman.

Fahey, Tony. 1995. "Privacy and the Family: Conceptual and Empirical Reflections." *Sociology* 29(4): 687–702.

Fay, Mary S. 1943. "Reading's Musicians of 1906 and Earlier." *The Vermonter* 48(8): 149.

Feintuch, Burt. 1981. "Dancing to the Music: Domestic Sphere Dances and Community in Southcentral Kentucky (1880–1940)." *Journal of the Folklore Institute* 18: 49–68.

Finnegan, Ruth. 1989. *The Hidden Musicians.* Cambridge: Cambridge University Press.

Flanders, Helen Hartness. 1937. *Country Songs of Vermont.* New York: G. Schirmer.

Flanders, Helen Hartness, et al. 1939. *The New Green Mountain Songster: Traditional Folksongs of Vermont.* New Haven: Yale University Press.

———. 1960–65. *Ancient Ballads Traditionally Sung in New England.* 4 vols. Philadelphia: University of Pennsylvania.

Flanders, Helen Hartness, and George Brown. 1931. *Vermont Folk Songs and Ballads.* Brattleboro: Stephen Daye Press.

Flanders, Helen Hartness, and Marguerite Olney. 1953. *Ballads Migrant in New England.* New York: Farrar, Straus, and Young.

Ford, Henry, and Benjamin Lovett. 1925. *"Good Morning": After a Sleep of Twenty-five Years, Old-fashioned Dancing is being Revived by Mr. and Mrs. Henry Ford.* Dearborn, Mich.: Dearborn Publishing Company.

———. 1941. *Good Morning: Music Calls and Directions for Old Time Dancing as Revived by Mr. and Mrs. Henry Ford.* Dearborn, Mich.: Dearborn Publishing Co.

Fowke, Edith. 1970. *Lumbering Songs from the Northern Woods.* Austin: University of Texas.

Gallagher, Nancy L. 1999. *Breeding Better Vermonters: The Eugenics Project in the Green Mountain State.* Hanover, N.H.: University Press of New England.

Gammon, Victor A. F. 1985. "Popular Music in Rural Society: Sussex 1815–1914." Ph.D. thesis, University of Sussex.

Gibbons, Roy W. 1981. *Folk Fiddling in Canada: A Sampling.* Canadian Centre for Folk Culture Studies Papers: Canadian Museum of Civilization Mercury Series, 35. Ottawa: National Museums of Canada.

Gifford, William H. 1970. *Colebrook: "A Place Up Back of New Hampshire."* Colebrook: The News and Sentinel.

Glover, Waldo F. 1955. "Old Scotland in Vermont." *Vermont History* 23(2): 92–103.

Goertzen, Chris. 1996. "Balancing Local and National Approaches at American Fiddle Contests." *American Music* 14(3): 352–81.

Gordon, Robert Winslow. 1938. *Folk-Songs of America.* New York: National Service Bureau.

Gray, Roland Palmer. 1924. *Songs and Ballads of the Maine Lumberjacks with Other Songs from Maine.* Cambridge, Mass.: Harvard University Press.

Green, Steven B. 1978. "Portland Fancy: Recollections of an Old Tradition." Unpub. ms.

———. 1981. "Fiddle Tunes in the Helen Hartness Flanders Ballad Collection." Unpub. ms.

Groce, Nora Ellen. N.d. "Dances as an Integrative Mechanism in the Rural New England Community." M.A. thesis, University of Michigan.

Grover, Carrie B. *A Heritage of Songs.* 1973. Norwood, Pa.: Norwood Editions.

Guest, Bill. 1985. "'Down East' Fiddling." *Canadian Folk Music Bulletin* 19(3): 11–12.

Guntharp, Matthew G. 1980. *Learning the Fiddler's Ways.* University Park: Pennsylvania State University Press.

Hahn, Steven, and Jonathan Prude, eds. 1985. *The Countryside in the Age of Capitalist Transformation: Essays in the Social History of Rural America.* Chapel Hill: University of North Carolina Press.

Halpert, Herbert. 1951. "Vitality of Tradition and Local Songs." *Journal of the International Folk Music Council* 3: 35–40.

Hansen, Karen V. 1994. *A Very Social Time: Crafting Community in Antebellum New England.* Berkeley: University of California Press.

Hardy, Anna Simpson. 1990. *History of Hope, Maine.* Camden, Maine: Penobscot Press.

Hareven, Tamara K., and Randolph Langenbach. 1978. *Amoskeag: Life and Work in an American Factory-City.* Hanover, N.H.: University Press of New England.

Hast, Dorothea. 1993. "Performance, Transformation, and Community: Contra Dance in New England." *Dance Research Journal* 25: 21–32.

———. 1994. "Music, Dance, and Community: Contra Dance in New England." Ph.D. thesis, Wesleyan University.

Hastings, Scott E. 1990. *The Last Yankees: Folkways in Eastern Vermont and the Border Country.* Hanover, N.H.: University Press of New England.

Hastings, Scott E., and Geraldine S. Ames. 1983. *The Vermont Farm Year in 1890.* Woodstock, Vt.: Billings Farm and Museum.

Hawes, Nicholas. 1981. "House Dances and Kitchen Rackets: Traditional Music Styles of the Northeast." In *Festival of American Folklife Program Book,* Washington, D.C.: Smithsonian Institution, 38–40.

Heart Songs. 1909. Boston: Chapple Publishing.

Hicks, Ivan C. 1985. "Old-Time Fiddling in New Brunswick." *Canadian Folk Music Bulletin* 19(3): 16–17.

Hidden, Mabel, and Jean Ulitz, comp. 1976. *Tamworth Recollections.* Tamworth: Tamworth American Revolution Bicentennial Commission.

Hill, Ellen C. 1983. *Across the Onion: A History of East Montpelier, Vermont, 1781 to 1981.* East Montpelier Historical Society.

Himes, Joshua. 1843. *The Millennial Harp: Designed for Meetings on the Second Coming of Christ.* Boston: J. V. Himes.

Historical Society of Temple, New Hampshire. 1976. *A History of Temple, New Hampshire, 1768–1976.* Dublin, N.H.: William L. Bauhan.

Holbrook, Stewart H. 1938. *Holy Old Mackinaw: A Natural History of the American Lumberjack.* Sausalito, Calif.: Comstock.

Horn, Dorothy D. 1970. *Sing to Me of Heaven: A Study of Folk and Early American Materials in Three Old Harp Books.* Gainesville: University of Florida Press.

Hornby, Jim. 1985. "A Survey of Fiddling on Prince Edward Island," *Canadian Folk Music Bulletin* 19(3): 7–10.

Howe, Elias. 1862. *American Dancing Master and Ballroom Prompter.* Boston: Elias Howe.

———. 1882. *Howe's New American Dancing Master: Containing about Five Hundred Dances.* Boston: E. Howe.

Hubka, Thomas C. 1984. *Big House, Little House, Back House, Barn: The Connected Farm Buildings of New England.* Hanover, N.H.: University Press of New England.

———. 1988. "Farm Family Mutuality: The Mid-Nineteenth-Century Maine Farm Neighborhood." In *The Farm,* ed. Peter Benes, 13–23. The Dublin Seminar for New England Folklife, Annual Proceedings, 1986. Boston: Boston University.

Hudson, John C. 2002. *Across This Land: A Regional Geography of the United States and Canada.* Baltimore: Johns Hopkins University Press.

Hughes, Charles W. 1980. *American Hymns Old and New.* New York: Columbia University Press.

Hull, Asa, and R. G. Staples. 1874. *The Golden Sheaf of Sunday School Music.* Philadelphia: Asa Hull.

Hutchinson, Patrick. 1985. "'You Never Think to Lose the "Nyah" . . .': Retention and Change in a Fiddler's Tradition." *Canadian Folklore Canadien* 7(1–2): 121–28.

Ives, Edward D. 1962. "The Satirical Song Tradition in Maine and the Maritime Provinces of Canada." Ph.D. thesis, Indiana University.

———. 1964. *Larry Gorman: The Man Who Made the Songs.* Bloomington: University of Indiana Press.

———. 1965. *Folksongs from Maine.* Northeast Folklore 7. Orono: University of Maine.

———. 1972. *Lawrence Doyle: The Farmer Poet of Prince Edward Island.* Maine Studies No. 92. Orono, Maine: University Press.

———. 1978. *Joe Scott: The Woodsman-Songmaker.* Urbana: University of Illinois Press.

Jabbour, Alan. 1971. *American Fiddle Tunes from the Archive of Folk Song.* Pamphlet for record L62. Washington, D.C.: Library of Congress.

Jackson, George Pullen. 1953. *Spiritual Folk-Songs of Early America.* 2nd ed. Locust Valley, N.Y.: J. J. Augustin.

Jewett, Candace. 1976. "Barn and Kitchen Dances in Troy, Maine." Unpub. ms. Maine Folk-life Center NAFOH #1045.

Keller, Kate Van Winkle. 1989. *Early American Dance and Music: John Griffiths, Eighteenth-Century Itinerant Dancing Master.* Sandy Hook, Conn.: The Hendrickson Group.

Keller, Kate Van Winkle, and Ralph Sweet. 1976. *A Choice Selection of American Country Dances of the Revolutionary Era, 1775–1795.* New York: Country Dance and Song Society of America.

Kern, Charles W. 1988. *God, Grace, and Granite: The History of Methodism in New Hampshire, 1768–1988.* Canaan, N.H.: Phoenix Publishing.

Kincaid, Bradley. 1928. *My Favorite Mountain Ballads and Old-Time Songs: As Sung Over WLS, the Prairie Farmer Station.* Chicago: WLS.

King, H. Thorn. 1965. *Sliptown: The History of Sharon, New Hampshire, 1738–1941.* Rutland, Vt.: Charles Tuttle.

Kingman, Daniel. 2003. *American Music: A Panorama.* 3rd edition. Belmont, Calif.: Thomson.

Koskoff, Ellen, ed. 2000. *Garland Encyclopedia of World Music, Vol. 3: The United States and Canada.* New York: Garland.

Kull, Nell M. 1961. *History of Dover, Vermont.* Dover: Book Cellar.

Lane, Brigitte. 1980. *Franco-American Folk Traditions and Popular Culture in a Former Mill-town: Aspects of Ethnic Urban Folklore and the Dynamics of Folklore Change in Lowell, Massachusetts.* New York: Garland Publishing.

Larkin, Ed. "The Music and Calls of Ed Larkin." Unpub. ms. VHS microfilm reel 16 (c. 1930–1954).

Laufman, Dudley, and Corinne Nash. 1992. *Dick Richardson: Old Time New Hampshire Fiddler.* Canterbury, N.H.: D. Laufman.

Laws, George Malcolm. 1950. *Native American Balladry: A Descriptive Study and a Bibliographical Syllabus.* Philadelphia: American Folklore Society.

———. 1957. *American Balladry from British Broadsides: A Guide for Students and Collectors of Traditional Song.* Philadelphia: American Folklore Society.

Lemon, James T. 1980. "Early Americans and Their Social Environment." *Journal of Historical Geography* 6: 115–31.

Leyshon, Andrew, et al. 1998. *The Place of Music.* New York: Guilford Press.

Linscott, Eloise Hubbard. 1939. *Folk Songs of Old New England.* New York: Macmillan.

Lomax, John A., and Alan Lomax. 1934. *American Ballads and Folk Songs.* New York: Macmillan.

Lorentz, Karen D. 2000. *Good Vermonters: The Pierces of North Shrewsbury.* Shrewsbury, Vt.: Mountain Publishing.

Lorenz, Ellen Jane. 1980. *Glory Hallelujah! The Story of the Campmeeting Spiritual.* Nashville: Abington.

MacArthur, Margaret. 1981. "The Search for More Songs from the Hills of Vermont: Songs and Ballads of the Atwood Family of West Dover, Vermont." *Country Dance and Song* 11/12: 5–19.

———. 1982. *An Almanac of New England Farm Songs.* LP recording. Green Linnet. SIF 1039.

MacKay, Donald. 1978. *The Lumberjacks.* Toronto: McGraw Hill Ryerson.

Mansfield, D. H. 1849. *The American Vocalist.* Rev. ed. Boston: Brown, Taggard, and Chase.

Marcoux, Omer. 1980. *Fiddle Tunes of Omer Marcoux.* Transcribed by Sylvia Miskoe and Justine Paul. Bedford, N.H.: National Materials Development Center for French.

Marini, Stephen A. 1982. *Radical Sects of Revolutionary New England.* Cambridge, Mass.: Harvard University Press.

———. 1983. "Rehearsal for Revival: Sacred Singing and the Great Awakening in America." *Journal of the American Academy of Religious Studies* 50(1): 71–91.

———. 1996. "Evangelical Hymns and Popular Belief." In *New England Music: The Public Sphere, 1600–1900,* ed. Peter Benes, 117–26. Boston: Boston University.

Martin, Philip. 1994. *Farmhouse Fiddlers: Music and Dance Traditions in the Rural Midwest.* Mount Horeb, Wis.: Midwest Traditions.

Martin, Stuart F., 1980. *New Pennacook Folks: A Historical Record of the Town of Rumford and the People Who Lived Here.* Rumford Point, Maine: S. Martin.

McCaskey, John, ed. 1881. *Franklin Square Song Collection: Songs and Hymns for Schools and Homes, Nursery and Fireside.* New York: Harper.

McIntire, Julia W. 1974. *Green Mountain Heritage: The Chronicle of Northfield, Vermont.* Canaan, N.H.: Phoenix Publishing.

McKernan, Michael. 1984. "Nineteenth-Century Leap-Year Balls in Central New England." *Country Dance and Song.* 14: 10–14.

McMurry, Sally. 1988. *Families and Farmhouses in Nineteenth-Century America: Vernacular Design and Social Change.* New York: Oxford University Press.

McNeil, W. K. 1988. *Southern Folk Ballads.* Vol. 2. Little Rock: August House.

Messer, Don. 1950. *Don Messer's Favorite Melodies.* Toronto: Canadian Music Sales.

———. N.d. *Backwoods Melodies: Don Messer and His Islanders.* Toronto: Canadian Music Sales.

Miller, Randy, and Jack Perron. 1983. *New England Fiddler's Repertoire.* Peterborough, N.H.: Fiddlecase Books.

Moody, Ed. 1968. "The Itinerant Fiddlers of New Hampshire." *Northern Junket* 9(2): 2–13.

Moore, Barrington. 1983. *Privacy: Studies in Social and Cultural History.* Armonk, N.Y.: M. E. Sharpe.

Moore, Pauline W. 1970. *Blueberries and Pusley Weed: The Story of Lovell, Maine.* Kennebunk, Maine: Starr Press.

Nissenbaum, Stephen. 1996. "New England as a Region and a Nation." In *All Over the Map: Rethinking American Regions,* ed. Edward L. Ayers, et al. Baltimore: Johns Hopkins University Press, 38–61.

Osborne, Lettie. 1952. "Fiddle Tunes from Orange County, New York." *New York Folklore Quarterly* 8 (3): 211–15.

Osterud, Nancy Grey. 1991. *Bonds of Community: The Lives of Farm Women in Nineteenth-Century New York.* Ithaca: Cornell University Press.

Overlock, E. Burnell. 1984. *Sixty-Six Years a Country Fiddler: Charles E. Overlock.* Milo, Maine: Milo Printing Company.

Page, Ralph. 1970a. "Those Were the Days." *Northern Junket* 10(1): 2–7, 10(2): 16–21.

———. 1970b. "It's Fun to Hunt." *Northern Junket* 10(3): 33–39, 10(4): 32–37.

———. 1971. "Contra Dance Background." *Northern Junket* 10(10): 2–9. 10(11): 7–14.

———. 1976. *Heritage Dances of Early America.* Colorado Springs: Lloyd Shaw Foundation.

———. 1983–84. "Traditional Dancing and Dance Music of the Monadnock (NH) Region (Parts I and II)." *Country Dance and Song* 13: 1–9, 14: 23–29.

———. 1984. *An Elegant Collection of Contras and Squares.* Denver: The Lloyd Shaw Foundation.

Patterson, Beverley. 1995. *The Sound of the Dove: Singing in Appalachian Primitive Baptist Churches.* Urbana: University of Illinois Press.

Phillips, Tom. 1983. "Chuck Luce: Old-Time Vermont Fiddler." *Country Dance and Song* 13: 10–16.

Pichierri, Louis. 1960. *Music in New Hampshire.* New York: Columbia University Press.

Pickering, Michael. 1983. *Village Song and Culture.* London: Croom Helm.

Pickering, Michael, and Tony Green, eds. 1987. *Everyday Culture: Popular Song and the Vernacular Milieu.* Milton Keynes, Pa.: Open University Press.

Pike, Robert E. 1935. "Folk Songs from Pittsburg, New Hampshire." *Journal of American Folklore.* 48(190): 337–51.

———. 1959. *Spiked Boots: Sketches of the North Country.* St. Johnsbury, Vermont: Cowles Press. Reprinted 1987: Dublin, N.H.: Yankee Publishing.

———. 1967. *Tall Trees, Tough Men: An Anecdotal and Pictorial History of Logging and Log-driving in New England.* New York: Norton.

Playford, John, ed. 1862. *American Dancing Master, and Ball-Room Prompter.* Boston: Elias Howe.

Pocius, Gerald L. 1991. *A Place to Belong: Community Order and Everyday Space in Calvert, Newfoundland.* Athens: The University of Georgia Press.

Porter, Gerald. 1992. *The English Occupational Song.* Stockholm: University of Umeå.

Porter, James. 1993. "Convergence, Divergence, and Dialectic in Folksong Paradigms: Critical Directions for Transatlantic Scholarship." *Journal of American Folklore* 106(419): 61–98.

Post, Jennifer C. 1983. *An Index to the Field Recordings in the Flanders Ballad Collection at Middlebury College, Middlebury, Vermont.* Middlebury College.

———. 1985. "Family Song Traditions: The Pierce-Spaulding Farm of West Bridgewater and North Shrewsbury (Northam), Vermont." *Northeast Folklore* 30: 57–89.

———. 1994. "Erasing the Boundaries between Public and Private in Women's Performance Traditions." In *Cecelia Reclaimed: Feminist Perspectives on Gender and Music,* Susan C. Cook and Judy S. Tsou, eds. Urbana: University of Illinois, 35–51.

Prosser, Albert C. 1968. *Sanford, Maine: A Bicentennial History.* Sanford Historical Committee.

Quigley, Colin. 1985. *Close to the Floor: Folk Dance in Newfoundland.* St. John's: Memorial University of Newfoundland.

———. 1988. "A French-Canadian Fiddler's Musical Worldview: The Violin Is 'Master of the World.'" *Selected Reports in Ethnomusicology* 7: 99–122.

———. 1996. "Folk Dance." In *American Folklore: An Encyclopedia,* ed. Jan Harold Brunvard. New York: Garland, 191–97.

Reed, Nita. 1955. "Country Dance Forty Years Ago." *Vermont History* 23(2): 133–35.

Renwick, Roger. 1980. *English Folk Poetry: Structure and Meaning.* Philadelphia: University of Pennsylvania Press.

Revival Melodies, or Songs of Zion. 1843. 20th ed. Boston: John Putnam; New York: Saxton and Miles.

Roerden, Chris. 1965. *Collections from Cape Elizabeth, Maine.* Town of Cape Elizabeth.

Ross, James. 1961. "Folk Song and Social Environment: A Study of the Repertoire of Nan MacKinnon of Vatersay." *Scottish Studies* 5: 18–39.

Russell, Ian. 1987. "Stability and Change in a Sheffield Singing Tradition." *Folk Music Journal* 5: 317–58.

Ryan, Mary P. 1981. *Cradle of the Middle Class: The Family in Oneida County, New York, 1790–1865.* Cambridge: Cambridge University Press.

Ryden, Kent C. 1993. *Mapping the Invisible Landscape: Folklore, Writing, and the Sense of Place.* Iowa City: University of Iowa Press.

Sawyer, Nina G. 1972. *A History of Island Falls, Maine: From Its Settlement in 1843 to Its Centennial Year 1972 and a Collection of Historical Sketches.* Nina G. Sawyer.

Sesquicentennial Committee of the Town of Hancock, Maine. 1978. *A History of the Town of Hancock, 1828–1978.* Town of Hancock.

Sharp, Cecil, and Maud Karpeles. 1932. *English Folk-Songs from the Southern Appalachians.* London: Oxford University Press.

Sher, Ruth. 1989. *And Everyone Would Sashay: The Remembrances of the Ed Larkin Contra Dancers.* Chelsea, Vt.: Gibby Press.

Shields, Hugh. 1993. *Narrative Singing in Ireland: Lays, Ballads, Come-all-ye's and Other Songs.* Blackrock, County Dublin: Irish Academic Press.

Shorey, Eula M., ed. 1974. *Bridgton, Maine, 1768–1968.* Bridgton Historical Society.

Somes-Sanderson, Virginia. 1982. *The Living Past: Being the Story of Somesville, Mount Desert, Maine and Its Relationships with Other Areas of the Island.* Mount Desert: V. Somes-Sanderson.

Spielman, Earl. 1975. "Traditional North American Fiddling: A Methodology for the Historical and Comparative Analytical Style Study of Instrumental Musical Traditions." Ph.D. dissertation, University of Wisconsin at Madison.

Steinberg, Judith T. 1973. "Old Folks' Concerts and the Revival of New England Psalmody." *Musical Quarterly* 59: 602–19.

Stokes, Martin. 1997. *Ethnicity, Identity, and Music: The Musical Construction of Place.* Oxford: Berg.

Strassner, Susan. 1982. *Never Done: A History of American Housework.* New York: Pantheon.

Szwed, John F. 1990. "Paul E. Hall: A Newfoundland Song-Maker and His Community of Song." In *Folksongs and their Makers,* ed. Henry Glassie, et al. Bowling Green, Ohio: Bowling Green University Popular Press. 147–69.

Taggart, John Adams. 1915. "Recollection of a Busy Life." Ms. New Hampshire Historical Society.

Taylor, Paul S., and Anne Loftis. 1981. "The Legacy of the Nineteenth-Century New England Farmer." *New England Quarterly* 54: 243–54.

Temperley, Nicholas. 1981. "The Old Way of Singing: Its Origins and Development" *Journal of the American Musicological Society* 34(3): 511–44.

Thorpe, Walter. 1911. *A History of Wallingford, Vermont.* Rutland: Tuttle.

Toelken, Barre. 1979. "Northwest Regional Folklore." In *Northwest Perspectives,* ed. Edward R. Bingham and Glen A. Love, 21–42. Eugene, Oregon: University of Oregon.

Tolman, Beth, and Ralph Page. 1976. *The Country Dance Book: The Best of the Square and Contra Dancers and All About Them.* Brattleboro, Vt.: Stephen Green Press.

Tolman, Newton F. 1937. *Quick Tunes and Good Times.* New York: A. S. Barnes.

Violette, Maurice. 1976. *The Franco-Americans.* New York: Vantage Press.

Wakefield, Alice Webster. 1985. *West Brookfield and Thereabouts.* Alice Wakefield.

Wakefield, Charles E. 1978. *Trademark, Music.* Cherryfield, Maine: Wakefield.

Walker, William. 1854. *The Southern Harmony & Musical Companion.* Philadelphia: E. W. Miller.

Warner, Anne, ed. 1984. *Traditional American Folk Songs from the Anne and Frank Warner Collection.* Syracuse, N.Y.: Syracuse University Press.

Warner, Jeff. 1978. "Lena Bourne Fish: New Hampshire Traditional Singer." *Country Dance and Song* 9: 5–11.

Washburn, Harrison Gray. 1863. *The Ball-room Manual of Contra Dances and Social Cotillons with Remarks on Quadrilles and Spanish Dance.* Belfast, Maine: H. G. O. Washburn; Boston: G. W. Cottrell.

Wehman Bros.' Good Old-time Songs. 1910–1916. New York: Wehman Bros.

Wells, Paul F. 1976a. Liner notes for *La Famille Beaudoin*. LP. Philo 2022.

———. 1976b. "Mellie Dunham: Maine's Champion Fiddler." *JEMF Quarterly* 12(43): 112–18.

———. 1978. "A Brief Social History of Fiddling in New England." In *New England Traditional Fiddling: An Anthology of Recordings, 1926–1975*. LP with accompanying booklet. JEMF 105. Los Angeles: John Edwards Memorial Foundation.

White, B. F., and E. J. King. 1859. *The Sacred Harp: A Collection of Psalm and Hymn Tunes, Solos, and Anthems, Selected from the Most Eminent Authors*. Philadelphia: Collins Printing House.

Whittemore, Edwin Carey. 1902. *The Centennial History of Waterville, Kennebec County, Maine*. Waterville, Maine : Executive Committee of the Centennial Celebration.

Williams, Raymond. 1973. *The Country and the City*. New York: Oxford University Press, 1973.

Williams, W. W. 1975. *Rochester, Vermont, its History, 1780–1975*. Rochester, Vt.: The Town of Rochester.

Wood, Thomas. 1997. *The New England Village*. Baltimore: Johns Hopkins University Press.

Index

Page numbers in **boldface** indicate musical examples.

McKeage, Robert (Kidderville, N.H.), 197, 199–201, 207

McNally, Jack (Stacyville, Maine), 252–53

men: and dance music, 198; and hymns, 74–75; and performance, 120–29; and social roles, 3, 10–11, 114–18; and song, 129–37; and work, 20, 22

Merrill, Orlon (Charlestown, N.H.), 176, 179, 262–63

Messer, Don, 170–171, 202–3

Millennial Harp: Designed for the Meetings on the Second Coming of Christ (Himes), 73

Millennial Harp: Or Second Advent Hymns, 68–69

"Millennial Hymn" ("The Judgment Hymn"), **70, 71**

Miller, William (1782–1849), 70

"Millerite Hymn," **72**

Millerites, 70–74

"Miss Clara Noble's Ball," 21

"Money Musk," 95, 197, 266

Moore, Mrs. Norris (Burlington, Maine), 21

"Moose Pond Song, The." *See* "Four Cousins, The"

Morgan, Ida (Jeffersonville, Vt.), 23, 70, 285n.22

Moses, Jonathan (Orford, N.H.), 26, 52–54

Mosher's Orchestra (Farmington, Maine), 84

"Murder of Sarah Vail, The" (Laws F9), 41, **43**

musical instruments, 81, 84–85, 94–95, 116. *See also* banjo; drums; fiddle; guitar; mandolin; organ; piano; trumpet

"My Papa Was a Woodman," 164

"Needle's Eye, The," **56–57**, 163, 287n.63

neighborhood, 3–4, 8–11, 17–19, 20–21, 23–24, 60–61, 74–75, 78–83, 115–20, 163–64, 169–71, 186–204, 206–7, 211–13, 235–38

Neill, Albert (Warren, Vt.), 78–79, 81–82, 236

Neill, Thelma (Warren, Vt.), 19, 75, 78–79

"Nellie Gray." *See* "Darling Nellie Gray"

Nelson, Thomas Edward (New Brunswick, Maine), 29–31

New Hampshire: Berlin, 41; Bristol, 105; Charlestown, 168, 174, 176, 178, 179, 262–63; Clarksville, 168, 191–92, 197, 204; Colebrook, 34, 62, 121–24, 129–30, 181–82, 192–95, 206–7, 242, 254, 284n.11, 296n.11; Columbia, 178–79, 258–59; Cornish, 57; E. Jaffrey, 39–40, 64–67, 240; Freedom, 91–92; Groveton,

269–70; Kidderville, 197, 199–201, 207; Manchester, 82, 95; Orford, 23, 36, 52; Pike, 250; Pittsburg, 7, 19, 45–47, 60, 75, 82, 119, 123, 126, 129–32, 168–234, 248–49, 257–58, 264–66, 268, 295n.30; Sharon, 96–97; Stark, 169, 171, 187, 205, 207–8, 235; Stewartstown, 168, 197, 199, 201; Stewartstown Hollow, 20, 186–90, 193, 204, 206; Tamworth, 79

"Newport Jail," 179

North Hill Church (Stewartstown Hollow, N.H.), 193

"Nothing Between," 171

"O Sing to Me of Heaven," **67**

"O Thou in Whose Presence," **193–94**

"Old Arm Chair," 208

"Old Black Joe," 205

"Old Dan Day Song, The," 190, 295nn.29–30

"Old Kelly's Blood." *See* "Irish Patriot, The"

"Old Maid the Burglar, The," **267–68**

"Old Oak Tree, The," 21

"Old Refrain, The," **162–63**

"Old Zip Coon," 98

Olney, Marguerite, x, 168, 184, 193, 201, 236

"On the Green Carpet," **56–57**, 206

"On the Green Hills of Old Vermont," **5–6**

organ, 17, 67, 75, 80–81, 87, 94, 193, 196, 199–203

"Orphan Children, The," 160, **268–69**

Osterud, Nancy, 114

"Outlandish Knight." *See* "Lady Isabel and the Elf Knight" (Child 4)

Page, Ralph, 93, 107

"Paper of Pins," 52–54, **269–70**

Parks, Beulah (Stark, N.H.), 174–78

parlor (living room), 17, 18, 63, 75, 78, 117–18, 120, 140, 158, 162, 207, 239, 268

parlor songs, 44–50

"Patronella." *See* "Petronella"

Pellettier, Mike (Old Town, Maine), 94–95

"Peter Emberley" ("Peter Amberley"; Laws C27), 36, 179, **271–72**

"Petronella" ("Patronella"), **272**

Pettingill, Grace (S. Royalton, Vt.), 56–58

piano, 48, 67, 80–81, 84–85, 87, 94, 116, 193, 199–203

Pickering, Michael, 7, 16–17

Pierce, Edwin (Shrewsbury, Vt.), 156–58

Pierce, Gertrude Spaulding (N. Shrewsbury, Vt.), 140, 142–55, 246

Stark, Harry (Cornwall, Vt.), 273
Stark Old-Time Fiddlers' Contest, 169, 235
Stebbins, Evelyn (Colebrook, N.H.), 199
step dancing, 18, 82, 87–88, 93, 116
"Sunbright Clime," 193
"Suncook Town Tragedy, The" (Laws F21), 41, 43–44, 126, 176, **260–61**
"Sweet Hour of Prayer," 74
"Sweet Trinity, The" (Child 286), 27

Taggart, John (Sharon, N.H.), 96–97
"Tailor and the Chest, The." *See* "Sailor and the Tailor, The"
"Tenting Tonight," **157**
"There's No One to Welcome Me Home," **276–77**
"They Never Told a Lie," **160–61**
"Three Little Kittens," 146
"Throw Out the Life Line," 74
Titus, Alice Dodge, 43–44
Titus, Walter (Johnson, Vt.), 10, 44, 260
"Tod and the Sow," **277–78**
Tolin, A. (Chester, Vt.), 43
Tolman, Beth, 91
traveling performers, 14, 45, 84, 95, 160
"Tree in the Wood," 126
"True Story, The," 140, **154–55**
trumpet, 81, 84–85, 94–95
"Turkey in the Straw," 98, 105, 205
Twitchell, B. L. (Shaftsbury, Vt.), 127–28
"Two Kittens, The," 146
"Two Little Girls in Blue," 47, **158–60**
"Two Little Orphans," **135**
two step, 76, 88, 102

"Uncle Hall's Barn," 23, 285n.22
urbanization, 13–14, 44–45, 84, 89, 107, 211

Vaara, Elizabeth (Middlebury, Vt.), 17–18
Vermont: Baltimore, 34–35, 52; Barnet, 58; Barre, 58; Bennington, 260–61; Benson, 9–10, 80, 85, 172–73; Brattleboro, 287n.63; Bristol, 84, 102; Burlington, 82, 94; Calais, 4, 41; Chelsea, 84, 91–92, 105–6; Cornwall, 273; Cuttingsville, 124–25; Dorset, 54; Dover, 10; E. Bethel, 23, 71, 101; E. Calais, 21, 51–52, 121–24, 132–34; E. Montpelier, 86; Fair Haven, 48, 78, 80, 85; Grafton, 5–6; Hardwick, 43–44, 51–52; Jeffersonville, 23,

70; Johnson, 10, 44, 260, 294n.15; Lincoln, 74, 113; Middlebury, 17–18; Milton, 36; N. Calais, 72; N. Montpelier, 121–24, 132–34, 276–77; N. Shrewsbury, 19, 45–46, 139–67, 176, 243–46, 268–69; Putney, 70; Quechee, 96; Reading, 272; Ripton, 279–80; Rutland, 162–63; Shaftsbury, 127–28; Shaftsbury Hollow, 21; South Royalton, 56–58; Springfield, 19, 21, 79–80, 238, 272–73; Vergennes, 127–28; Warren, 3–4, 19, 75, 78–79, 81–82, 236; W. Bridgewater, 139–67; Woodstock, 62
Vermont Commission on Country Life, ix
"Vermont Farmer's Song," 1
visiting, 9–10, 60, 115, 142

"Wabash Cannonball," 102, 205
Wakefield, Charles (Cherryfield, Maine), 83
Walker, Arthur (Littleton, Maine), 40–41
"Walking the Floor Over You," 172
waltz, 87–88, 93, 102, 128, 156, 208, 236
"Waltz You Save for Me, The," 205
Washburn, Abe (Pittsburg and Colebrook, N.H.), 184–85, 191–92
"Water, Water Wild Flowers," **57–58**
Weeks, Luther (Springfield, Vt.), 272–73
Wells, Paul, 94
"When the Roll Is Called Up Yonder," **67–68**
"Whispering Hope," 74
"Wild River Tragedy," **41–42**
"Willie O Winsbury" (Child 100), 29, 121
"Will the Weaver" (Laws Q9), 172
Wilson, Bill (Pike, N.H.), 250
women: and dance, 90–91, 93; and dance music, 198; and hymns, 60, 74–75; and performance, 120–29; and social roles, 3, 10–11, 81, 114–18; and song, 129–37; songwriting, 186, 208, 212; and space, 113–38; and work, 10, 19–20, 22, 24
"Woodsman's Alphabet," **279–80**
Woodward, Bill (Bristol, N.H.), 105
work bees, 20–21, 78–79, 117–18
work songs, 54–55

"Young Beichan" (Child 53), 26–27, 140
"Young Charlotte" (Laws G17), 124, 140, **147–51**, 208
"Young Monroe." *See* "Jam on Gerry's Rock, The"

Music in Rural New England
Family and Community Life, 1870–1940

Recordings 1939–1988

1. "The Backwoodsman" (Laws C19), Asa Davis, Milton, Vermont (9/25/42).
2. "The St. Alban's Tragedy" ("James MacDonald," Laws P38), Edward Dragon, Ripton, Vermont (7/41).
3. "A-Walking and A-Talking" ("The Cuckoo"), Myra Daniels, Hardwick, Vermont (7/1/54).
4. "The Female Smuggler," Charles Finnemore, Bridgewater, Maine (9/30/41).
5. "The Darby Ram," Charles Finnemore, Bridgewater, Maine (n.d.).
6. "The Paper of Pins," Floyd and Bea Shatney, Groveton, New Hampshire (8/87).
7. "The Tod and the Sow," Murchie Harvey, Houlton, Maine (8/30/42).
8. "There's No One to Welcome Me Home," Jack McNally, Staceyville, Maine (8/28/42).
9. "Cabbage and Meat" ("The Half Hitch," Laws N23), Marjorie Pierce, North Shrewsbury, Vermont (11/84).
10. "Beulah Land," Marjorie Pierce, North Shrewsbury, Vermont (11/84).
11. "The Woodsman's Song" ("Lumberman's Alphabet Song"), Edward Dragon, Ripton, Vermont (7/41).
12. "The Alphabet Song" ("Lumberman's Alphabet Song"), Florence Scott and Flora Campbell, Pittsburg and Stark, New Hampshire (5/88).
13. "The Little Mohea" (Laws H8), Ellen Hoadley, Johnson, Vermont (10/23/54).
14. "The Little Mohea" (Laws H8), Flora Campbell, Stark, New Hampshire (5/88).
15. "Chippewa Stream" ("The Chippewa Girl," Laws H10), Maude Covill, Pittsburg, Newe Hampshire (9/5/41).
16. "The Four Cousins," Maude Covill, Pittsburg, New Hampshire (9/5/41).
17. "The Bulldog Song," Abe Washburn, Colebrook, New Hampshire (11/21/41).
18. "Lord Banner" ("Little Musgrave and Lady Barnard," Child 81), Clyde Covill (two verses, 7/88) followed by Maude Covill (6/3/41).
19. "Arise My Soul Arise," Lena Bourne Fish, East Jaffrey, New Hampshire (9/18/45).
20. "The Land of Canian (Canaan)," Lena Bourne Fish, East Jaffrey, New Hampshire (9/18/45).
21. "The Bower," Belle Luther Richards, Colebrook, New Hampshire (9/24/45).
22. "Boston Fancy" (with calls), Robert McKeage, Pittsburg, New Hampshire (1942).
23. "Chorus Jig" (with calls), Edwin Larkin, Chelsea, Vermont (11/39).
24. "Devil's Dream," Elmer Barton, Quechee, Vermont (8/13/45).
25. "Portland Fancy," Luther Weeks, Springfield, Vermont (1932).
26. "Buckwheat Batter," Leo Brooks, Pittsburg, new Hampshire (7/18/87).
27. "Black Velvet Waltz," Leo Brooks, Pittsburg, New Hampshire (7/18/87).